Romi Behrens
A Painting Life

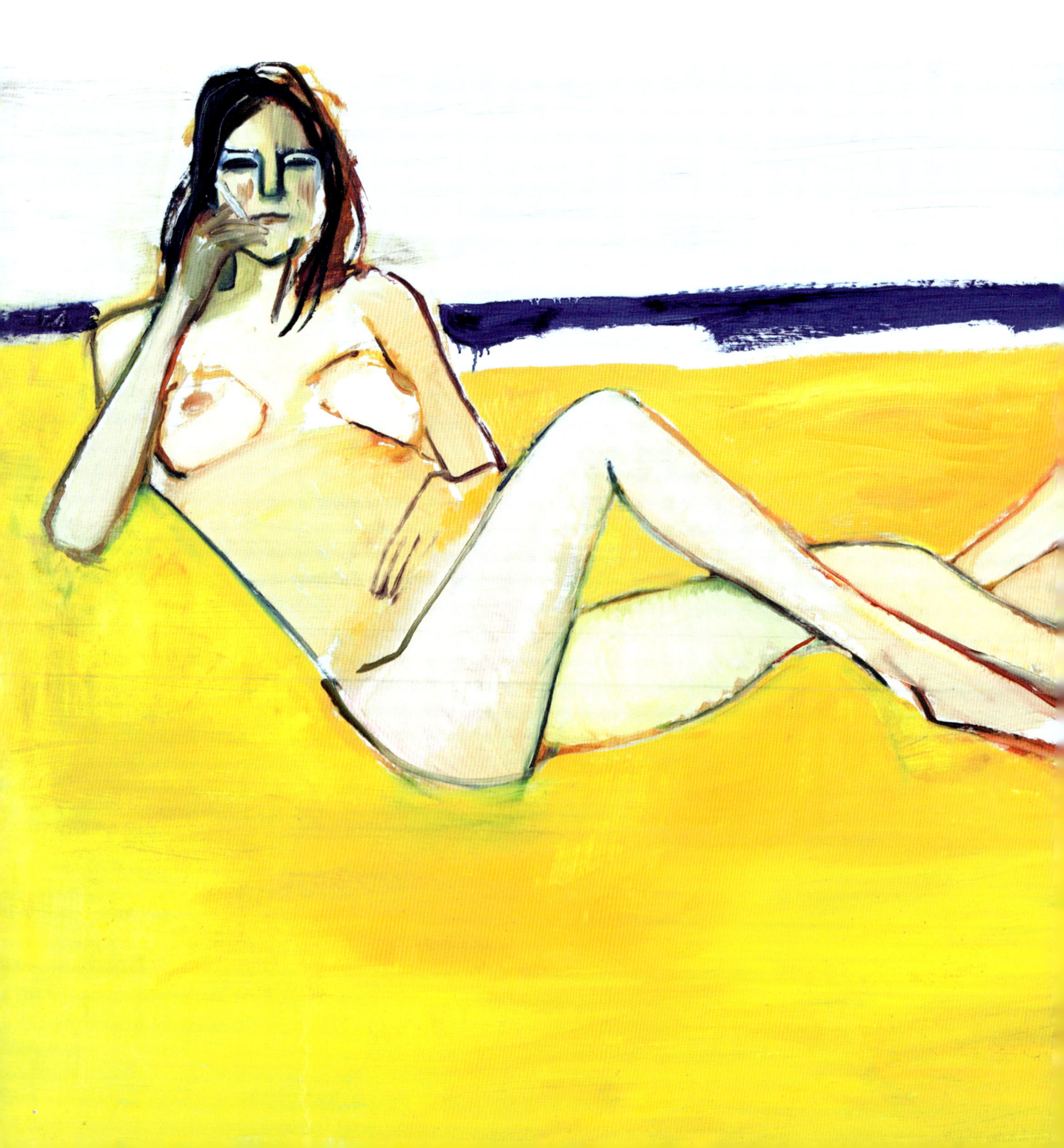

Romi Behrens

A Painting Life

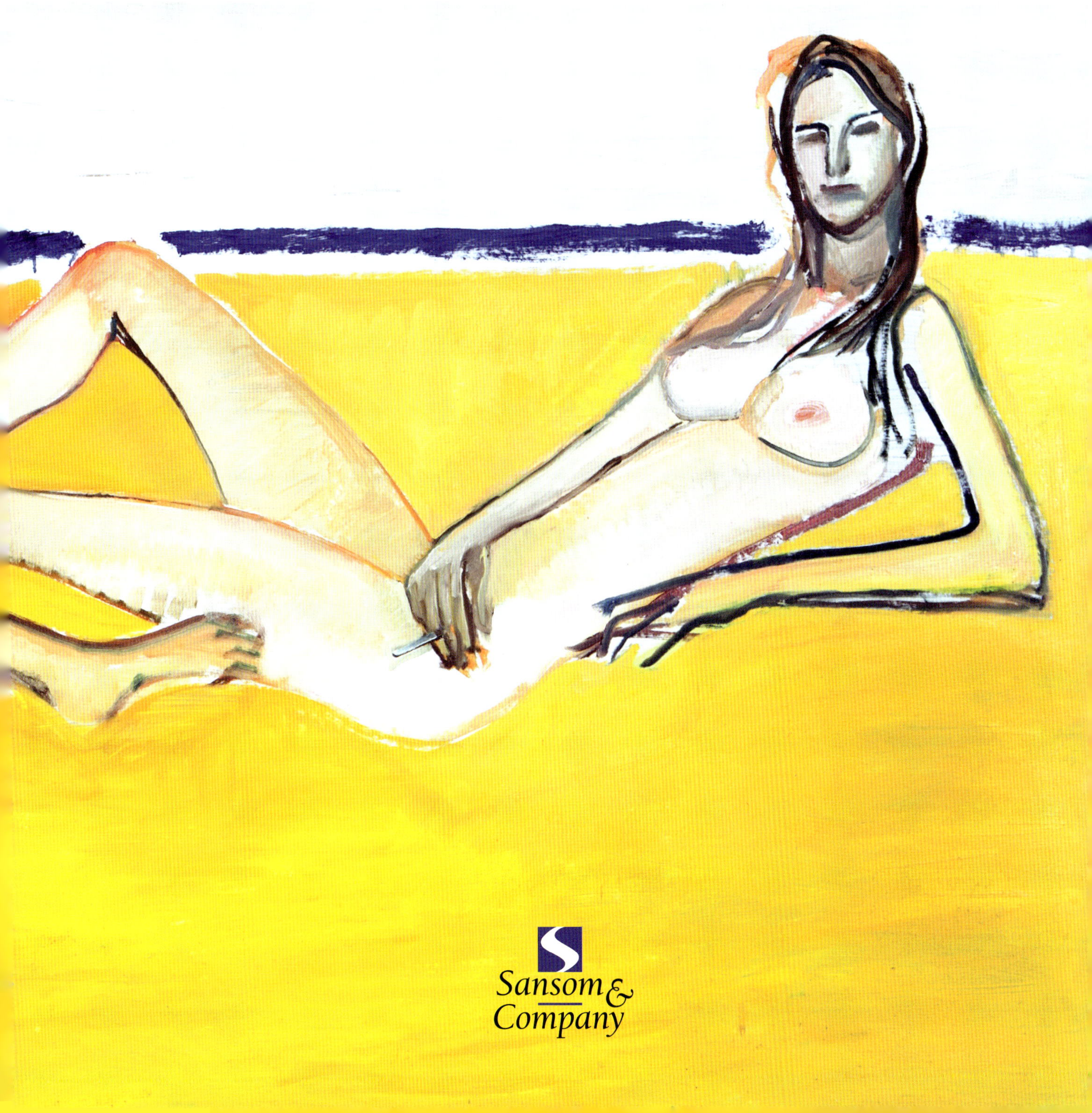

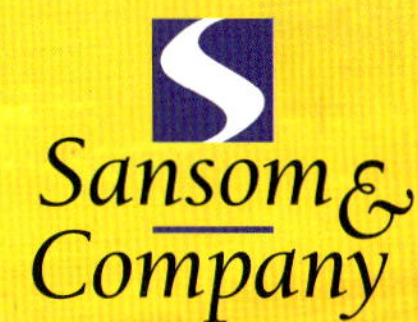

Sansom & Company

First published in 2024 by Sansom and Company,
a publishing imprint of Redcliffe Press Ltd.,
81G Pembroke Road, Bristol BS8 3EA
www.sansomandcompany.co.uk · info@sansomandcompany.co.uk

ISBN 978-1-915670-16-8

Edited by Rebecca Derry-Evans, Ann Kay and Emily Saner
Design and typesetting by E&P Design, Bath
Printed and bound by Akcent Media

Frontispiece: *Sophie and Scarlett (The Sirens)*
2011 · oil on board · 122 x 244 cm

Contents

Foreword

Chris Stephens

I am delighted and honoured to be invited to provide a foreword for this, the first commissioned book on the art of Romi Behrens. It is wonderful to see an artist's achievement set out in this way, complemented with a thorough account and analysis by Rachel Rose Smith and with such considered reflections and reminiscences from several of the artist's friends.

I first came across Romi's painting at the last exhibition of her lifetime at the wonderful Tremenheere Sculpture Gardens near Penzance. It was the private view and a convivial occasion with Romi surrounded by friends, family and admirers. I was sorry not to have met her before that day. It is surprising that I hadn't, given the fact that we had many friends and acquaintances in common after my thirty years of researching, writing about and exhibiting the artists who had made west Cornwall one of the most exciting places for art in the post-war period. By 2018, of course, those artists, and their partners and friends, were a dwindling band, though Romi was of a younger generation and closer in age, in many cases, to the children of the artists of the 1950s. It felt, in any case, as if she was the inheritor of a much longer tradition of creative and distinctive expression than simply that of her friends.

I was struck by how at home the works seemed at Tremenheere, perched as it is above the sea, tucked under the shadow of the moors, with glorious views of St Michael's Mount and Mount's Bay beyond, surrounded by fields of agapanthus and dahlias. Romi's paintings had a freshness and clarity that seemed perfectly to reflect their setting. Bright sprays of flowers – tulips, camellias, love-in-a-mist, for example – landscapes, trees, jaunty buildings and street scenes, household ornaments. Animated by her lively brushwork, and all modest in scale and set in clean, white frames, they seemed to speak to and of West Penwith, not just through the subject-matter but also in their clear, fresh luminosity. Many artists and writers – not least Romi's friend Patrick Heron – have spoken of the special, clear light of west Cornwall, surrounded as it is by sea on three sides, and whatever the subject-matter her paintings seem to embody that sharp, white light.

Just as its warm climate provides a fertile home for the earliest spring flowers, so west Cornwall has nurtured many artists over numerous generations. In the late nineteenth century some were drawn by the picturesque labour of the fisherfolk of Newlyn and other ports. For others it was the drama of the sea. The attraction of a simple, rural existence has been a recurring theme for successive waves of artists, as has the attraction of a community of like-minded individuals and the infrastructure of galleries and studios. As the wonderful accounts of her life and art that follow describe, none of those were the reason for Romi moving to Cornwall, or for staying there. But it seems hard not to conclude that it was that place and some of the people she knew there that both encouraged her to make art and affected the way in which she did so. As the wife of a local gentleman farmer, when she first studied painting in Penzance she must have been very aware of the area's fertility, both agricultural and artistic. While the art she came to make feels very much of that place, it is not necessarily more closely related to that of her friends and neighbours than to art from other places, other times.

Superficially, Romi's paintings seem to have a certain *naïveté*. An authenticity that derives from an apparent lack of over-trained sophistication. To that extent, she might be most obviously compared to an artist like Christopher Wood. Wood was, of course, closely associated with art in Cornwall, an intimate friend of Ben and Winifred Nicholson, and it was with Ben that he met the amateur painter Alfred Wallis in St Ives in 1928. Wallis became a talisman for both that generation and the next, his wobbly-edged paintings of boats and

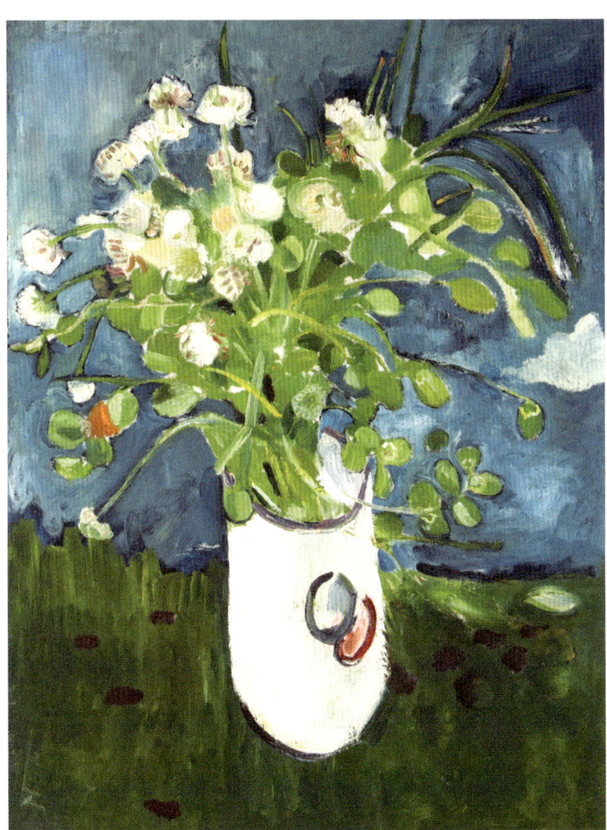

White Clover · c.1984 · oil on board · 76 x 60 cm

harbours occupying many of the mantlepieces of the artists and their friends in the 1950s and beyond.

Wood had died in 1930 but his work remained known and his spirit lived on. He was a vital presence in David Brown's landmark exhibition 'St Ives: Twenty-Five Years of Painting, Sculpture and Pottery' in 1985. Wood strove to achieve an art that had the innocence of Wallis's, though it was, unavoidably, imbued with all that he'd learnt from

those who had gone before him, such as Pablo Picasso and Henri Matisse. Similarly, Romi's paintings have the freshness and sincerity of the untutored maker but are informed by her knowledge and appreciation of artists of the past. Her marks are so lively, swift and confident that one might believe them to be entirely instinctive. At the same time, she was knowledgeable and surrounded by knowledgeable friends. Of course her work was informed by what she knew and saw of others' art. Often, artists like Romi are portrayed as singular figures, intuitive individuals set apart from other artists and dominant histories. But nothing comes from nothing. Great artists always recognise that they stand on the shoulders of those who came before. The strength of Romi's art derives from her absorption and understanding of others' art, not its separateness from it. That is not to deny her a distinctive, talented and poignant voice. There is, unquestionably, something unique to her work.

As David Ward suggests, Romi painted pretty much everything. Yes, traditional subjects like flowers in vases, land-/seascapes, boats in harbour, but the range of subjects and their specificity bears witness to a constant need to paint, forcing her to capture whatever, or whoever, was in front of her there and then. She had a keen eye for forms that she found occurring in the world around her. More importantly, her art tells of her love of life and of the joy she clearly found in the things she encountered day to day: particular cups, mugs or jugs, fresh wild flowers, china dogs, the packaging of a Christmas panettone; her street scenes give an unmistakeable sense of someone finding visual interest in the mundane buildings passed frequently, the hidden corners and funny features of her local towns. Regardless of the quality and power of her means of expression and her technique, that palpable love of all that is around is enough to make Romi's art one that will surely stay fresh and alive and speak to many of us for a long time to come.

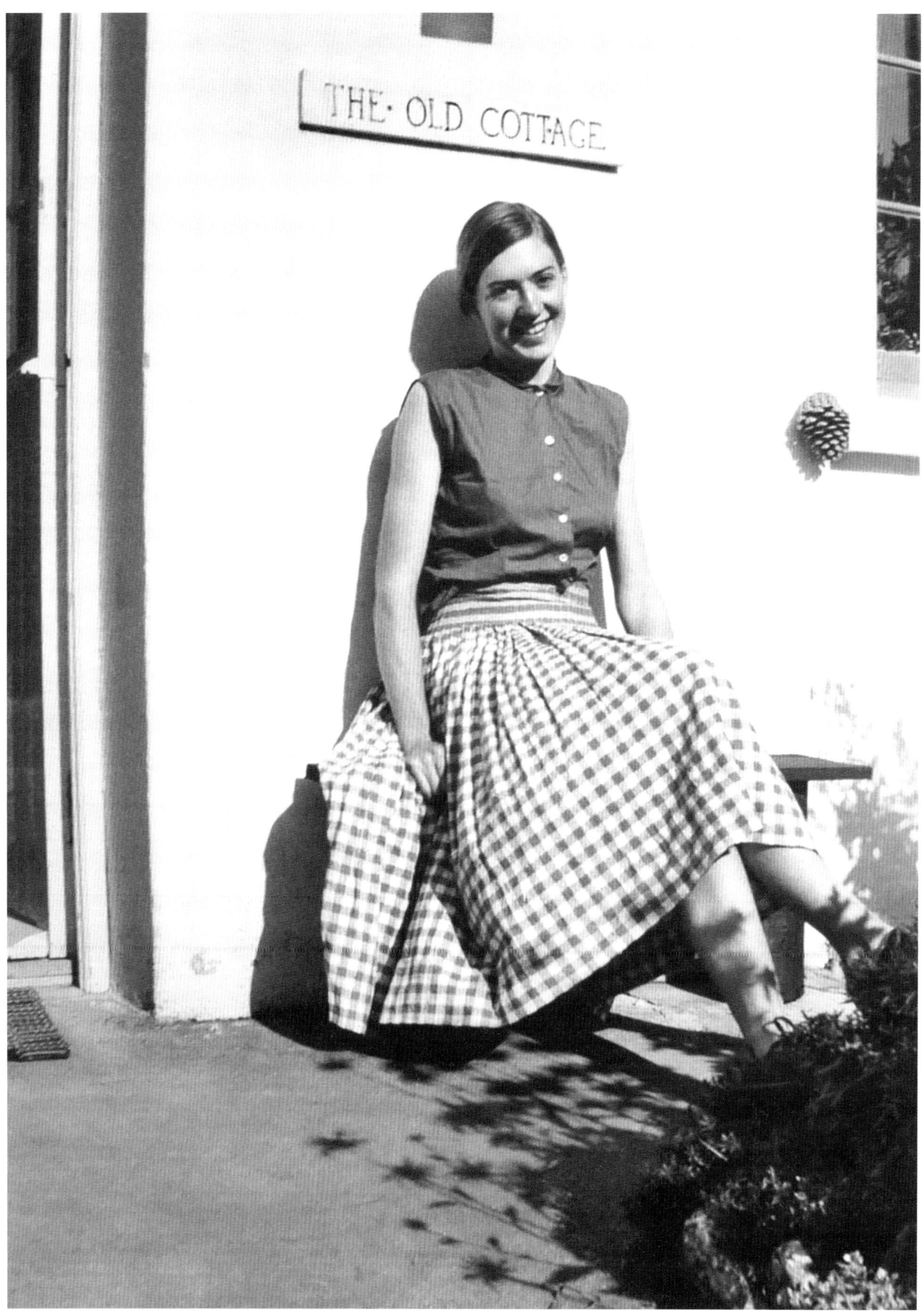

Romi, probably Cornwall, summer 1959

Becoming Romi Behrens

Rachel Rose Smith

For an artist as prolific as Romi Behrens, relatively little has been laid out publicly of her life and work. I offer an introduction to her early life and career in the hope that it helps others to begin to approach her work with some understanding of who she was and how she painted. In the process, I provide some thoughts about the kinds of paintings Romi made and how we might understand her relationally, as an artist actively conversing with long traditions of painting. I hope that this helps us to see the uniqueness of her work in her day, as well as how both its unusualness and variety might have contributed to how it has, or hasn't been, joined up with a broader art historical picture.

It feels important to try to put some of Romi's work into words, to encourage us to look closely at it, to appreciate the boldness of marks made and colours chosen. I am most astonished by the speed at which she came to her own painting style, as well as how she continued to get bolder in her choices of viewpoint, composition, colour and handling. I focus on the first half of her output here – culminating in 1979, when she was 40 years old – only because there is so much to say. Hopefully it will offer a foundation for others to build on when approaching her later achievements.

¶

Romi was born on 3 July 1939, the third daughter of Philip Humphrey Hall (known as Humphrey) and Marjorie (née Alcock). Humphrey, who hailed from Newcastle, had met Marjorie while studying at theological college. Marjorie was the daughter of Sir Walter Alcock, the organist at Salisbury Cathedral who was renowned for having played at three coronation services in Westminster Abbey, and a keen musician herself. Although a brilliant preacher, Humphrey, the young curate, was known to have lacked the academic ability and mental constitution to get

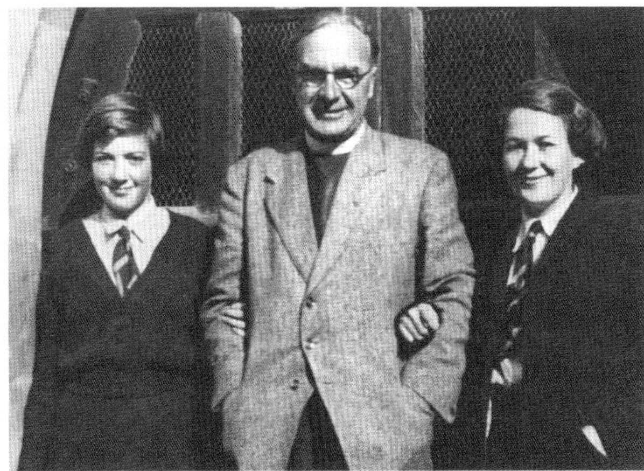

Romi, Humphrey and Gillian, c.1950–1

through rigorous priesthood exams. Encouraged instead to take a more vocational training path, he and Marjorie moved to Australia, where, between 1933 and 1938, they saw through the building and founding of a new Anglican church in the Wongan Hills, a remote area outside Perth. Romi's two sisters, Susan and Gillian, were born there, as well as a brother, Stephen, who sadly did not survive beyond a few months. Upon the family's return to England, Humphrey became vicar at Ramsbury, north Wiltshire. Romi (officially Rosemary, a name she never liked) was born in London and brought to Ramsbury ten days later.[1]

Romi's early years were thus spent in a village vicarage with a respected, gentle father and a generous and active mother, kept busy by three young girls, community responsibilities (including organ-playing in church) and, during the war, hosting evacuees. The girls all attended St Brandon's Clergy Daughters' School in Clevedon, Somerset, where Romi boarded from a young age.[2] Her time there was, however, cut short when, as a young teenager, she was expelled in 1954 for talking

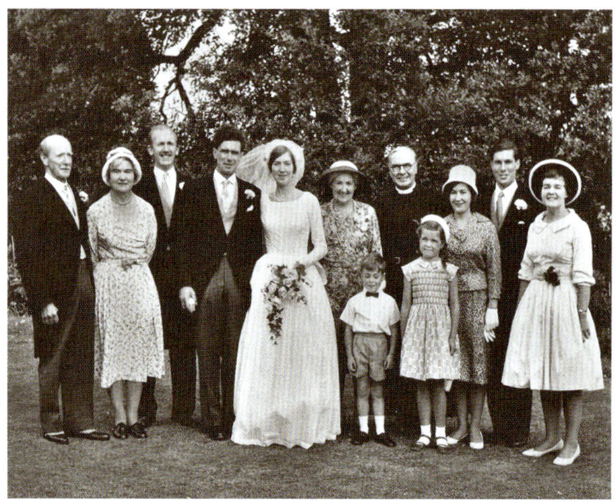

Mike and Romi with families on their wedding day, 11 July 1959

back to the headmistress about her boater hat. She had a strong Christian faith from a young age and was not without ethical principles, but she clearly struggled to comply with institutional rulebooks.

Then followed the most formative change in Romi's life. Humphrey's brother, Giles, a doctor, and his wife, Joan, agreed to host Romi in Penzance, Cornwall, where she was to attend the School of St Clare (Romi's sister, Susan, was already there, teaching music). She was, therefore, sent to experience a very different place and to be under the guidance of new semi-parental figures. However, it was not long before her elders had renewed concerns. In the summer of 1955, Romi found herself picking apples on the estate of Porth-en-Alls, inherited a couple of years earlier by young farmer Michael Tunstall-Behrens upon turning 30. Michael (called Mike) would have been known to Dr Hall and his eldest niece, Susan, through musical connections and both families' links with Wiltshire. Porth-en-Alls estate is located about nine miles east of Penzance, in an area known as Prussia Cove. Mike's grandfather, L.W.F. Behrens, a German gentleman, had bought the estate during the second half of the nineteenth century. He had married an Englishwoman, Emily Tunstall, and became a naturalised British citizen. Before taking on Porth-en-Alls, Mike had studied engineering at Cambridge and spent time in Burma with the Bengal Sappers and Miners, followed by the study of estate management in Plymouth.

A keen cyclist, Romi would frequently push her way along the 18-mile round trip between Penzance and Porth-en-Alls in one day. While Mike was, in many respects, a good match – he was handsome, hardworking and musical – the age difference (Romi was 16 and Mike 32 when they met), probably not helped by Romi's track record for impulsivity, meant that her parents did not immediately approve, and Romi was forbidden from marrying until she turned 20. In the meantime, she had to leave the School of St Clare

and Cornwall, and was sent to a different uncle, this time in Northern Ireland. Mike continued learning to farm his land and struggled to make it financially sustainable. Though he let some estate buildings to long-term tenants and rented some cottages in the holidays, the dominant stream of income during these years came from the very difficult work of running a coastal dairy and sheep farm.

Despite geographical hindrances, Mike and Romi corresponded regularly during the late 1950s and even had some secret meetings, enabled mostly by the Thomas family.[3] They were married at Bishopstone church in

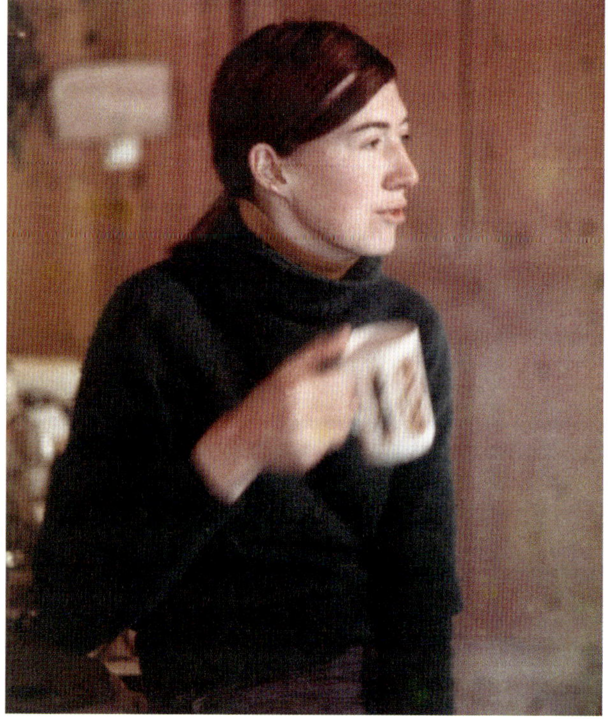

Romi at Trenalls, c.1960

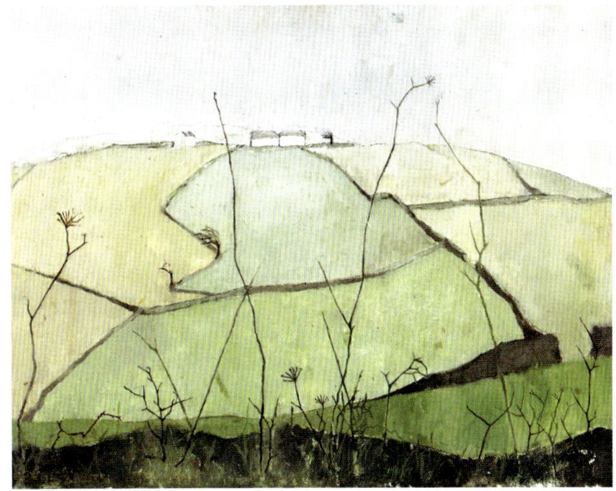

Green Fields · 1960 · oil on board · 38 x 51 cm

Wiltshire on 11 July 1959, one week after Romi's twentieth birthday, with her parents' approval, after which she went to live with her new husband at Porth-en-Alls.

Mike and Romi lived in Trenalls, a house on the estate, lit by oil lamps and candles.[4] In many ways Romi seems to have taken cheerfully to the requirements of being a gentleman farmer's wife, applying herself to the countless manual duties in and around the many cottages on the estate. Her diaries from the early 1960s remind us of the range of tasks to be undertaken for a young couple in this situation, learning to run a house and farm and managing tenants. On 25 January 1960 Romi recorded briefly and objectively her achievements of the day: 'Down to post. M [Mike] fencing. I brought up seven lambs … masses to do. Fire. Painted a tub white. Sausage rolls.'[5] Two days later: 'Made a big rock cake … Filled hens' nesting boxes.'[6] Romi also regularly helped to move the cows from one field to another, which she did alongside learning to cook and struggling to make preserves and bread, as well as much knitting, patchwork, cleaning, polishing and general mending around the house. Though they had the relative security of owning land and buildings, there was hardly enough money for spending, or time for resting, a situation which Romi appears to have handled practically and generously (she was known for rising early to make buns or sandwiches for the day's visitors). Furthermore, the road network surrounding the estate was poor, and there was no electricity until it was run underground and installed in November 1961. At this milestone Romi was relieved that it wasn't too bright.[7]

It was in this context of applying herself creatively but also matter-of-factly to a range of practical tasks at Porth-en-Alls that Romi became a painter. Between her marriage to Mike in July 1959 and the birth of their firstborn, Rebecca, the following August, she seems to have decided to apply herself with intent to this new skill. With so much

to do, it is unlikely that she would have devoted time and thought to learning a new craft had it not been a strong priority. We know that Romi passed an Art O-Level in Salisbury before moving to the remote farm in Cornwall and embarking on a new stage in life.[8] This seems to have provided extra motivation to use painting as a means of maintaining some private focus and personal creative development. Moreover, learning to paint was probably, for Romi, not dissimilar from a culture of learning with which she would have been infinitely more familiar: that of gaining, maintaining and improving one's skills in playing a musical instrument, done not just for the sake of performing but also with an understanding that such practice contributed to one's own well-being and life force. In 1963 she wrote in her diary, 'Cannot go through life without an instrument.'[9]

By the end of January 1960 Romi was taking some classes at Penzance School of Art, recording that she had finished a painting of green fields there. This, one of her earliest works, already contained distinctive hallmarks of her painting. It is a humble and simple view of the shapes of agricultural land in the middle and far distance, seemingly seen and painted from behind a hedgerow, sprouting from which is a series of long stems. Not obscuring the view, they provide it with scale, grounding, perspective and visual rhyme – the delicate lines are more frontal and painterly than those describing the field boundaries in the distance but, through their painterliness, they remind us that the artist's brushstrokes created all of the marks. The restricted use of colour in *Green Fields* (above) further encourages focus on the dark, upwardly reaching sprigs and helps to create an atmosphere of bare winter spindliness. The painting introduces us to Romi's gifts of perception, showing how she would often give a scene a particular focus, chosen not without humour, on characterful though distinctly everyday features, and paint them with a quiet vividness and flair.

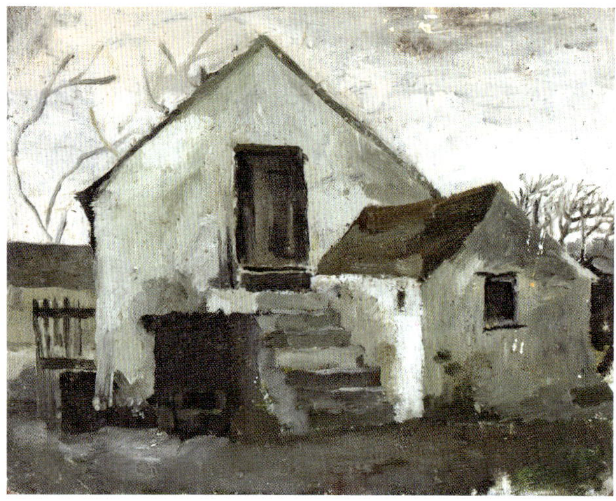

The Barn, Trenalls · c.1961 · oil on board · 36 x 46 cm

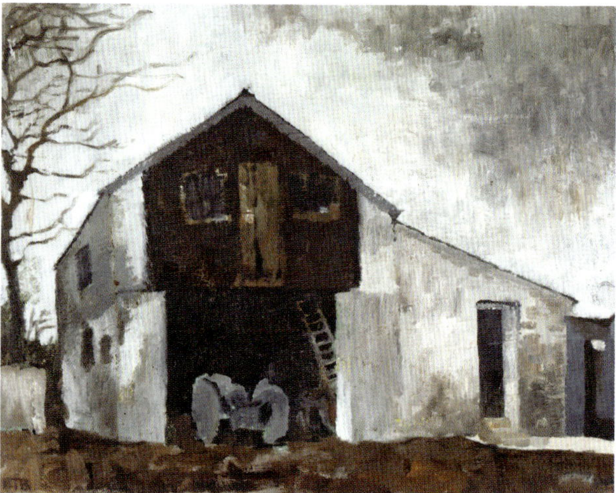

Tares Tractor Shed · early 1960s · oil on board · 35 x 46 cm

Penzance School of Art was, from 1881, situated on Morrab Road in a large purpose-built granite Victorian building that had originally been paid for by public subscription. Romi benefitted from the structure of attending occasional classes, as well as the opportunities the school offered to show work and to discuss it with others. As with learning an instrument, it is likely that she appreciated the need for private practice and learning from those around her, whether formally or informally, through discussion with friends. For someone mostly painting in her kitchen for the first ten years, dedicated studio space would have been extremely welcome. Regarding materials for her work, Romi bought cheap oil paints from local art shops, including W.H. Smith's, and received some as gifts from family.[10]

Throughout her life she bought hardboard in bulk from the hardware store Parkers of Penzance and cut this herself, usually without much measuring, so that the edges of panels were rarely straight. Mike would make her frames when he had the time. In the early 1960s Romi's diaries rarely mention her teachers. When she began at the art school, she worked under a tutor called Mrs Gage, though the references to her are sparse and mostly involve lines such as 'Sketched for Art School. Mrs Gage mad, nothing worked and I got fed up.'[11] Indeed, from the start Romi was her own harshest critic. She could compliment her own efforts but more often noted her failures.[12] Despite this, her persistence and passion for painting prevailed, suggesting that she allowed herself a good deal of understanding that learning a craft called for patient experimentation and practice.

Romi attended classes quite regularly for the first couple of years of painting, although she had an energetic desire to make work which far surpassed that of engaging with a new hobby. She appears to have had a need to paint, and to continue painting even though being a farmer's wife

and mother proved most demanding. Romi's responses to her situations were relatively inventive and probably quite unusual at the time. She would often sketch or paint a scene while her baby daughter was asleep under a tree or in a car parked nearby (her diaries note a surprising number of car parks frequented to paint). Not to be restricted by walls, she would also paint views from windows in the house and looking across the yard from the house towards the tractor shed (above).

At art school she mostly painted still lifes, probably because of their suitability for group classroom supervision. Despite noting regular failings at painting flowers throughout 1960, she made her earliest surviving still-life painting the following year: *Poppies (First Flower Painting)* (see facing page). The flowers seem decidedly more alive than still, springing close towards us at a jaunty angle from the lower edge, as if the vase had just been handed to us and we are first taking in the poppies' sprawling shapes. It contains large areas of thicker paint that are heavy with the trails of broad brushstrokes, which mostly describe the negative space, enlivening the whole area and also filling the volume that the poppies take up with animated thickness and energy.

While clearly taking to this genre, Romi was never just a still-life painter, always thriving on being able equally to be outdoors and engaging with the structures of the town, buildings and landscapes around. She sketched in her local fields, sometimes with friends, and enjoyed taking herself into Penzance to sketch and paint more urban scenes. As early as 21 January 1960 she noted that she had sketched the bottom of Morrab Road, below the art school, and by the middle of May she had finished a painting of it (facing page).[13] Working between different genres, furthermore, seems to have enhanced her ability to appreciate different subjects and to have kept her motivated.

Romi's tuition in painting arguably benefitted from
the relatively strong and long-standing artistic culture
in Penzance and Newlyn, which meant that there were
not only other artists around, but also galleries regularly
mounting exhibitions of historic and contemporary work.
In February 1960 she visited an exhibition at Penlee
House, which included work by her peers, describing
what she saw there as 'okay', and in April she wrote about
visiting an open art exhibition, also including peers'
work.[14] In other respects, too, living on a farm outside of
Penzance did not prevent her from being aware of cultural
developments further afield. She and Mike often saw contemporary films, and listened to classical music and radio
plays. From the Easter of 1962 Mike's younger brother,
Hilary, arranged a classical music festival at Porth-en-
Alls, which took place annually and for which esteemed
musicians from around the country were invited to stay.
This festival gave way to the renowned International
Musicians Seminar (IMS) in 1972.

Romi was also alert and responsive to important national
and international events, regularly noting them down in
her diary in ways which indicate her empathy for people
much further away. Diary entries include references to
a deadly earthquake in Morocco (March 1960), the first
man going into space (April 1961) and, in her own words,
'President Kennedy is assassinated. Too horrible for words.
Poor America' (November 1963). While it seems obvious
to point out that Romi was not just a painter leading a
busy family life in Cornwall but also a person aware of
international events, keeping this in mind can help us
to appreciate the strength of her desire to paint local
subjects and, by doing so, to make sense of the shapes
and qualities of her own life and immediate environs.
These were the subjects that she had found herself living
around; they were the things closest to her and the means
through which she was most able, at this time, to express
parts of herself and her life. This life was also by now much

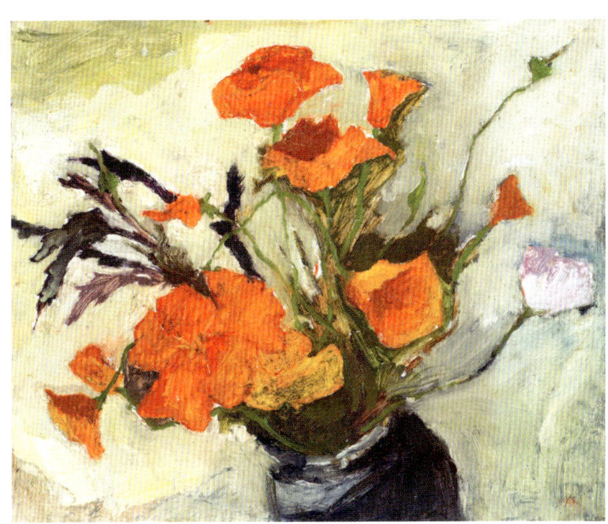

Poppies (First Flower Painting)
1961 · oil on board · 41 x 48 cm

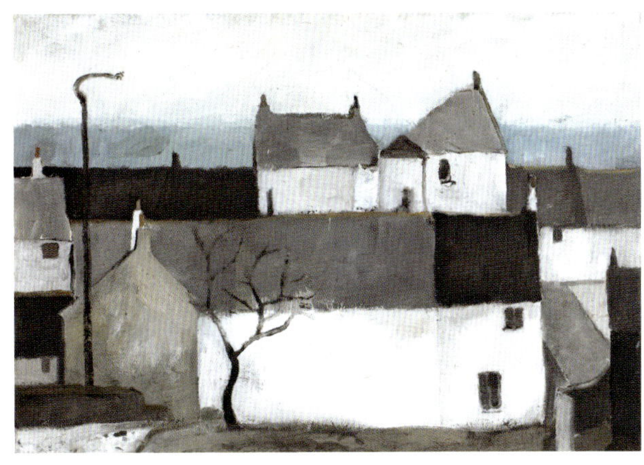

Morrab Road · 1960 · oil on board · 50 x 76 cm

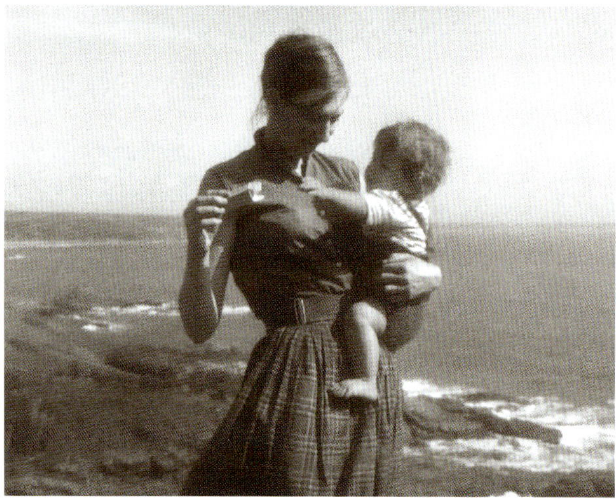

Romi and Rebecca on the farm, 1961

changed, taking her to a new home, as well as a new family and wider community, in which she was having to play a leading, responsible part.

Living at Porth-en-Alls, Romi arguably had first-hand access to an enviable range of rural subjects for painting, as well as the more urban (though not at all city-like) townscape of Penzance. Thus, while many of her contemporaries nationally were responding to the gritty cityscapes of London and other urban metropolises, Romi's haystacks and more orderly (even if grey) scenes of corners of Penzance were her reality. It is tempting to read into her choice of agricultural subject-matter the influence of nineteenth-century painters who painted similar subjects, most notably Claude Monet and Vincent Van Gogh, whose haystacks and cornfields must have been known to her, even if she had not studied them formally. Romi would have visited the National Gallery during the 1960s, and, though it is not known when she acquired it, her collection of art books includes a book of 16 full-colour plates illustrating the work of Van Gogh, published as an '*Express* Art Book' in 1958. This book must have been fairly close at hand, as at some point Romi used its back cover as a palette.[15]

I would suggest that the precedents of Impressionist and Post-Impressionist rural scenes bolstered Romi's natural inclination to see the landscape around her with a creative eye. Whether that agricultural landscape was especially evocative – to an art world at least – of contemporary Britain or nineteenth-century France, she clearly felt there was no need to avoid her rural reality as a painting subject. Instead, it seems that Romi was not at all troubled about whether the facts of her life provided contemporary or outmoded subject-matter for painting – cornfields and haystacks (also, slightly later, a portrait of her postman) were not just artistic subjects to her, they were as much a part of her daily life as were her children,

friends, house and trips to town. Some of these scenes are to me the most touching records of Romi's faith in the power of painting personally – more precisely, of *not* grasping for subjects which explicitly speak of modernity and contemporary change. Furthermore, they are testament to her ability to paint any subject around her with such vividness and human attention that our own powers of perception are refreshed. Later in life, Romi copied out for herself the dictionary definition of the word 'microcosm', which she outlined in a striking red box. The

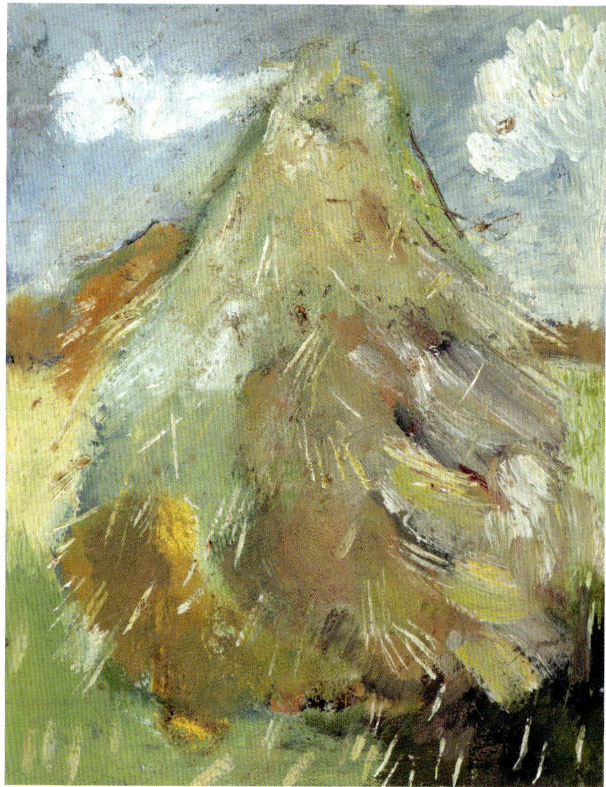

Mike's Hay Stooks · mid-1960s · oil on board · 39 x 33 cm

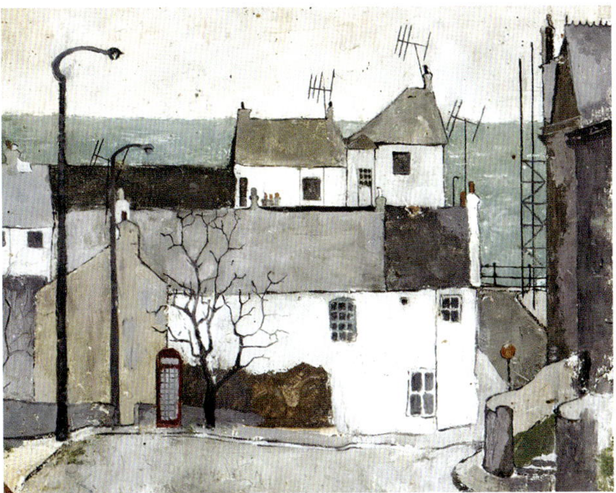

Morrab Road · 1962 · oil on board · 30 x 35 cm

definition begins 'n. a little universe or world, an object, situation, etc. contained within another + displaying all its characteristics on a smaller scale'.[16] Her paintings of even the smallest subjects often suggest the fullness of the world around them, including its light, colour and atmosphere, as well as patterns of human behaviour.

Romi's sense of the value of small things is inseparable not only from her strong Christian faith (always attending church on Sundays and often mid-week, too), but also from the sense of rightness and purpose she gained from living her life at Porth-en-Alls with Mike. In December 1960 she wrote appreciatively, 'Lovely walk with M all around. Life is very good to me and I feel v happy.' In January the following year: 'Lovely things to draw, life isn't long enough.'[17] In a cyclical turn, the paintings she made also provided decoration for her home and further visual stimuli. Although she was decidedly not always joyful and experienced periods of mental struggle (overcome through housework, faith and painting), it is also clear that Romi enjoyed being a mother. A second daughter, Emily, was born in May 1962 and a son, Peter, in March 1965. Her diaries from these years are full of happy perceptions, recording what her children had been like and what they had done, as well as what she had been painting and doing around the home.

From the start, Romi also seems to have enjoyed the challenge of painting more complex combinations of buildings and other structures in Penzance, often with a focus on specific corners or cropped views of a street. Among these scenes, a later painting of one of her earliest subjects, *Morrab Road* (above), has an unusually large number of elements. A bare tree stands out as the most organic shape in an otherwise grid-like composition of buildings and infrastructure, though its verticality and thin dark lines also echo a range of other features, especially the straight upward lines of scaffolding,

communication aerials and thicker lamp posts. A telephone box is lightly paired with a circular red sign on the other side of the road. It is a recognisable and distinctively sloping part of the town with the blue sea beyond; a relatively unremarkable corner painted with an eye for compositional balance and character. Despite the absence of figures, the place and the buildings feel active and occupied.

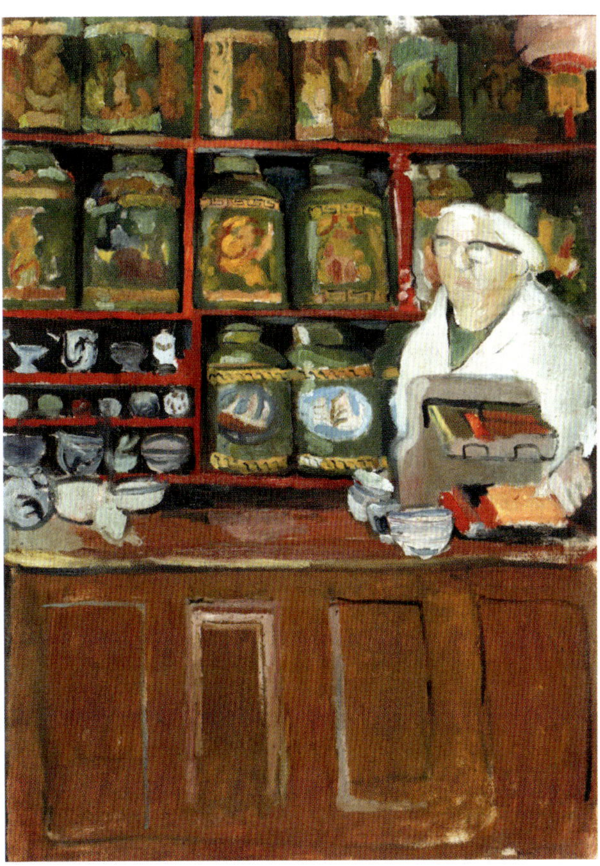

The Old Tea Shop, St Ives · early 1960s · oil on canvas · 92 x 66 cm

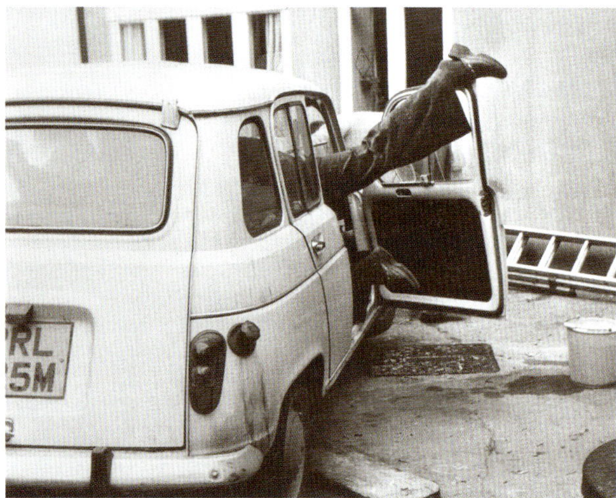

First Renault 4, early 1970s

Other views of town buildings painted during the 1960s have a busier feel and offer compelling records of the local people and businesses. On a visit to St Ives in 1963 she painted the interior of the Old Tea Shop (see previous page), complete with a white-haired, white-coated shopkeeper, whom she probably knew, who stands between a till and a shelf full of cup-like objects and large decorated jars. As with Romi's paintings of buildings, strong horizontal and vertical lines (of the countertop, wooden panels and shelves, for example) give her painting balance and symmetry, as well as intimacy – we feel we are inside and directly in front of this tightly ordered display, full of things to choose from. In places, Romi let herself apply paint more freely: the lower part of the counter, the patches of red and orange on the till, the striped cup standing in front of it, and the freely outlined receptacles on the left. These don't distract from the main impetus of the scene – our eyes are still drawn to the golden rope-banding on the glistening jars and to the details of the shopkeeper's face and hands, as well as the neatly spaced lines of smaller objects on the left. These freer sections, however, also bring vividness and tenderness; they have been painted not simply as incidental objects, but elements to be thoroughly enjoyed as colours, shapes and characters. I have a sense of Romi seizing the opportunity to make something alert out of everything there.

From at least 1964, but possibly earlier, Romi was also painting the exteriors of local shop fronts in ways which reveal a similar love for the detail and character of these places, as well as the people she associated with them. Though this painting is not currently known, in January 1964 Romi recorded having painted her own Utrillo, namely a painting of Clark's shop, in Marazion, just outside Penzance. She wrote of it: 'Utrillo in Mz. Lovely fun'.[18] French painter Maurice Utrillo (1883–1955) specialised in cityscapes of Paris, painted with a certain illustrative naivety, often focusing on corners of the city and on shops with handwritten signs, which invite us to imagine the buildings as places run by people and inhabited by community life. In November 1960 Romi had purchased, probably from a house clearance, a Utrillo print, which Mike framed and which was then hung on a wall at home.[19] Romi's reference to her own 'Utrillo in Mz' suggests total awareness of the relationship between her painting and the work of this older artist, who had worked similarly but in a different place and some decades before.

Many more of Romi's shop paintings survive from around the 1970s, one of the earliest being a painting of S. Curnow's fish shop in Causewayhead, Penzance (below). The building takes up most of the available

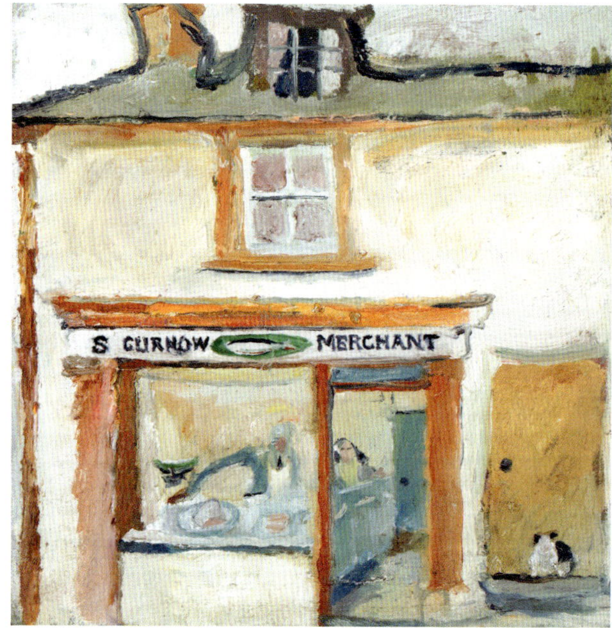

Fish Shop, Causewayhead · late 1960s · oil on board · 32 x 32 cm

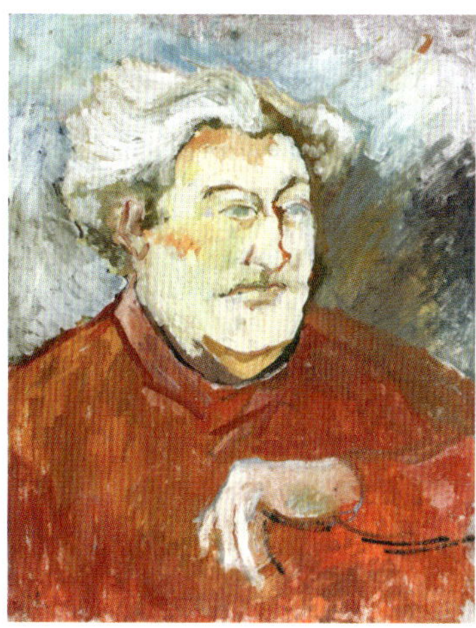

First or Second Portrait Ever
1964 · oil on board · 80 x 61 cm

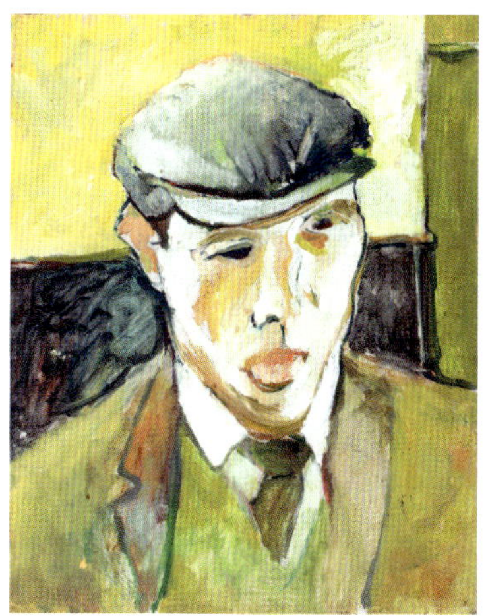

First or Second Portrait Ever
1964 · oil on board · 75 x 61 cm

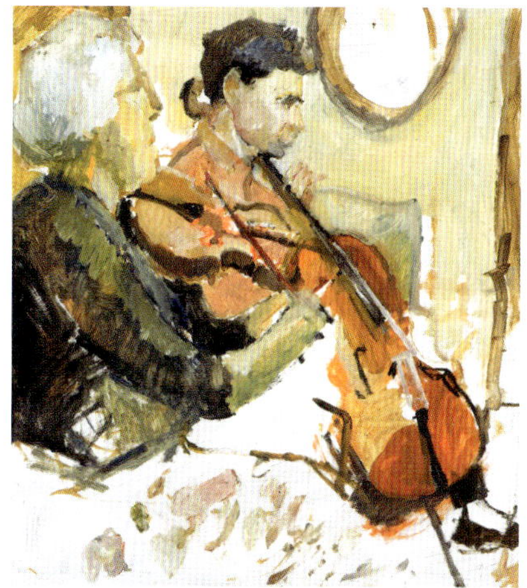

Faith Harris and Mike
c.1965 · oil on board · 61 x 56 cm

space, matching almost exactly the hard-board square Romi selected as her support. Confident outlines in blue and rusty red describe the building's distinctive shape; we read the lettering as we would come across it in the street and, through the door and windows, can see the fishmonger, pink fish on ice and weighing scales inside. One of the fishmonger's arms reaches beyond its natural line and a cat has been brusquely but characterfully described on the adjacent doorstep. Looking at the brushstrokes, it is clear that Romi did not always want her paint to be applied neatly but preferred to use generous application to make the painting more of an object in itself. In this, her work resonates with that of another artist, Alfred Wallis (1855–1942), who used household paints and rough-edged hardboard to depict landscapes and fishing scenes in ways which were not indebted to traditional painting techniques or perspectival systems, but which were widely praised as both freshly evocative scenes and painted objects. Wallis's paintings would have been known to Romi through the local art scene, as well as through appearances in galleries and reproductions. Romi probably would have seen (indeed she owned the catalogue for) an exhibition of his work mounted by the Arts Council in 1968, which was shown at the Penwith Gallery in St Ives.

Romi's shop paintings are undoubtedly connected with a genre to which she remained committed throughout her life: portraiture. Even paintings of buildings not titled after their inhabitants or owners were clearly connected in her mind with these people – they were part of the identification system and language she used to describe them. The first mention of portraiture in Romi's diaries appears at the beginning of 1961. That January, she made what she described as a 'bad self-portrait' and appears to have been painting family members when they would allow it.[20] By July 1963, she had painted a self-portrait that she was pleased with, and, by the following year, she was confident

enough to start painting people she didn't know, taking paints with her to the Tolcarne Inn in Newlyn and the Lamb and Flag pub outside Hayle.[21] A work now known as *First or Second Portrait Ever* (above left) – one of two works from 1964 with the same title – gives a weighty presence to its sitter, whose name is unknown. It is vivid and boldly painted (especially in its use of colour, including a red outline to his nose, slightly green jowls and a dark brown shadow under his chin), even though the man's left hand appears comparatively flat and sketchily drawn, as if in slight movement. Romi had written about the challenges of working with colour over the previous two years, but by this time she was experimenting quite liberally with it.[22] In 2010 she narrated the event:

> *I'd been painting lots of big old barns + chapels, + flowers … when a friend asked why I didn't try portraits? I said 'Never thought of it, not interested etc etc' – <u>However</u>, only a week later I was in Newlyn, a familiar hunting ground, when the heavens opened; I had to shove everything back into the car + make for the nearest pub, the Tolcarne, hoping the rain would stop + I'd soon be outside again … I always look to the right even now, as that was where these 2 chaps were sitting. The only people there – I found myself getting paints etc <u>out</u> of the car again. My first 2 portraits, but they opened the flood gates + from then on I wanted to paint every single person I met!*[23]

Working from home and painting people who knew her – that is, under presumably less intense but more intimate conditions – seems to have allowed for a greater fluidity and confidence in Romi's portraits. A picture of Faith Harris, leader of the Penzance Orchestra, and Mike (above) playing music together reflects the musicality and creative spontaneity of the event. Both figures share their focus, though perhaps Mike is not at this moment playing – we are not able to see his hand or bow. His cello

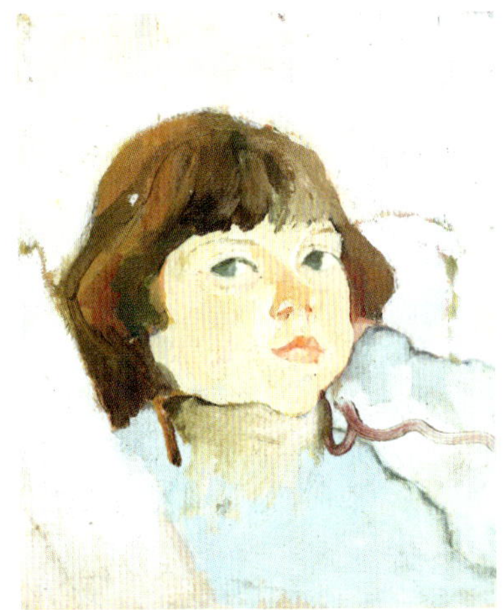

Emily, Askance
c.1967 · oil on board · 46 x 38 cm

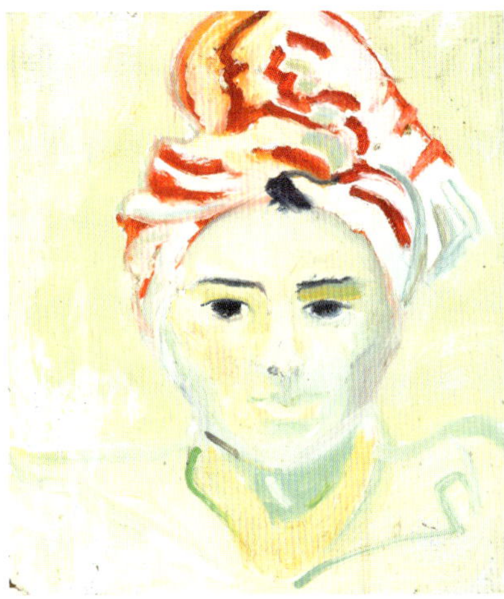

Rebecca with Towel on Head
c.1971 · oil on board · 30 x 27 cm

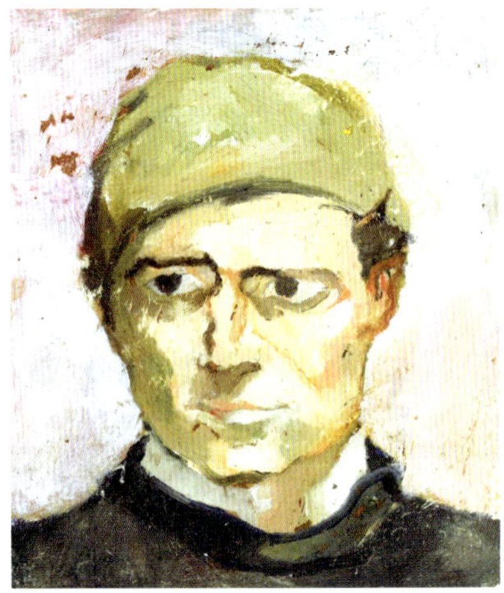

Young Dad
c.1965 · oil on board · 42 x 32.5 cm

is portrayed distinctly and made more prominent and beautiful because of the way in which its lines reach out somewhat towards the surrounding empty space. Perhaps Faith was wearing a light, patterned skirt; nevertheless, Romi felt the need to make only light daubs of pale colour on the empty primed white surface for almost a third of the composition, creating a semi-abstract fluttering that might express something of the lightness or beauty of the musicians' sounds. Romi situates this practice or performance in a real interior space, marking it out simply in the same brown paint. Even if this corner of the room does not end with the vertical brown line which runs along the composition's right-hand edge, that line helps to enclose the duo in a relatively tight space, while we look on.

Romi's early family portraits also show her confident exploration of different gazes. Her subjects variously acknowledge the artist's/viewer's presence: *Self-Portrait* (right); *Emily, Askance* (above); *Rebecca with Towel on Head* (above) – at times appearing a little self-conscious and avoiding of it (*Young Dad*, above). The works share powers of characterisation and a malleability of style or boldness to suit the character or atmosphere needed. Romi's *Self-Portrait*, for example, is delicate yet bold. Her gaze directly addresses the viewer (or herself, while she was painting), with a slight smile of recognition. One eye is outlined with a ring of lighter thick paint, which contrasts with a peachy eyelid, pink cheek and darker pink shadow down the left-hand edge of her face. The contrast between the sides of her face gives it shape and draws our attention to the work as a composition of colours on a flat surface. Seen as a whole, the pinks also pair with those at the opposite corner of Romi's head, the right-hand section of her hair. As with her earliest still life, the surrounding space is thickly and expressively painted; her bold use of colour and handling, however, ensures that attention is held foremost with the acknowledging features of her face.

Despite having only begun to paint the previous year, Romi was exhibiting work by the early summer of 1961, taking part in a group exhibition at Penzance School of Art.[24] She also benefitted from the encouragement of Michael Canney, then curator of Newlyn Art Gallery, who would go on to ask her to submit paintings for exhibitions at the gallery. In February 1962 Canney asked her to send 10 paintings. Although Romi worried that they were not up to standard, they were all accepted.[25] She appreciated the encouragement and took great courage from being told

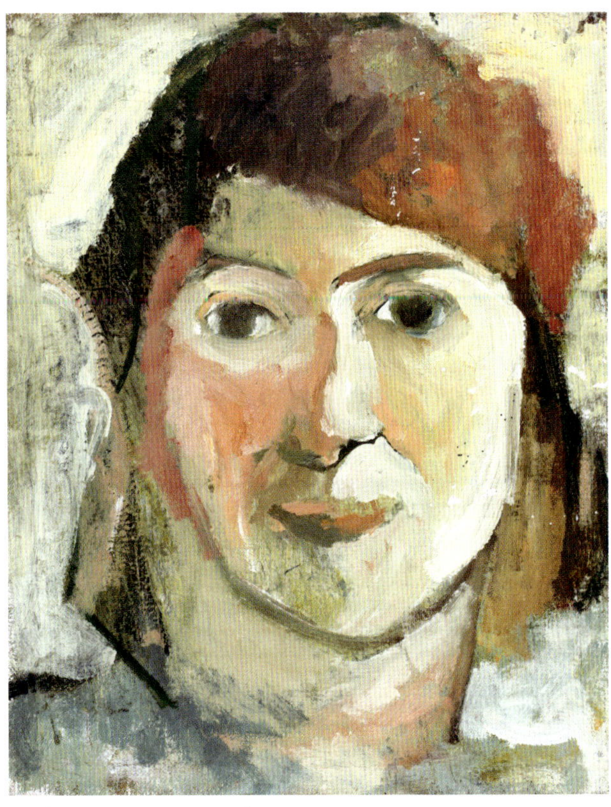

Self-Portrait · c.1968 · oil on canvas · 51 x 41 cm

her works had been admired. In July 1962, she noted that
Canney had rung her up to let her know that artist Peter
Lanyon (1918–1964) had especially picked out her work
as worthy of praise.[26] Romi never got to know Lanyon well,
but she admired his work (she saw a 1963 exhibition of
his in St Ives) and was devastated when he died in 1964.[27]
Opportunities to exhibit not only gave Romi confidence
and motivation to continue, they also occasionally brought
sales and further opportunities. In March 1964 she was
invited to exhibit paintings at Fore Street Gallery, St Ives,
the same venue where she had seen Lanyon's work the
previous year.[28]

Although living almost 200 miles away, Romi would
sometimes visit her parents in Wiltshire, from where
she had easier access to London. In November 1962 she
took her two children to stay with her parents, venturing
into London with just Rebecca. Eager to see as much as
possible, she recorded going to 'all the Cork St Galleries',
as well as the Kaplan and Leicester galleries, before
taking a bus to the Tate, where she reported that Oskar
Kokoschka's retrospective exhibition (of portraits, landscapes and imaginative scenes) was 'tremendous'.[29] In
June 1964, she visited the exhibition '54–64: Painting
& Sculpture of a Decade', at the Tate Gallery, which
celebrated the work of some of the most internationally
recognised artists from the last ten years. Romi particularly noted enjoying Lanyon's work (his large gestural
and abstract work, *Wreck*, 1963, was included), as well as
the work of French artists and J.M.W. Turner downstairs.[30]

Romi also later recalled the importance for her of seeing
a Matisse exhibition at the Hayward Gallery in 1968,
on what she described as 'one of her rare escapes to the
metropolis'.[31] While the experience of his work in person
clearly had a huge effect, she was probably already familiar
with Matisse through various publications. By the end of
her life, Romi owned at least 12 books on Matisse, as well

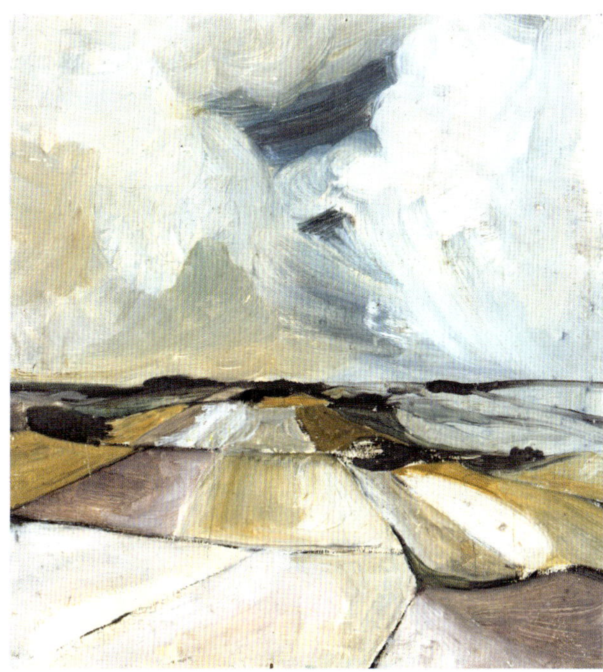

Berkshire Fields III · c.1964 · oil on board · 39 x 37 cm

as some much-thumbed general surveys of modern
European painting.[32]

Romi's engagement with Matisse, and her exposure to
a range of work which would have been notably bold in
colour and non-dependent upon strictly figurative subject-
matter (encountered at the Tate in 1964, among other
places), coincided with a period in her own painting which
can be described as increasingly flamboyant and bright,
as well as more simplified and eye-catching in compositional design. Though Romi, as we have seen, often used
coloured paints before 1970, comparing works made before
and after this date, one can see why she recalled that in
her early career she had painted mostly in black and white.

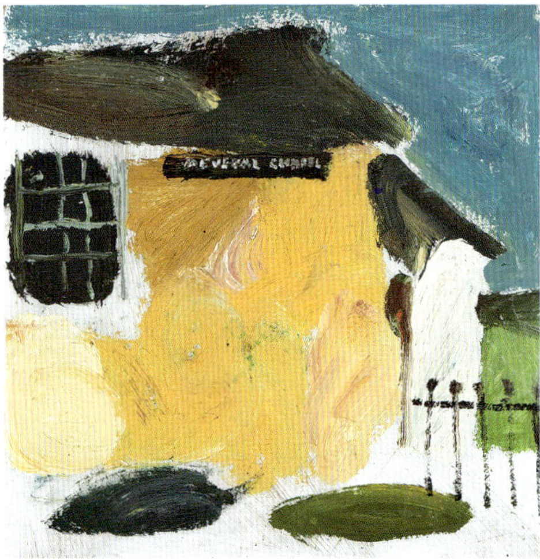

Deveral Chapel · 1970 · oil on board · 45 x 45 cm

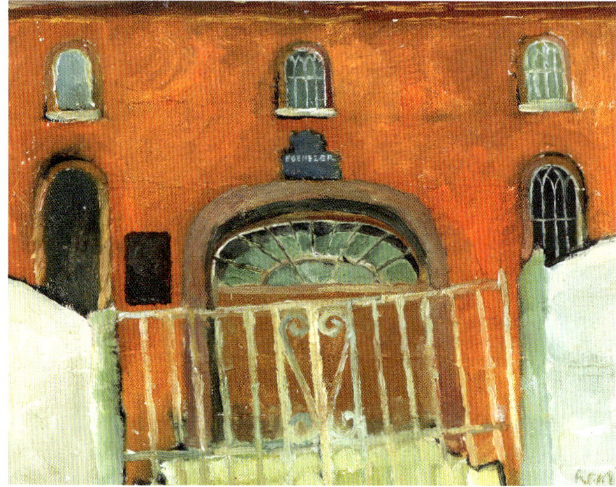

Ebenezer Chapel, Newlyn · c.1973 · oil on board · 33 x 44 cm

Deveral Chapel (above), Reawla, is especially flamboyant, the bulk of its side painted in a range of yellows, each applied with a broad brush in circular motions. The dark slate roof has been painted similarly – joyfully reluctant to be neat, non-uniform in texture (and colour), and without tidy lines. Two broad ovals in different greens at the bottom, where they are surrounded only by white primer, almost declare the painter's objective: to allow painted colour not only to be descriptive, but also to be enjoyed for the shapes, blends and textured residues of movements that an artist's broad and loaded brush can make.

Many of Romi's paintings of buildings from this time pay particular attention to doors and gateways, to the extent that her repertoire can feel like a collection revealing to us the variously changing and standardised shapes and sizes of these passageways, and of their associated paths, gates and other trimmings. I cannot help but think that part of the appeal of these works is how they remind us of the scene's humanness, shaped to our scale and designed according to ritual behaviours as well as various people's needs. It seems that Romi appreciated such features for providing her with strong punctuating shapes, as well as views on to buildings beyond, often seen through the veil of vertical (even if rather jaunty) bars of metal gates. Looking at *Ebenezer Chapel, Newlyn* (above), our eyes are drawn to the straight and swirling lines of the sloping – perhaps slightly open – gate, as well as the bands on the doorway arch, which fan outwards towards the other windows. The picture is probably based on the Primitive Methodist Chapel on Boase Street, Newlyn, most likely then already a dullish rusty brown rather than vibrant orange and quite recently decommissioned, which could explain the blackness of some of the windows and idiosyncratically angled gate. By depicting buildings front-on to the picture plane, Romi could align her brushwork (here, especially, with faint swirls of yellower tones on the

front) with the texture of a building's walls. Although, as we have seen, she used similar brushwork to describe negative space (around her earliest poppies, for example), she appears also to have enjoyed the way in which her relatively free application could help to suggest the texture, feeling or multifaceted nature of a surface.

As with her paintings of buildings and gateways, Romi was drawn to other opportunities to depict subjects or details with a greater degree of simplification and symmetry of composition. She painted her son, Peter, around this time (below), face-on and crowned by the thin spindles and round top of a Windsor kitchen chair.

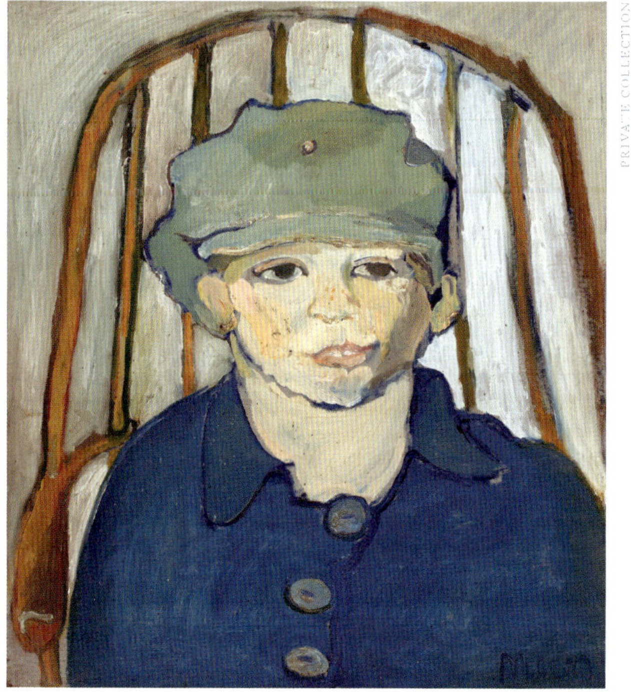

Peter · c.1971 · oil on board · 61 x 56 cm

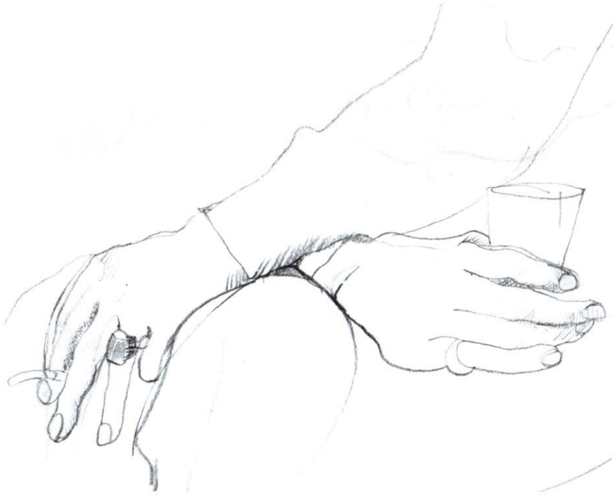

Hands · c.1972 · pencil on paper · 21 x 30 cm

Wearing a blue top and blue-green hat, his whole form is outlined confidently in a bright blue, which ensures his presence sitting forward from the chair's back. Although he sits a touch off-centre and looks slightly to our right, the overall symmetry of composition provides a calm clarity and focus on the young child, patiently sitting.

Her figurative studies of the 1970s also begin to focus on pairs of legs and shoes, often painted from the obvious human position of another person: to the front and looking down, and distinctly cropped from the rest of the figure. Focus is kept on the shape of each leg, the angles at which each emerge and the various ways they are held and adorned. Plain, though still thickly painted, backgrounds, strong outlines and a relatively restricted palette further keep the focus on particularities of shape.

Romi's fascination with legs extended to her obsession with photography. By the end of her life, she had compiled albums full of photographs of human legs (often cropped from the waist, at least), mostly belonging to people she knew and loved, who were attired and positioned in relaxed, informal ways (right). Her joy at capturing the telling postures of these limbs extends also to her later full-length portraits and group portraits, where limbs are often painted with boldness and verve.

As her good friend Jeremy Le Grice wrote: 'Arms and legs, feet and fingers, are all there for the asking.'[33] Although works such as *Italian Shoes* (overleaf) and *Paddy's Boots* (overleaf) might consciously connect with the tradition of shoes and other personal accoutrements appearing in still lifes (most obviously by Van Gogh, but also William Nicholson), Romi's paintings of shoes are always still partial portraits, inhabited by human limbs. As such their cropping often has a more humorous, playful and human effect, inevitably inviting viewers somewhat into a mental game of 'exquisite corpse'.[34] From the early 1970s,

if not earlier, Romi was also drawing prolifically, often capturing details, such as curling fingers or resting limbs, with a few firm pencil lines (above).

Romi approached objects with a collector's eye for idiosyncratic shapes and characters. From the early 1960s she would acquire, very cheaply, humorous and interesting objects to paint. Family members recall her particularly romanticising these objects, keeping them to hand and often painting them multiple times, as well as in combination with other items. *Christingle* (p. 23) shows one such object, which was probably constructed by Mike for Romi, as an Advent decoration symbolising the Light of

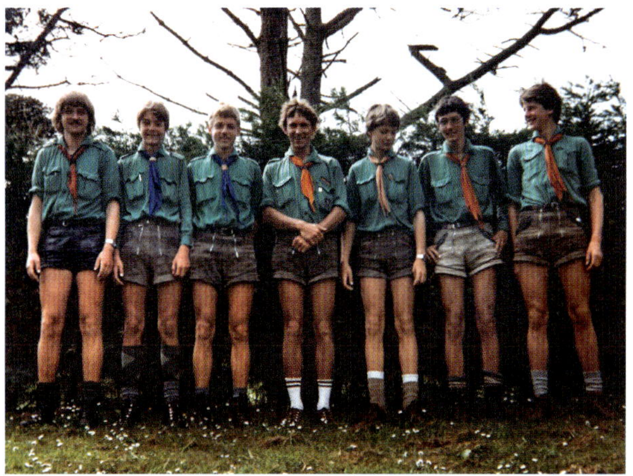

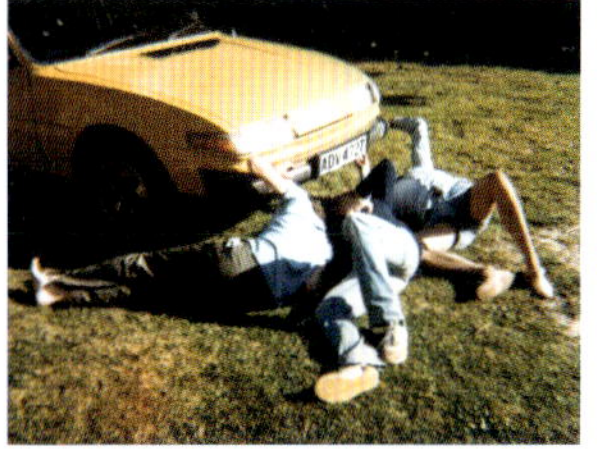

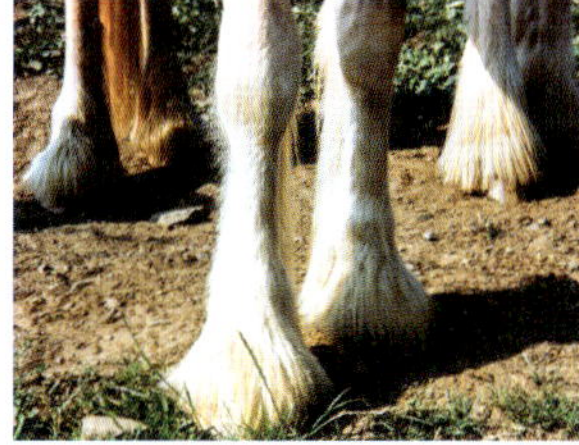

A fascination with legs: German scouts; yellow Rover; horses

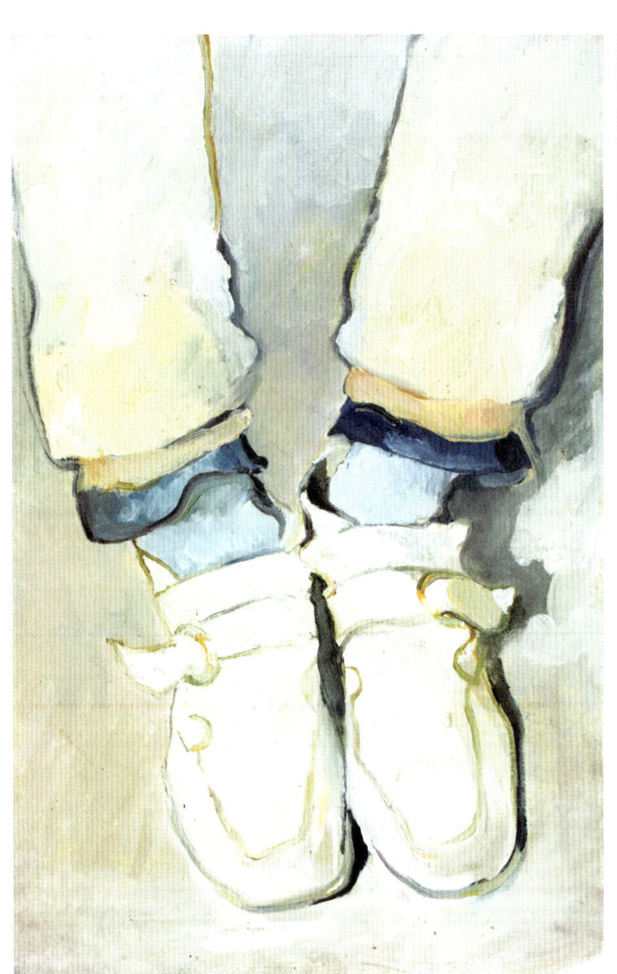

Italian Shoes · c.1976 · oil on board · 63 x 40 cm

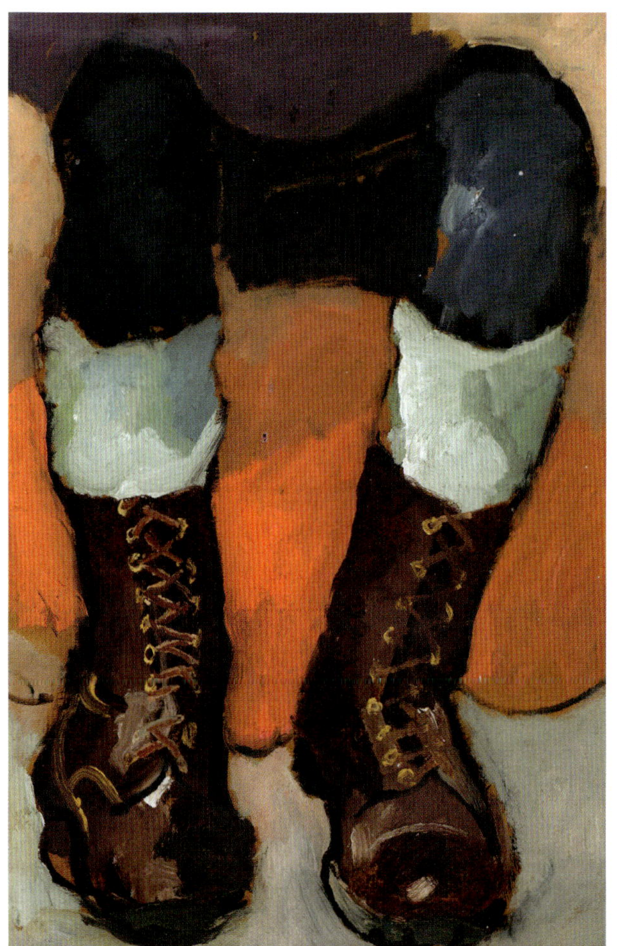

Paddy's Boots · c.1977 · oil on board · 65 x 55 cm

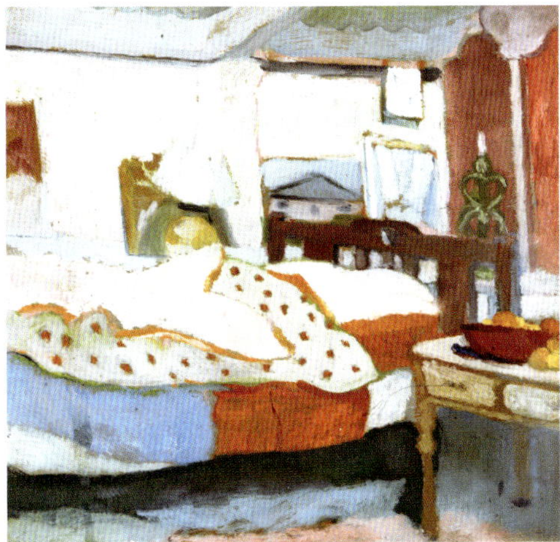

The Old Studio, Trenalls
1972 · oil on board · 28 x 30 cm

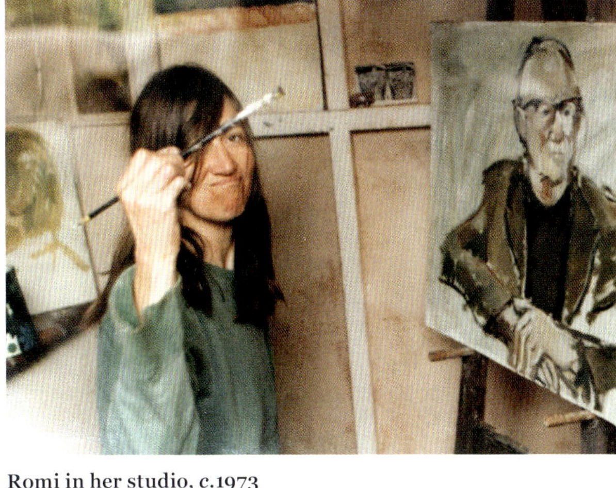

Romi in her studio, *c.*1973

Christ. In the 1970s, and possibly connected to
her enjoyment of shop fronts, she was particularly
attracted to subjects with typographical elements,
relishing the challenge of recording labels printed with
words or logos affixed to three-dimensional objects. *Los
Arcos Sherry Bottle* (overleaf) is one of the simplest of
these, the symmetry of the bottle's placement enhancing
the whole product's modest but stylish design and shape.
As a painting it is not especially humorous, but lightly
subversive, revealing somewhat intimate facts about
the artist's life, and awarding a bottle of sherry that
she might share with others an almost iconic status.

The humour of Romi's choice of subjects can also be
felt in her landscapes, which she approached with an eye
for detail and combination, and which were often joyful
in effect. In more than one, a house peers a bit sheepishly
from behind a dominating bush, which mirrors its blocky
shape (*Cottage at Godolphin*, p. 25). In *Windmill in Suffolk*
(overleaf), long white blades project upwards to double
the height of the building, at the same angle as one of
two neighbouring bushes that squeeze into the picture's
narrow space. There is some humour in the tallness and
slope of each element.

From about 1970 Romi began to have her own dedicated
painting space, built by Mike, partly to reduce the risk
of oil paint mixing with other kitchen activities. The
studio was basic, built in the old pigsty, with clear plastic
corrugated panels for natural light and windows taken
from a nearby barn. It was so cold that she would often
paint in full outdoor clothes, but it contained a basin and
a bed and had electric lights for the evenings. In 1972
she painted a corner of it (above), bringing some features
into relief by using thick white paint: the edge of a pillow,
light falling on a lampshade and the white wall at the
back. The area describing the bedsheets and rear wall is
almost patchwork-like in its clusters and layers of shapes,

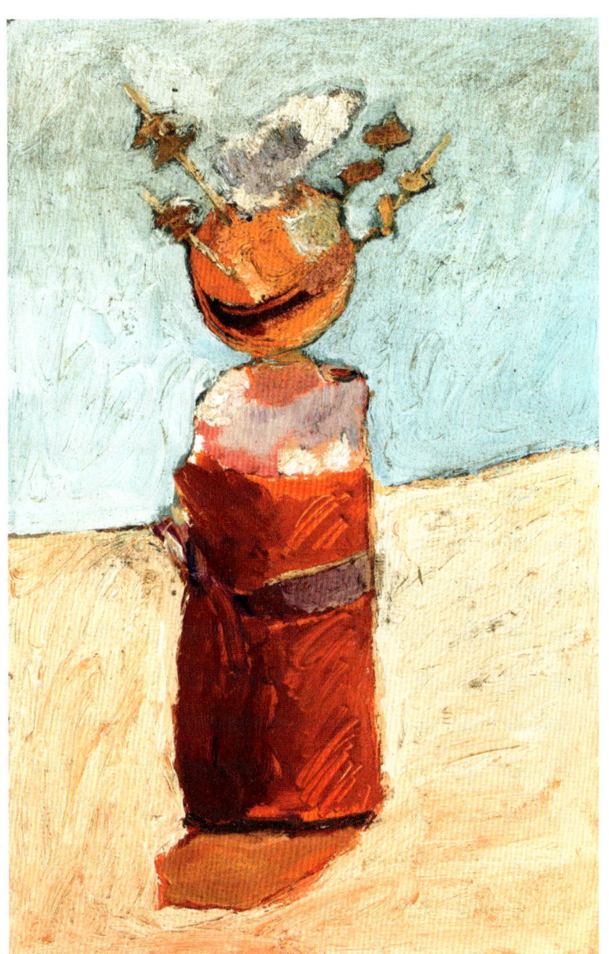

Christingle · *c.*1977 · oil on board · 42 x 29 cm

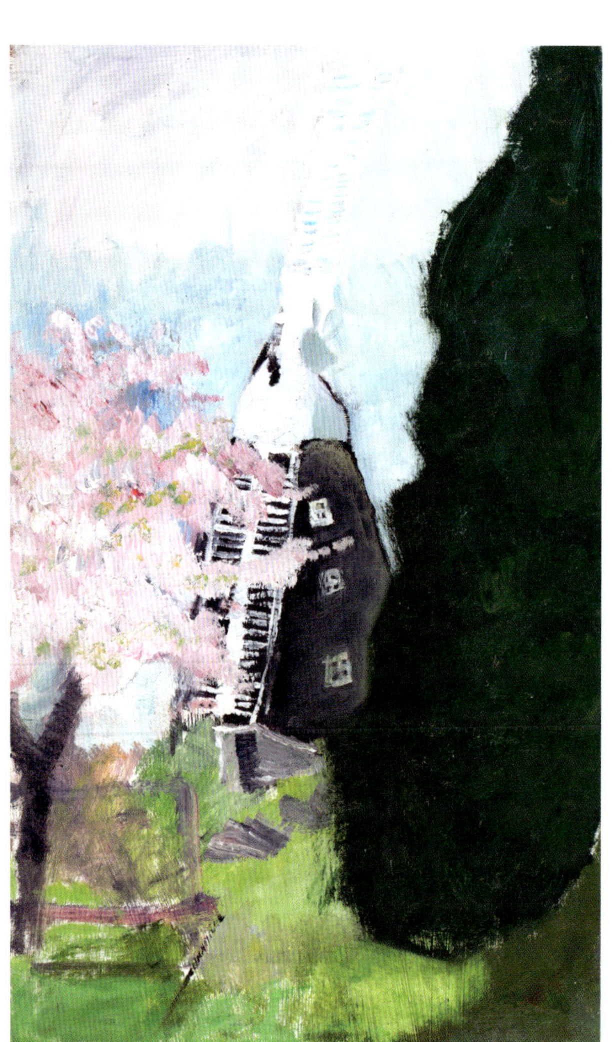

Windmill in Suffolk · mid-1970s · oil on board · 61 x 37 cm

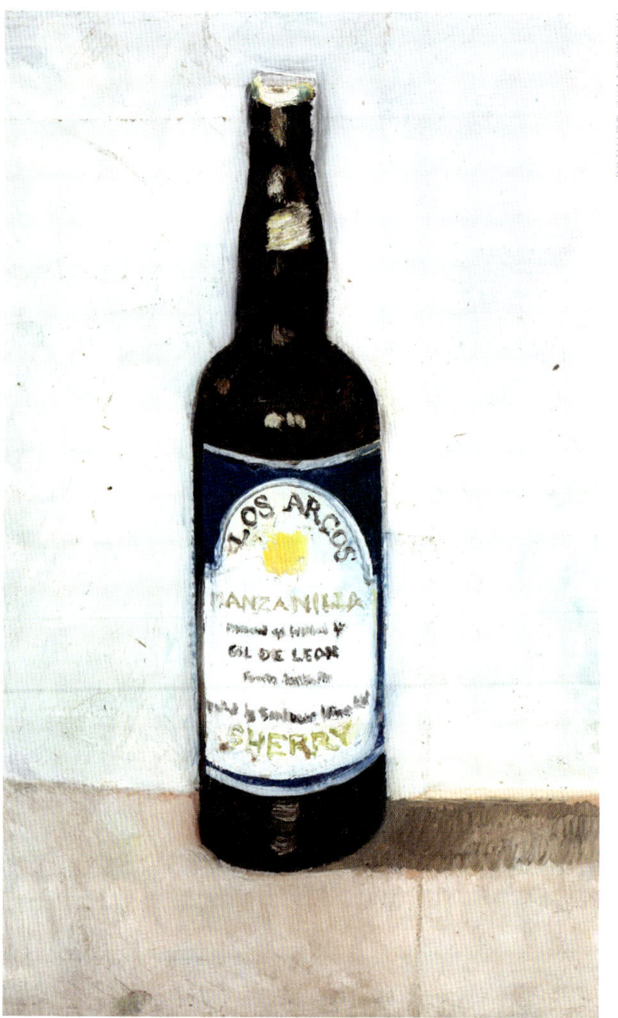

Los Arcos Sherry Bottle · c.1976 · oil on board · 60 x 46 cm

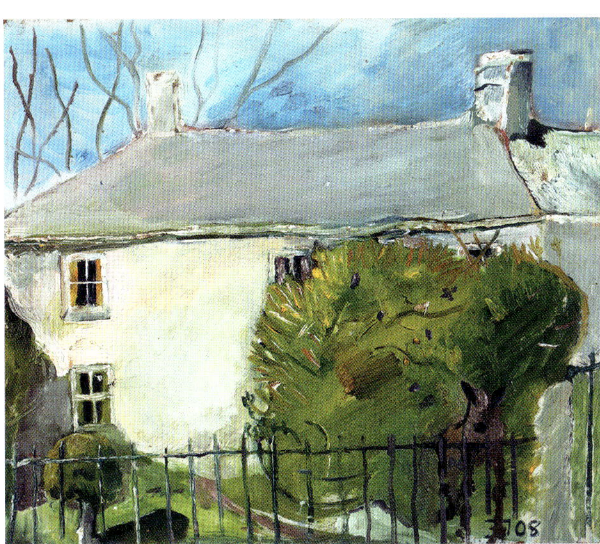

Cottage at Godolphin · c.1973 · oil on board · 42 x 51 cm

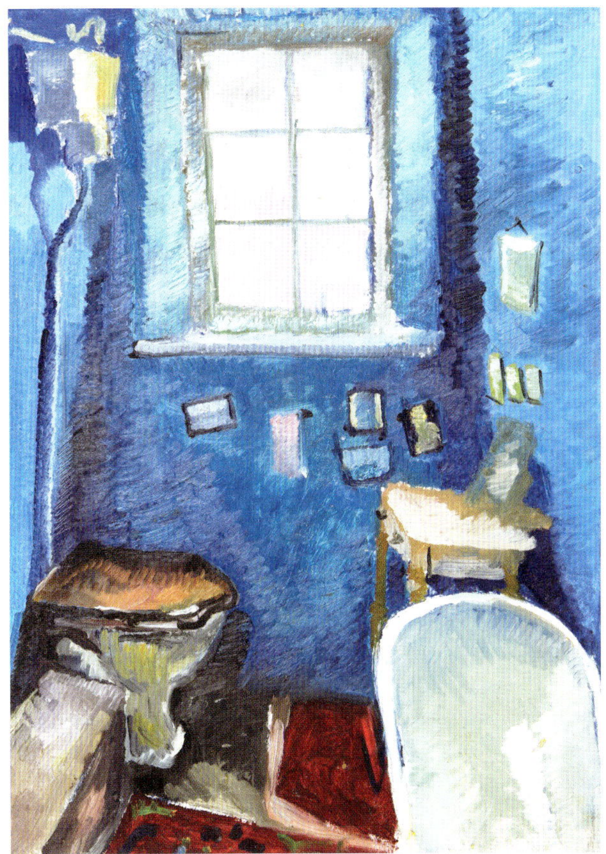

Trenalls Bathroom · c.1974 · oil on board · 81 x 59 cm

whereas in other areas the room's features are more spatially distinct.

In 1974, she painted the bathroom at home (right) with a similar combination of perspectival rendering (creating some depth of space) and techniques which make the distance seem closer to us. The bathtub tilts slightly upwards as it recedes, and the density of short, repeated blue brush-strokes describing the rear wall and air in front of it visually align that space with the picture plane. The resulting effect is that the whole scene appears rich with vibrant light and energy. A small collection of Romi's postcards and at least one image framed in a passepartout decorate the corner opposite the loo. She must surely have been aware of relevant traditions of modern French painting, including the technicolour bathroom scenes of Pierre Bonnard, if not the dense patterning of Édouard Vuillard's interiors. For someone interested in painting

these interior scenes, it seems unlikely that she would not have encountered artists like Bonnard through books, and then again when she visited Paris in 1973, journeying on to Arles, Avignon and Italy with Mike. The influence of such French artists, working about half a century before, seems to have seeped subconsciously into parts of her work, which nevertheless remained very much her own – raw, and truthful to her life and love for painting.

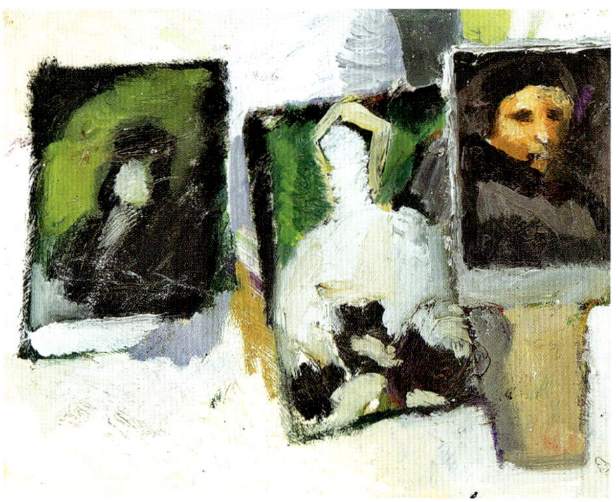

Three Postcards · c.1978 · oil on board · 30 x 37 cm

*T*hree Postcards (above) offers a helpful endnote on some of the themes dealt with above. It shows Romi responding to the things around her, and especially to her love for painting as a tradition and as a living practice. Later, her son Peter asked Romi to try to paint an Old Master type of portrait. While she had 'great fun' trying, she also concluded that what they had achieved was, actually, 'Magic'.[35] While she gradually collected books, prints and postcards, and, like an art historian, must have developed a vast visual catalogue in her mind of ways of seeing and depicting, her relationship with precedents was largely subconscious in the moment of painting and based more on respect for their work than on any kind of analysis. Writing of the importance for her of absorbing the work of 'Great Masters' via the local library, she described this process succinctly: 'Not thinking too much, just letting myself absorb what they did.'[36]

In terms of her contemporaries, Romi has, to my knowledge, never been aligned with a wider group or artistic movement, despite her proximity to one of the strongest regional artistic cultures in the country. She was learning to paint while the main movement of modern art in St Ives was in a late phase, with critics mourning the deaths of a few of its protagonists, including both Barbara Hepworth and Bryan Wynter in 1975. Factors contributing to her never having been considered among these artists include her independent character, geographical location and style of work. The traditions she responded most readily to in her work were arguably most aligned with those also built upon by Patrick Heron, with whom she became great friends from about 1979. It was at around this time that she also developed significant friendships with other artists, including Jeremy Le Grice and Catharine Armitage, and that her career entered its next stage, marked by a 1980 solo exhibition at the Arnolfini Gallery in Bristol.

What this wider comparative context perhaps helps to draw out is how relatively 'unmannered' Romi's practice stayed. To my eyes she never performed a particular modernist style, but continued to work with variety and humility, propelled foremost by a sustaining desire to respond to things around her and to work out how to make paintings from them. The scene of these three postcards, whether tacked on a wall or propped up on a table, is transplanted into her own painting. Although recognisable to many as a painting by Behrens, whether because of its slightly jaunty composition or of what it reveals about the alertness of its maker to her own life or studio, it has a directness of representation, incomparable to the work of those other artists, staying instead with the fundamental act of painting: the rendering of actual things by applying paint to a support. Later in life, Romi explained how the circumstances of her life helped her in this respect, encouraging her to work with naturalness, spontaneity and speed, but also in ways which remained qualitative, full of judgement and decision. She explained:

I also think I was lucky because I was extremely busy with a 7 day a week, 52 weeks a year farming husband, 3 children, and cows, pigs and sheep … There was no time to worry about whether it was right or wrong, it was just a painting … There are a thousand ways of painting and we have to find what we feel happiest with …[37]

Romi wanted people to see, enjoy and respond to her work, yet the relative obscurity in which she stayed might have paradoxically enabled her to continue her own relationship with the discipline in an especially free and intensely personal way. For me, this is evident in the works and in how people respond to them, as pieces made by a particular person set on appreciating everything by committing them to paintings. For someone whose identity was so dependent on her work ('I am a painter and I paint every day!'[38]), this was both a persistent need and a generous act of faith.

1. I am grateful to the artist's daughters, Rebecca Derry-Evans and Emily Saner, for providing me with information concerning Romi's family background and early life. Rebecca and Emily, as well as David Ward, kindly commented on draft versions of this text.
2. As it was called around that time; that is, a school for daughters of the clergy.
3. Howard and Dee Thomas (who had six daughters) owned a cottage in nearby Canon's Town, where they spent all the school holidays and were regular visitors to Porth-en-Alls. Romi Behrens (RB) archive.
4. Mike and Romi lived in Trenalls until 1995, when they moved to Tares, a converted tractor shed across the yard, and then in 2000 to Trewartha, a farmhouse on the edge of the estate.
5. Typescript of diaries 1960–64 by Rebecca Derry-Evans. RB archive.
6. Diary entry 27 January 1960.
7. Diary entry 12 November 1961.
8. A newspaper clipping explains that she was a student at the Salisbury School of Art and Crafts, where she was the subject of a portrait by John Barker, a member of the Salisbury Group of Artists. *Salisbury and Winchester Journal*, 20 March 1959. RB archive.
9. Diary entry 3 January 1963. Romi first played the violin as a child, stopping around age 13 or 14. She recommenced lessons in 1963. During the 1960s, Mike played the cello and later the French horn. Romi's sisters played the bassoon and cello. Her mother played the cello and organ.
10. Diary entry 3 April 1962 mentions buying paints from [W.H.] Smith's.
11. Diary entry 28 September 1960.
12. Diary entries – 18 September 1960: 'Tried to paint the Shippan, not good. Ticked off about standards.' 20 September 1960: 'Painted in Newlyn, no good.' 15 April 1961: 'Painted another failure.' 29 October 1960: 'Painted Trenalls Cottage in oils – not bad.'
13. Diary entry 13 May 1960: 'Finished Morrab Rd painting.'
14. Diary entries 6 February 1960, 9 April 1960.
15. A diary entry from 8 June 1961 also mentions her enjoyment of a 'Van Gogh tribal trip book'. A framed reproduction of a cypresses painting by Van Gogh was also displayed at home.
16. Handwritten definition of 'microcosm'. RB archive.
17. Diary entries 10 December 1960 and 29 January 1961.
18. Diary entry 6 January 1964.
19. Diary entry 7 November 1960.
20. Diary entry 25 January 1961.
21. Diary entries – 10 July 1963: painted a 'self-portrait and was pleased'. 19 August 1964: 'After lunch M and Crick, [Chris Aarvold] Beck and I in Lag. I painted at Lamb and Flag.'
22. In her diaries, Romi mentioned having painted her first 'colour' picture ('Fun') on 9 June 1961. 23 November 1961: 'Changing from non-colour to colour isn't easy.' By 11 January 1962, she was writing 'V pleased about painting and can't wait to start again.'
23. Handwritten notes, 2010. RB archive. During Romi's exhibition at the Brunswick Gallery on Judd Street, London, in 1978, she released a flyer offering to paint visitors. Flyer, RB archive.
24. Diary entry 22 June 1961: 'To art school with all paintings for

exhibition under Mrs Gage.' On 29 June 1961 she reported having five paintings in the exhibition.
25. Diary entry 13 February 1962. Romi became a life member of the Newlyn Society of Artists, enabling her to show work regularly in mixed exhibitions.
26. Diary entry July 1962: 'Mike rang Canney who says I have three in exhibition and Peter Lanyon thinks one is the best there??? Don't believe it.'
27. After attending his 1963 exhibition, in early February, Romi wrote, 'Marvellous. Colour and movement. Most exciting.' In September 1964 she wrote: 'Peter Lanyon dies. A really, really, really unfillable gap. Awful, awful.' She also mentioned Lanyon's presence at an event in June 1961. Lanyon had studied at Penzance School of Art during the 1930s.
28. Diary entry 7 March 1964: 'Letter from Fore Street Gallery [St Ives] asking me to exhibit! Phew. Excitement.'
29. Diary entries – 8 November 1962: 'Left EF with Mum and took RR to London … Did all the Cork St Galleries.' 9 November 1962: 'Went to the Kaplan Gallery, not too thrilling … and Leicester Gallery … free bus ride to the Tate. Kokoschka Exhibition tremendous.' The exhibition was 'Oskar Kokoschka: A Retrospective Exhibition of Paintings, Drawings, Lithographs, Stage Designs and Books' (Tate Gallery, 14 September– 10 November 1962).
30. Diary entry 25 June 1964.
31. She narrated the event in the third person, describing how 'on one of her rare escapes to the metropolis, [she] found herself face to face with Matisse at the Haywood [*sic*] … That was the he + the she of it.' Romi appears to have misremembered the date of this encounter, suggesting it had been earlier, in 1960–61. Handwritten notes, 2010. RB archive. Romi also made drawings of Matisse's sculptures, possibly when attending the same gallery in 1984–5.
32. RB Library.
33. Jeremy Le Grice, 'Romi Behrens', undated text, late 1990s. RB archive. 'People's real features, the glimmer in an eye, glimpse of a nostril, curl of the lips, are devastatingly accurate and recognisable in their observation. Arms and legs, feet and fingers, are all there for the asking.'
34. Exquisite Corpse (*Cadavre Exquis*) is typically used to refer to a collaborative way of working with images (or writing) that often produces intuitive and bizarre results. It was popularised by the Surrealists.
35. Handwritten notes, 2010. RB archive.
36. Ibid. 'Because I only very rarely went to London, or big exhibitions, I think I have learnt most from going to the library + looking at The Great Masters. Not thinking too much, just letting myself absorb what they did.'
37. Ibid.
38. There was a piece of paper, with this statement written in capital letters, and in characteristic thick red felt pen, that Romi had Blu Tacked above the kitchen sink to prompt herself to keep at it. RB archive.

'I paint every day!'[1]

David Ward

If you suddenly and unexpectedly feel joy,
don't hesitate. ...
Mary Oliver, 'Don't Hesitate'[2]

The poetics of Romi Behrens' paintings are found in relationships. In relationships between the painter and her subjects; between objects in the paintings themselves; between the very touches of her brush on the surface of canvas or board and in relationships between ourselves and the paintings before us.

An aspect of the modern in painting is sometimes referred to as 'repetition with variation', and in Romi Behrens' work important repetitions and variations occur over considerable spans of time. Her themes, her preoccupations, recur across decades and the nature of their reappearance is significant. Working within the traditional genres of a figurative painter, she painted still lifes, landscapes and portraits. And within these genres other returns or revisitings emerge.

Within the still-life paintings, a small repertoire of very personal and idiosyncratic objects appear and re-appear, sometimes years apart: the figurine of a toucan; panettone cakes in their wrappings; an angular candle-stick; flowers in various vessels – and more flowers. Then pairs: two Chinese porcelain bowls; two plough shears; two sculptures by different friends; a pair of Staffordshire dogs; a flatfish chopped in two. It is conspicuous how many pairings occur. Poignant indeed is the frequent appearance of the pairing of a violin and bow, lying side-by-side together, mute yet resonant partners. These objects are not ornaments. Rather they appear almost as icons, frequently invested with a curious sense of identity, as with the strangely totemic toucan figure. And within these sometimes humorous encounters there is also a gravitas to be found. Within the celebratory energy of

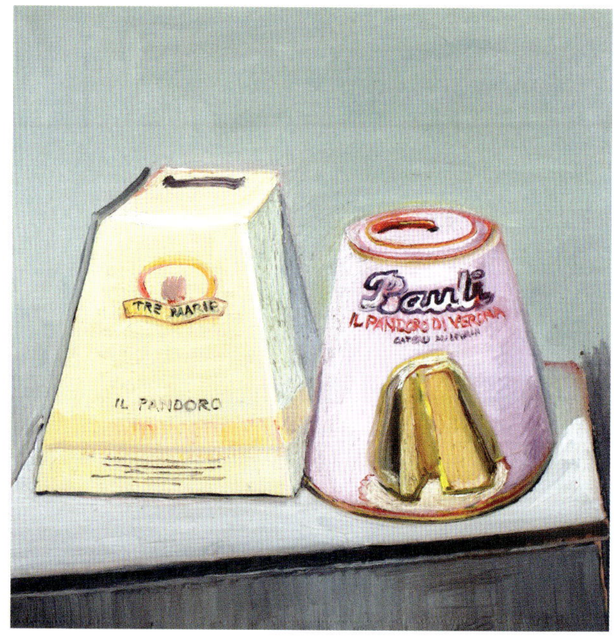

Panettone · c.1985 · oil on canvas · 77 x 76 cm

her painting an acknowledgement of mortality may be present – a gravitas that relates some of her still-life paintings to those of Manet.

If the poetic of the iconography in her still-life paintings is inclined towards the metaphorical, allegorical and reflective, then the gregarious nature of her portraits is altogether more extrovert. Amongst the spectrum of these, for example, are close family and relatives; intimate friends; friends of friends; strangers; briefly encountered visitors to Porth-en-Alls; celebrated musicians and artists. And portraits of dogs. Time, in many of these paintings, is compressed in the uninhibited immediacy of sittings. Visitors, before introductions were complete, might have found themselves being drawn from across the kitchen table. She seized those moments. As Mary Oliver urges: *don't hesitate.*

Landscapes range from authoritative vistas to speedy sketch-scapes, rolling field-scapes, inconspicuous farm-yard corners, astonishing tiny nocturnal seascapes. Within this genre a particular focus emerges towards trees, with particular attention to solitary trees. As the painter Christopher Le Brun has succinctly proposed, when Cézanne painted an apple, the apple was not the subject of the work. The subject of the work was painting. The apple was the motif.

How appropriate is this to Romi Behrens' work? As a painter she was what is sometimes called 'a natural'. By that I mean that sometimes the painting is risky, but she handled paint with a rare spontaneity, ease and loose-ness (like a dancer) that is simultaneously balanced with decisive control. Gazing at the tree paintings, the balance between the subject (painting) and the motif (the tree) is deeply expressive. Yet, when I asked her one day, as we drove in her car past a line of silhouetted pines, what it was, about particular trees, that stirred her to paint them, she replied: 'I suppose it must be to do with the shapes.'

Looking at her paintings you can tangibly feel the way her free brushwork is physically finding and forming these arresting shapes. The choreography of arm and wrist is at work in the swerve that persuades the brush to find the line that defines the trunk, the bough of the tree. Then the dexterity of the fingers, dabbing another brush in, to animate the canopy.

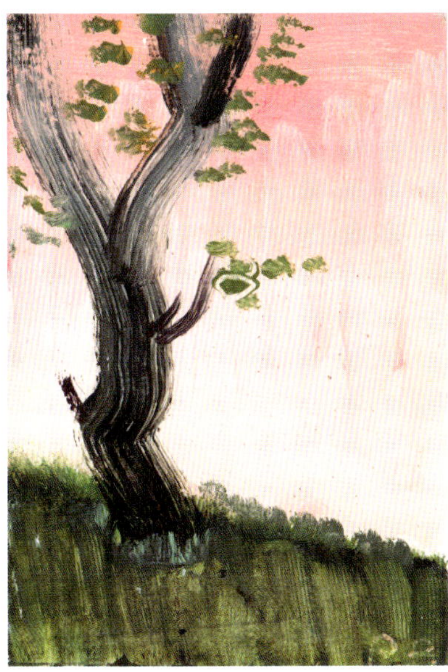

Tree on Pink
*c.*2004 · oil on board · 17 x 11 cm

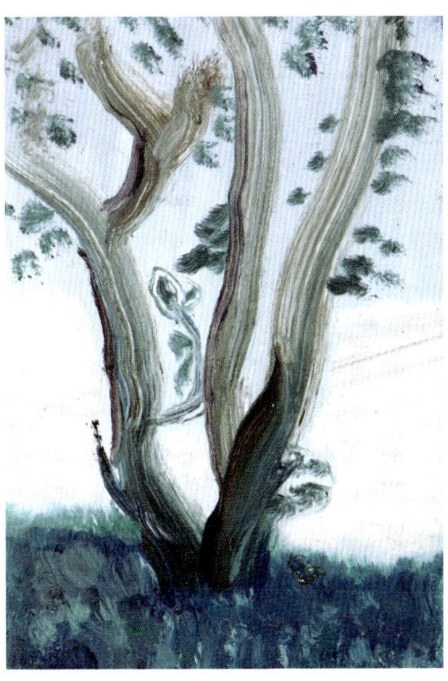

Tree on Grey
*c.*2004 · oil on board · 17 x 11 cm

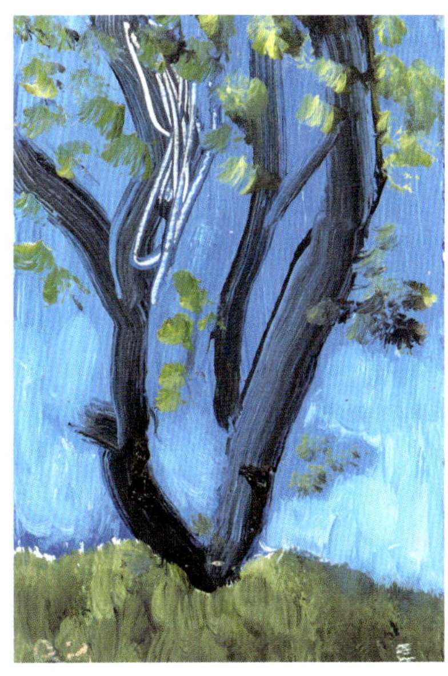

Tree on Blue
*c.*2004 · oil on board · 17 x 11 cm

The motif of the tree has a long tradition, including
the vaporous forms of Turner's Mediterranean trees;
the abundant, lofty crowns of Constable's elms or a line
of pollarded willows in an austere Monet winter scene.
Cézanne's attention to individual trees comes to mind
but Behrens' brush lays down an altogether different
physicality. Some paintings suggest an association
between the tree and a human presence, though not
in a direct representational sense. Yet the ancient myth
of Daphne's metamorphosis into a laurel tree, or the
imagery of the Tree of Jesse, speak to us of a profound
identification between tree and being human.

Across all the genres of painting that she applied
her eye and hand to is a virtuosity akin to that of the
violinist that she also was. There is a dynamic in this
that can appear effortless. But as Matisse (also a violinist)
said: 'I have always tried to hide my efforts and wished
my works to have the light joyousness of springtime ...'³
For a painter as prolific as Romi Behrens, what we see
is a lifelong, daily labour of love. The works can be the
source of life-affirming pleasure, of jouissance within
us, yet they may be hard-won for the artist.

Here was a painter whose dexterity, in lucid strokes
of paintwork, brought forth the forms of a vibrant pink
camellia flower with deep green leaves in a blue and white
china pot with consummate skill. She could also dash in
the line of a hipped carafe with the single stroke of a laden
brush against a flat black background and fill it with sticks
of carnations in seconds. She conveys the awe and wonder
of a red lunar eclipse over the sea and then holds our gaze
in the gaze of a sitter who looks out at the painter, and
through the painter's eyes, to us.

I began with the first words of a Mary Oliver poem and
end with her closing lines: '... Anyway, whatever it is,
don't be afraid of its plenty. Joy is not made to be a crumb.'

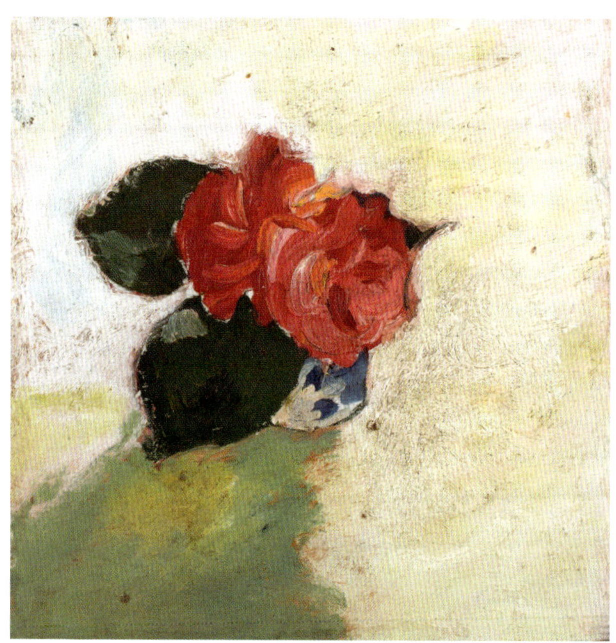

Camellias · c.1988 · oil on board · 39 x 40 cm

Notes
1. Thanks to Rachel Rose Smith for finding
this quote in the RB archive.
2. Mary Oliver, 'Don't Hesitate', *Swan*
(Bloodaxe Books, 2011), p. 42. Reprinted by
permission of The Charlotte Sheedy Literary
Agency as agent for the author. Copyright
© 2010, 2017 by Mary Oliver with
permission of Bill Reichblum.
3. Henri Matisse, 'Letter to Henry Clifford,
1948' [Vence, 14 February], in Jack D. Flam,
Matisse on Art (Phaidon, 1973), p.120.

Plates

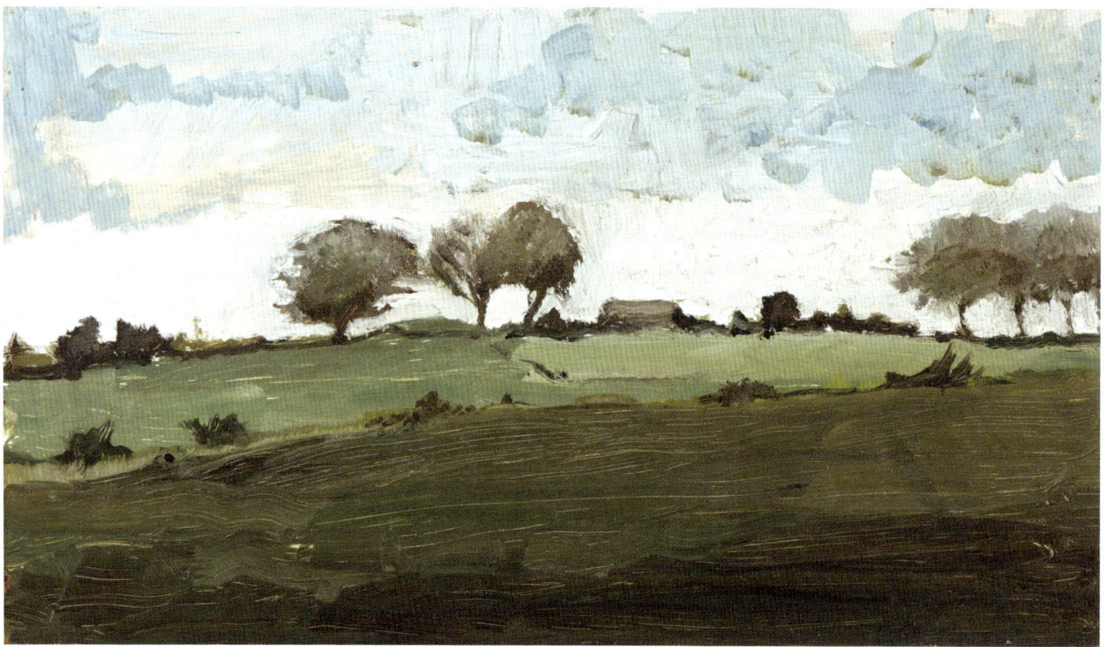

Trees, Bishopstone Down · c.1962 · oil on board · 20 x 36 cm

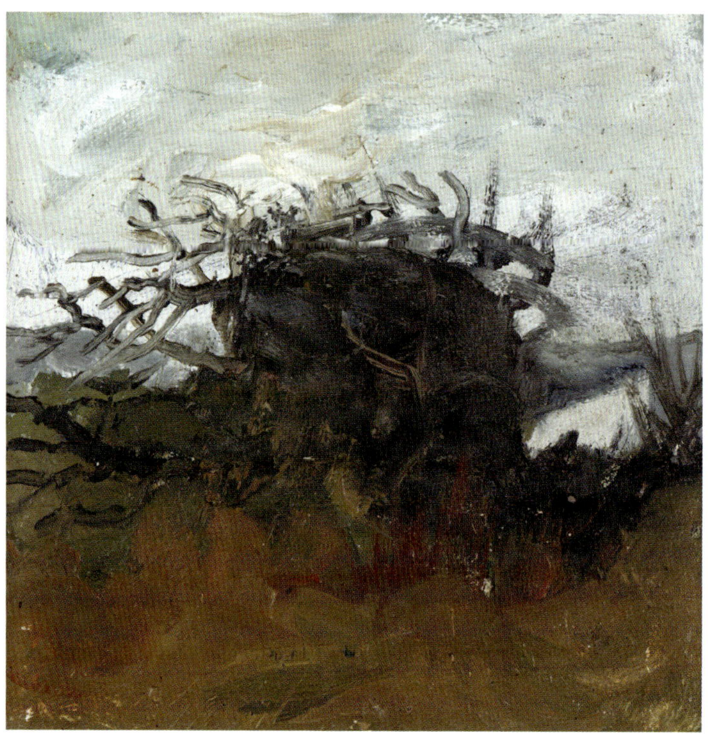

Bush on the Downs · c.1965 · oil on board · 26 x 26 cm

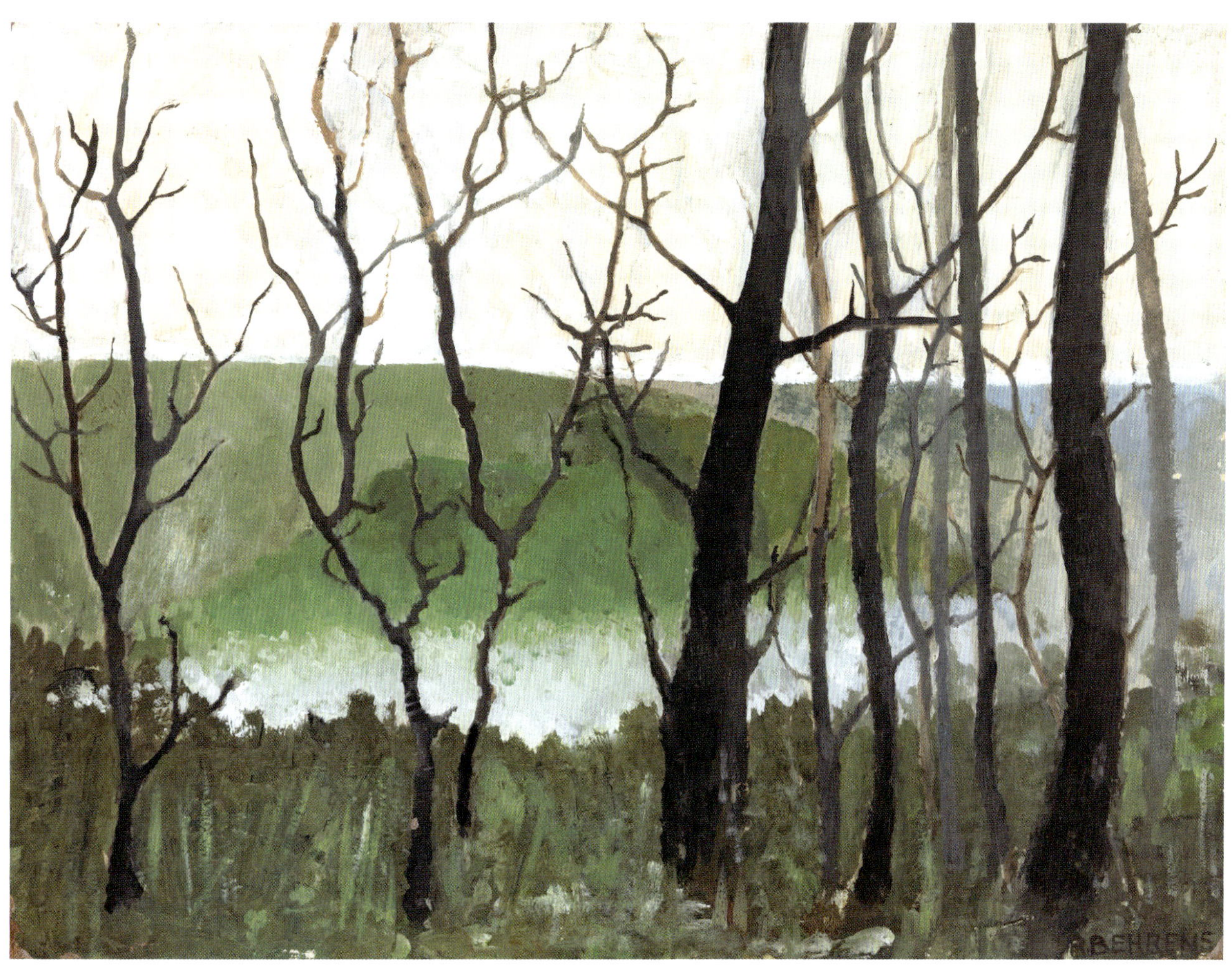

Through the Wood to the Hoe · c.1962 · oil on board · 31 x 41 cm

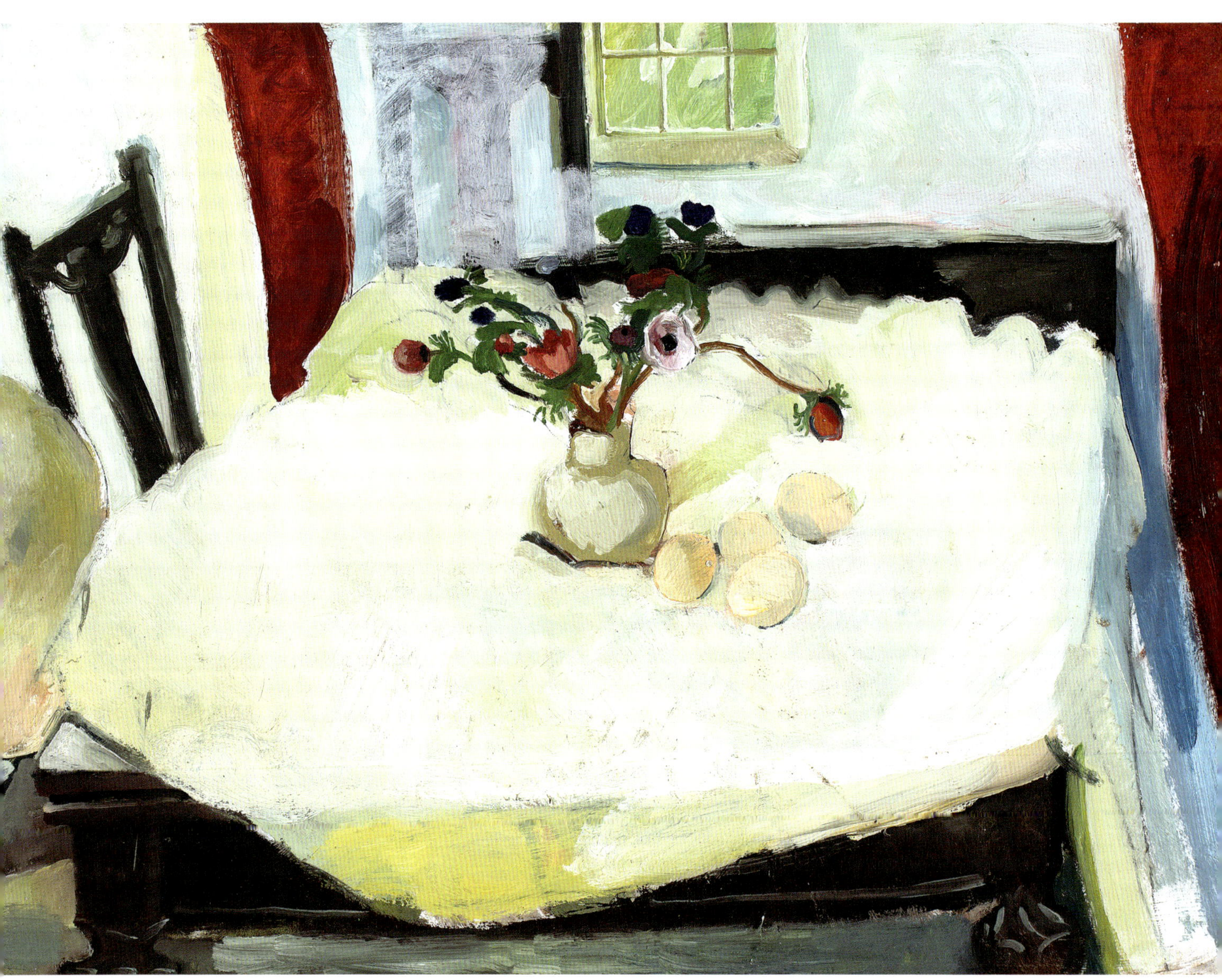

Anemones with Table and Chair · c.1973 · oil on board · 64 x 91 cm

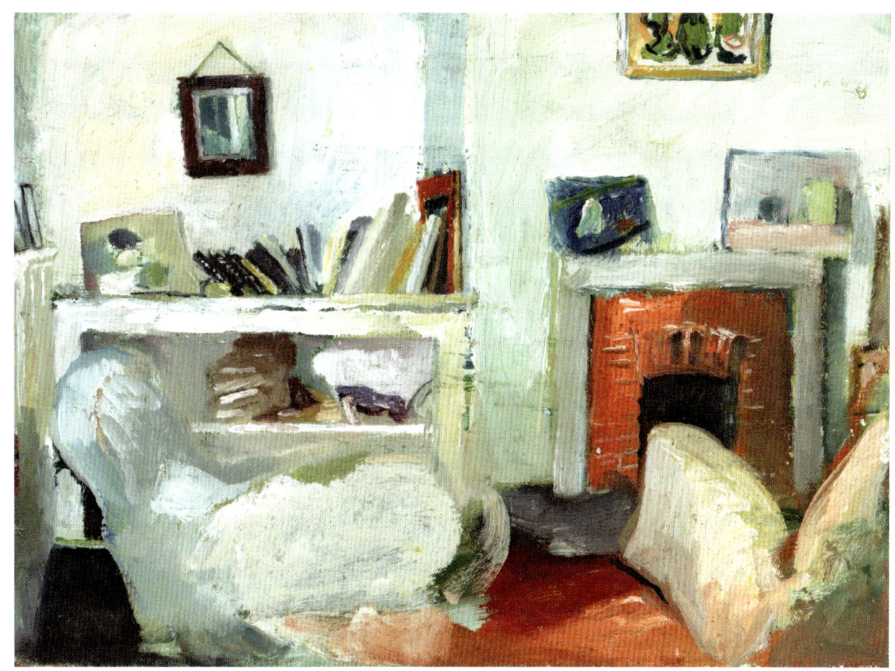

Coastguards No. 6, Fireplace · c.1973 · oil on board · 31 x 42 cm

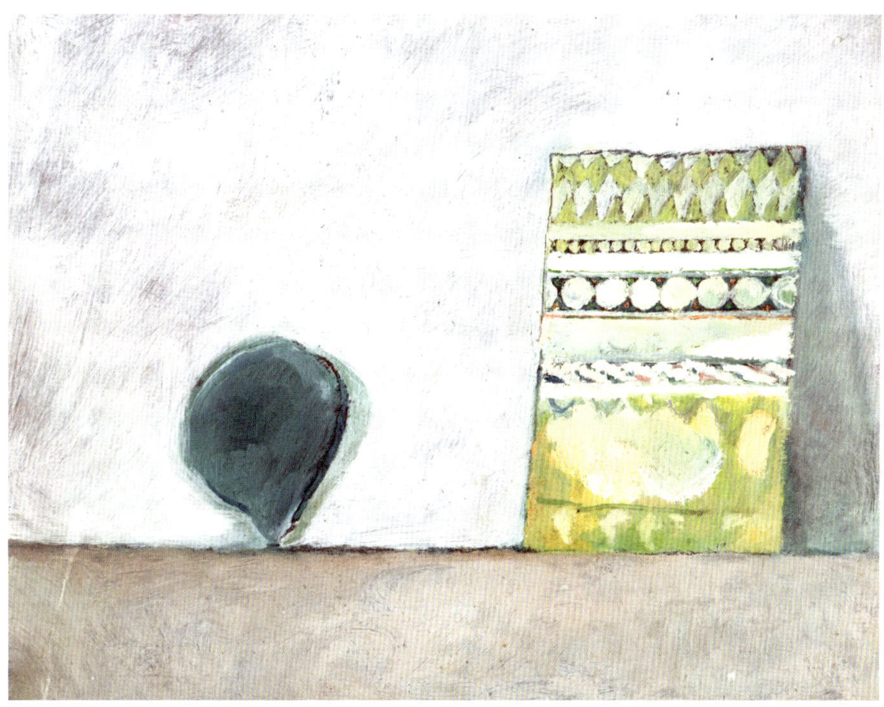

Pebble and Postcard · c.1972 · oil on board · 33 x 42 cm

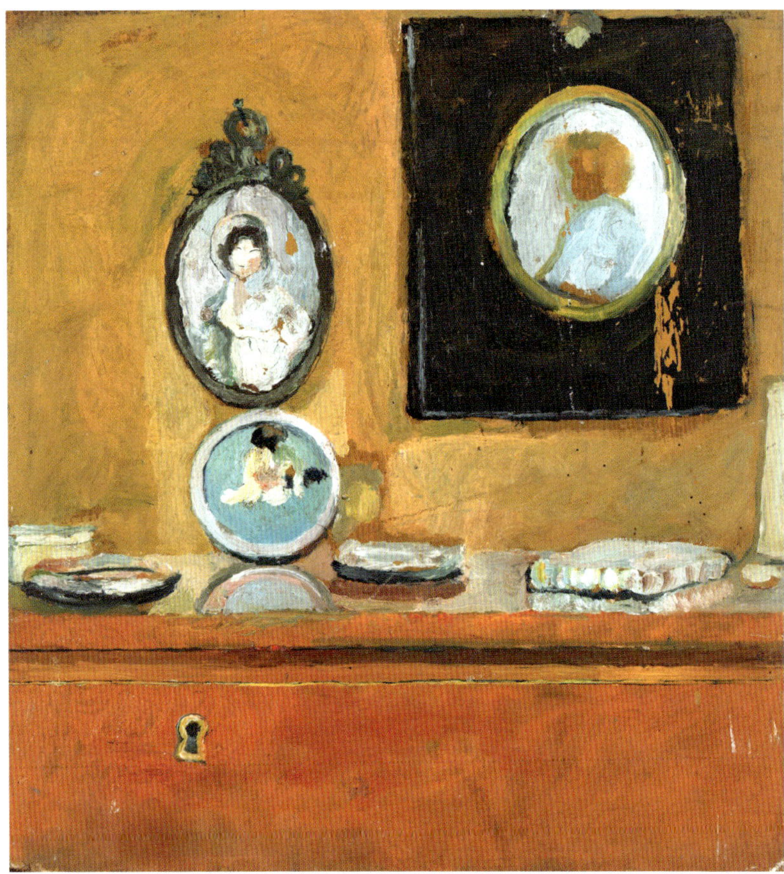

Tregarne · early 1970s · oil on board · 31 x 28 cm

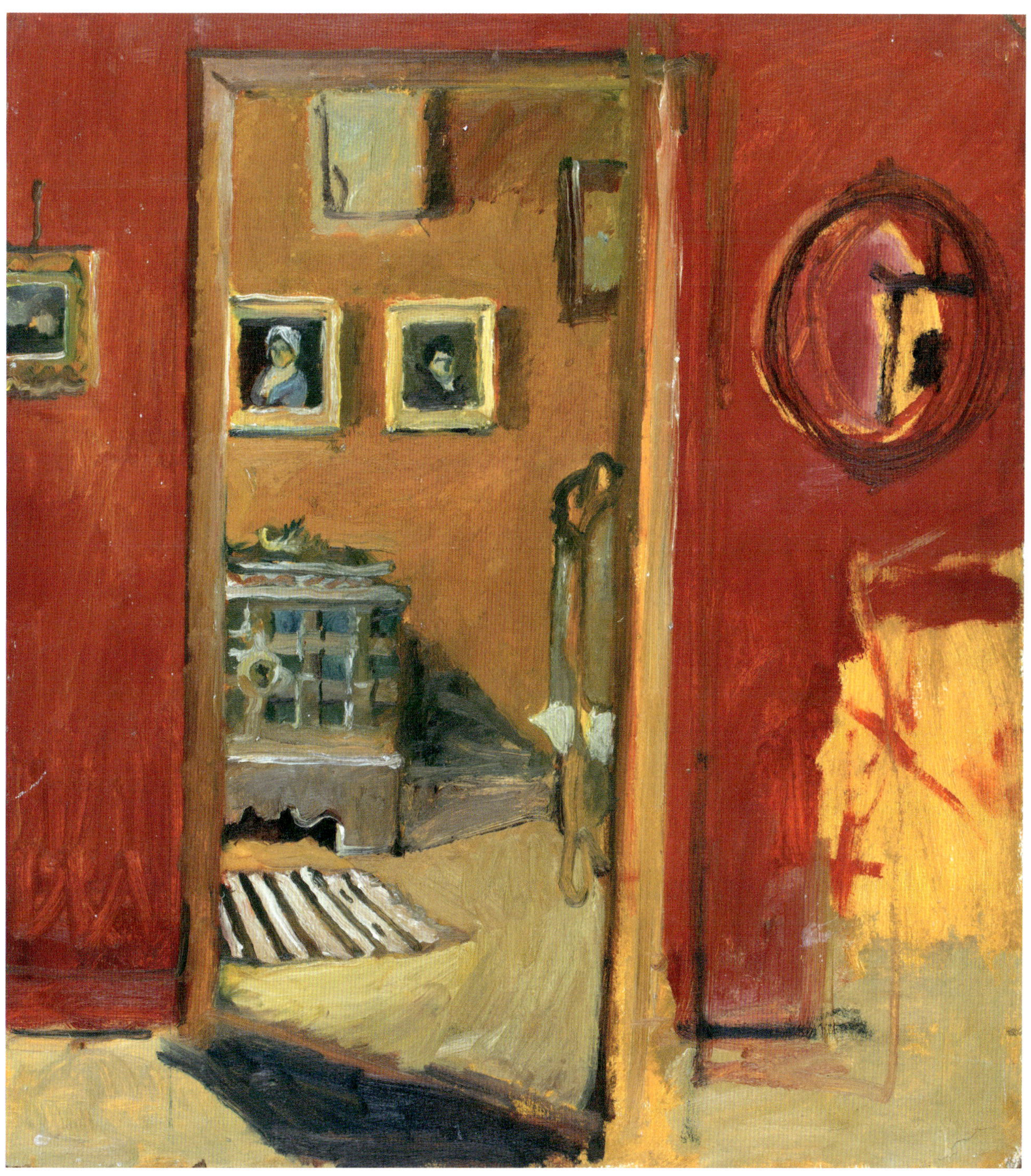

View from the Drawing Room, Trenalls · c.1975 · oil on board · 61 x 56 cm

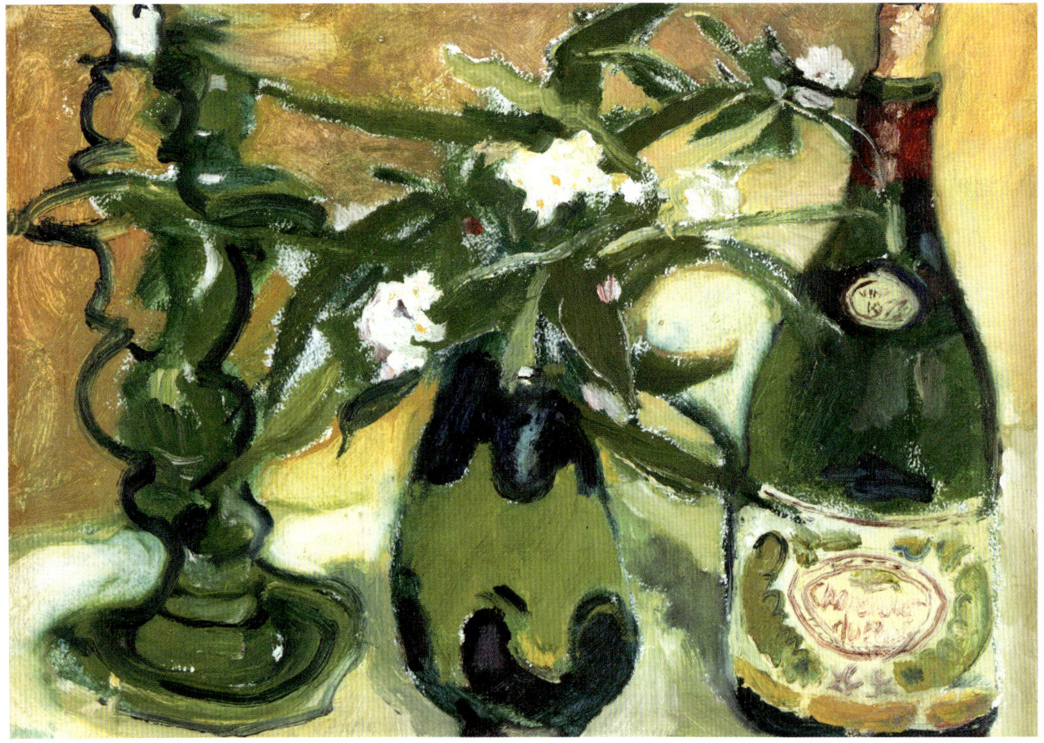

Candlestick, Vase, Côte · early 1970s · oil on board · 31 x 43 cm

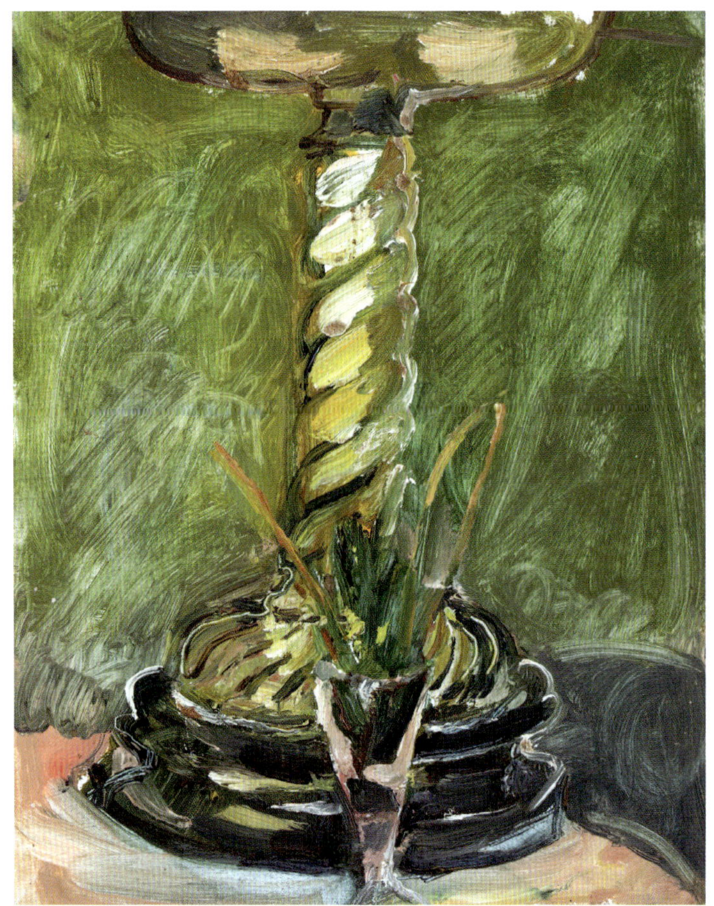

Brass Lamp and Grasses · c.1972 · oil on board · 38 x 31 cm

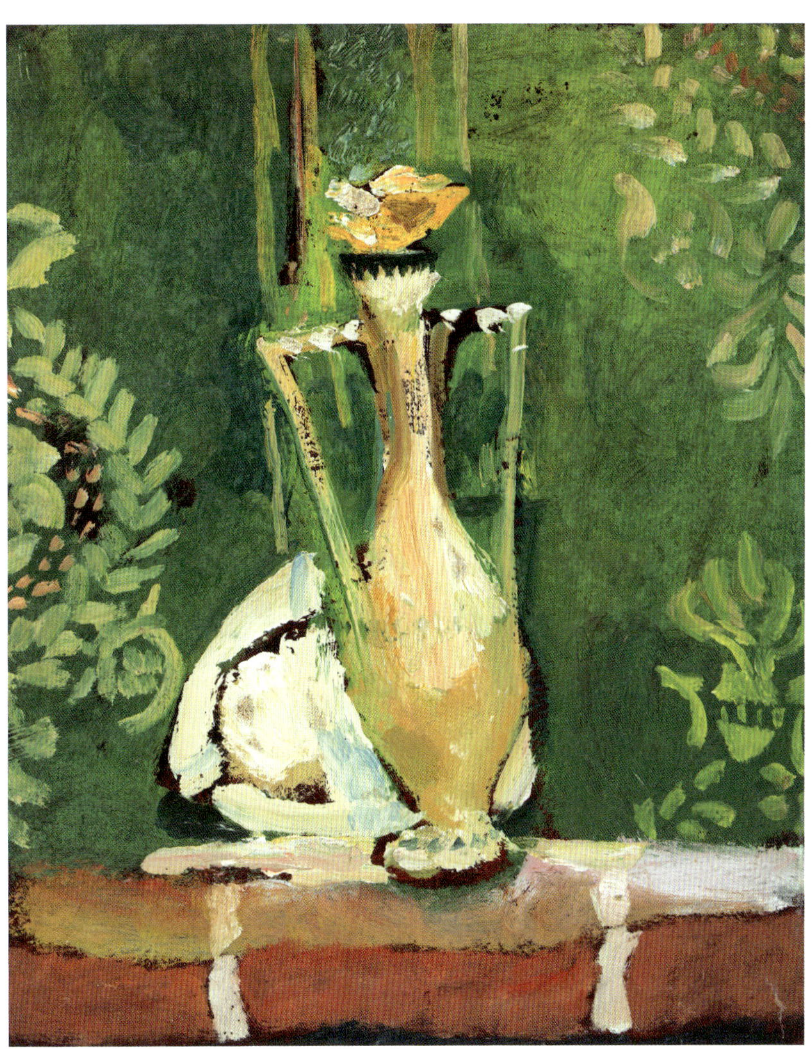

Pot at Coastguards No. 2 · c.1971 · oil on board · 41 x 33 cm

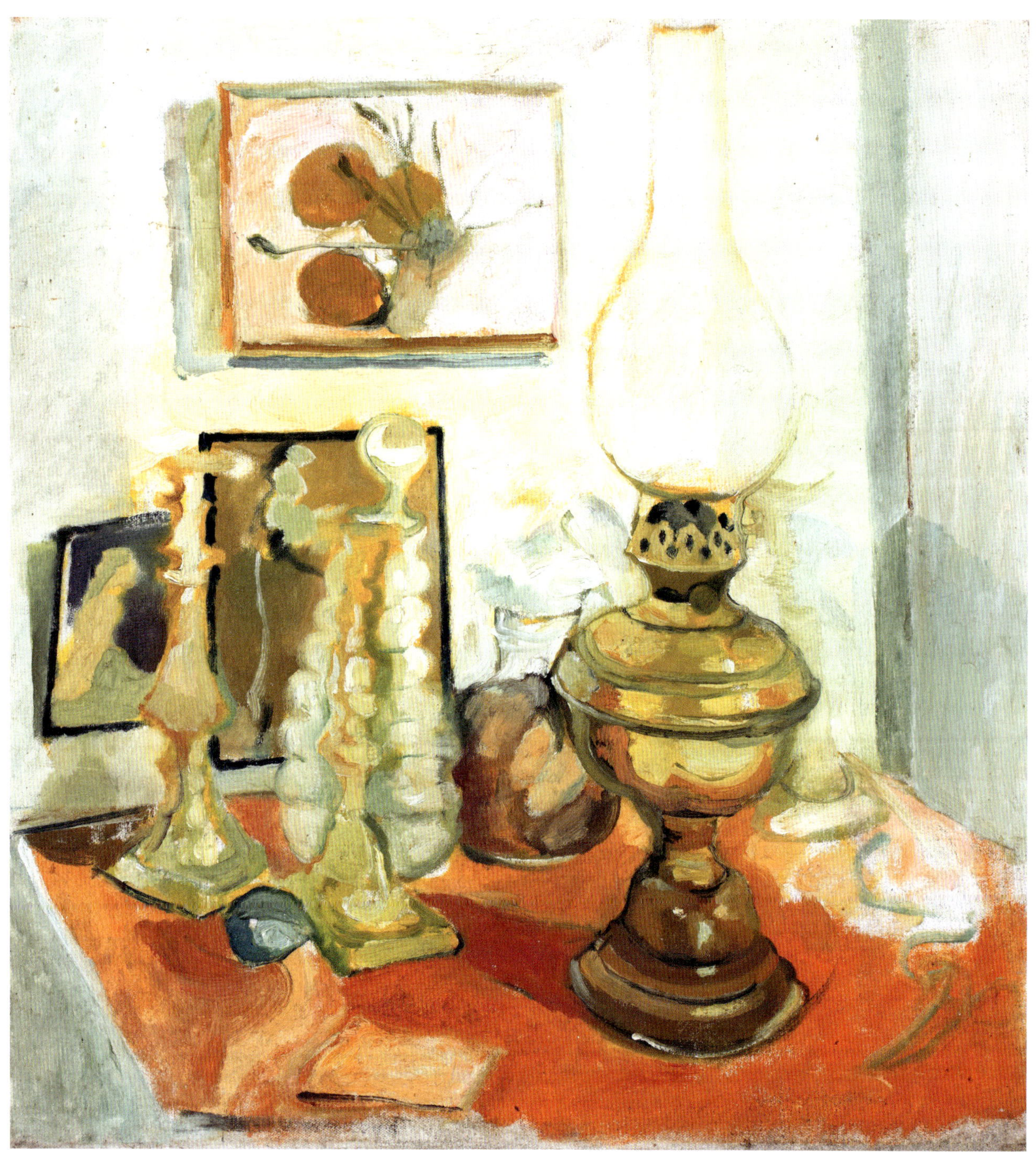

Lamp on Fridge · c.1973 · oil on board · 64 x 61 cm

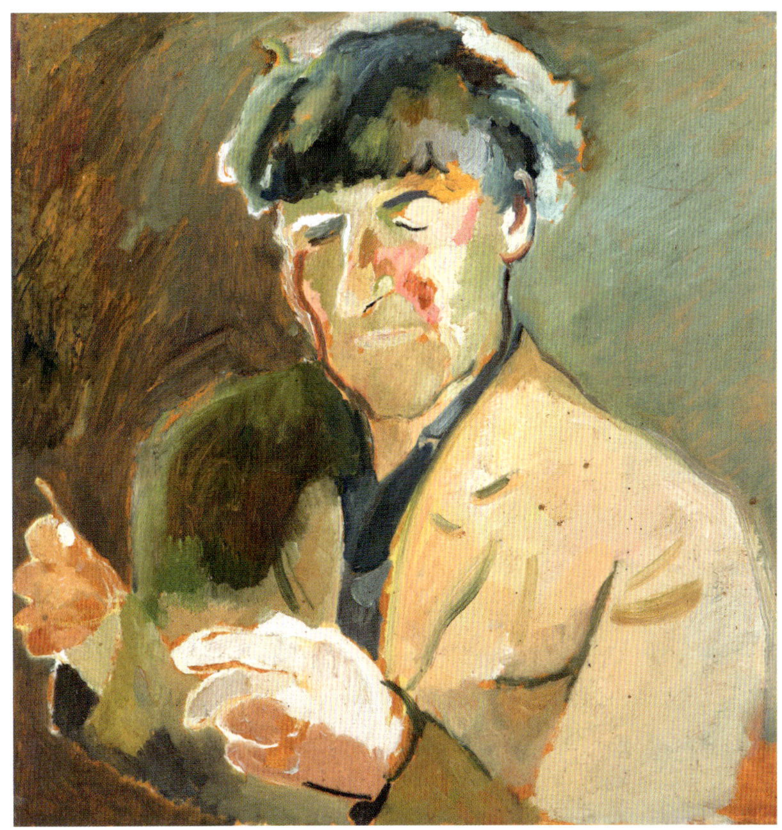

John Wells · c.1973 · oil on board · 62 x 61 cm

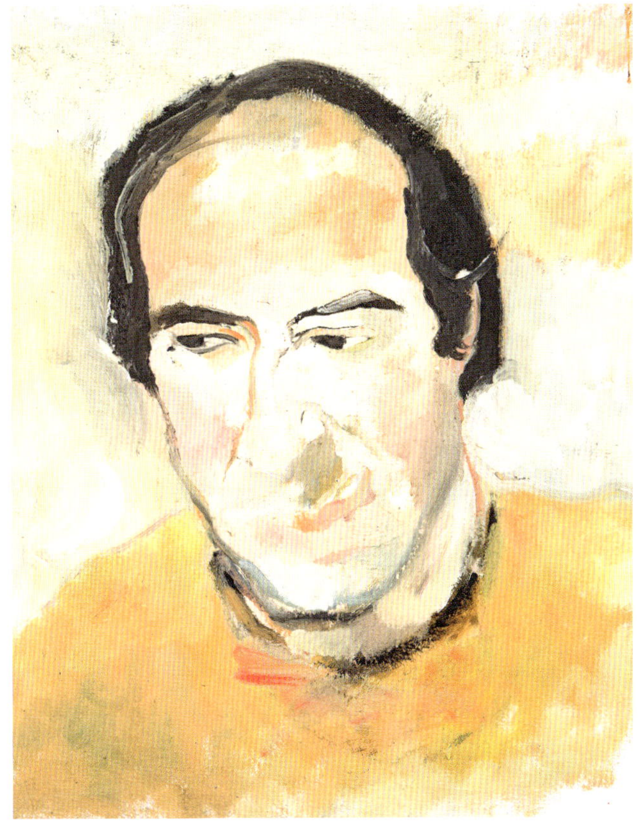

George Misiewicz · c.1975 · oil on canvas · 61 x 51 cm

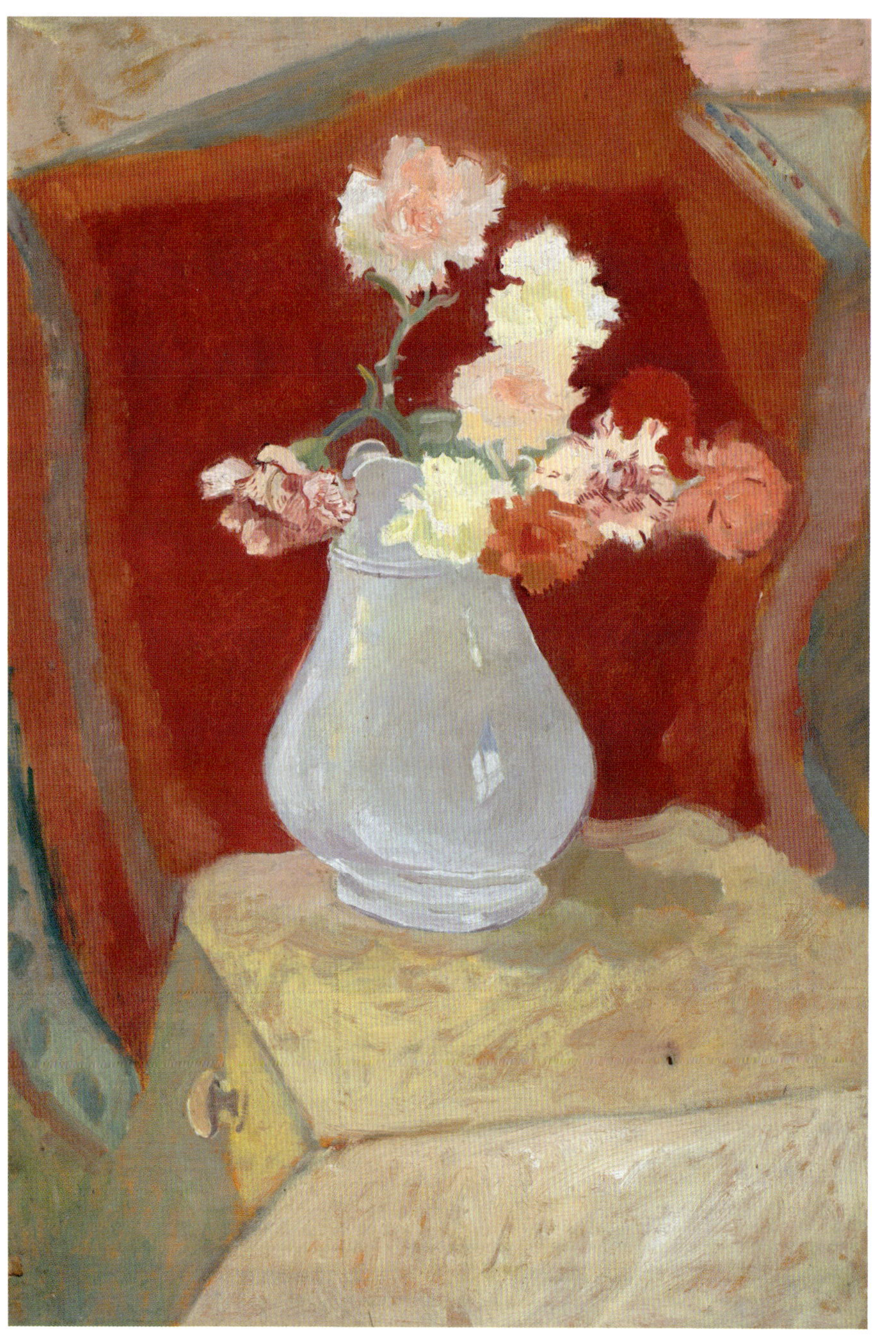

Carnations in White Jug · c.1967 · oil on board · 77 x 52 cm

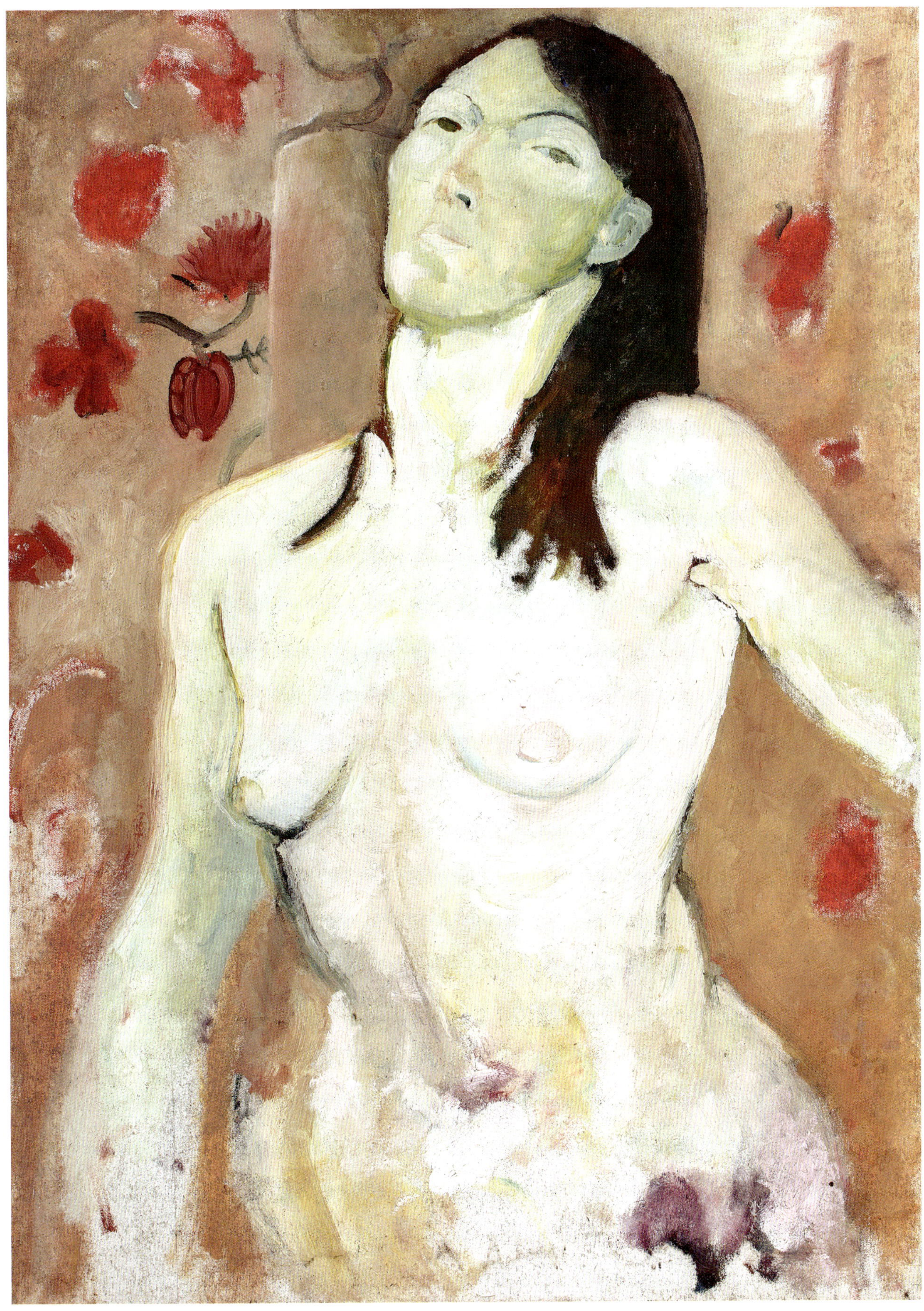

Self · 1971–72 · oil on canvas · 91 x 66 cm

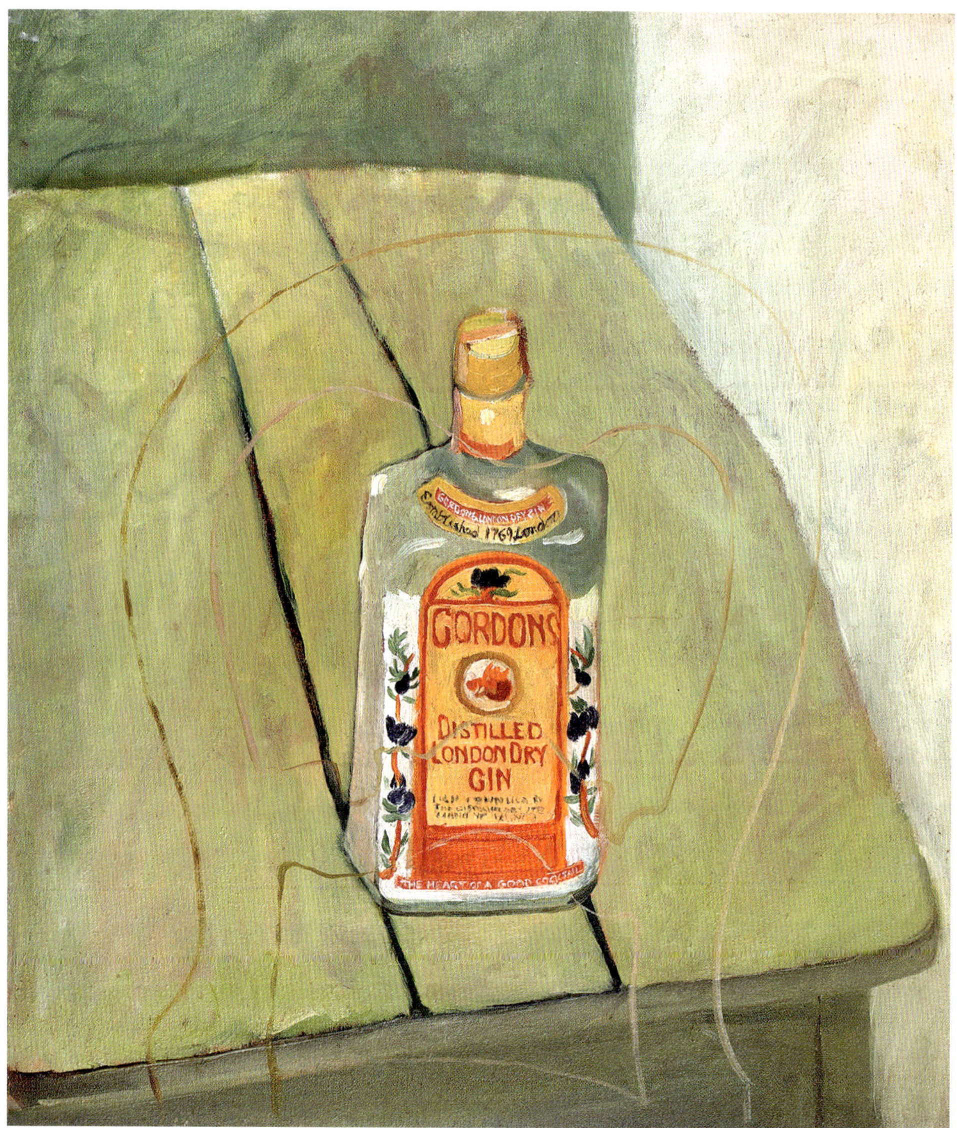

Gordon's and Chair · early 1970s · oil on canvas · 71 x 64 cm

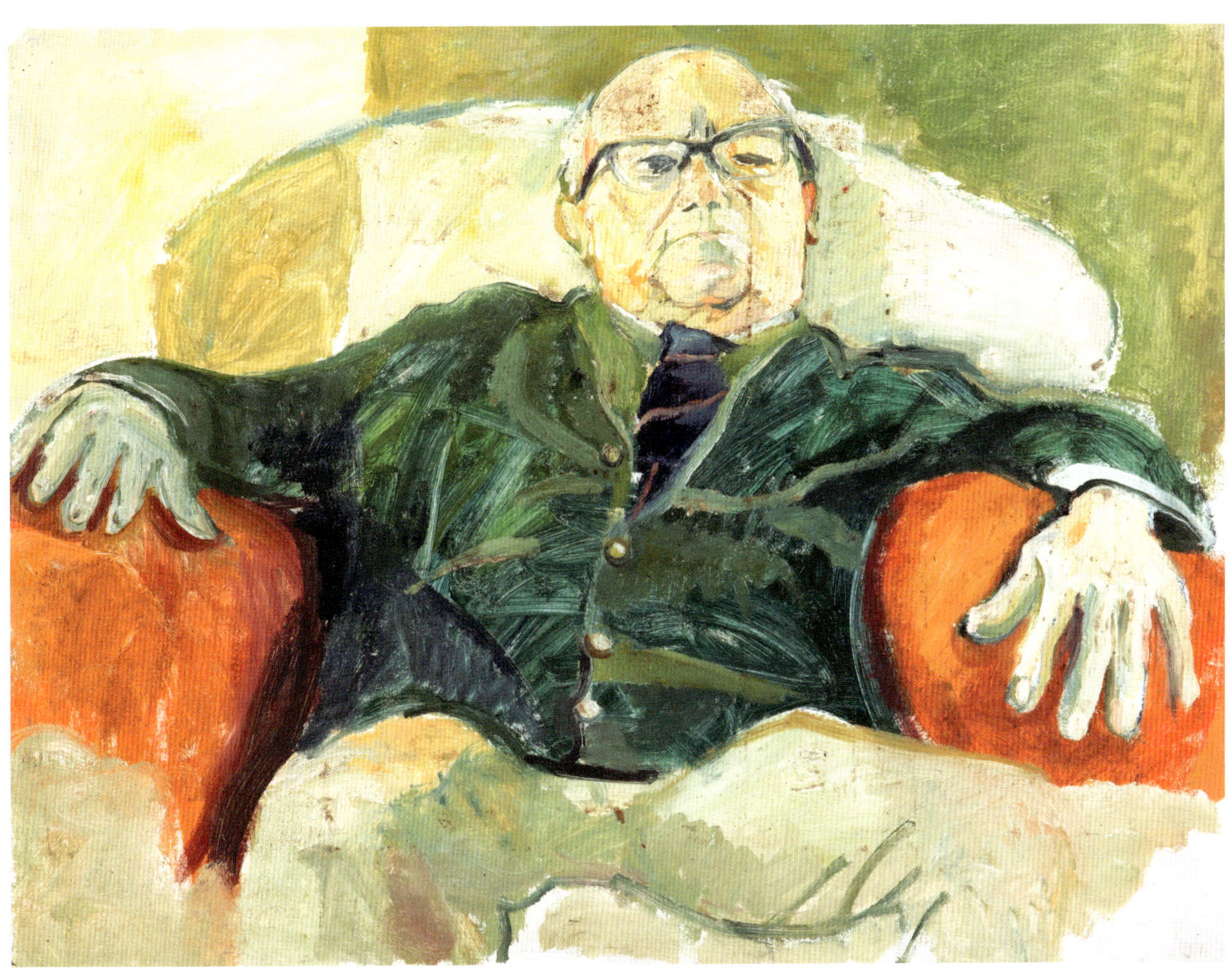

Rev. John Griffen · c.1970 · oil on board · 61 x 82 cm

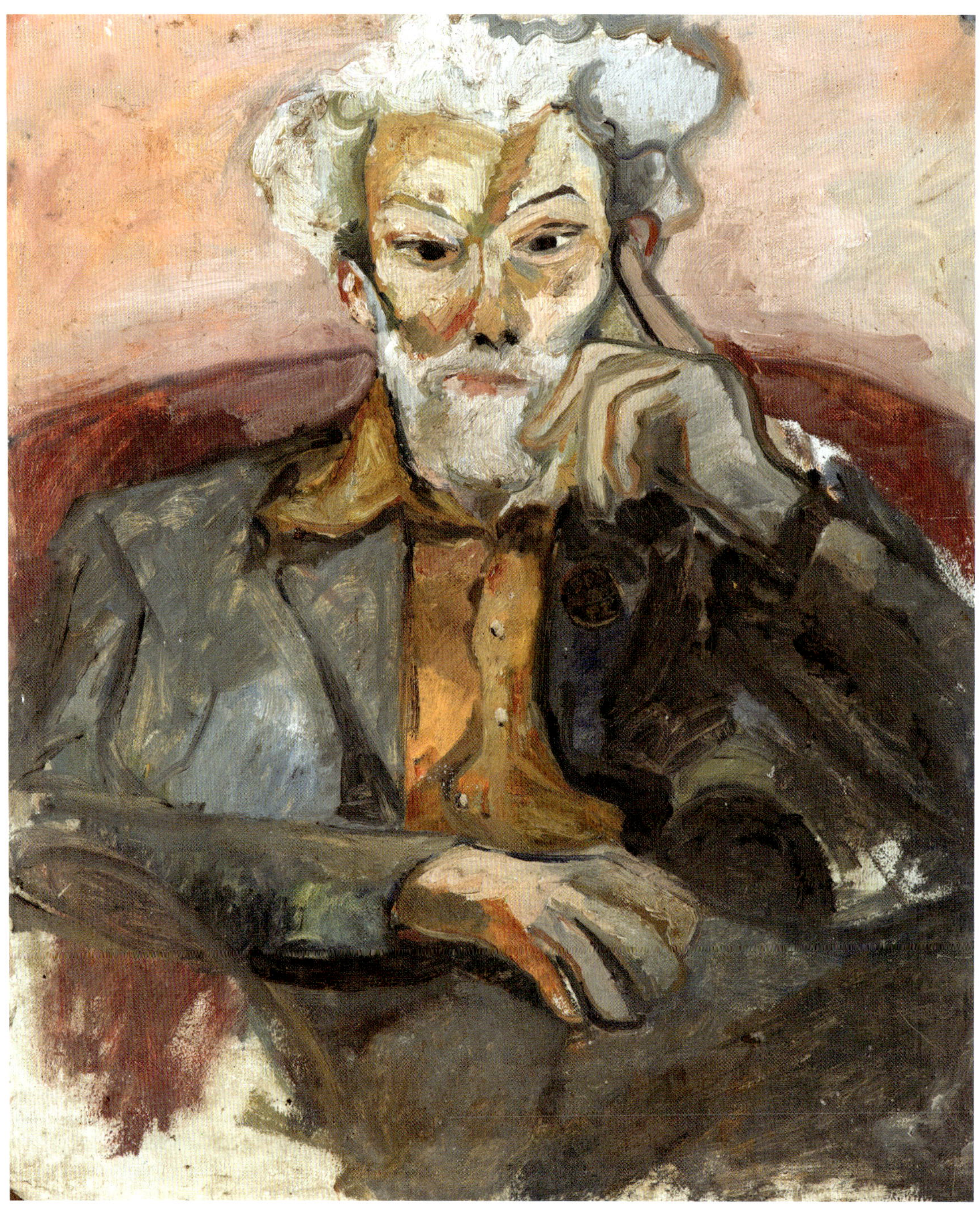

The Postman · c.1972 · oil on board · 82 x 64 cm

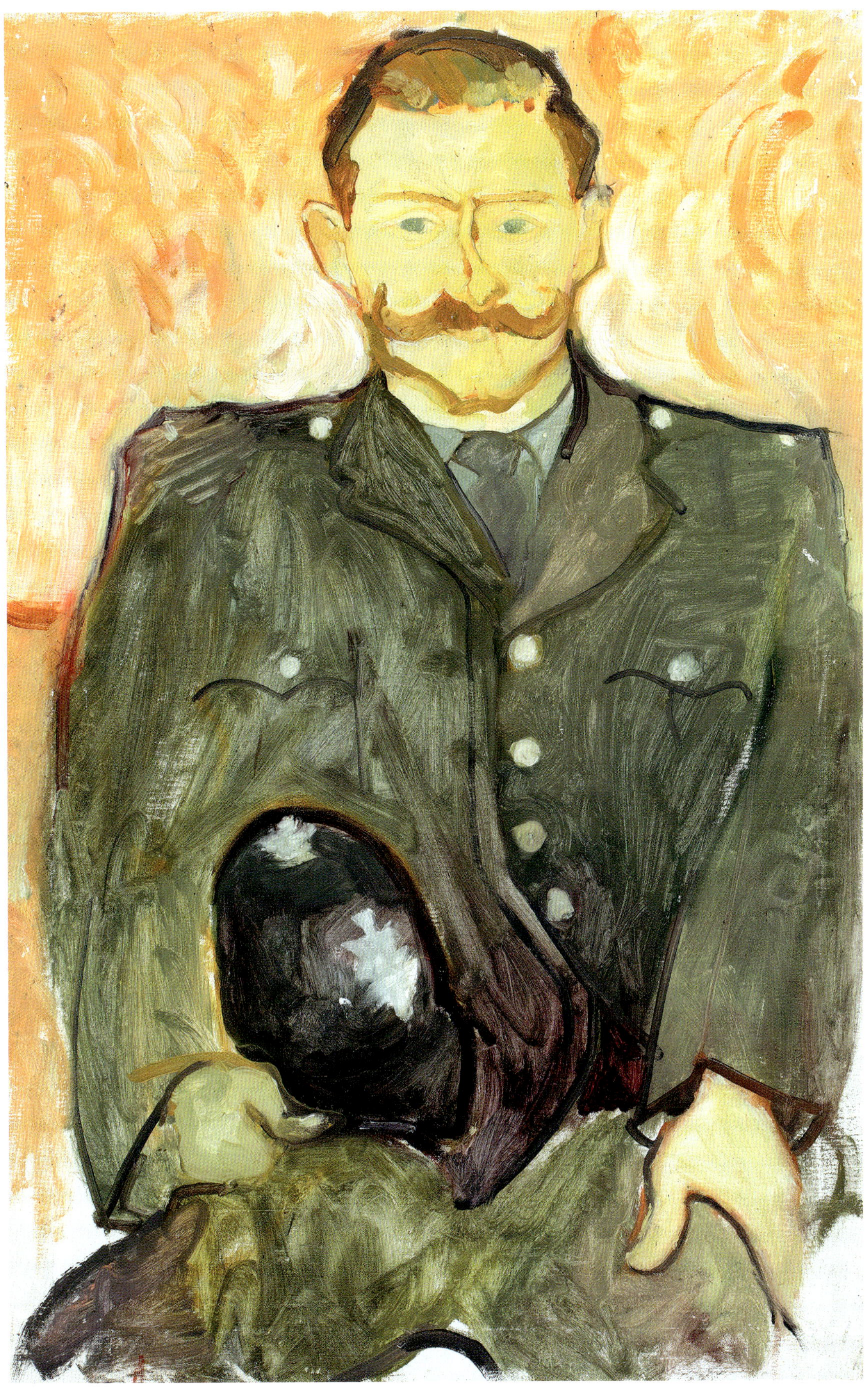

P.C. Collins · c.1970 · oil on canvas · 102 x 67 cm

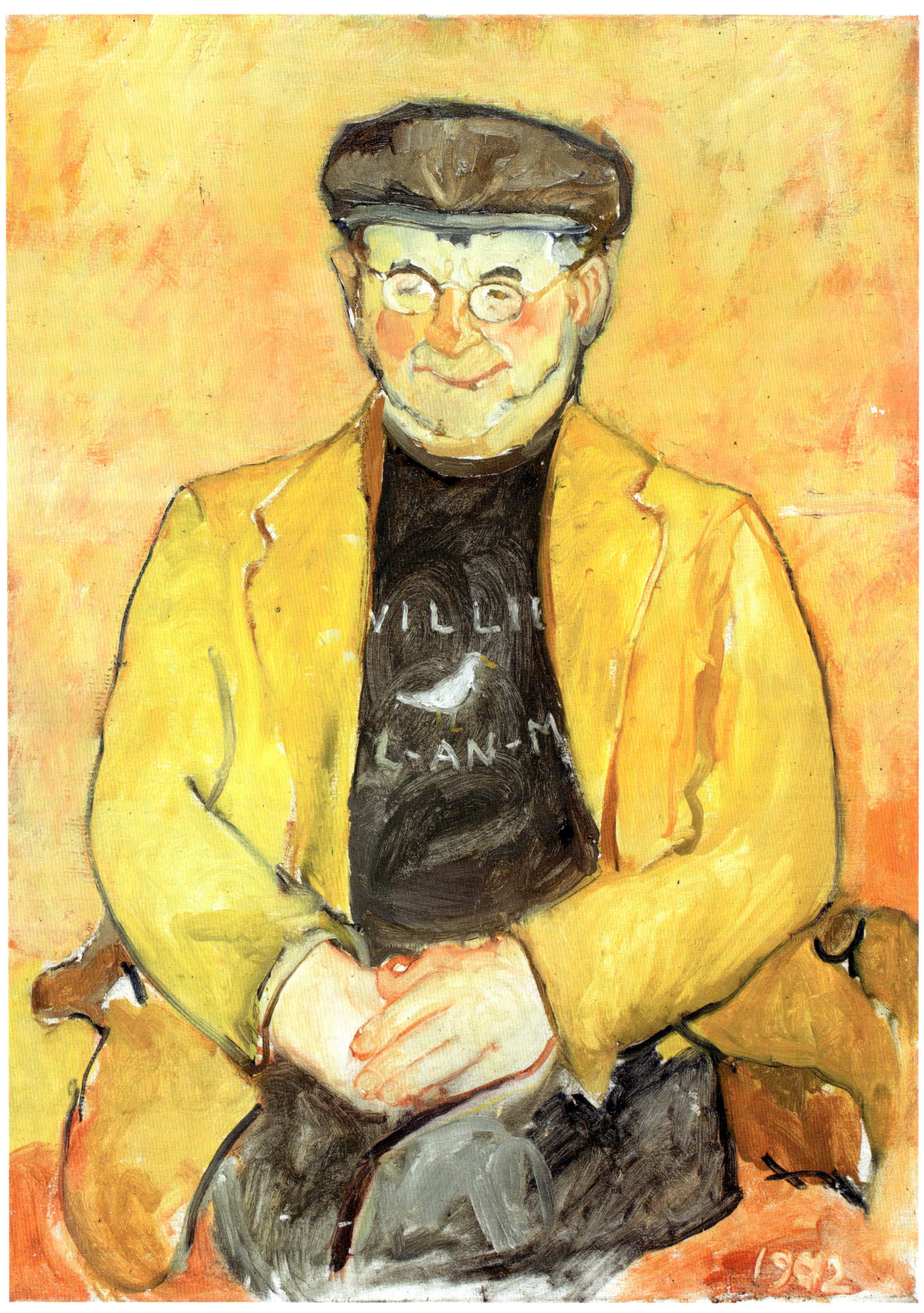

Willie Brek · c.1971 · oil on canvas · 91 x 66 cm

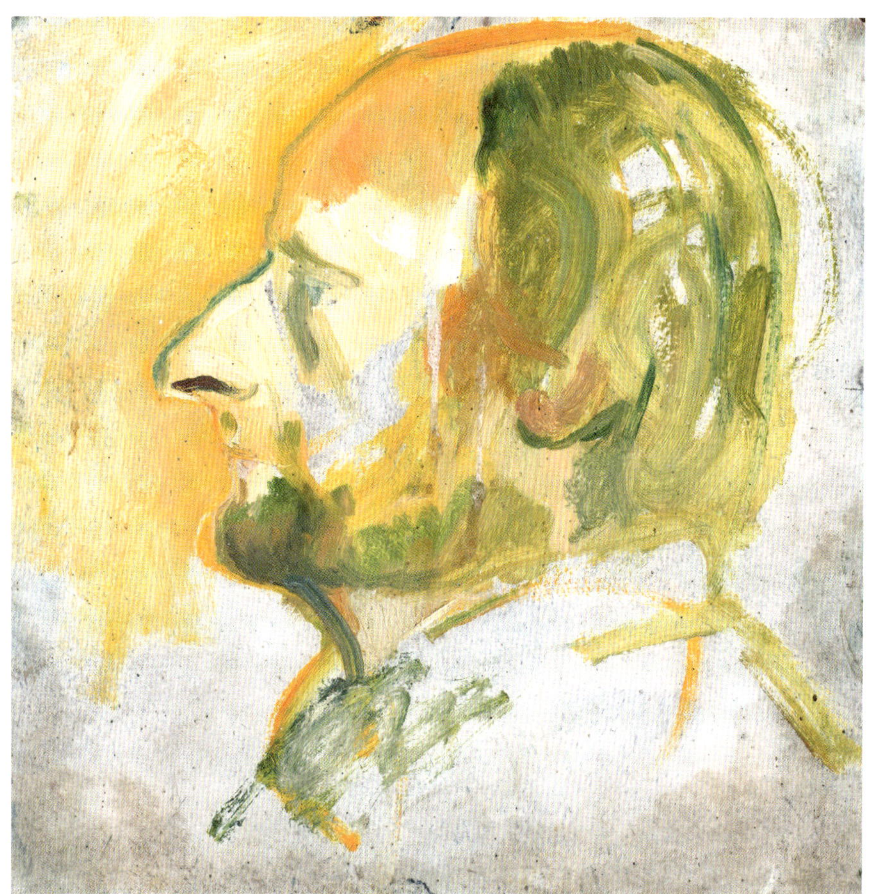

Roger Norrington · c.1971 · oil on board · 41 x 41 cm

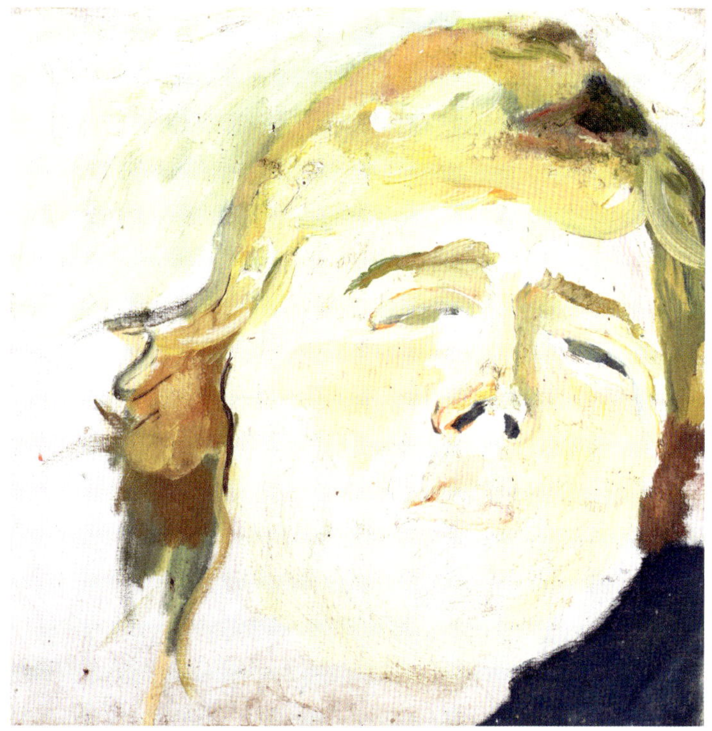

'Peanuts' (Charles Turner) · c.1972 · oil on canvas · 36 x 36 cm

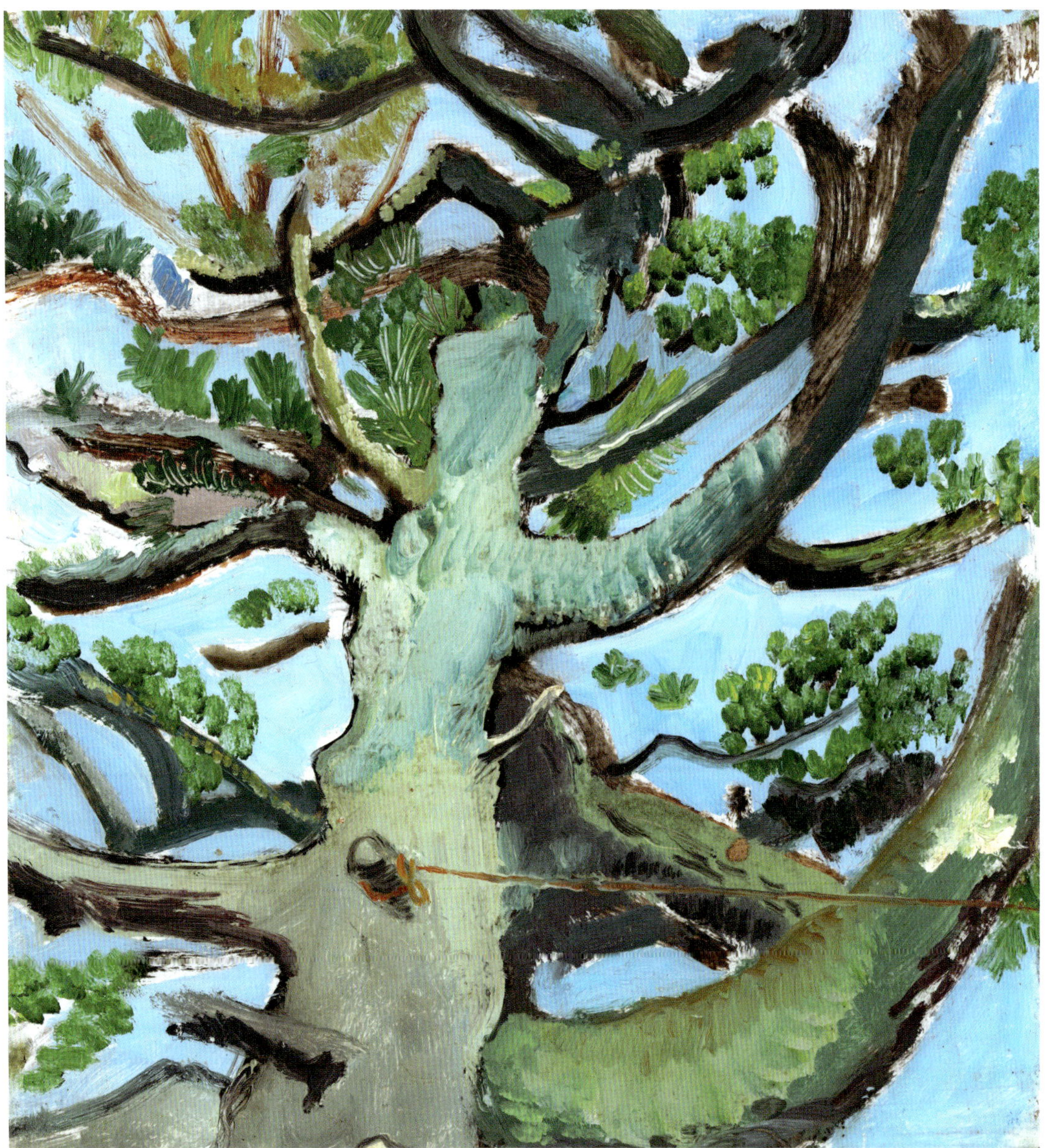

Clothes Line Fir Tree at Lodge · mid-1970s · oil on board · 38 x 36 cm

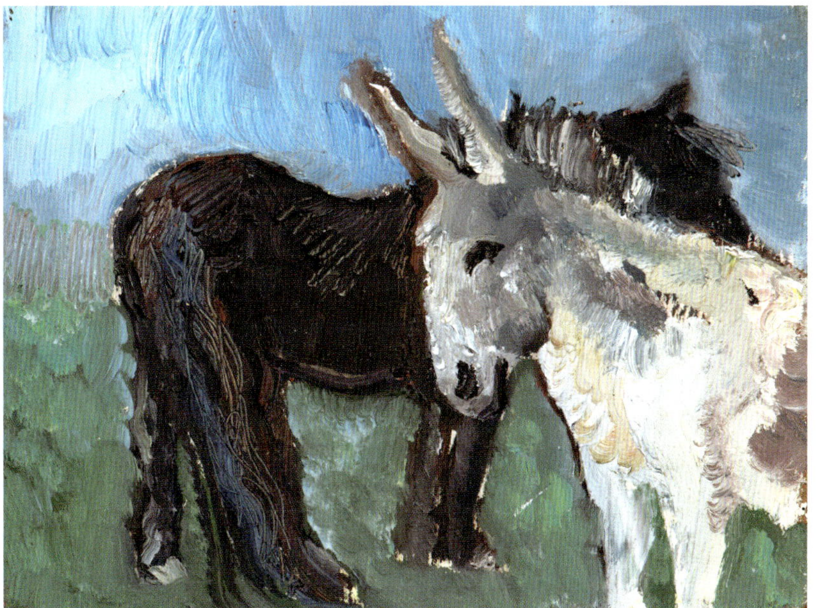

Rebel and Curly I · c.1975 · oil on board · 20 x 28 cm

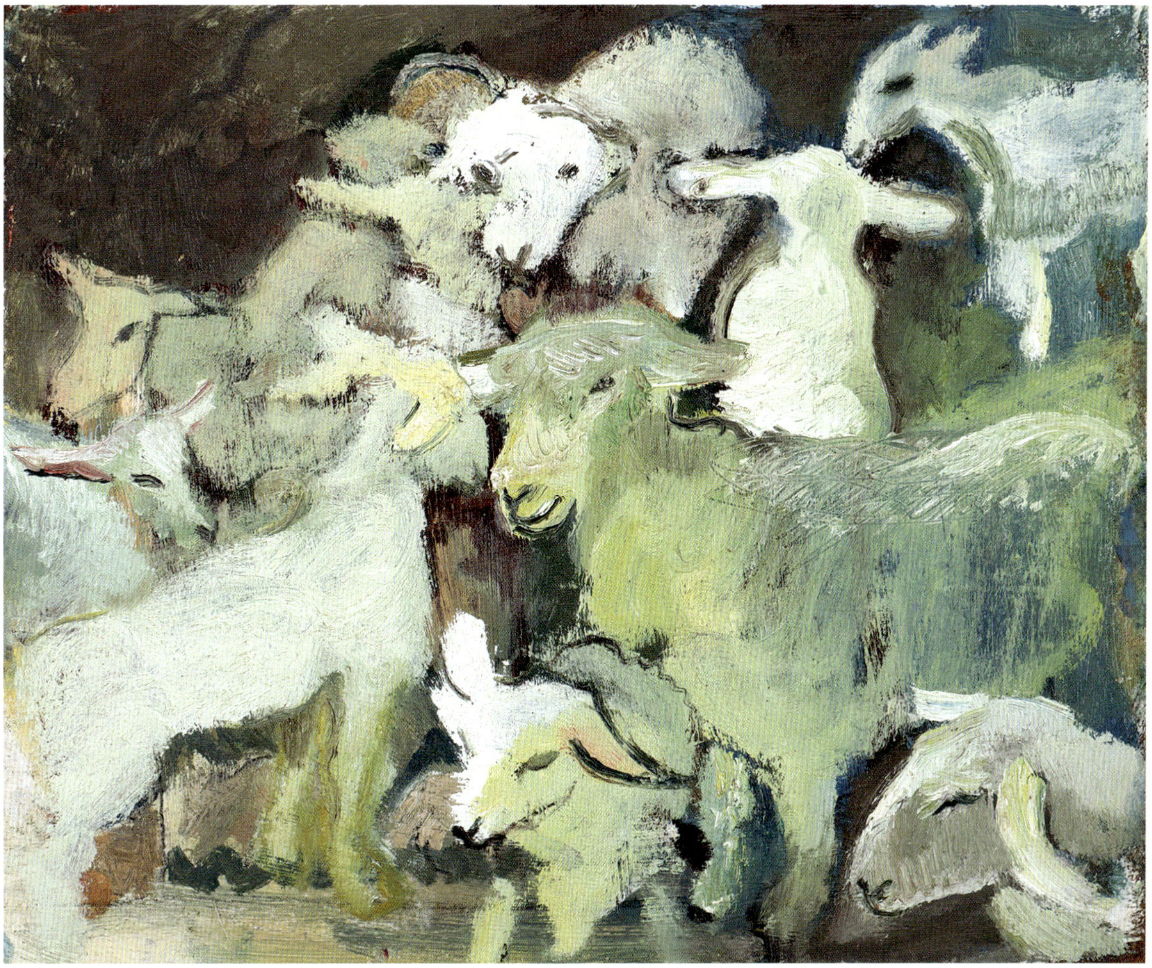

Mike's Sheep · c.1978 · oil on board · 31 x 38 cm

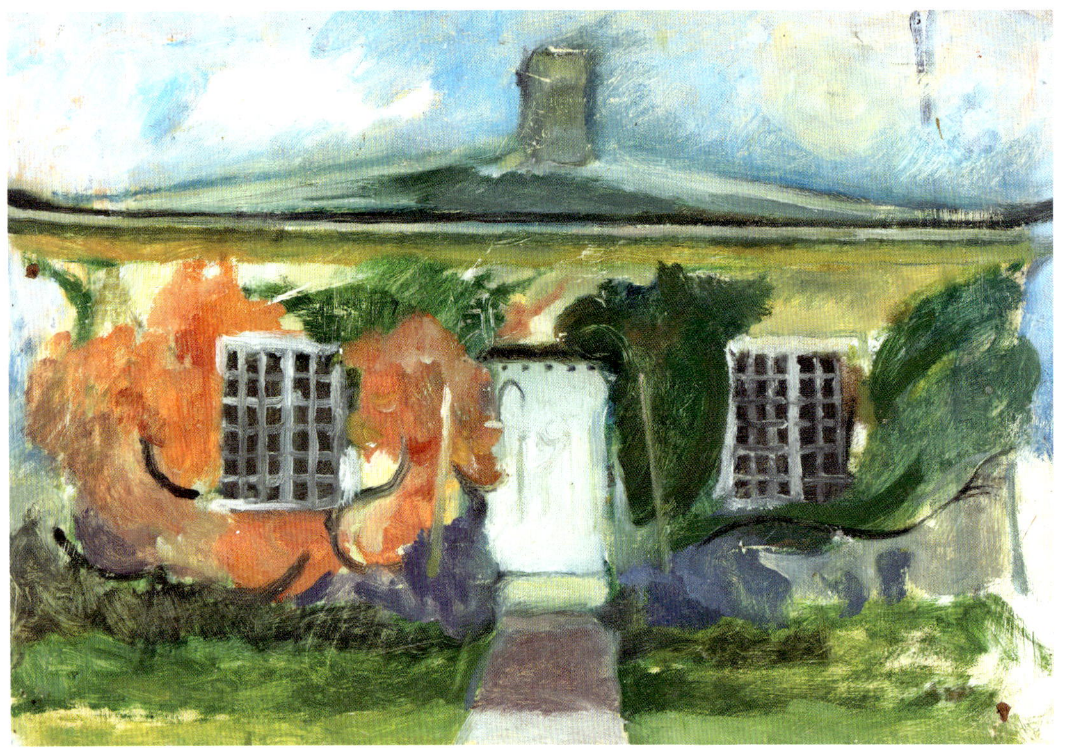

Summer House at Rosemary, Yorkshire I · c.1975 · oil on board · 31 x 43 cm

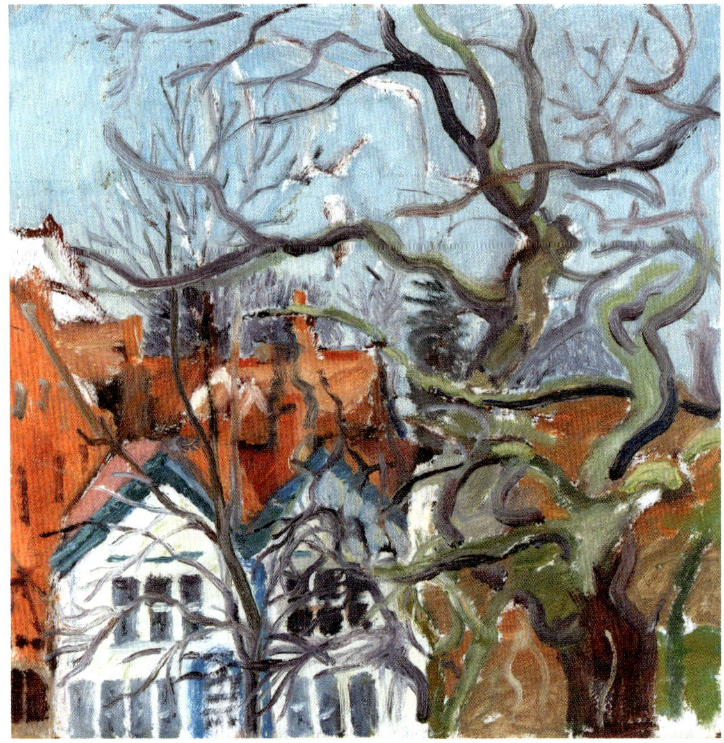

Oxford House, Northmoor Road · c.1979 · oil on board · 31 x 31 cm

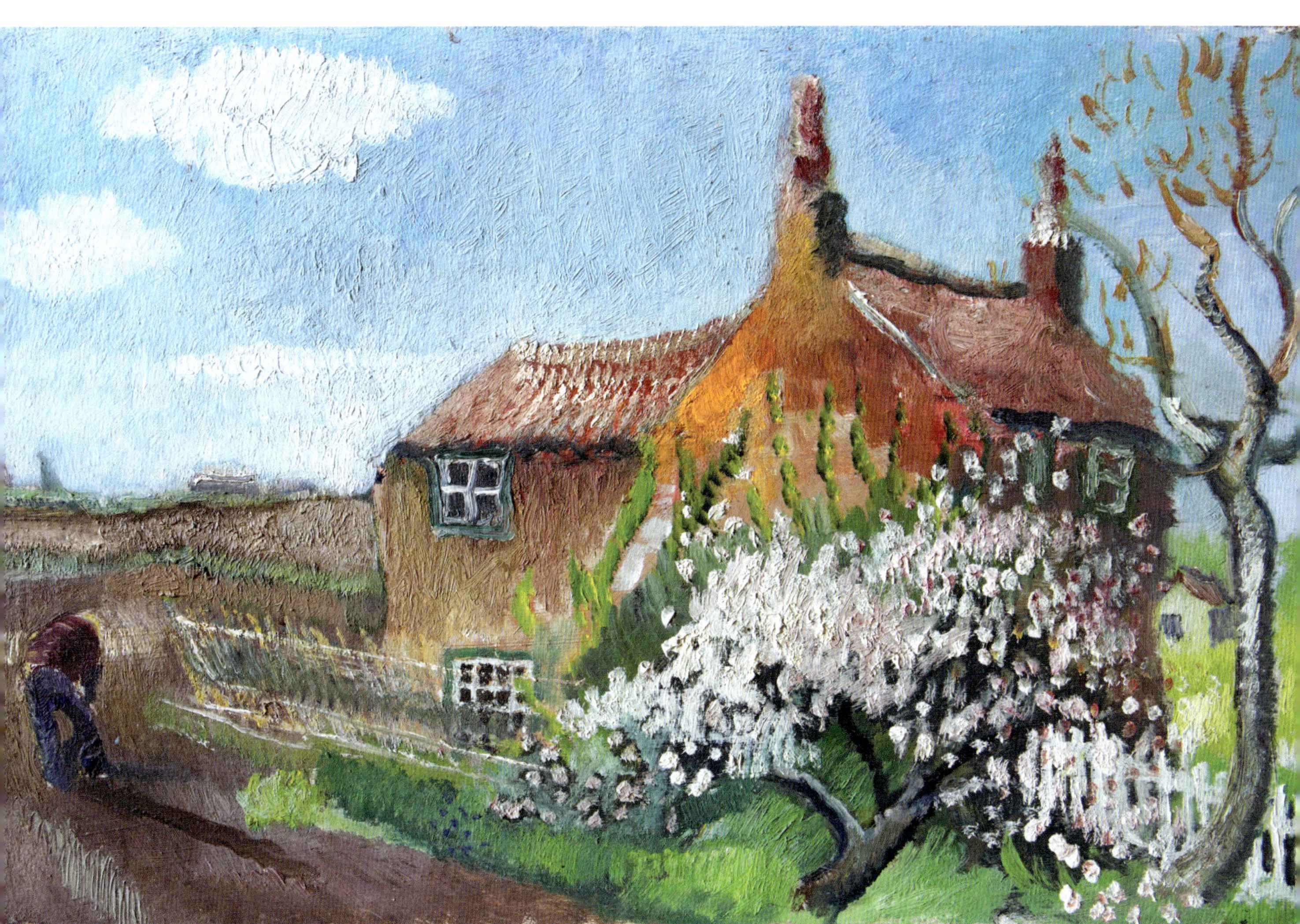

House in the Fens · c.1982 · oil on board · 38 x 61 cm

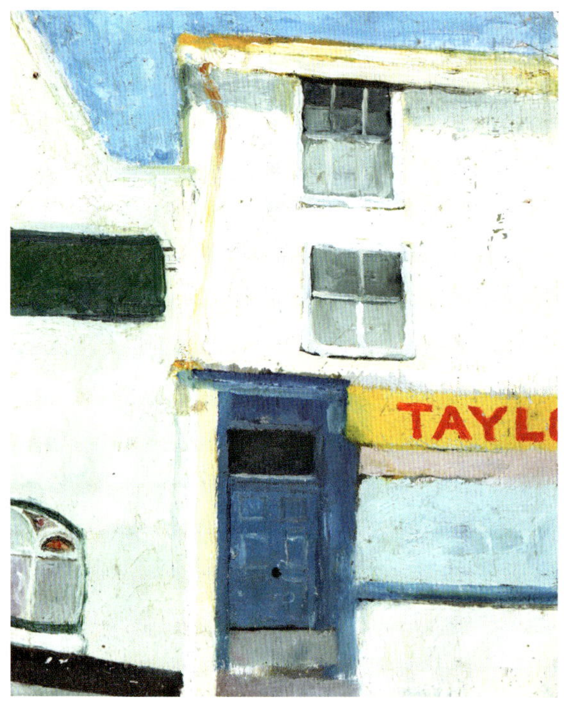

Taylors, Penzance · early 1970s · oil on board · 37 x 30 cm

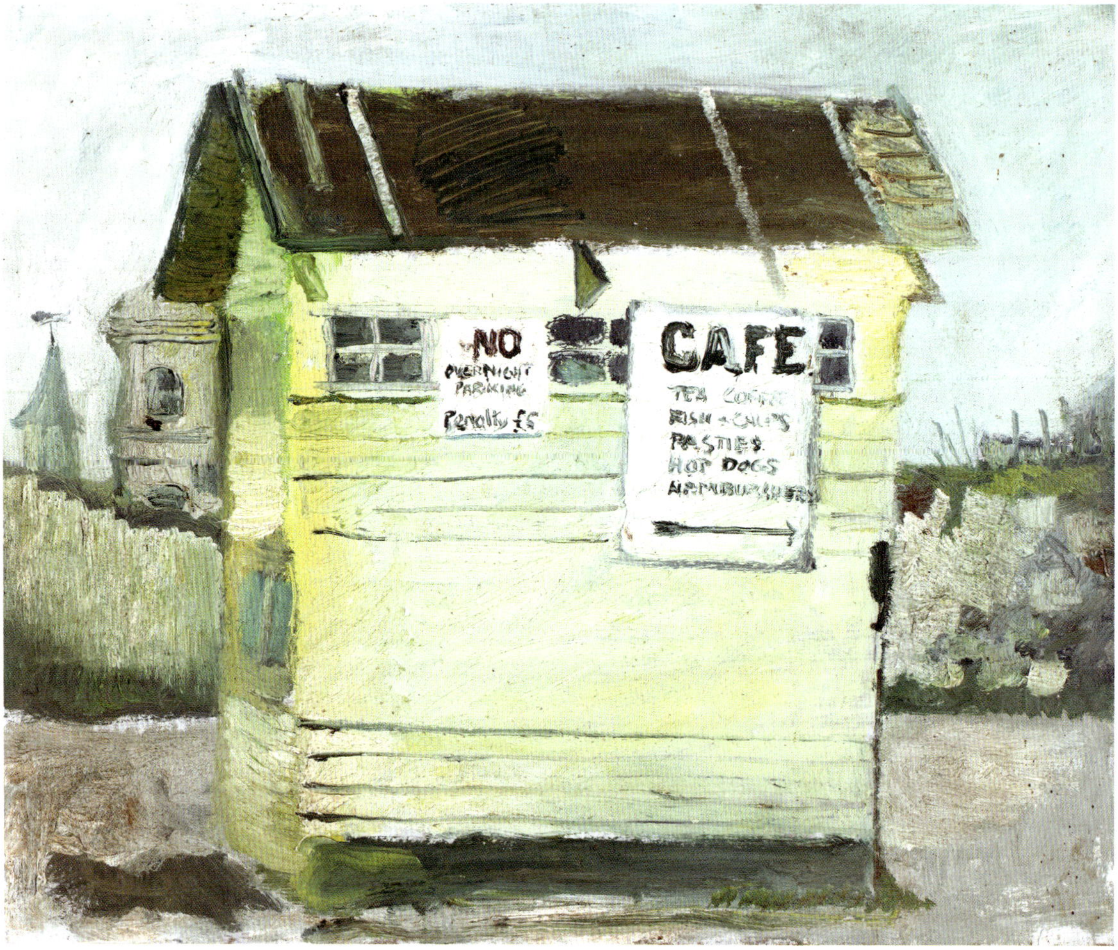

Marazion Cafe · c.1974 · oil on board · 49 x 61 cm

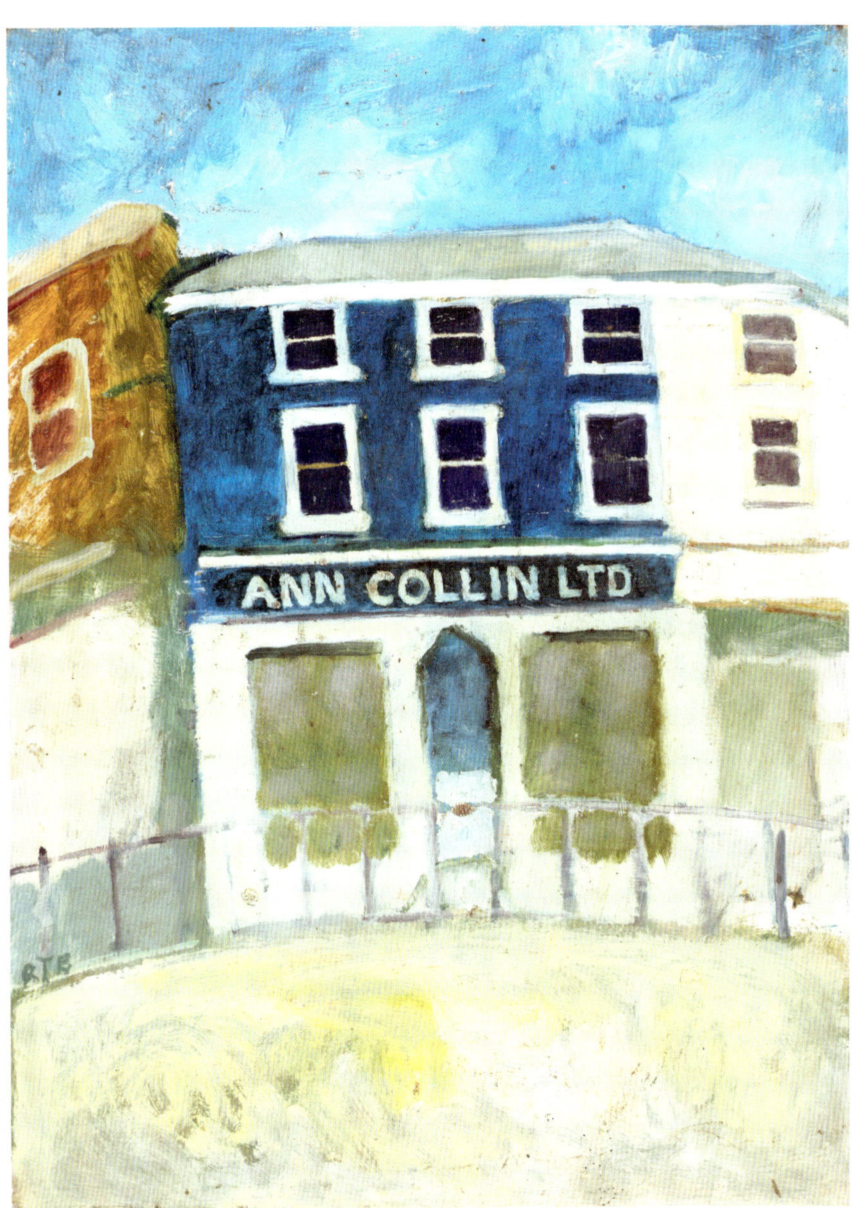

The Terrace, Penzance · c.1972 · oil on board · 61 x 46 cm

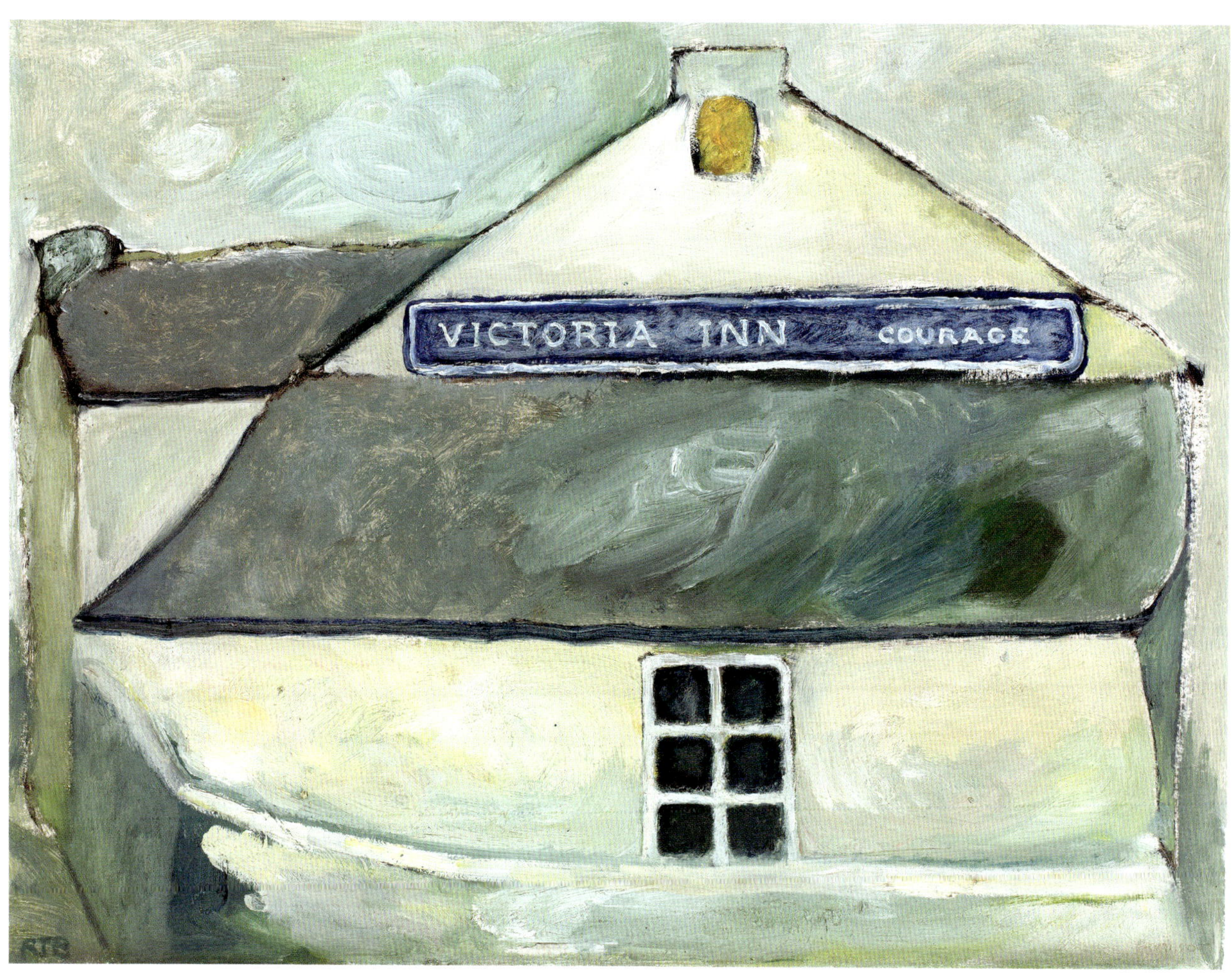

Victoria Inn, Perranuthnoe · c.1977 · oil on board · 61 x 81 cm

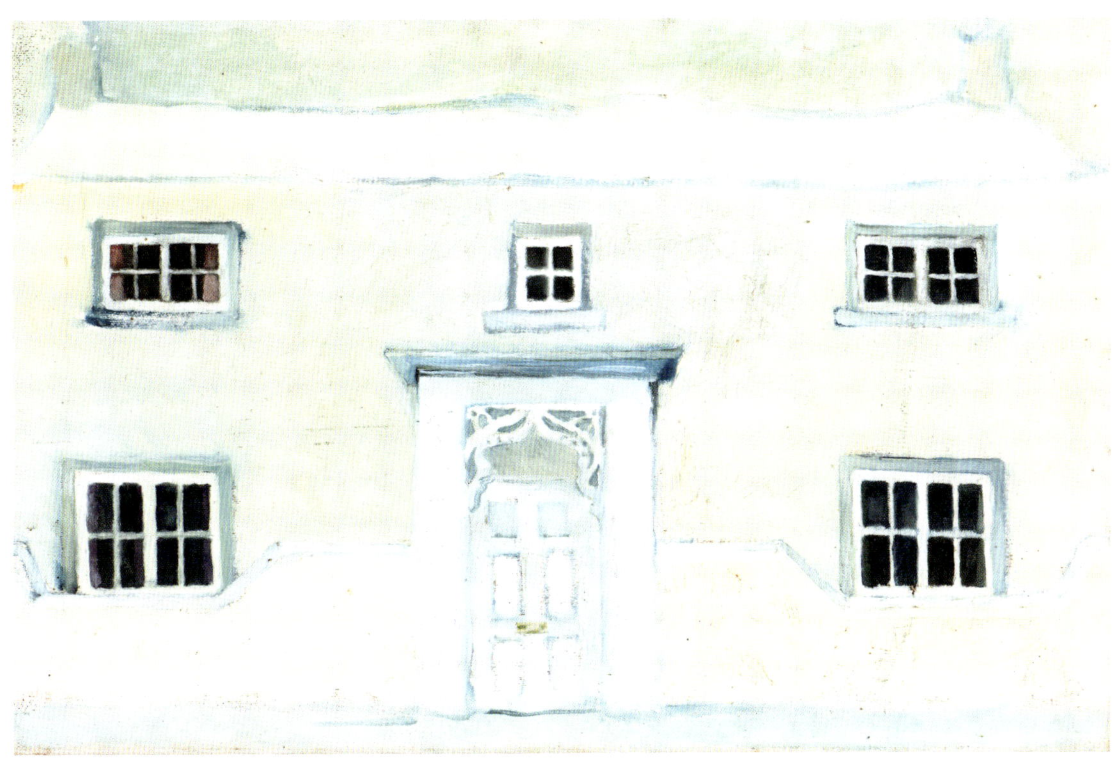

The White House · c.1975 · oil on canvas · 41 x 64 cm

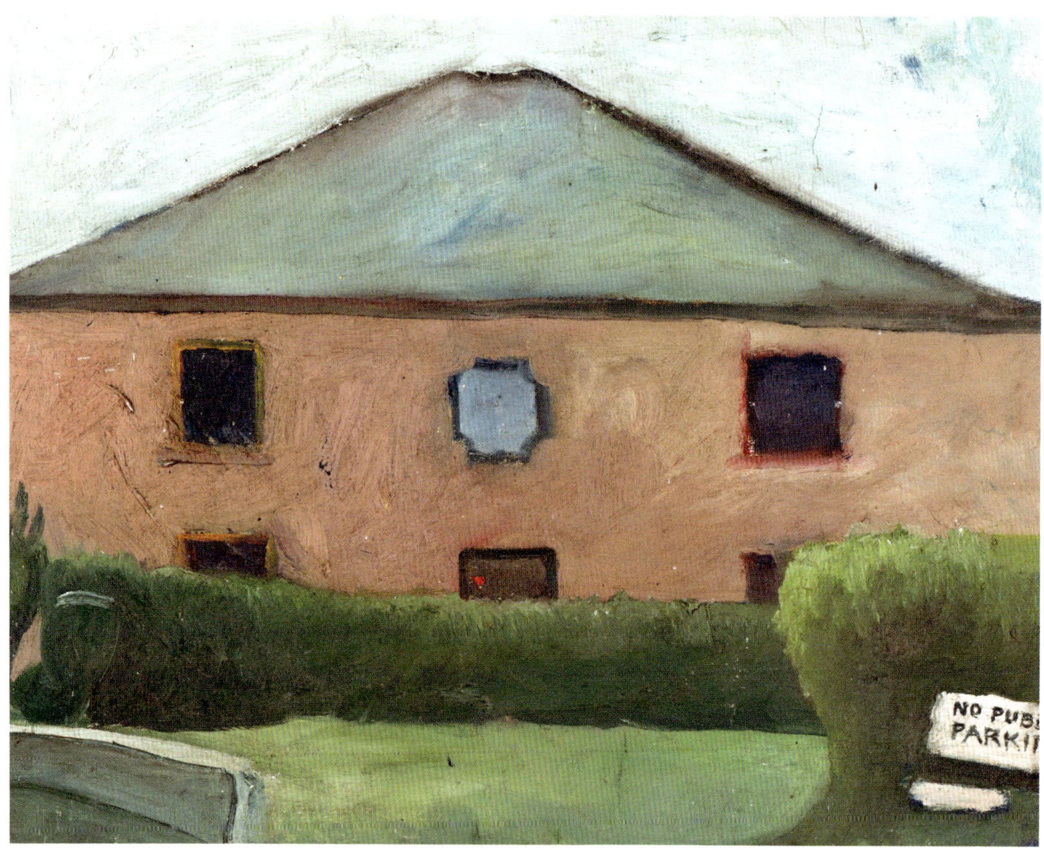

Masonic Hall, Hayle · c.1973 · oil on board · 39 x 50 cm

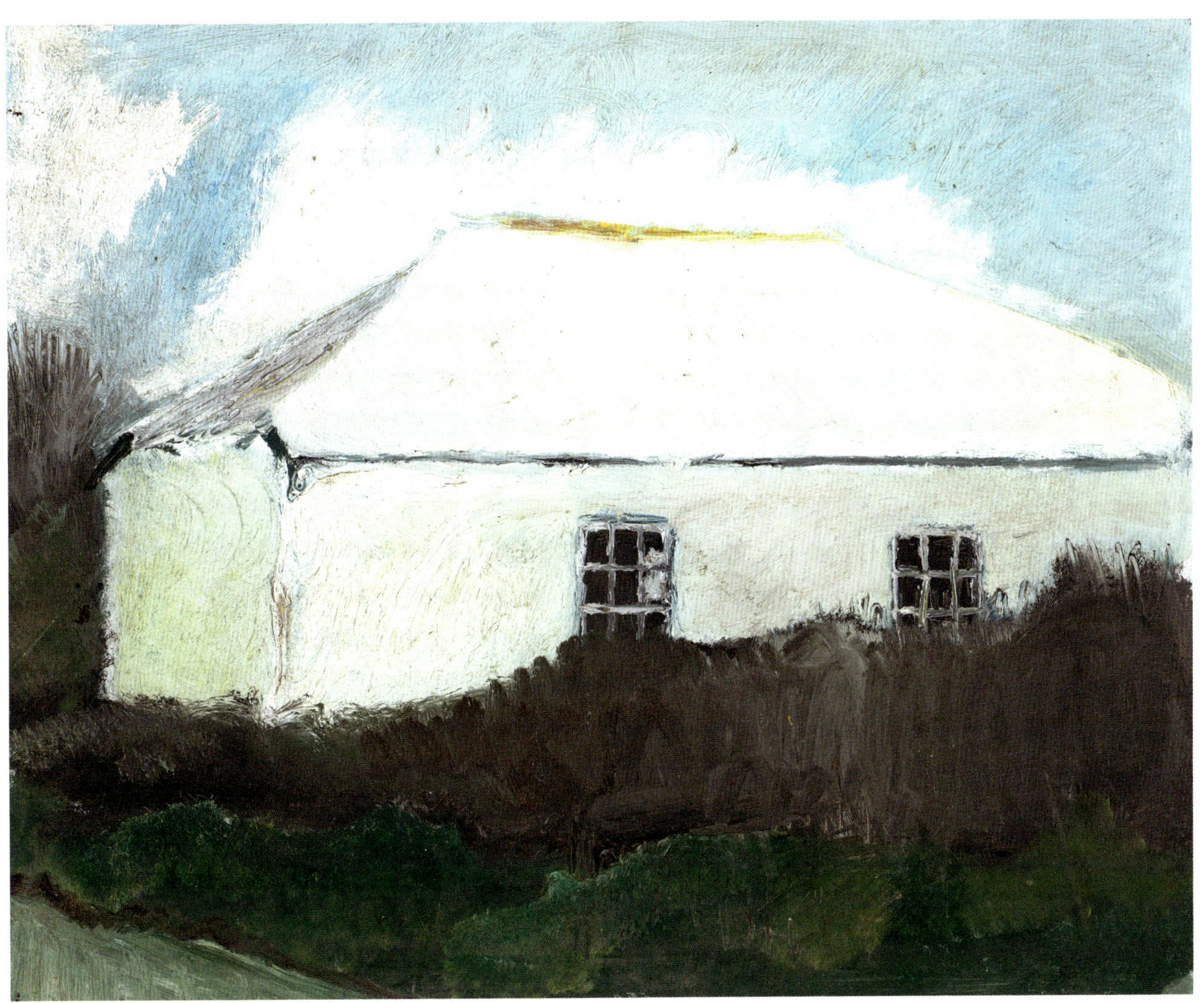

Rosudgeon Chapel · late 1970s · oil on board · 50 x 59 cm

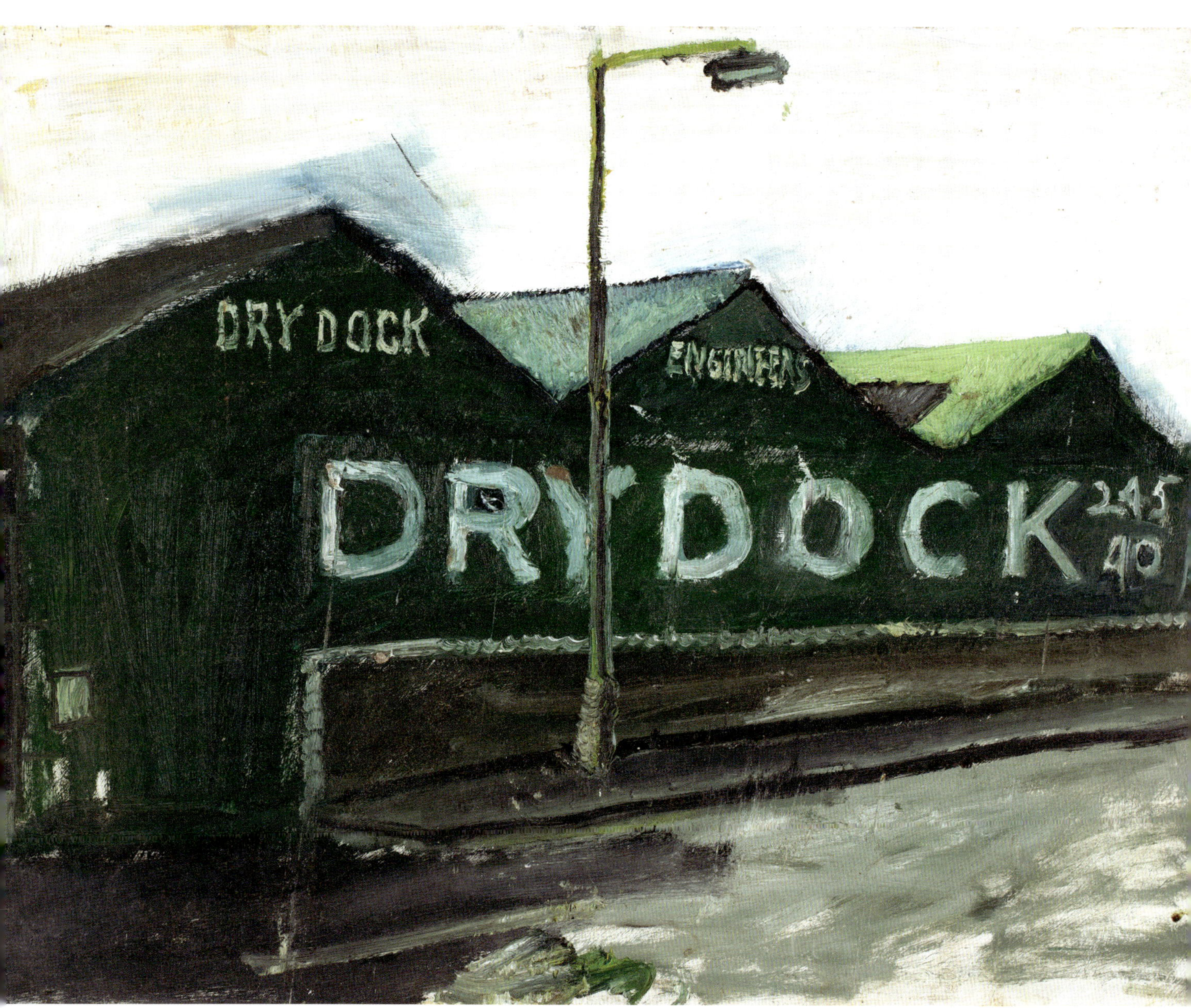

Dry Dock, Penzance II · late 1970s · oil on board · 61 x 84 cm

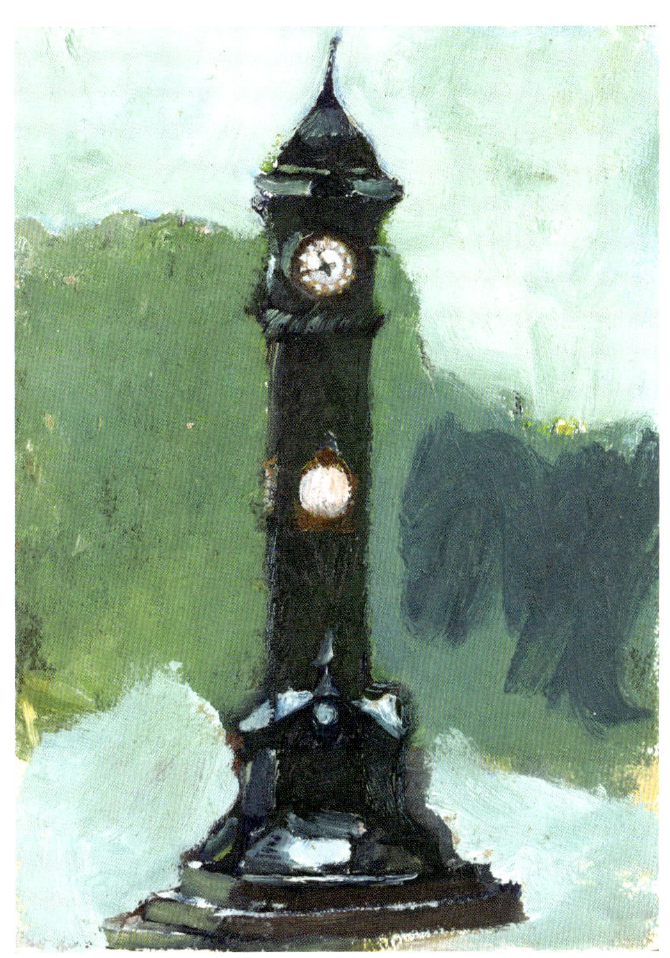

Highbury Clock, Islington · c.1978 · oil on board · 30 x 22 cm

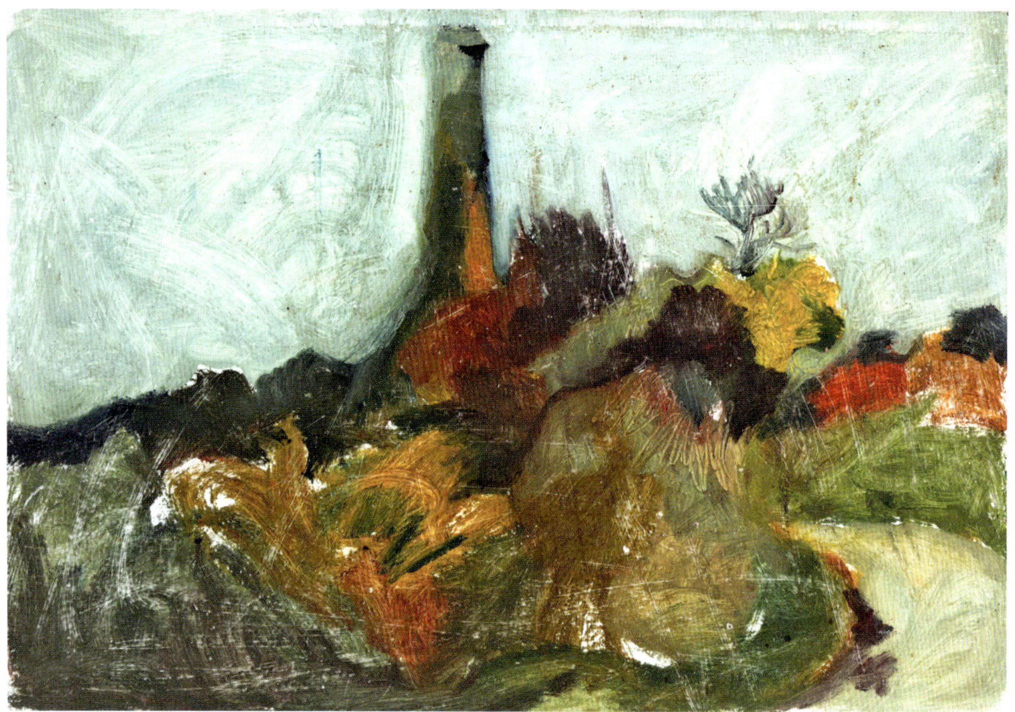

Mine at Tresowes · c.1982 · oil on board · 31 x 45 cm

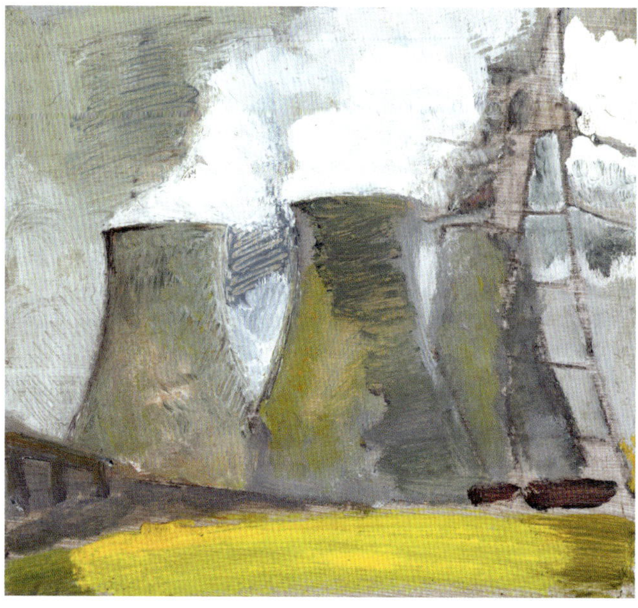

Didcot Power Station · c.1994 · oil on board · 26 x 28 cm

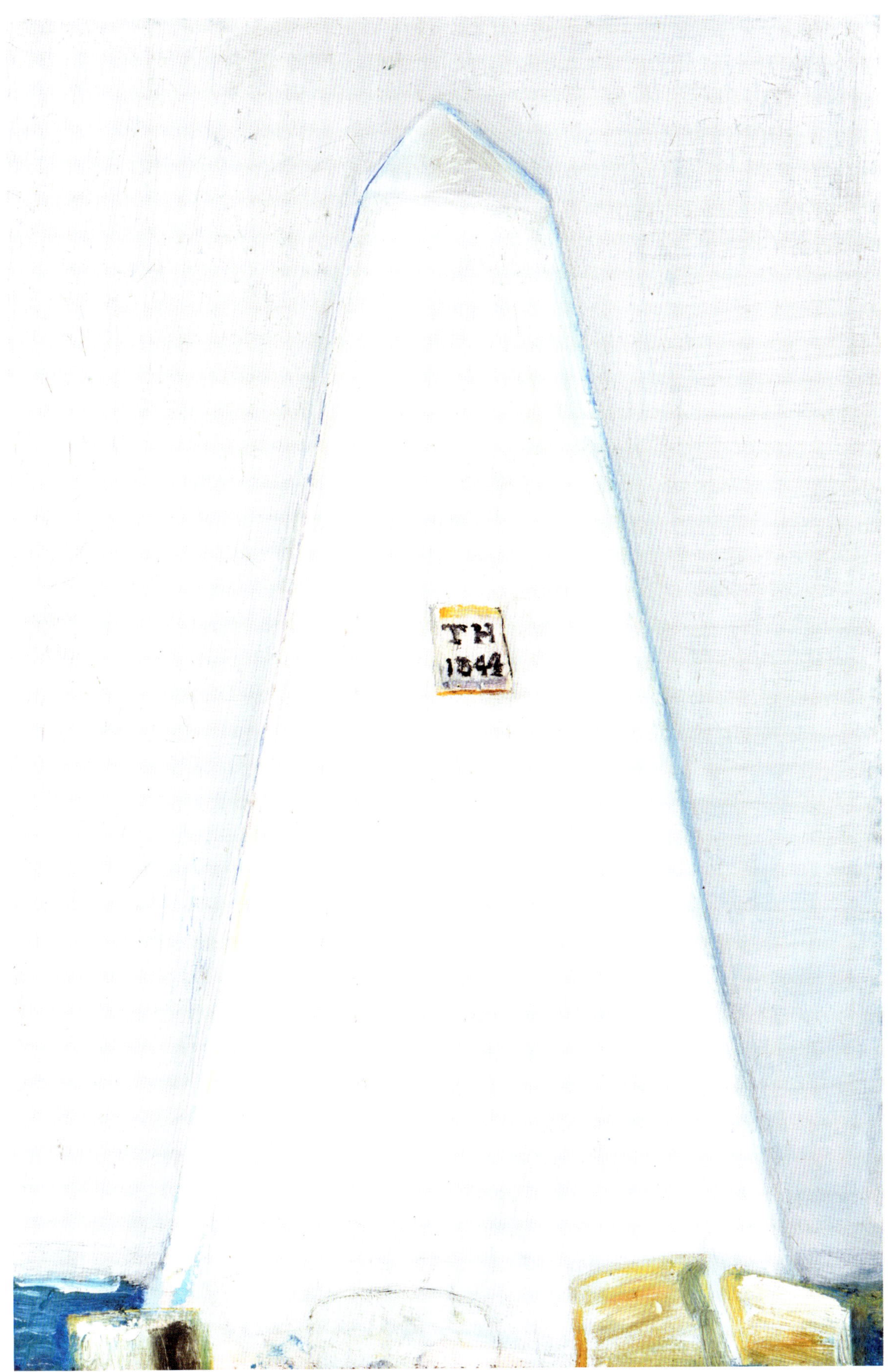

The Daymark, Portland III · c.2000 · oil on board · 76 x 51 cm

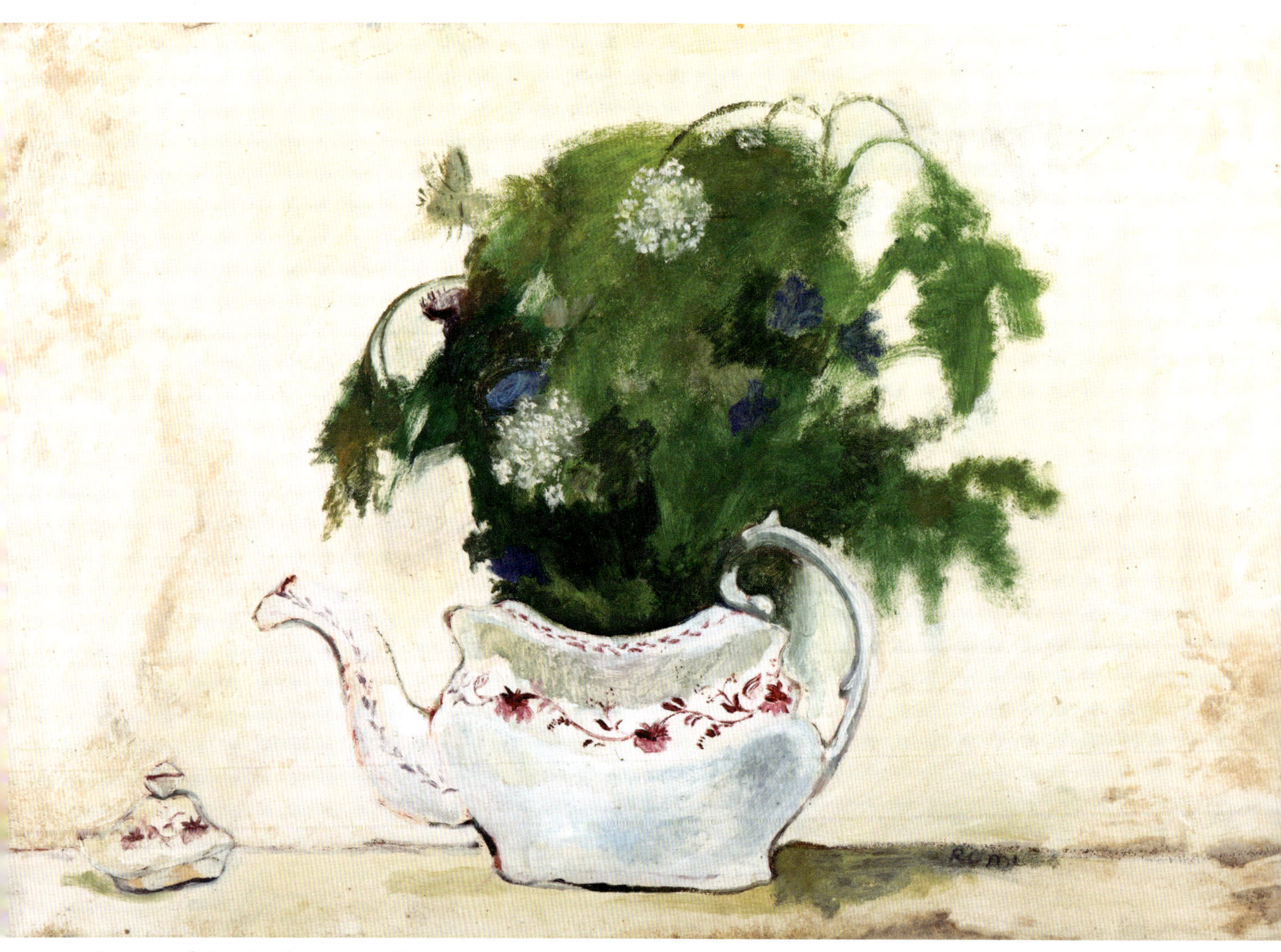

Teapot and Cow Parsley · c.1975 · oil on board · 61 x 91 cm

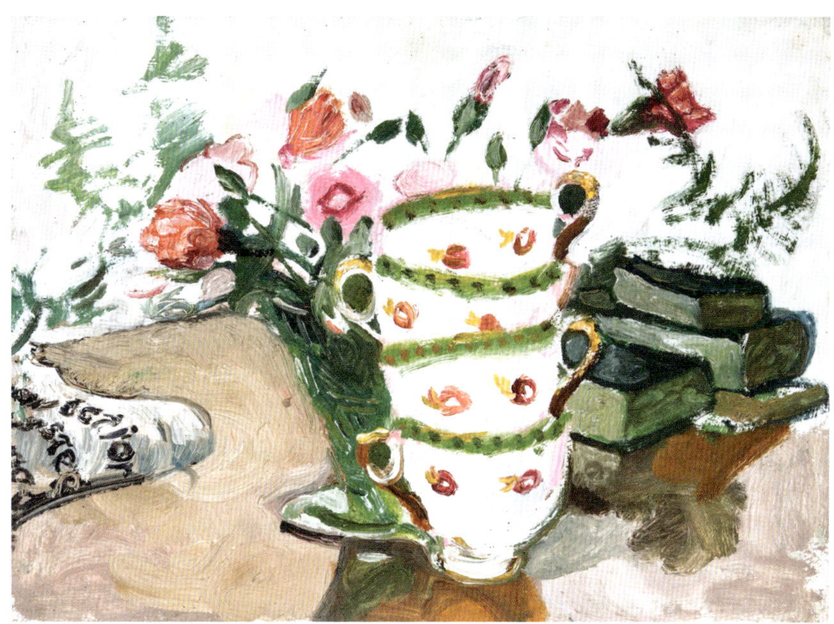

Still Life at St Nicks · c.1977 · oil on board · 38 x 51 cm

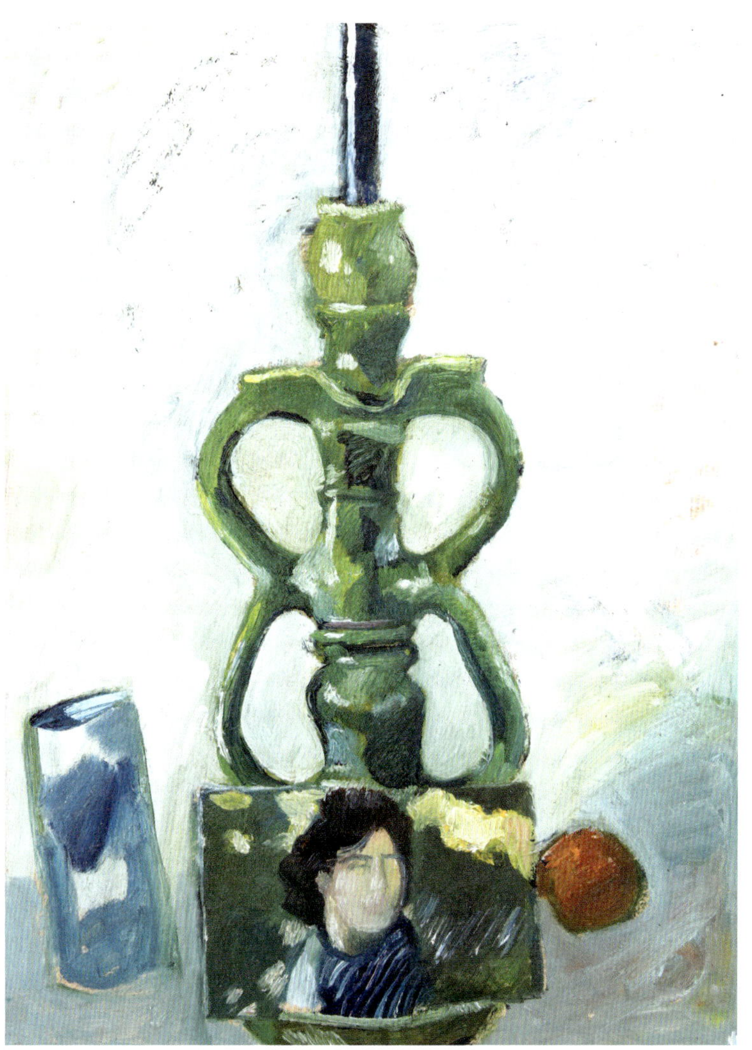

Green Candlestick with Bex · c.1978 · oil on board · 61 x 45 cm

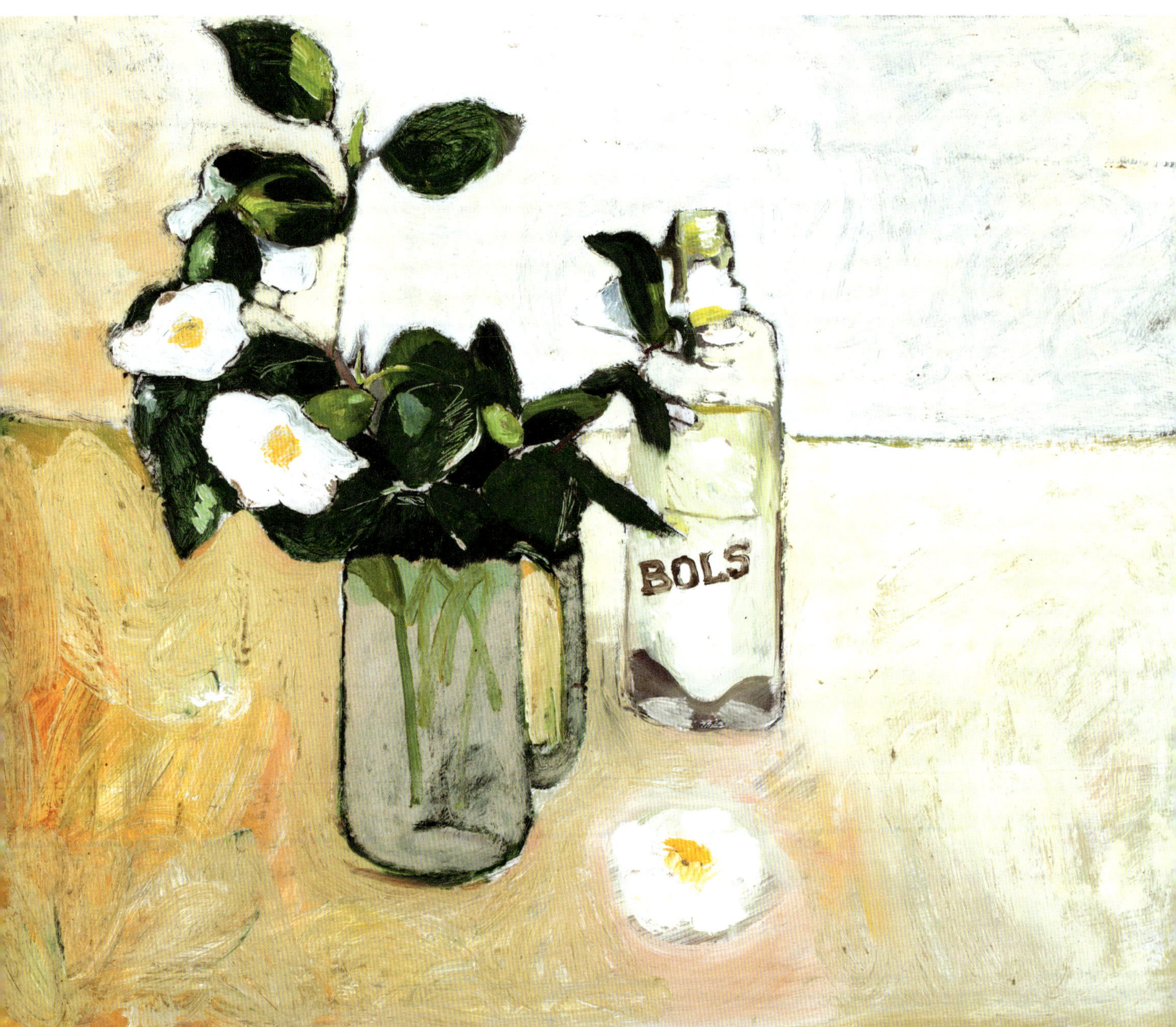

Bols and Camellias · c.1990 · oil on board · 72 x 88 cm

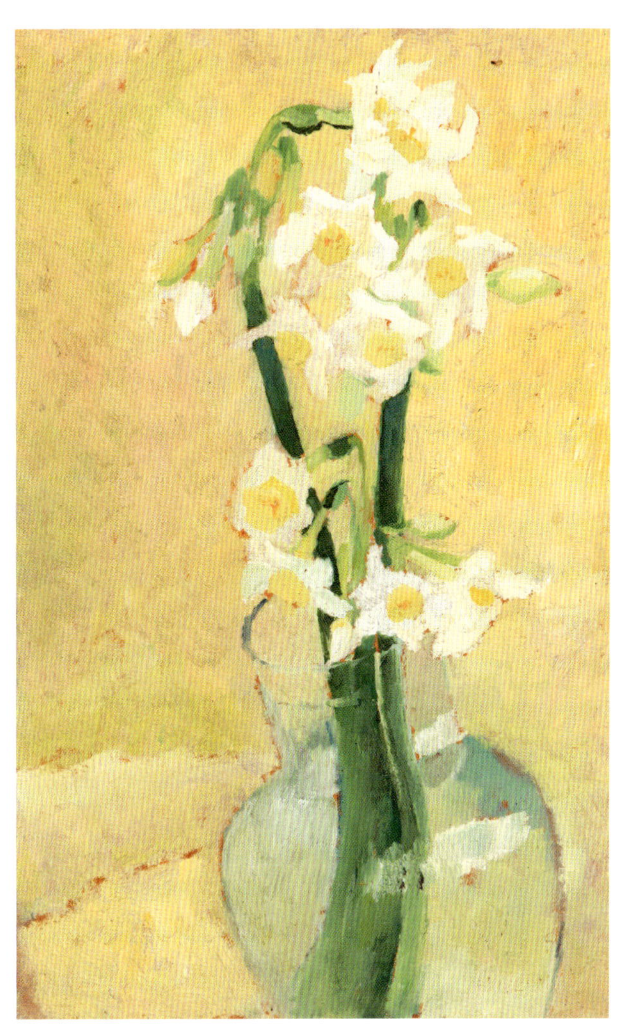

Narcissi · late 1960s · oil on board · 33 x 27 cm

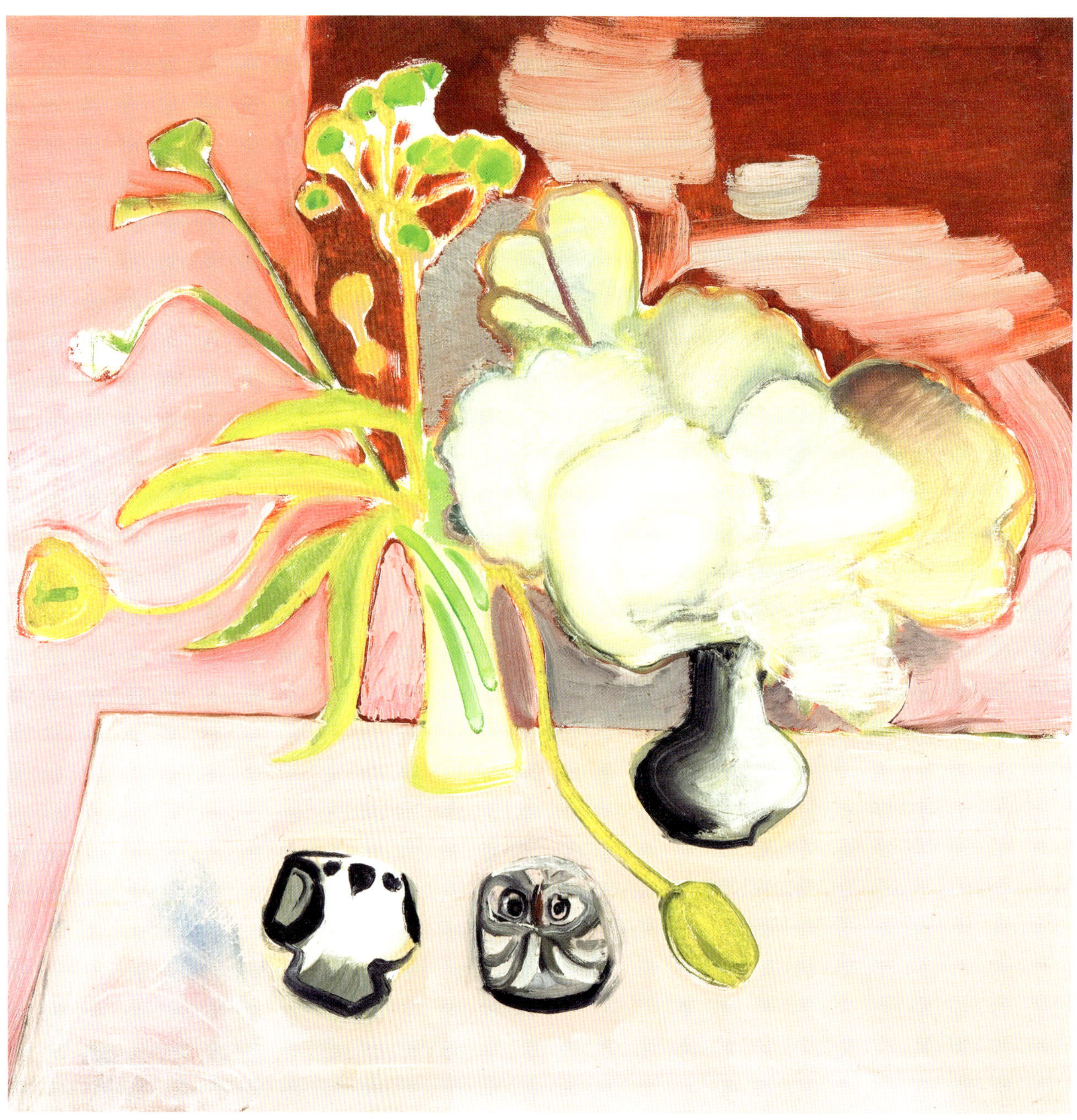

Mixed Flowers with Figures · c.1982 · oil on board · 76 x 76 cm

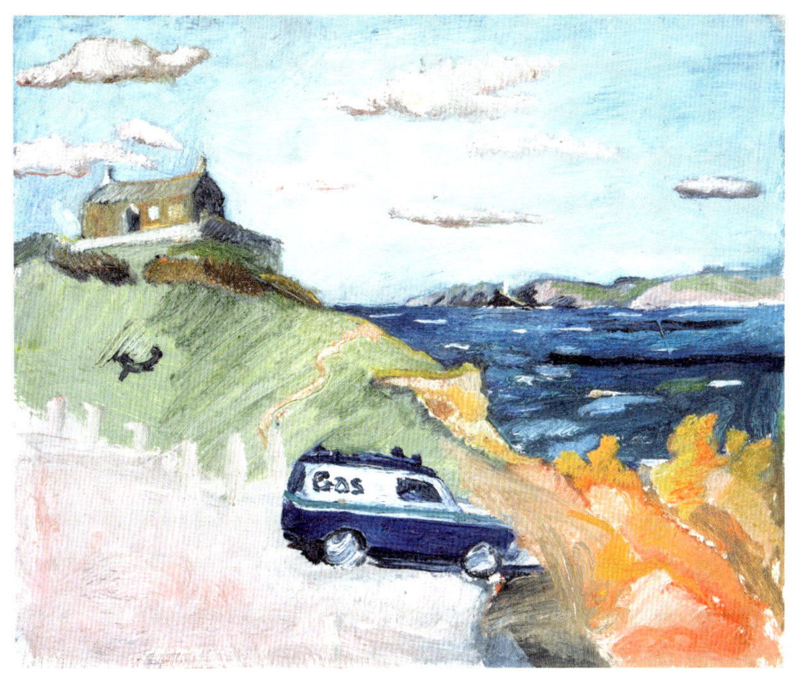

Gas Van at St Ives · c.1975 · oil on board · 45 x 50 cm

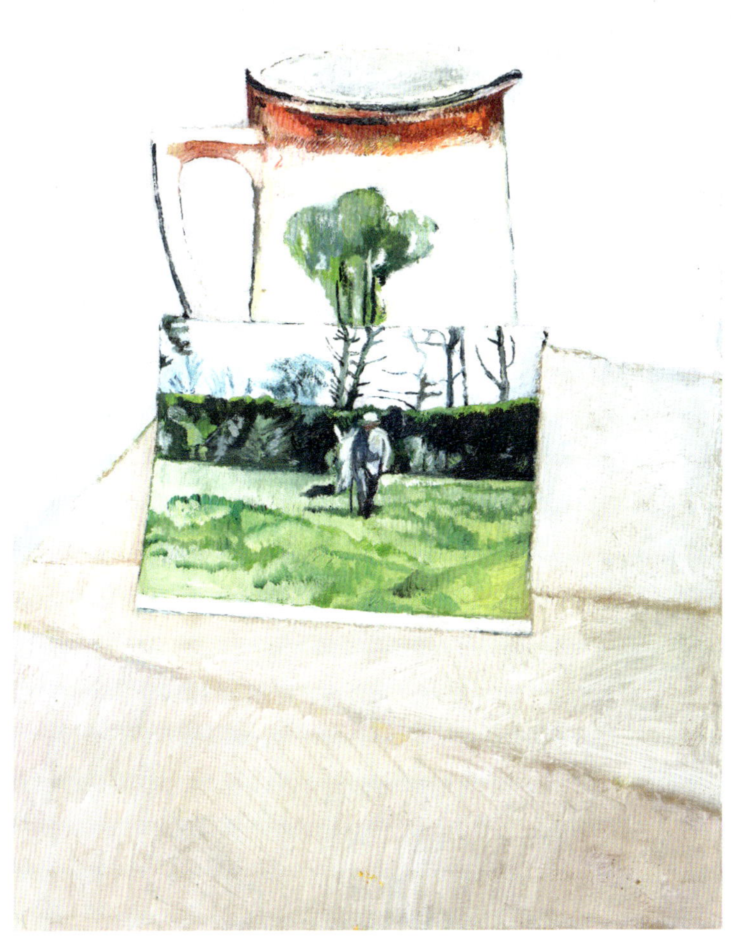

PHH and Norfolk Jug · c.1980 · oil on board · 61 x 45 cm

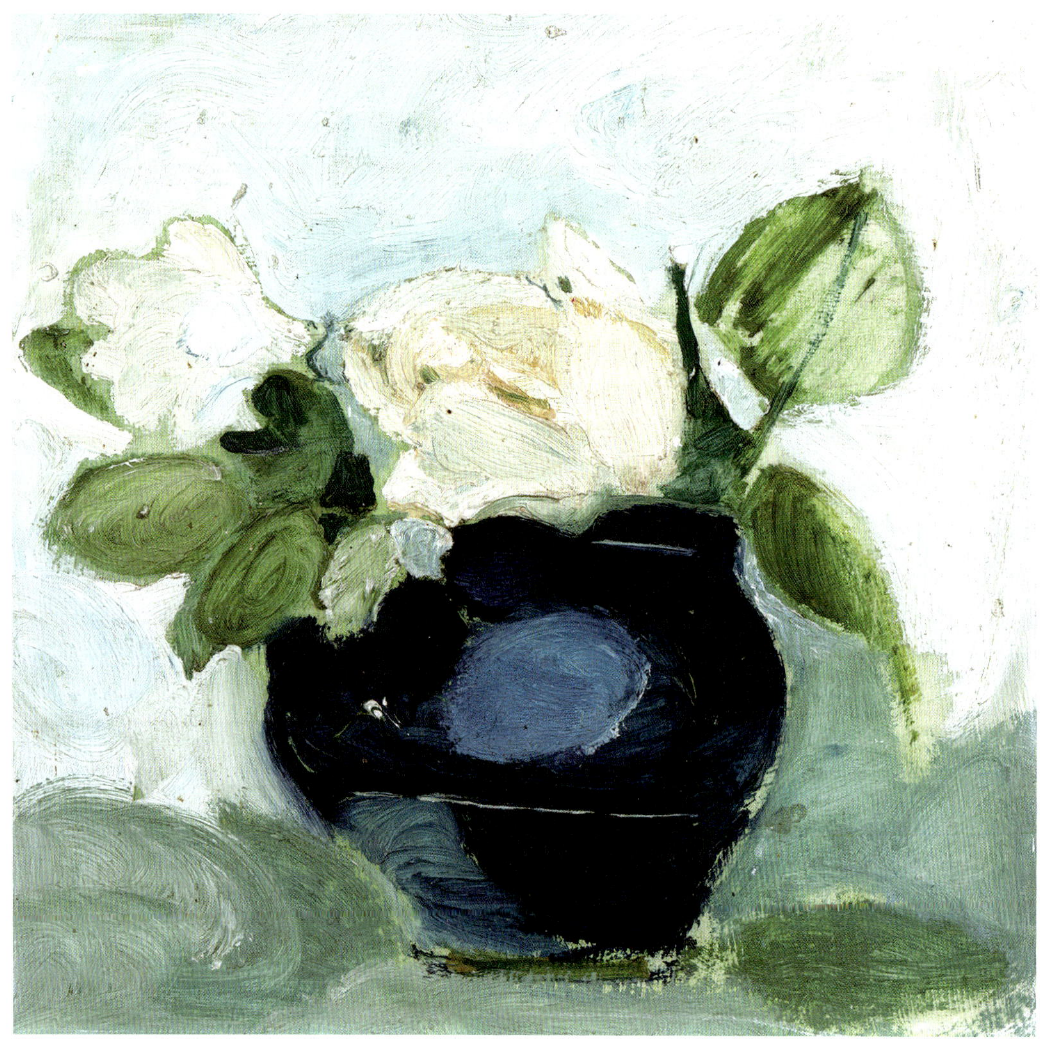

Camellia in Blue Vase · c.1978 · oil on board · 28 x 29 cm

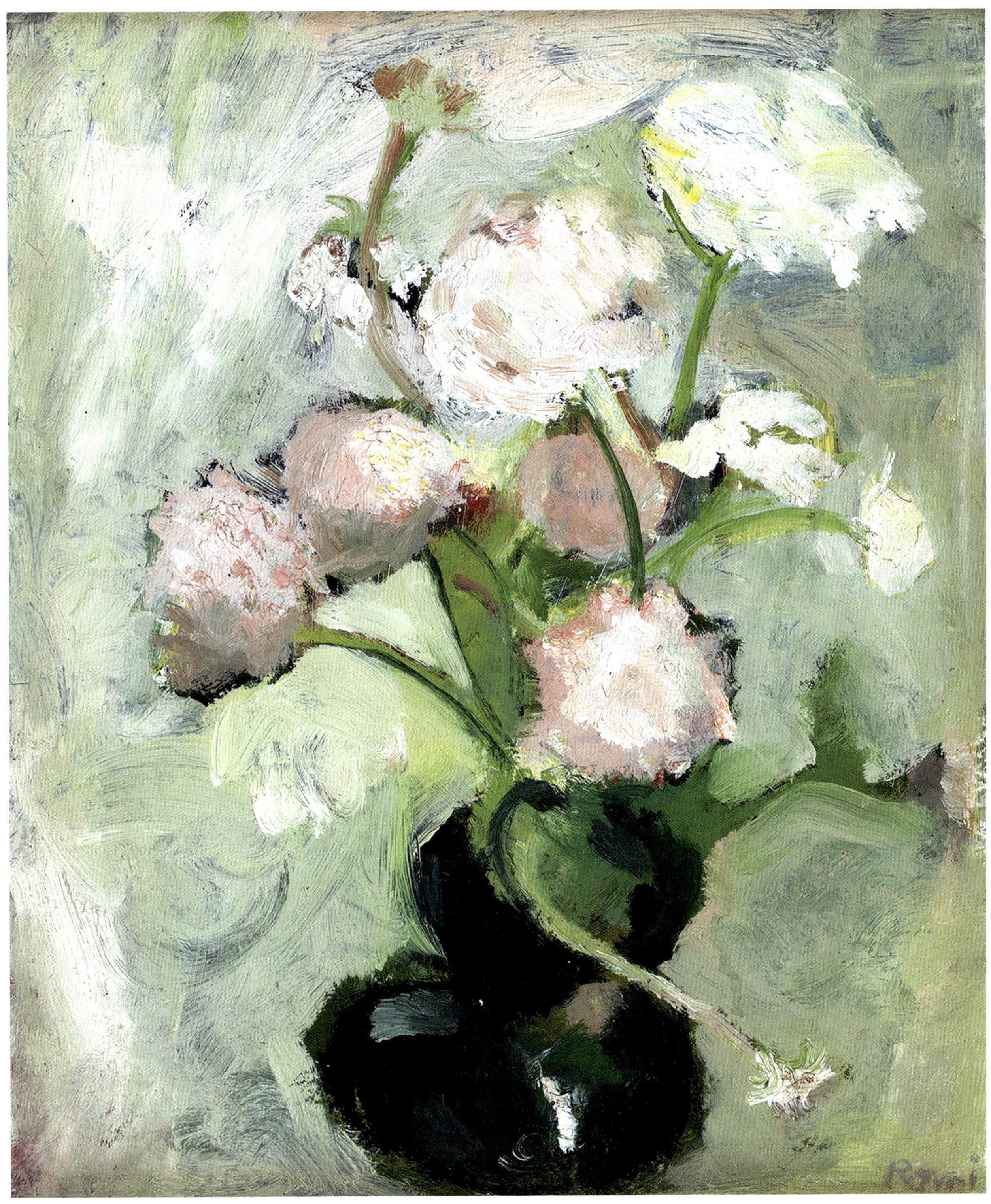

Cow Parsley · c.1977 · oil on board · 40 x 34 cm

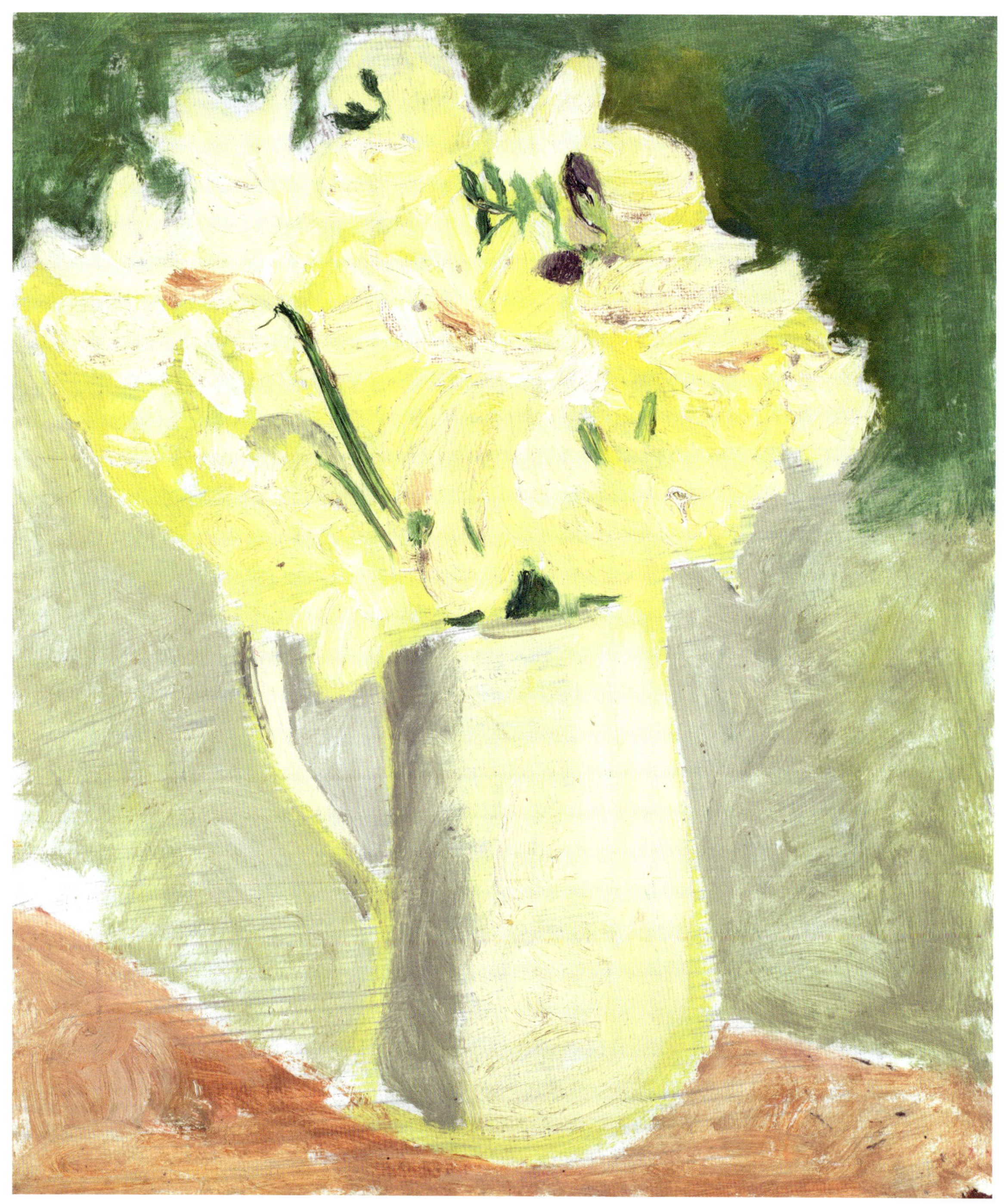

Daffs I · c.1998 · oil on board · 53 x 46 cm

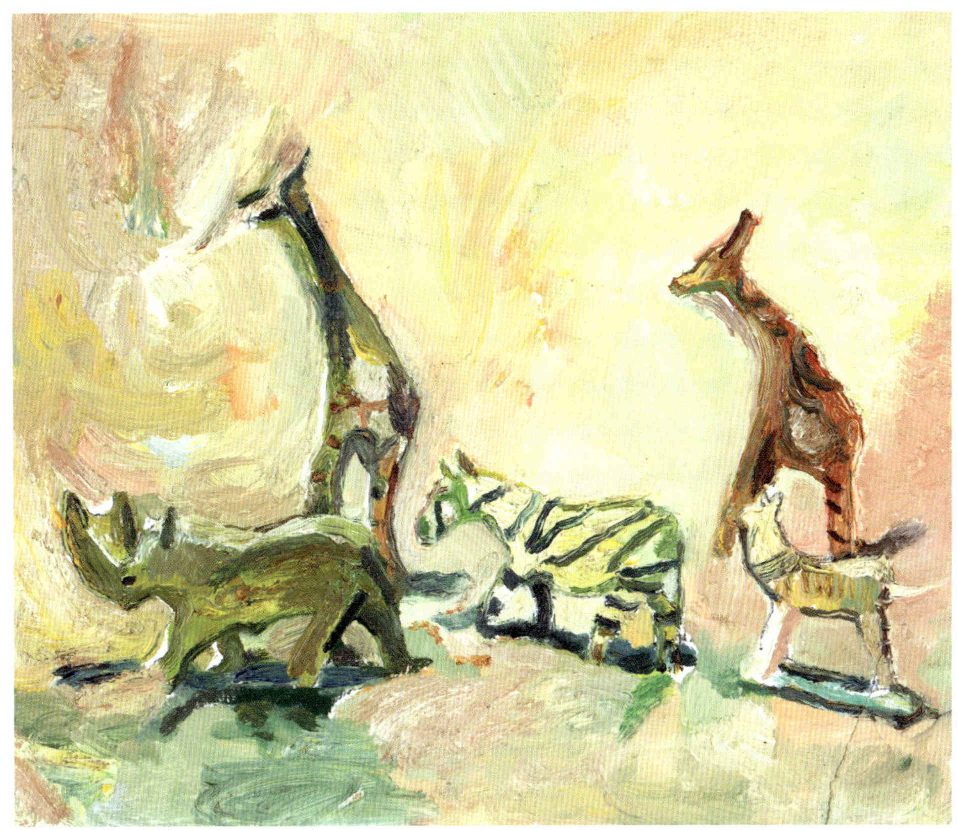

The Zoo · c.1982 · oil on board · 31 x 38 cm

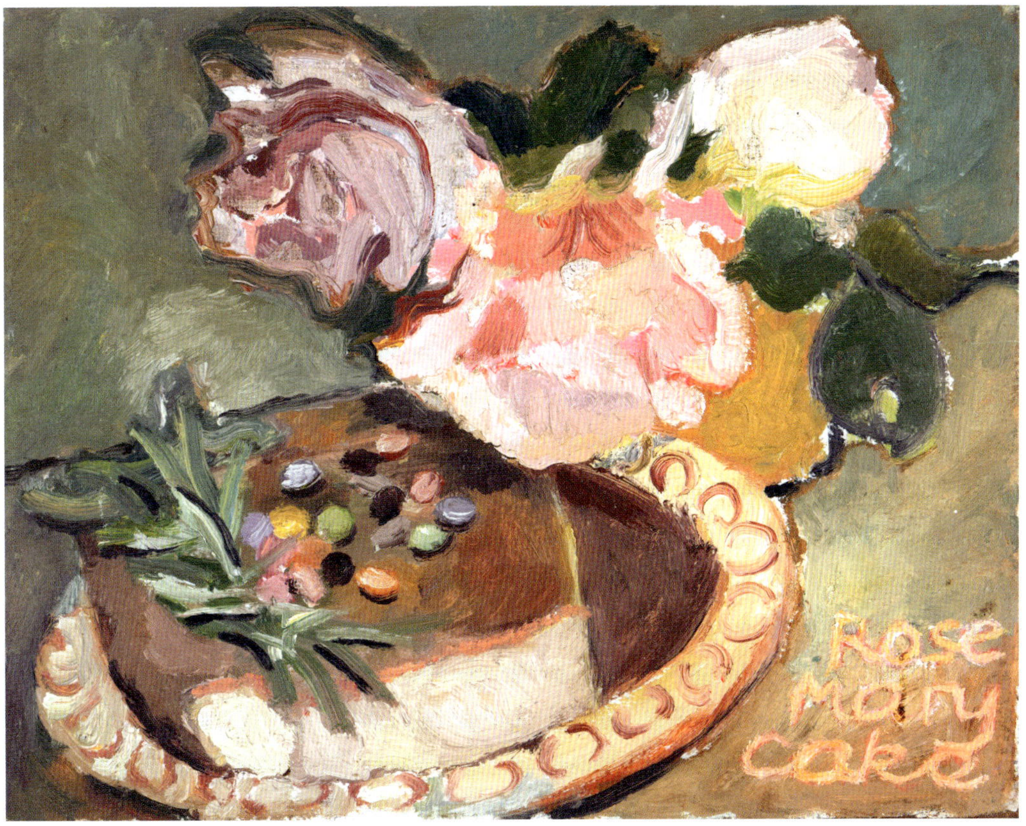

Roses and Smarties I · late 1970s · oil on board · 31 x 41 cm

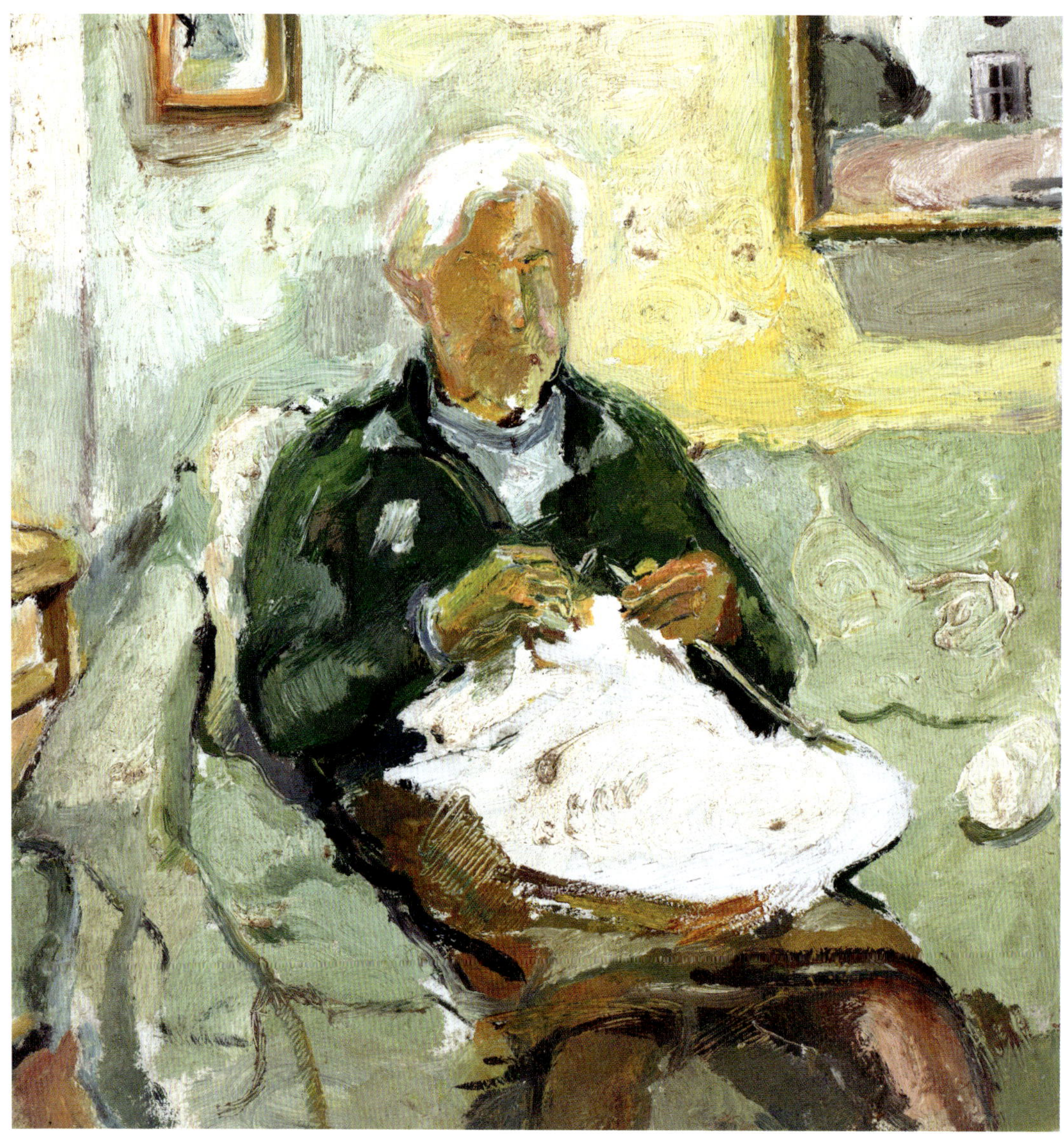

Mum (Marjorie) · c.1979 · oil on board · 37 x 36 cm

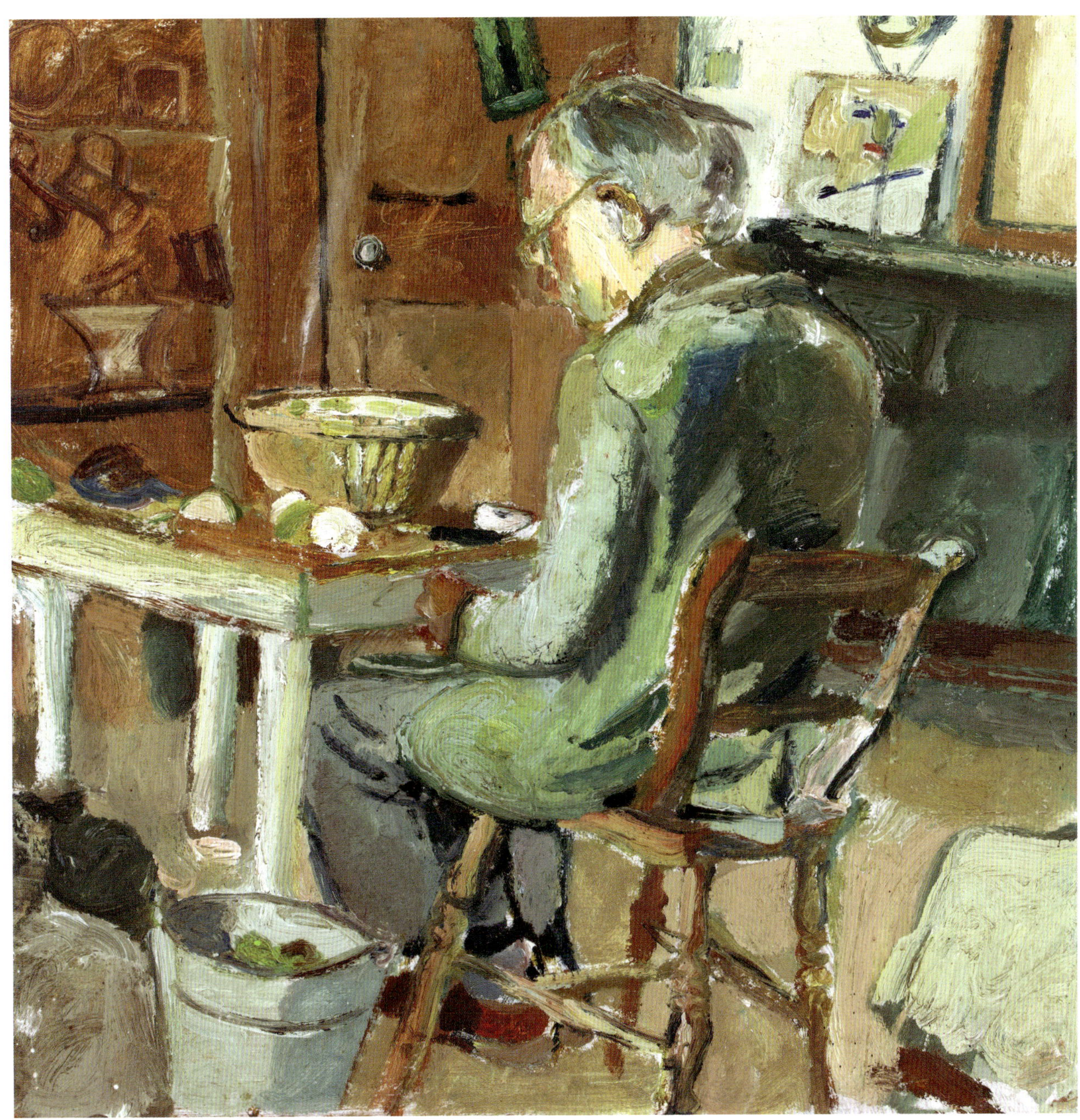

PHH, Peeling Apples · c.1973 · oil on board · 43 x 43 cm

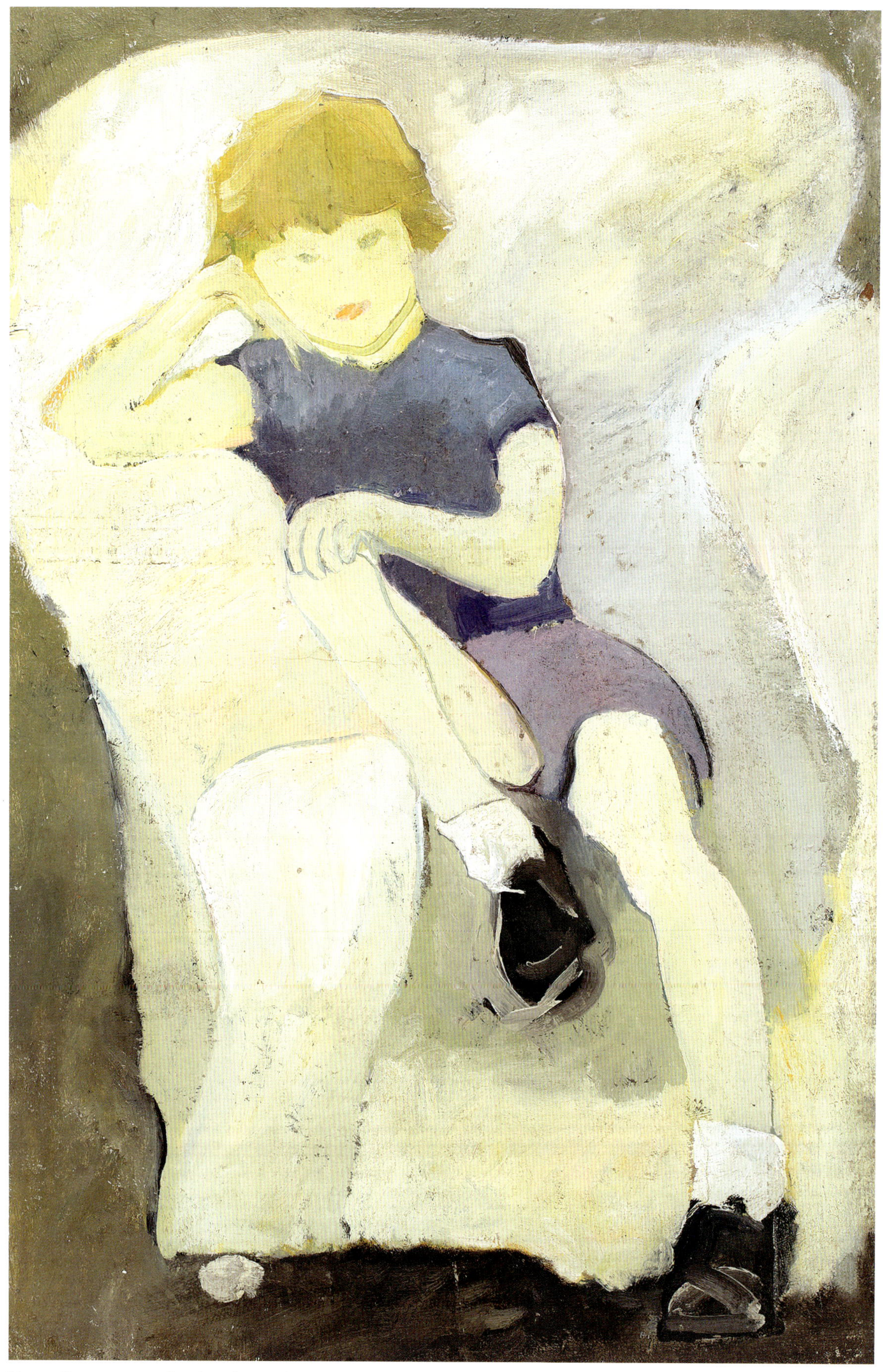

Young Boy · c.1975 · oil on board · 91 x 60 cm

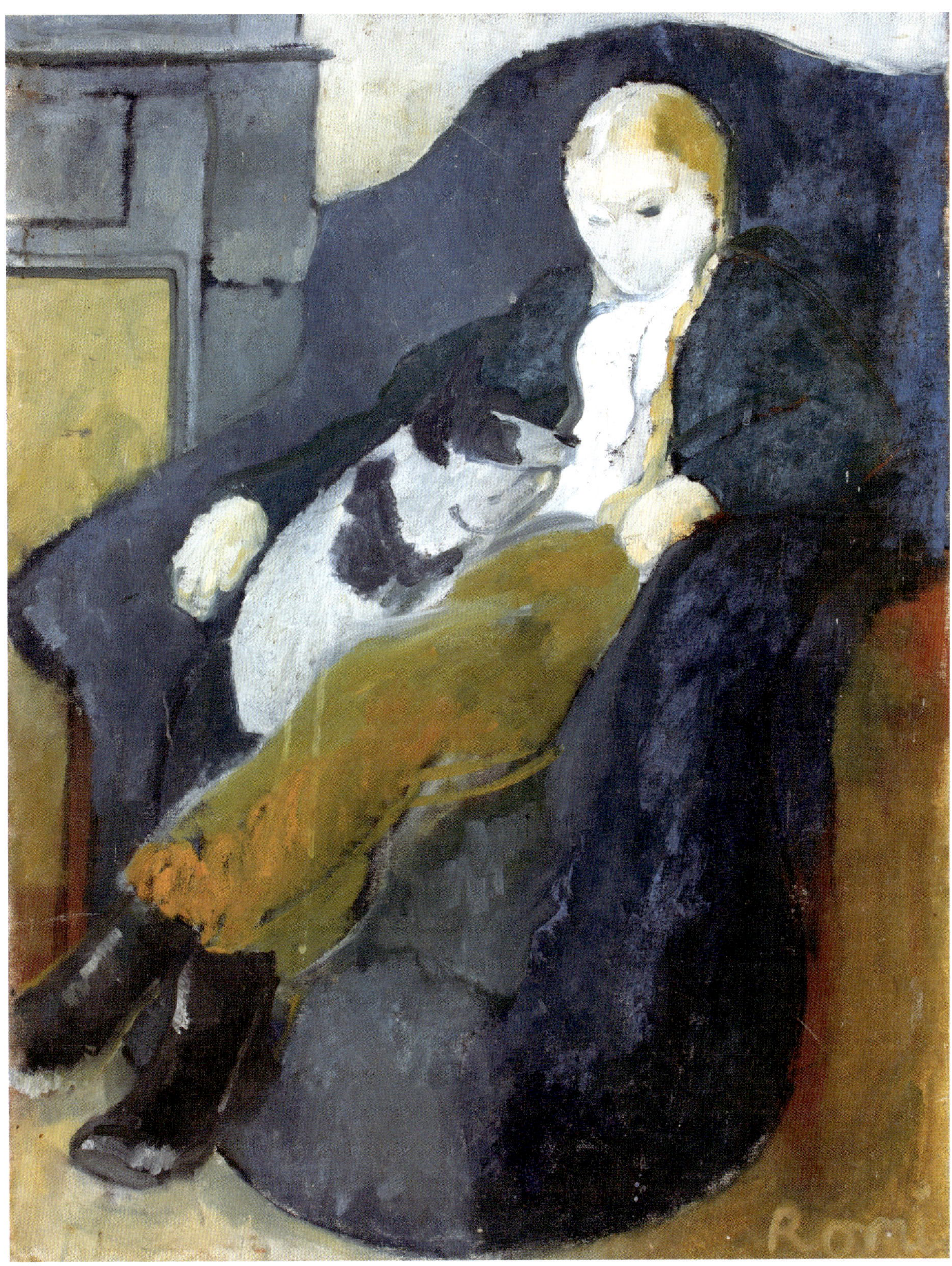

Caroline (USA) and Freddie · mid-1970s · oil on canvas · 82 x 64 cm

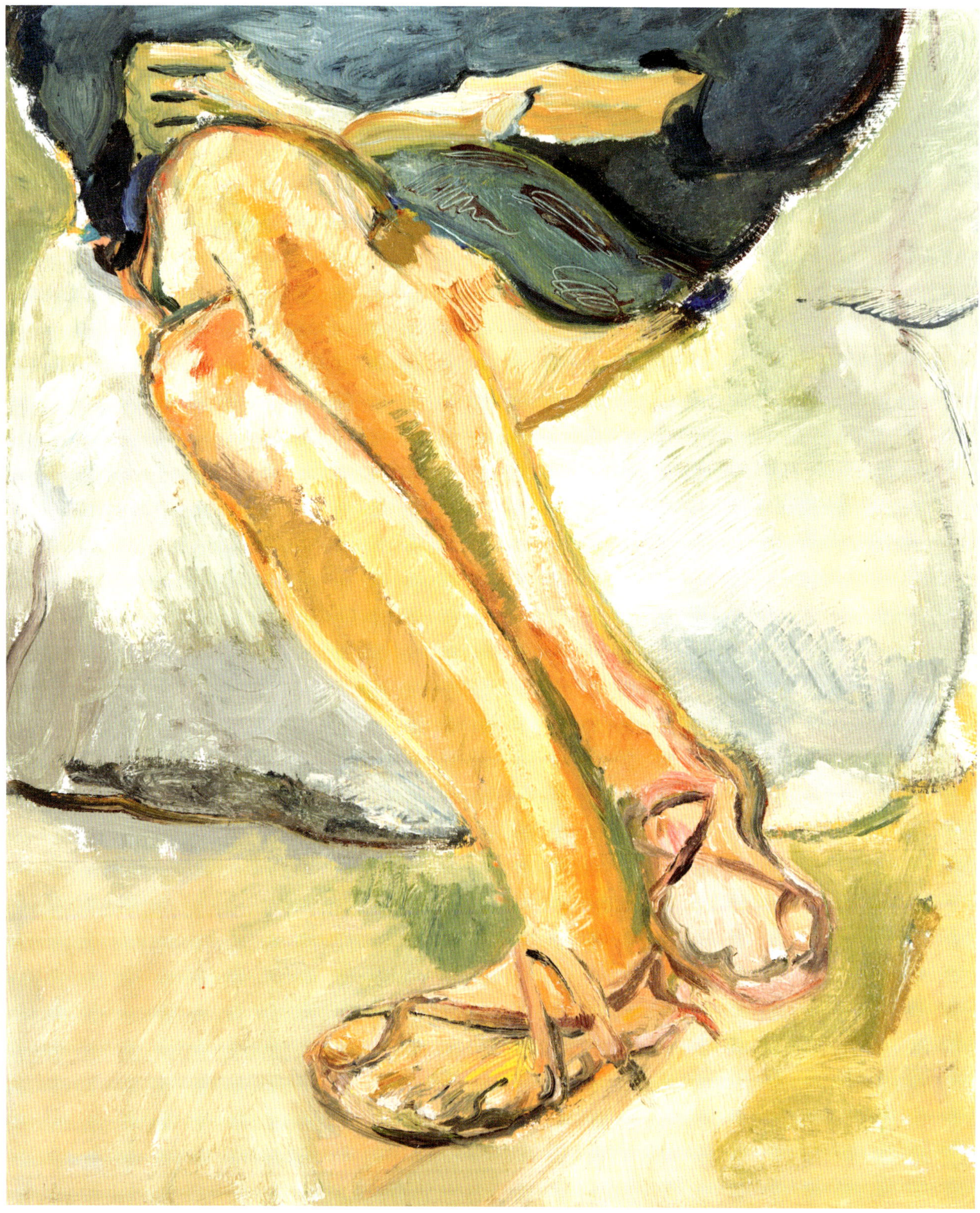

Emily's Legs in Sandals · c.1981 · oil on board · 76 x 62 cm

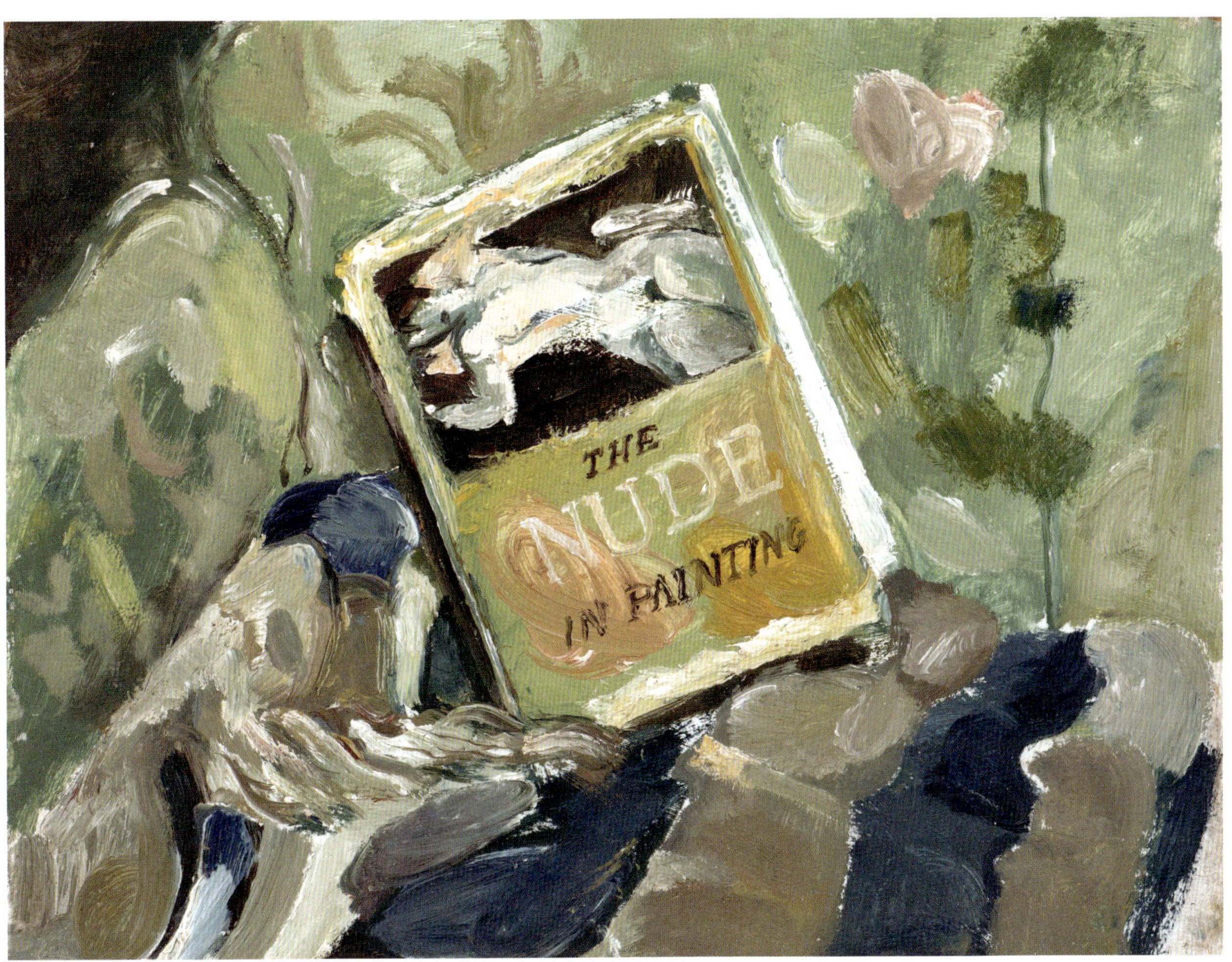

Book of Nudes · c.1996 · oil on board · 49 x 61 cm

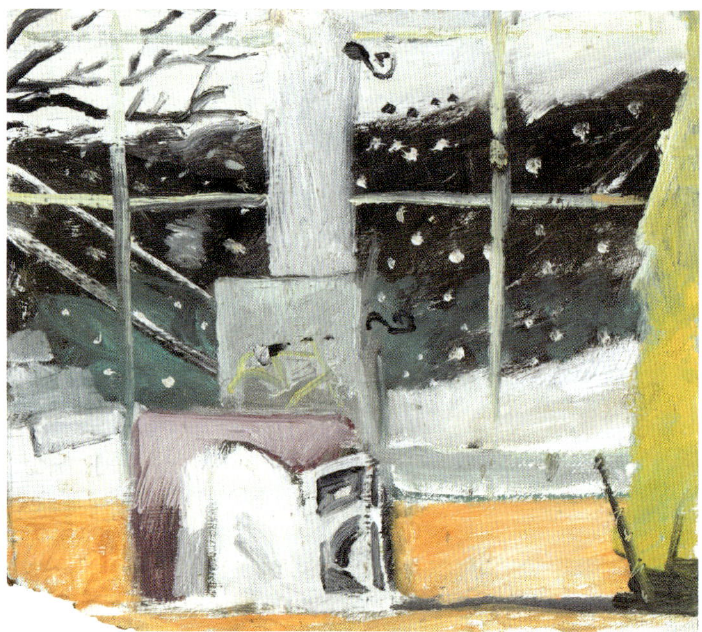

Trenalls Window II · c.1982 · oil on board · 31 x 36 cm

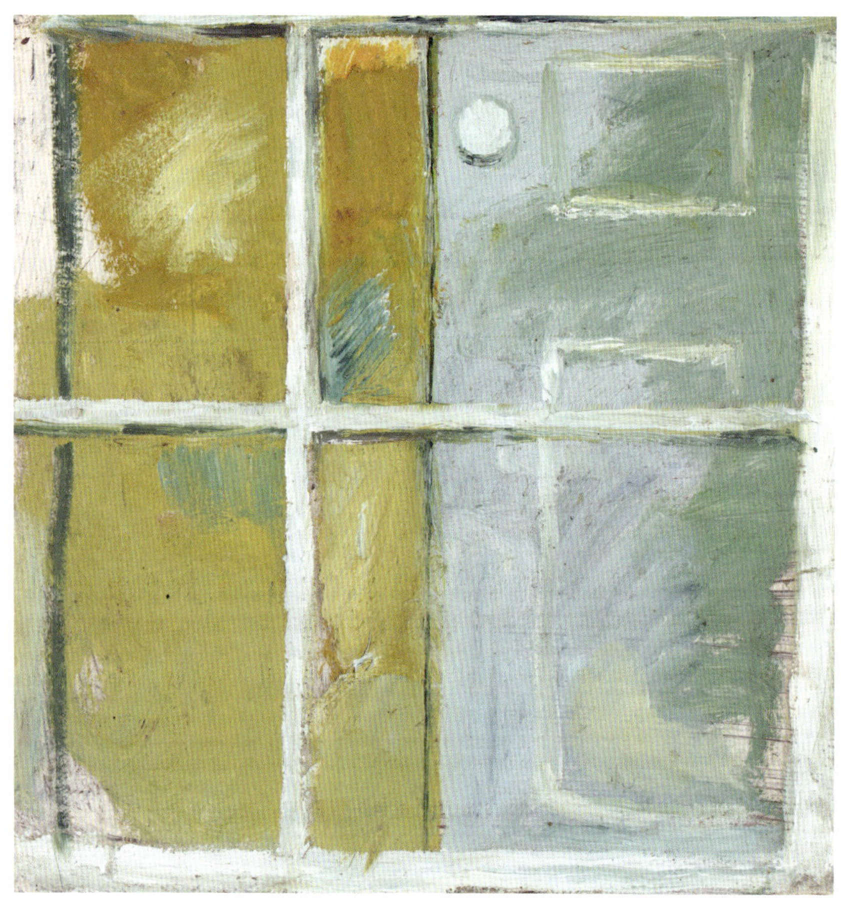

Window at Clevedon, Plumber's House · early 1980s · oil on board · 42 x 41 cm

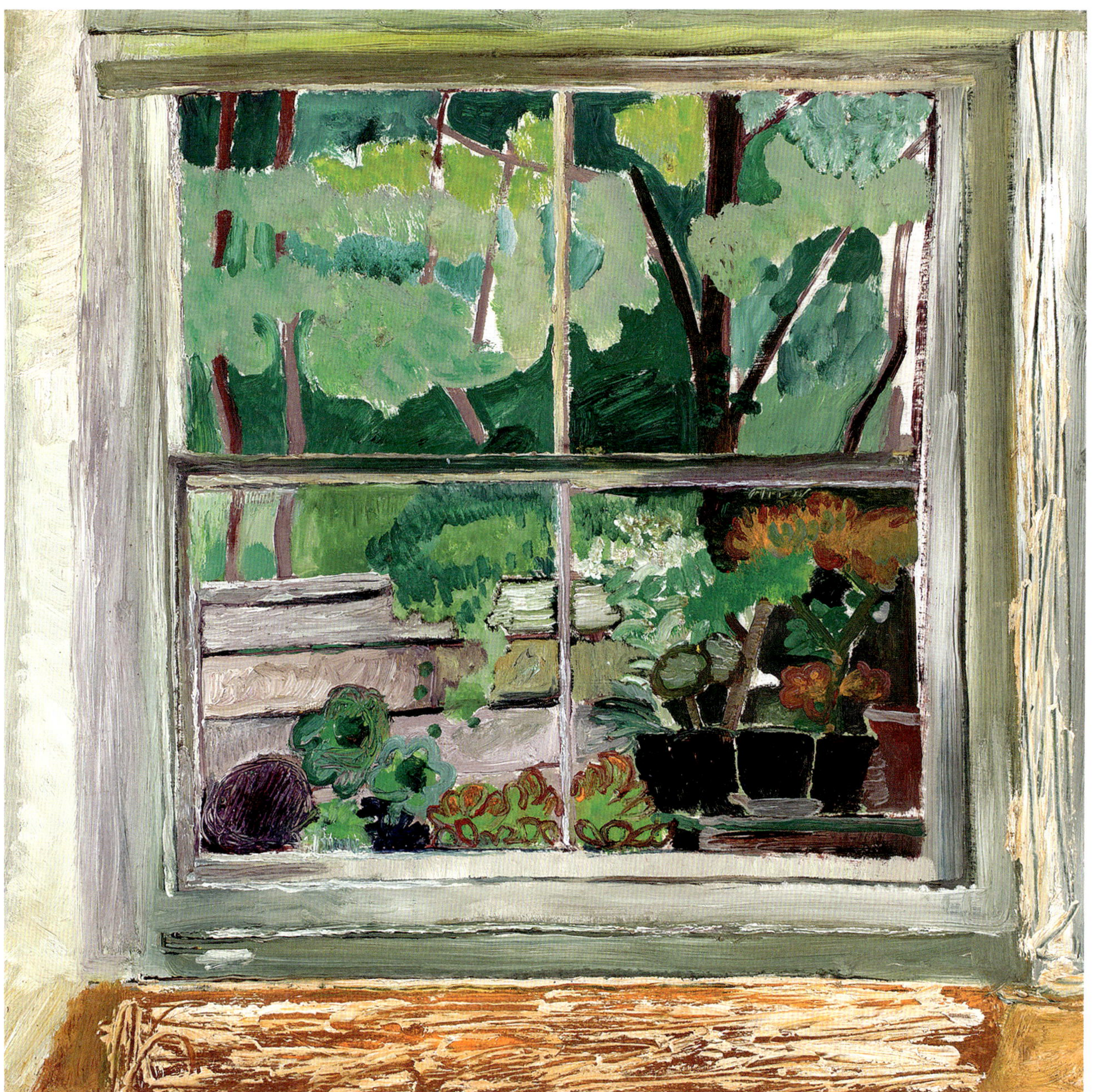

View through Tares Window · c.1997 · oil on board · 59 x 61 cm

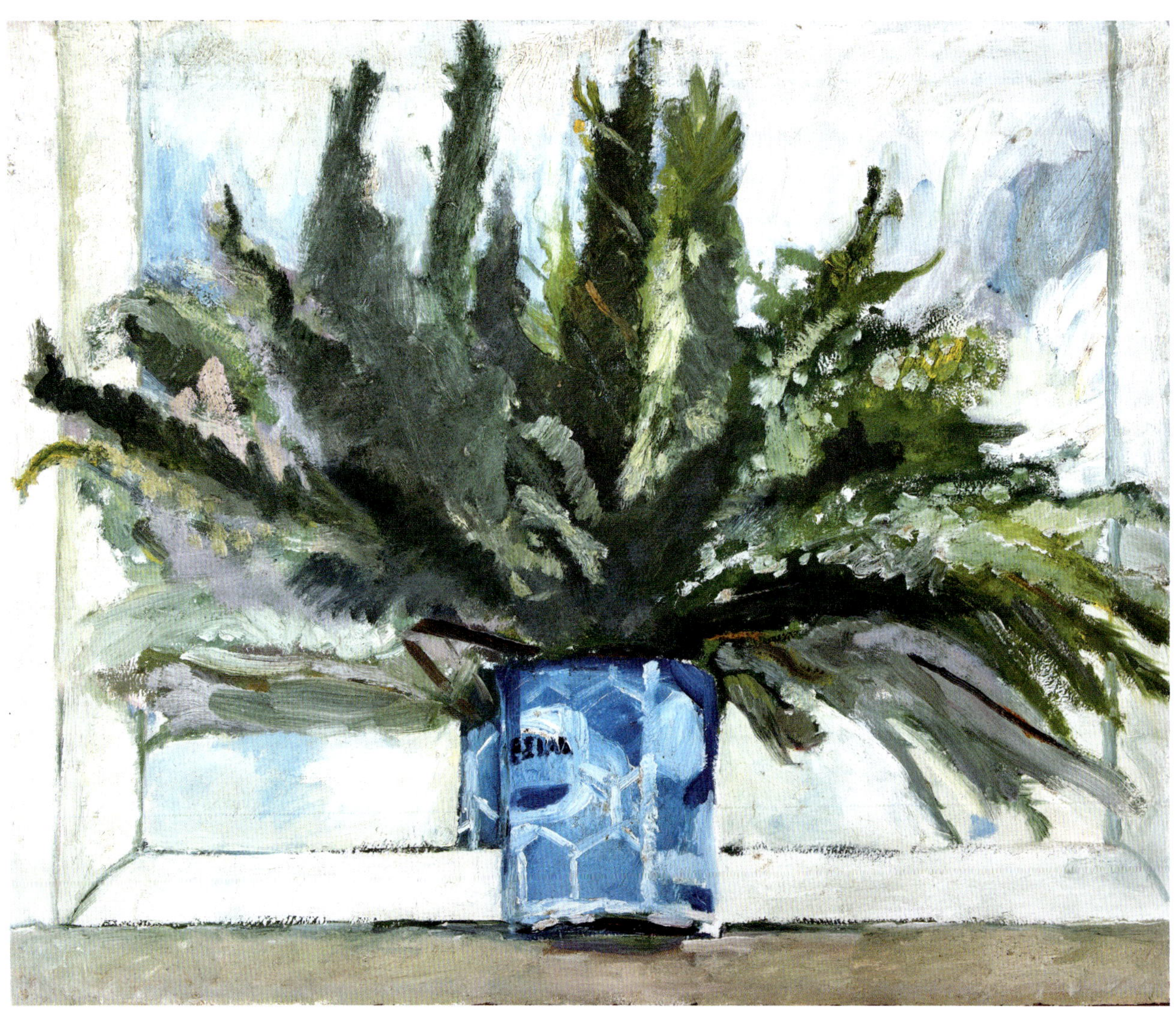

Heather in (Greek) Honey Tin · c.1983 · oil on board · 61 x 76 cm

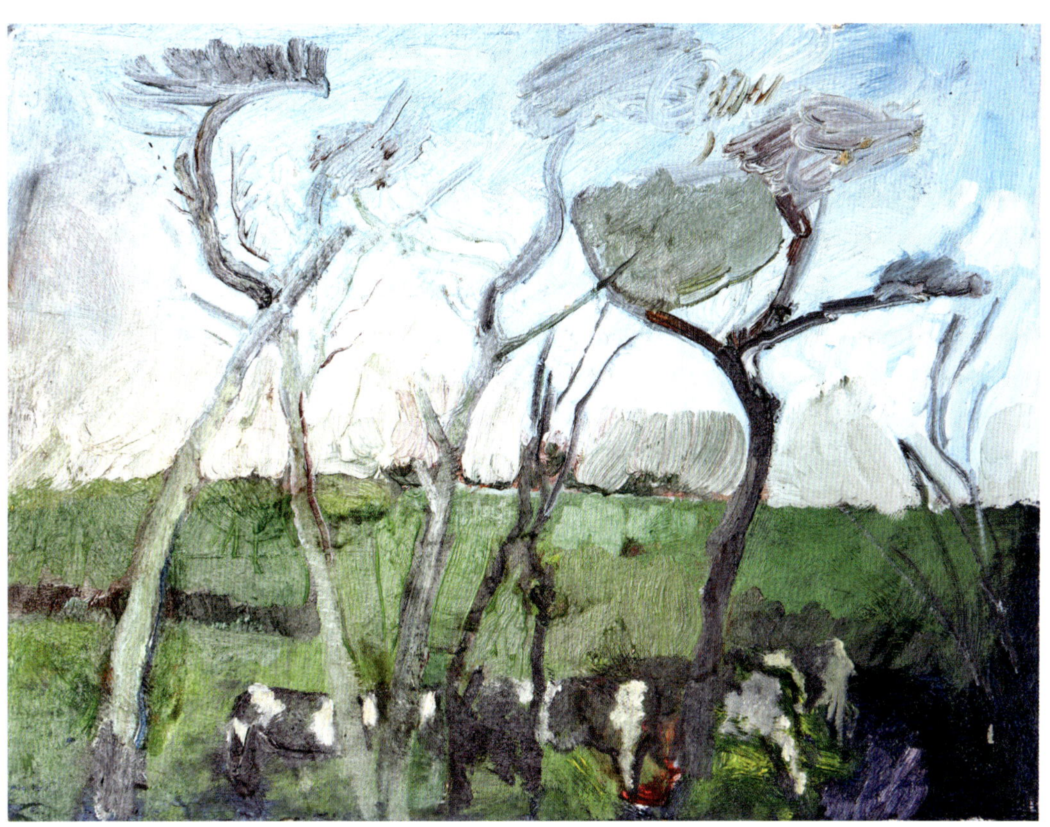

Friesians in the Pines · c.1987 · oil on board · 46 x 61 cm

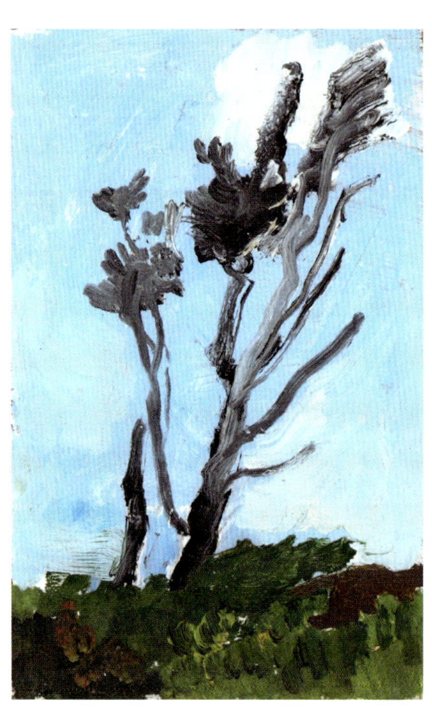

Sándor II · *c.*1980 · oil on board · 36 x 23 cm

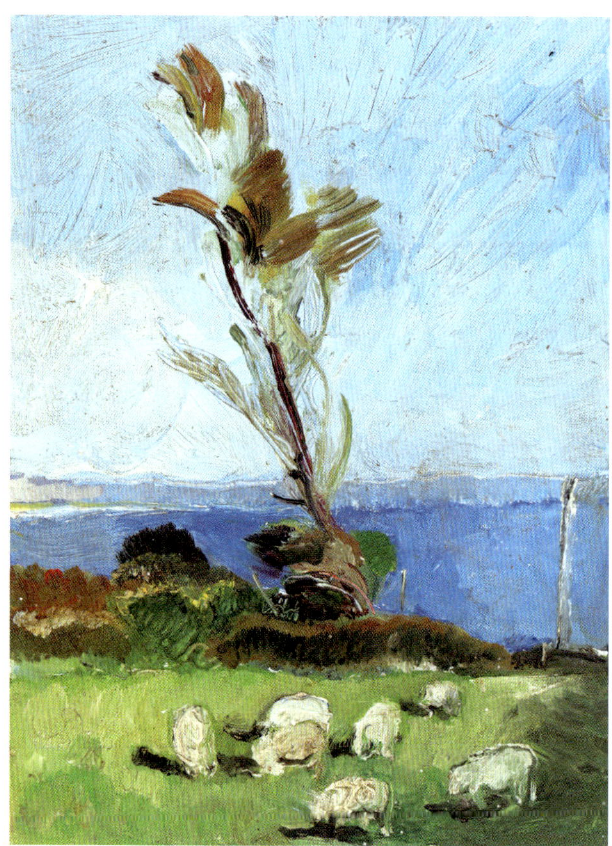

Sándor with Sheep · *c.*1982 · oil on board · 41 x 31 cm

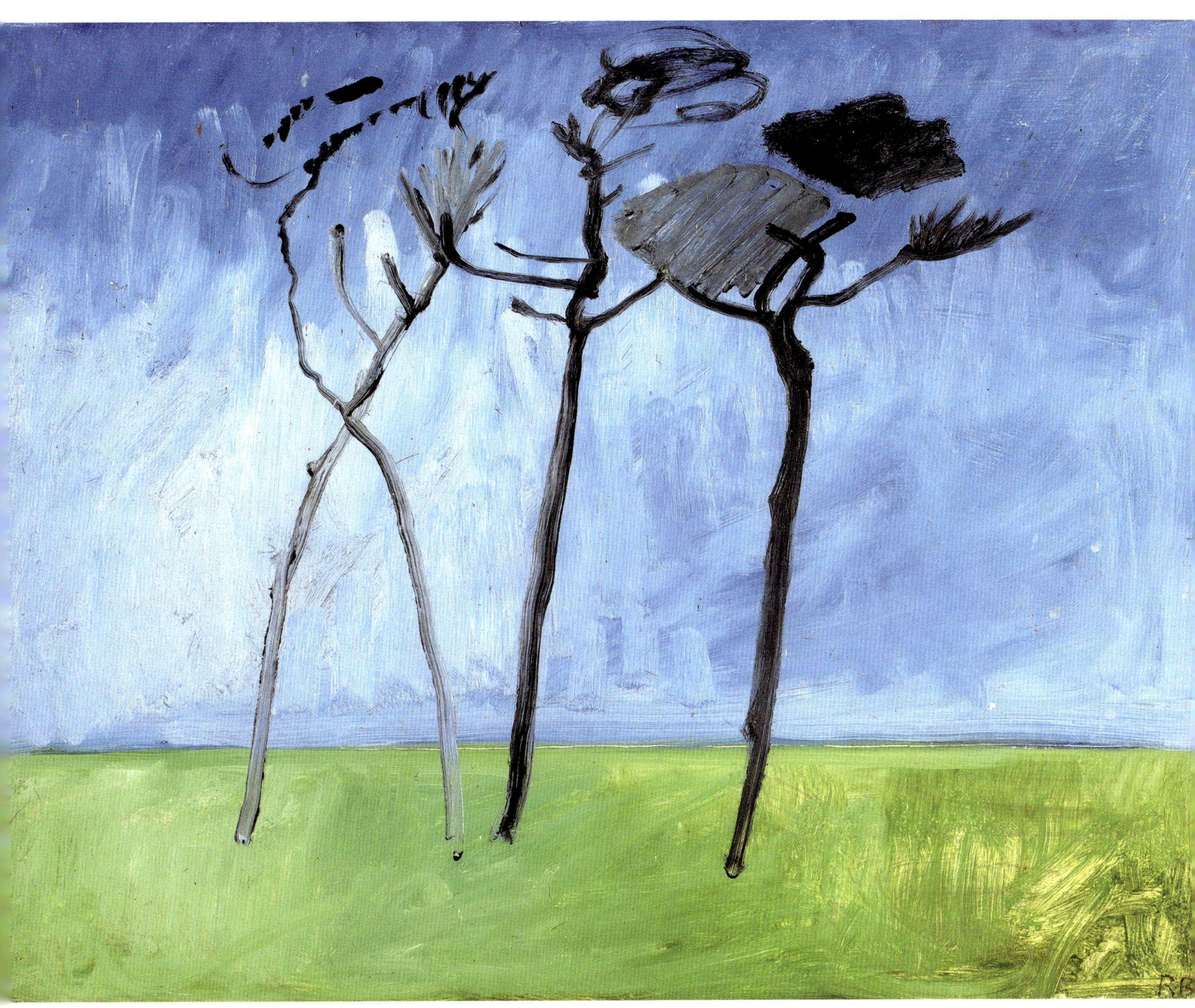

Dancing Grove · c.1987 · oil on board · 61 x 81 cm

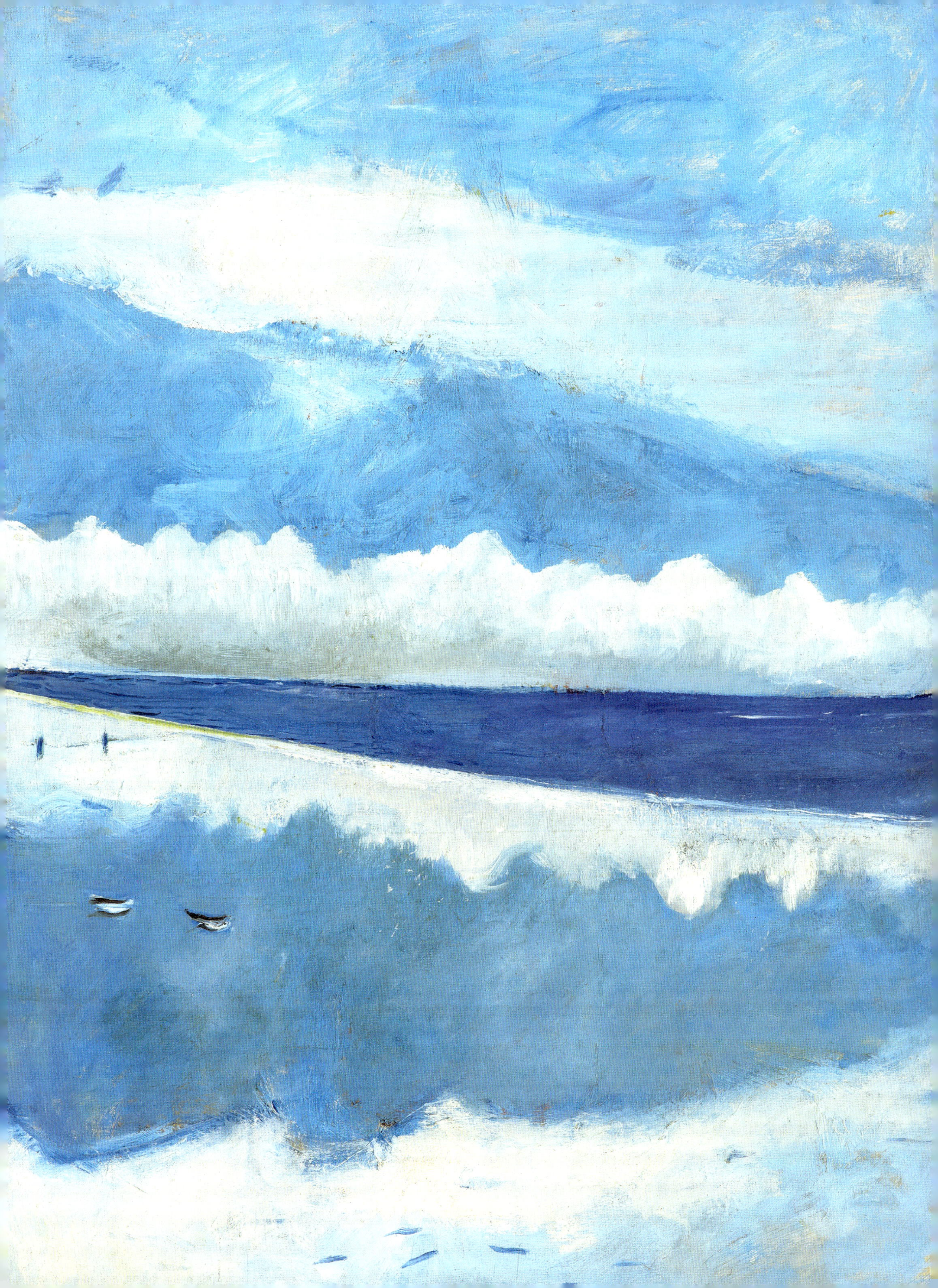

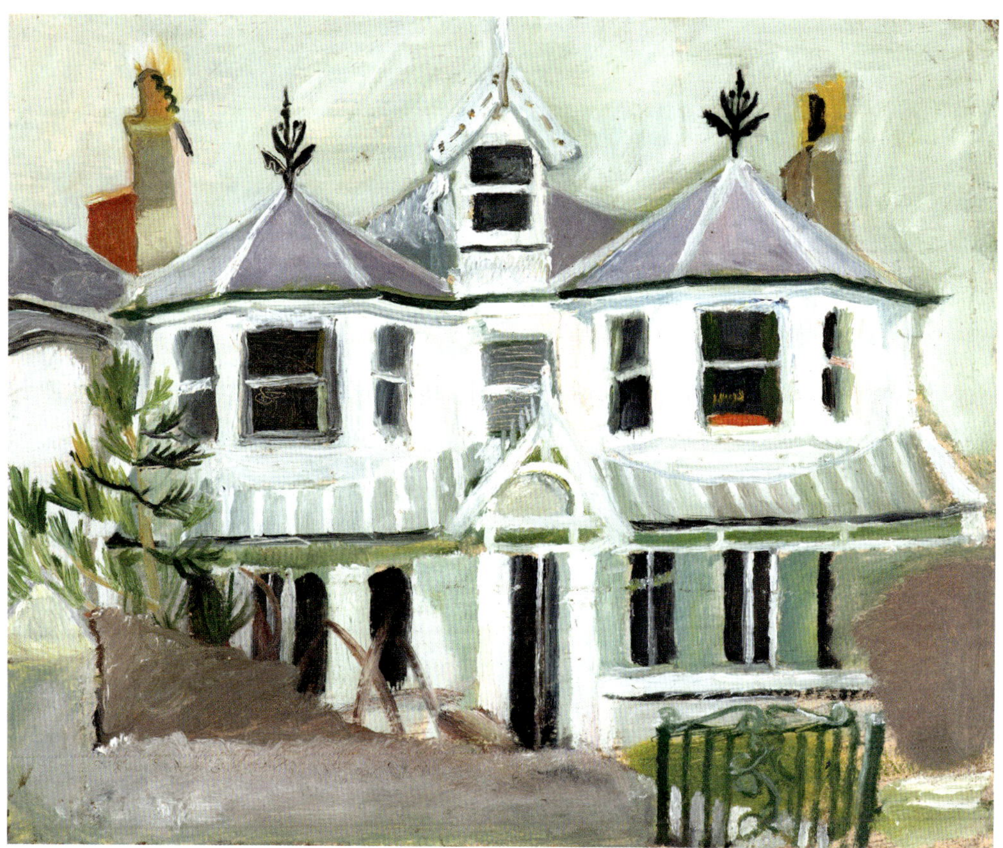

Clevedon Pottery · c.1982 · oil on board · 36 x 43 cm

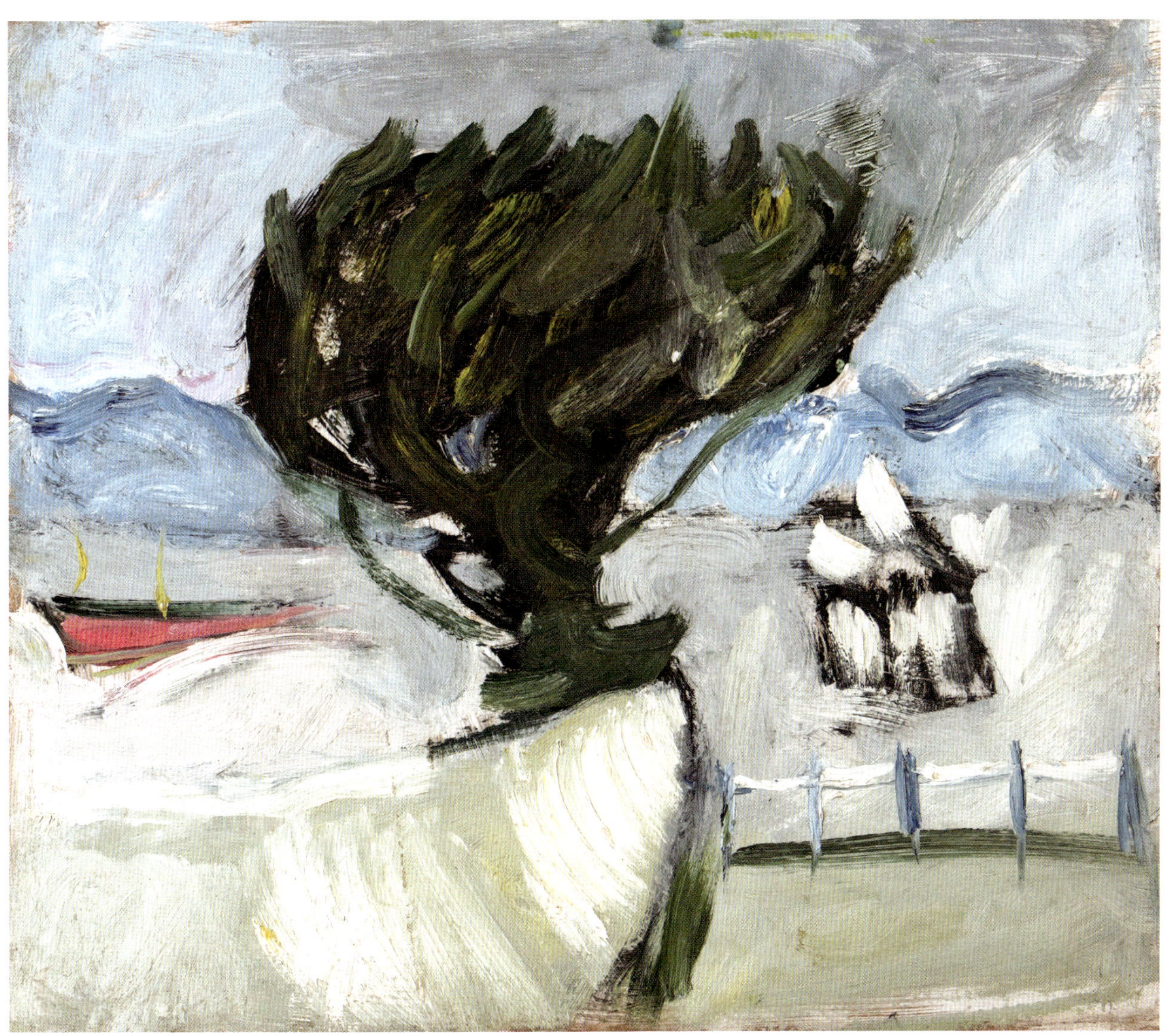

Clevedon Pier with Tree II · c.1989 · oil on board · 61 x 70 cm

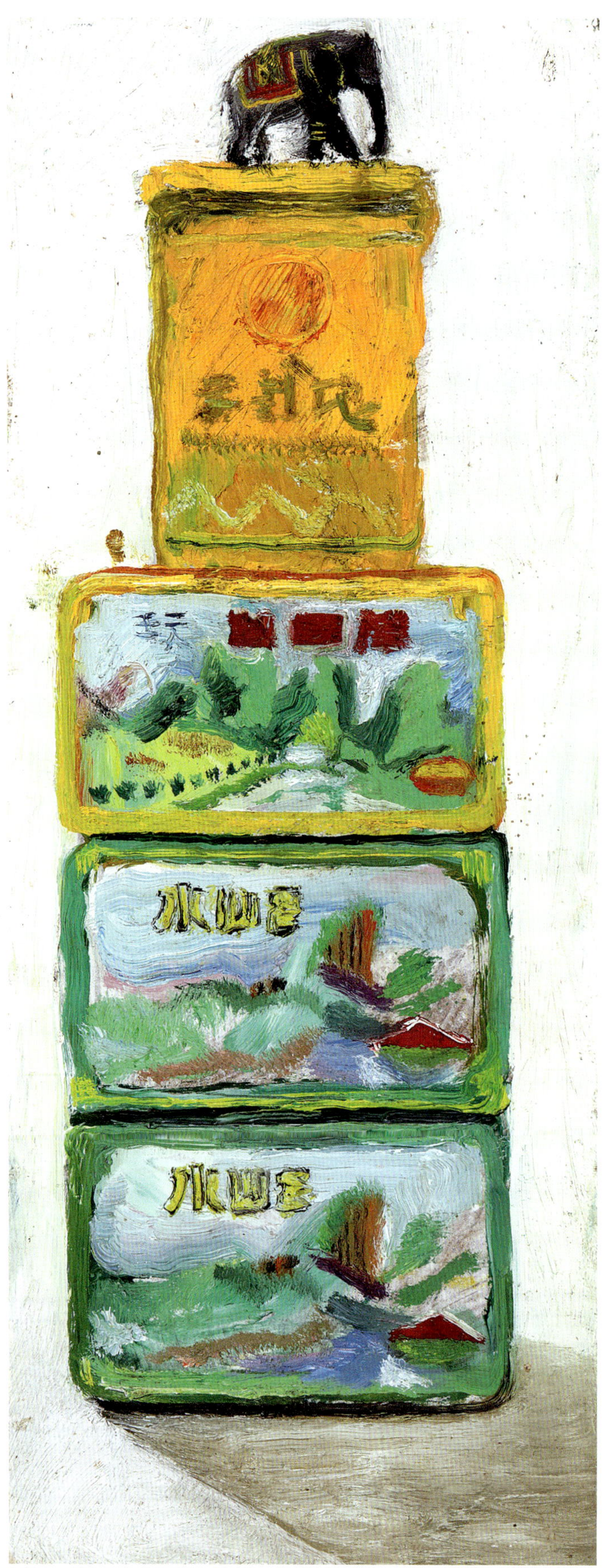

Chinese Tins with Elephant · c.1987 · oil on board · 41 x 17 cm

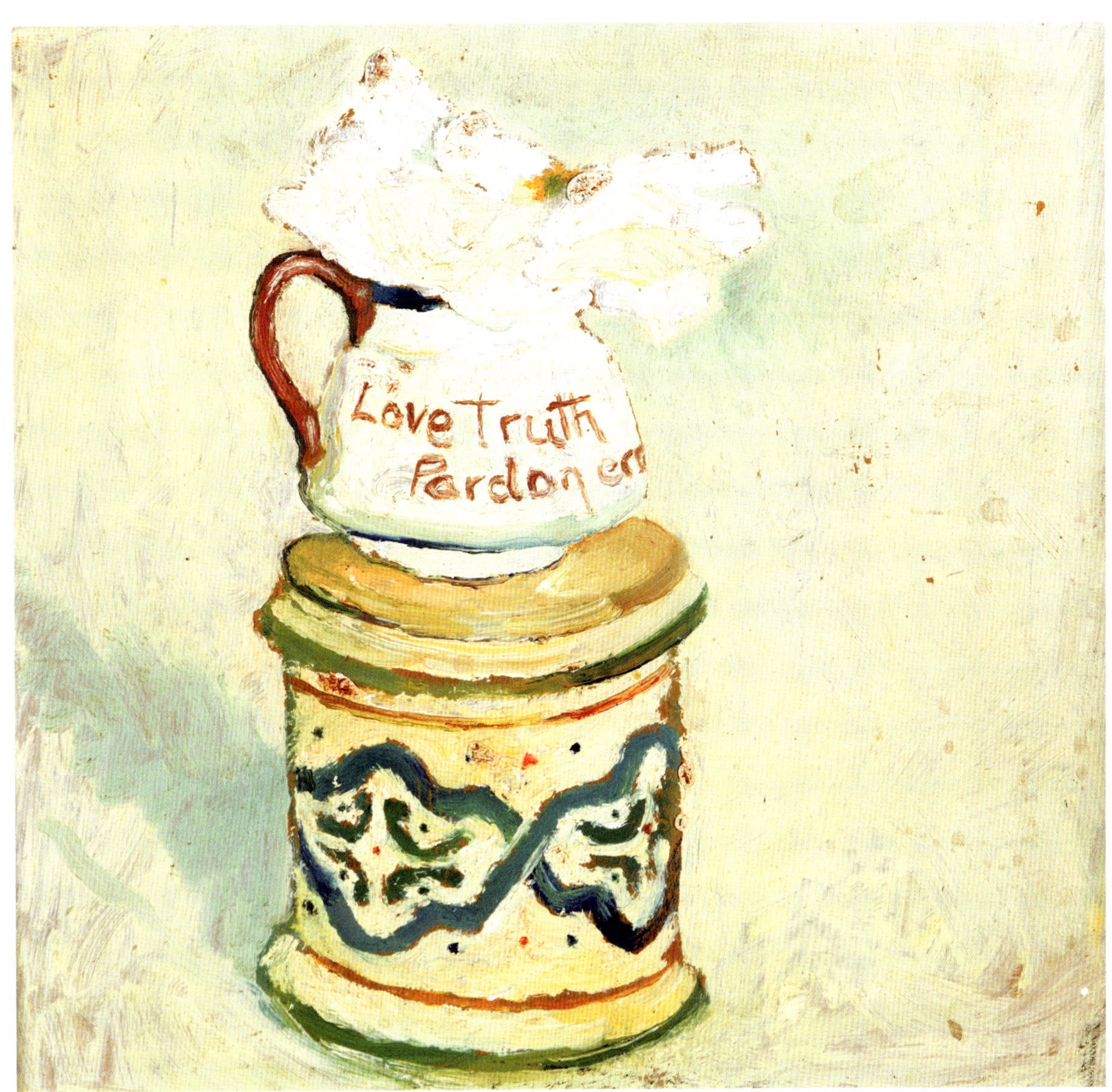

The Marmalade Pot · c.1974 · oil on board · 26 x 27 cm

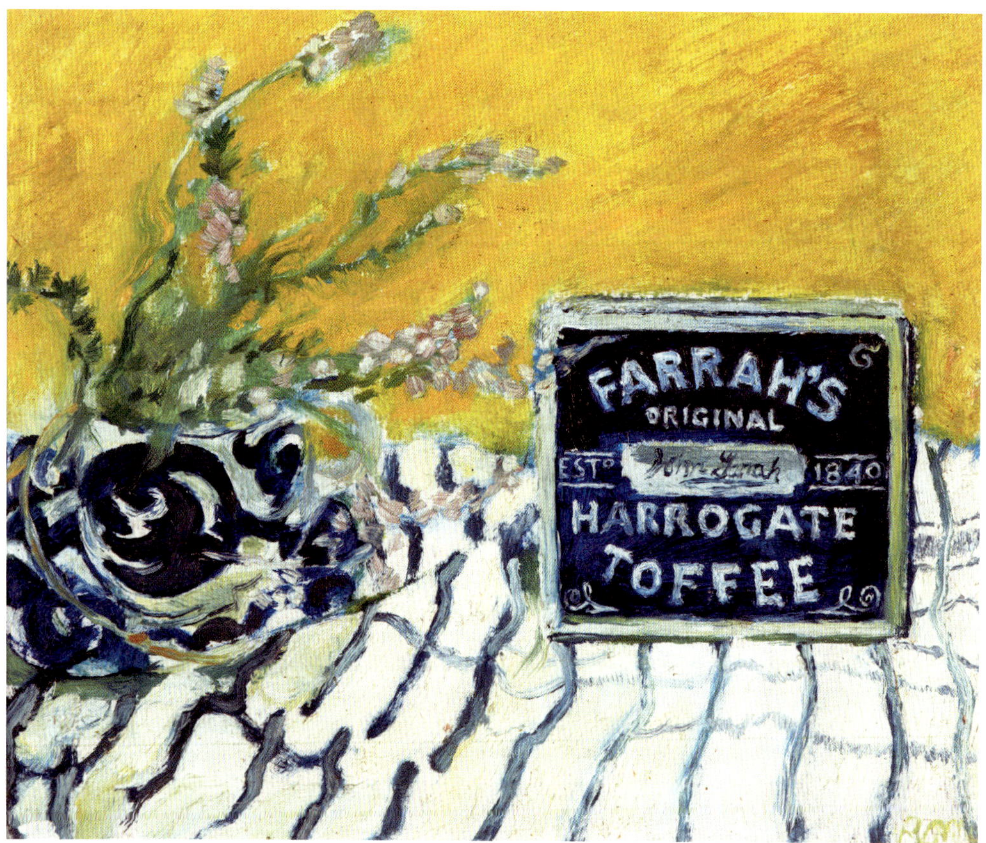

Farrah's Harrogate Toffee · c.1976 · oil on board · 25 x 31 cm

Ferreira · c.1979 · oil on board · 61 x 46 cm

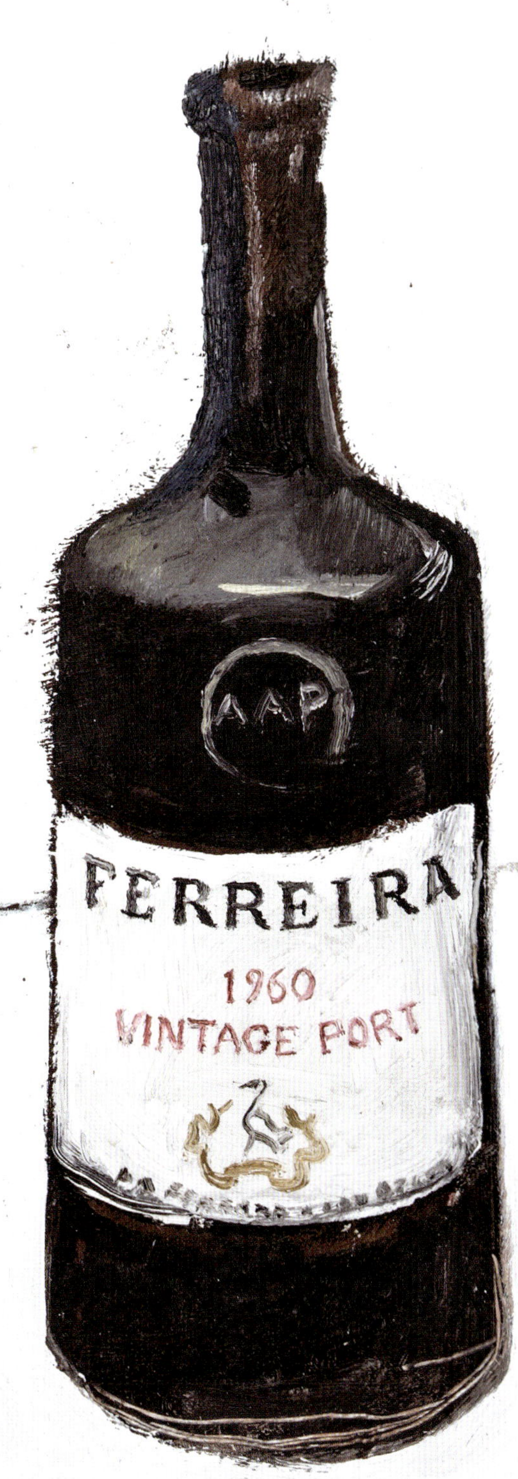
FERREIRA
1960
VINTAGE PORT

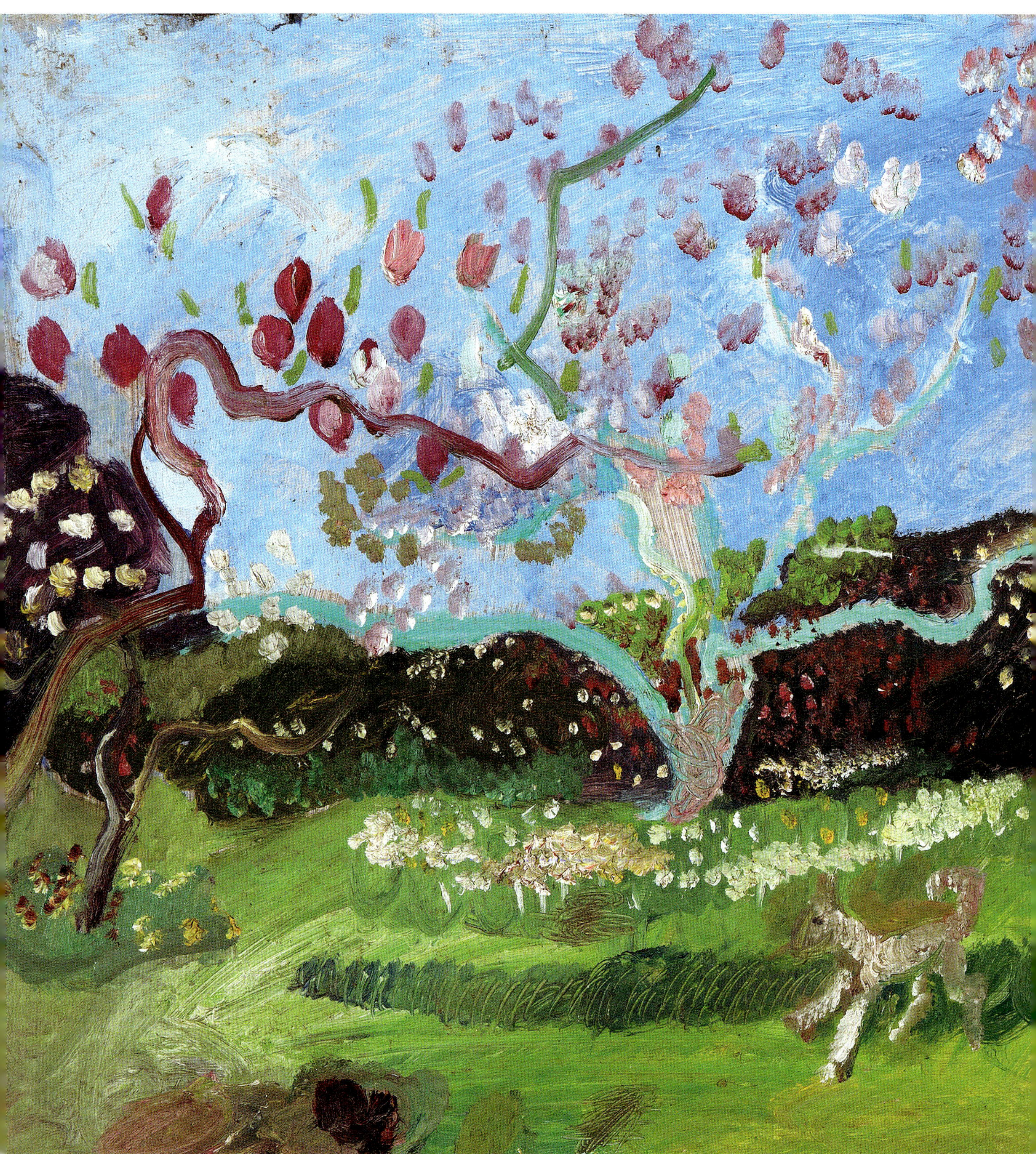

Morrab Gardens · c.1987 · oil on board · 59 x 122 cm

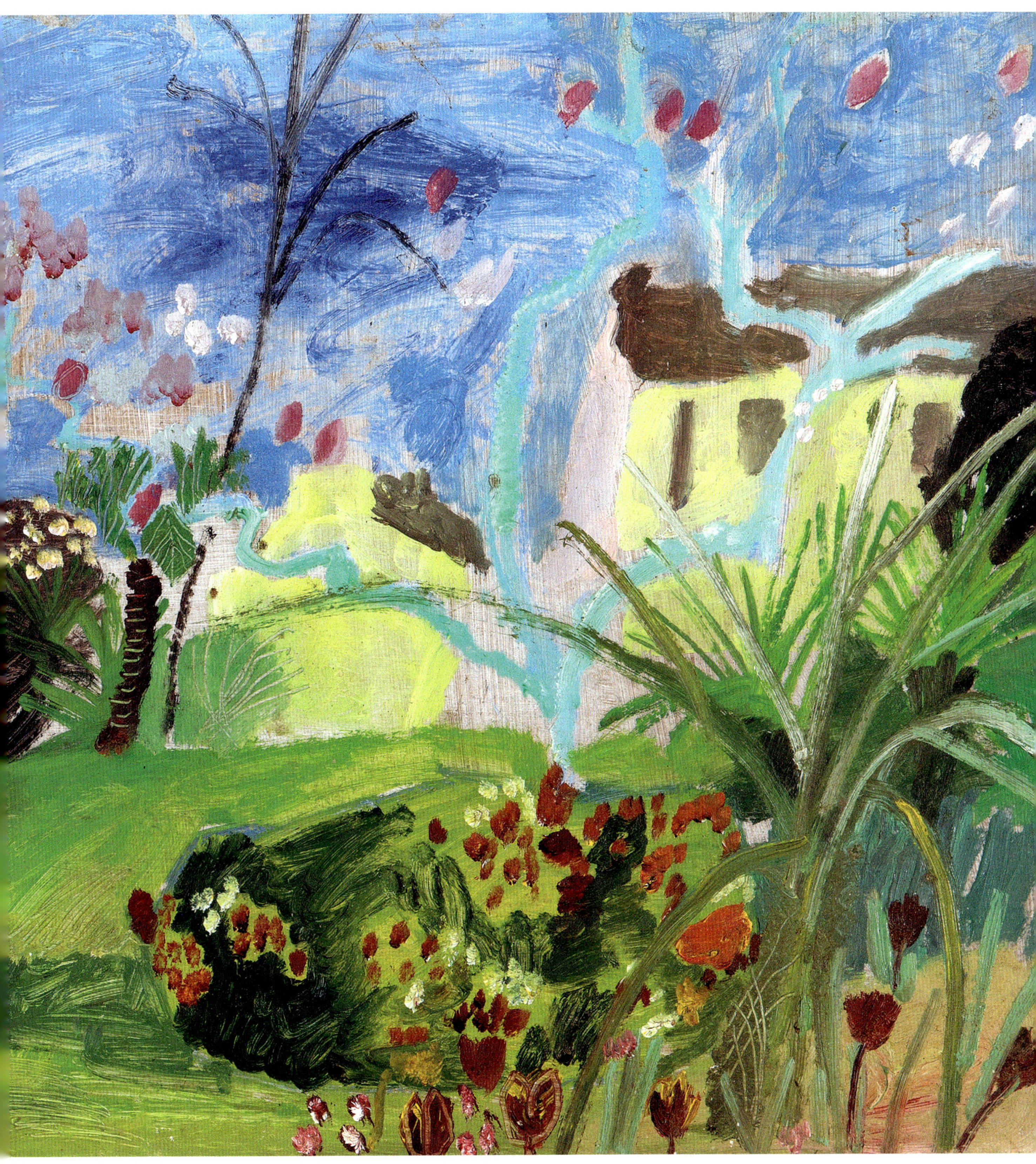

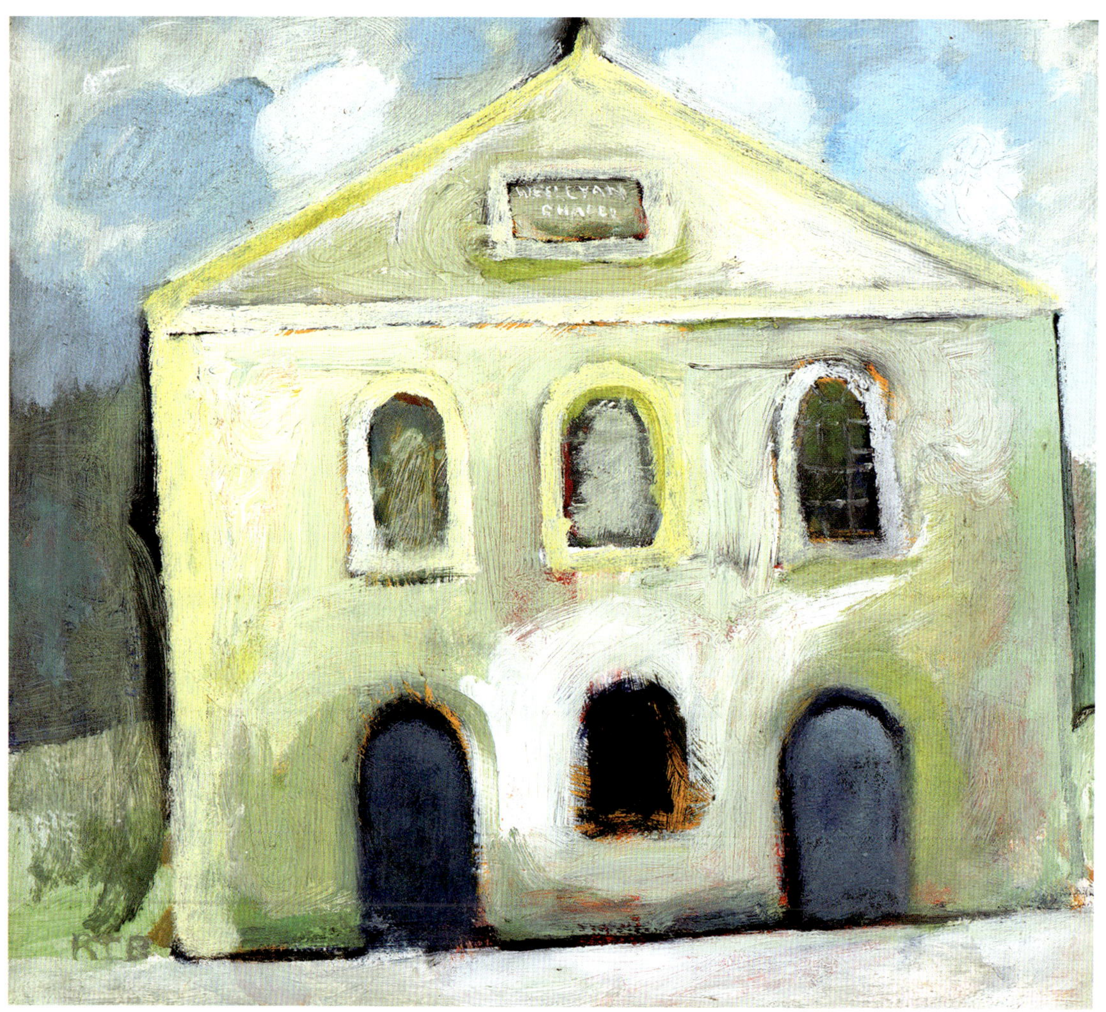

Wesleyan Chapel · late 1970s · oil on board · 36 x 41 cm

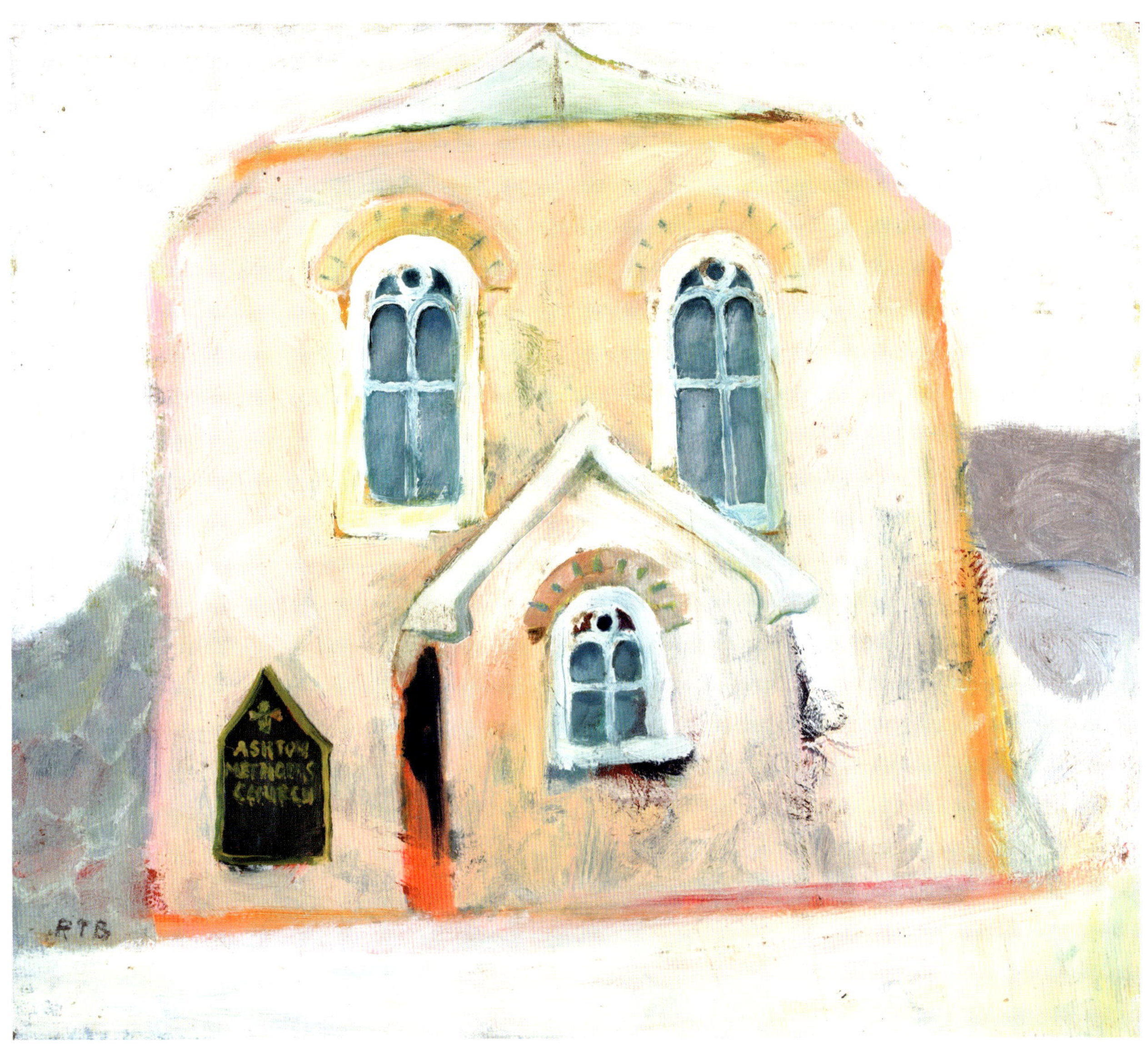

Ashton Methodist Church · late 1970s · oil on board · 41 x 46 cm

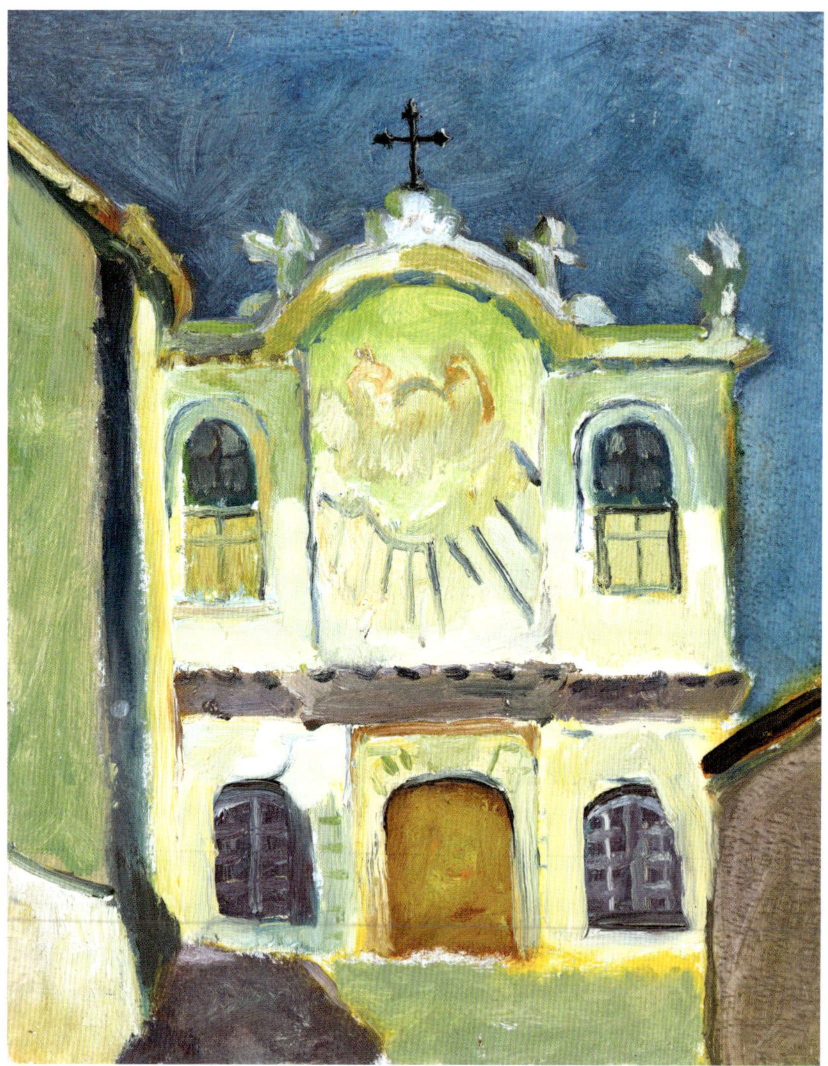

Church, Avignon · c.1973 · oil on board · 30 x 28 cm

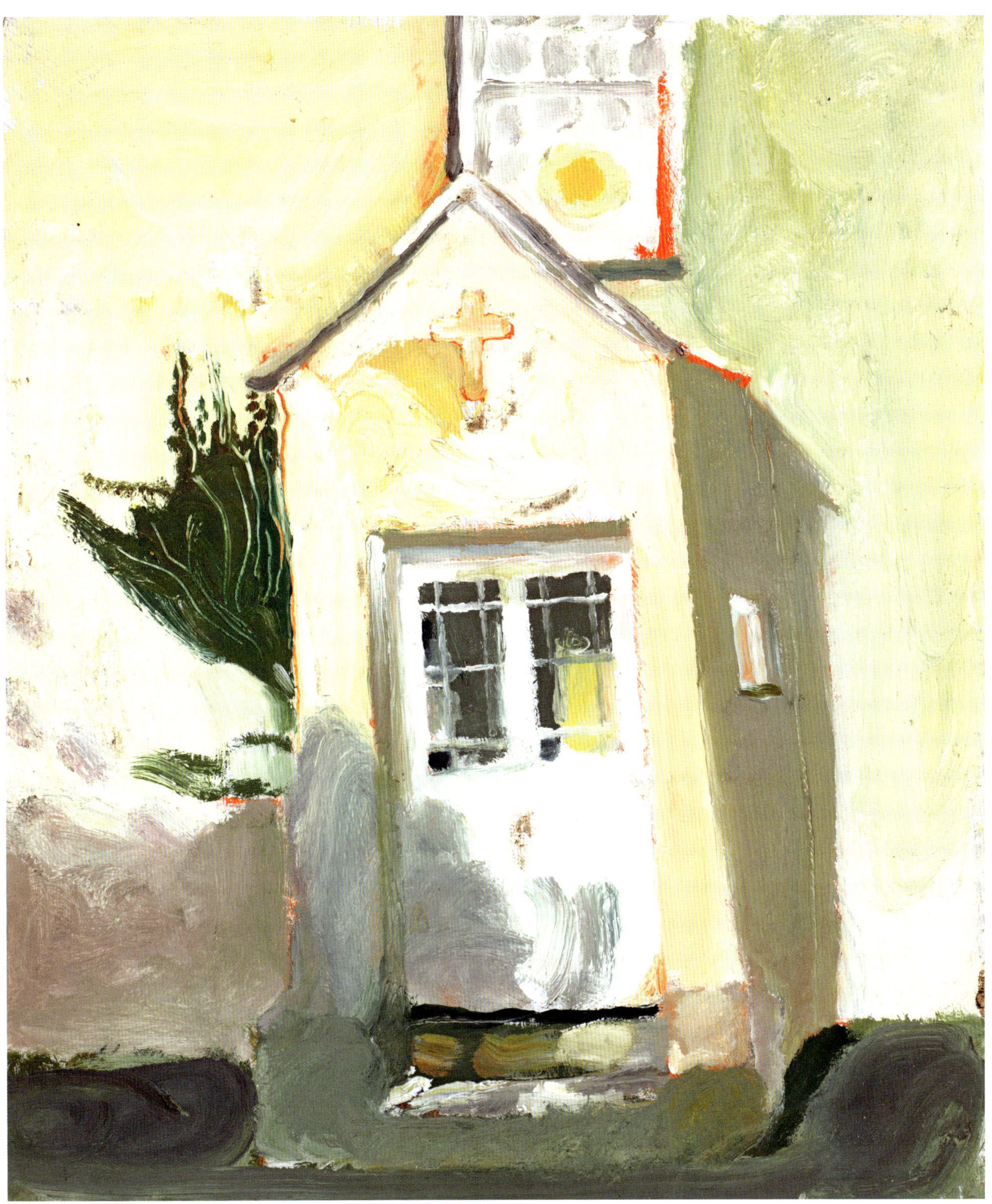

Seaview Porch · *c.*1978 · oil on board · 54 x 46 cm

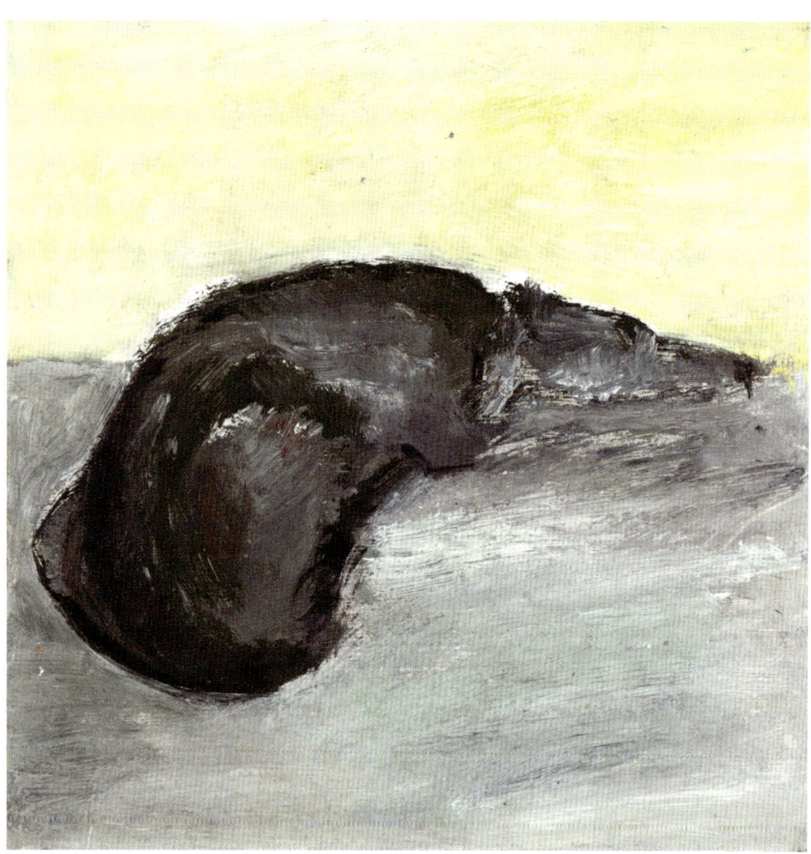

Fosse V · c.2001 · oil on board · 31 x 31 cm

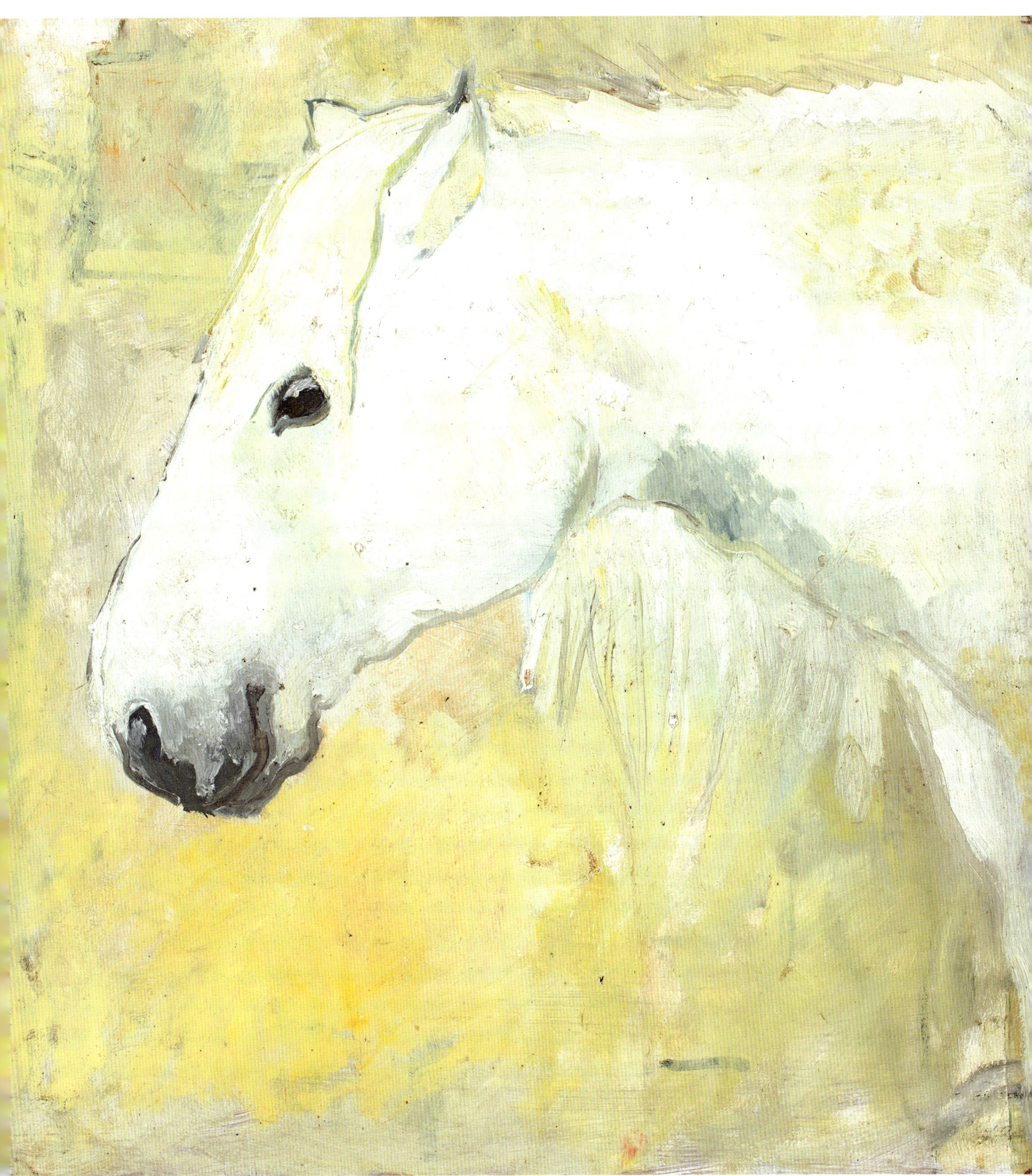

Glen · early 1970s · oil on board · 66 x 61 cm

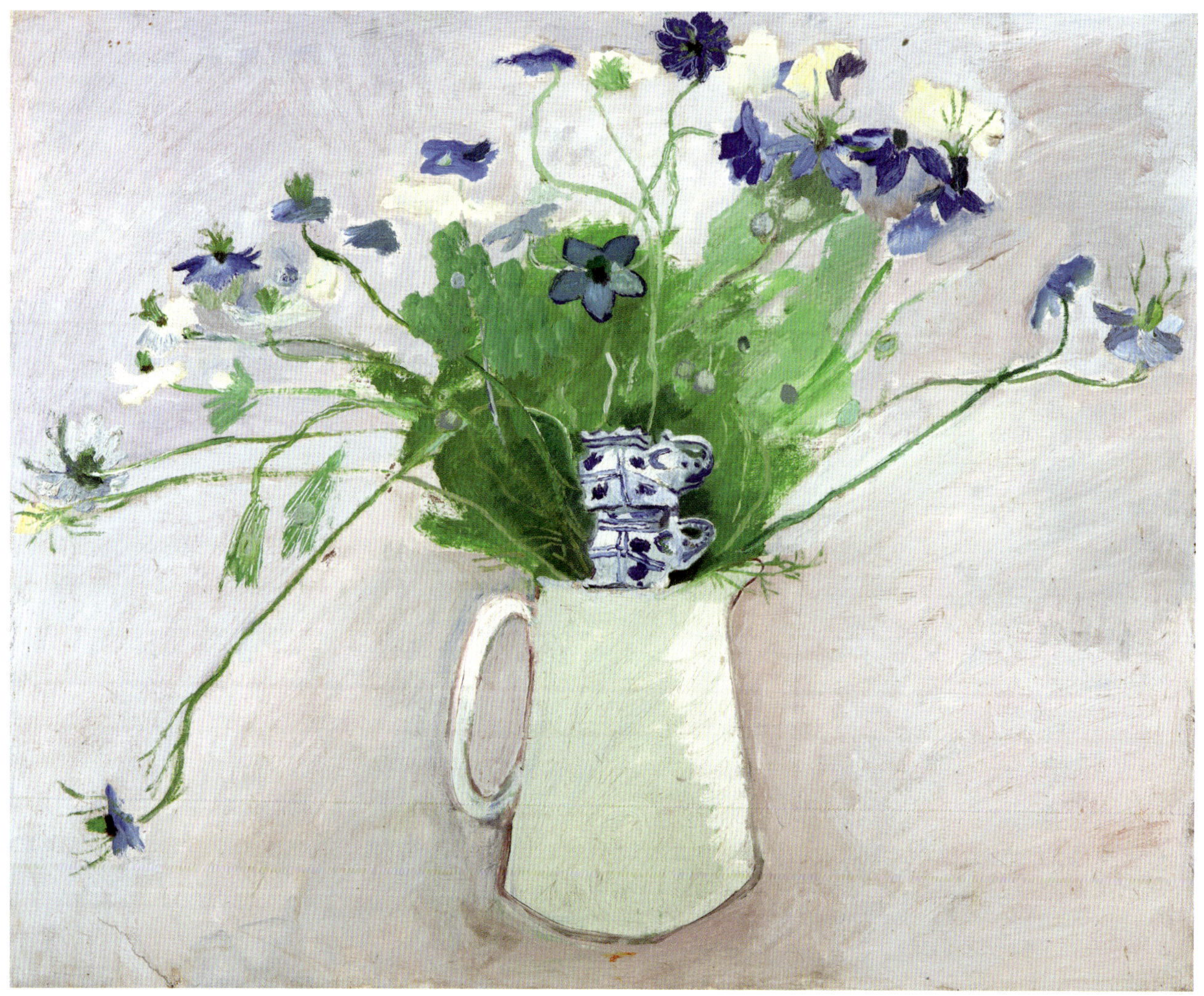

Love-in-a-Mist · c.1974 · oil on board · 60 x 75 cm

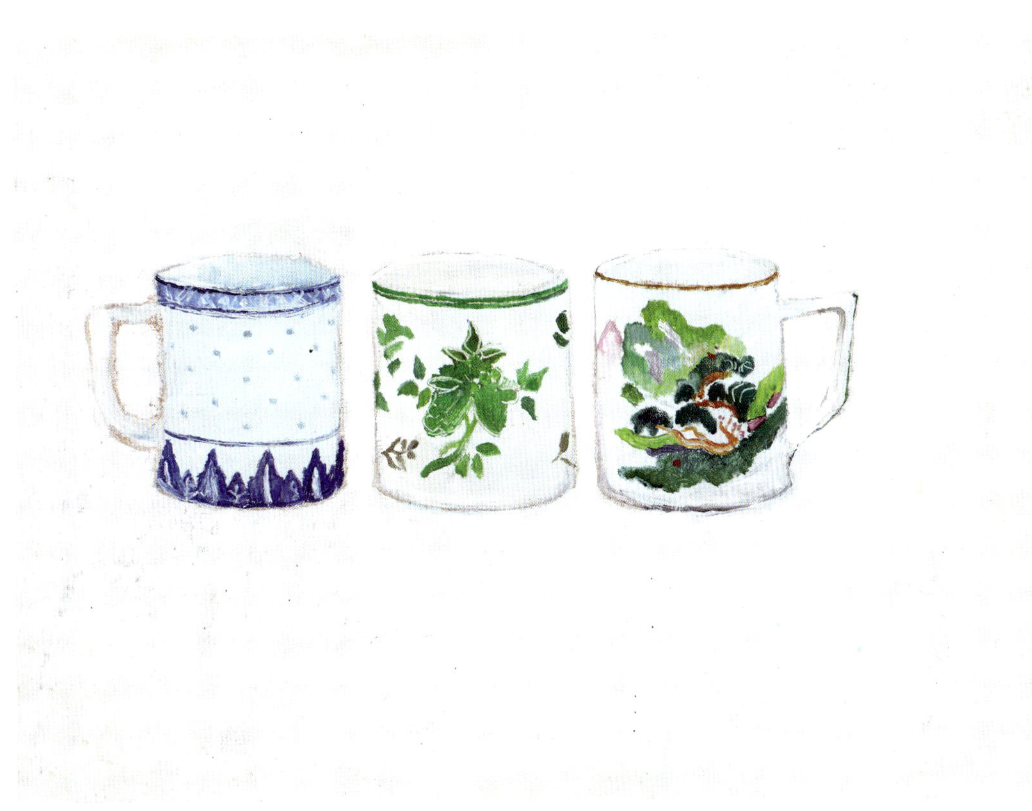

Three Mugs · c.1989 · oil on board · 45 x 61 cm

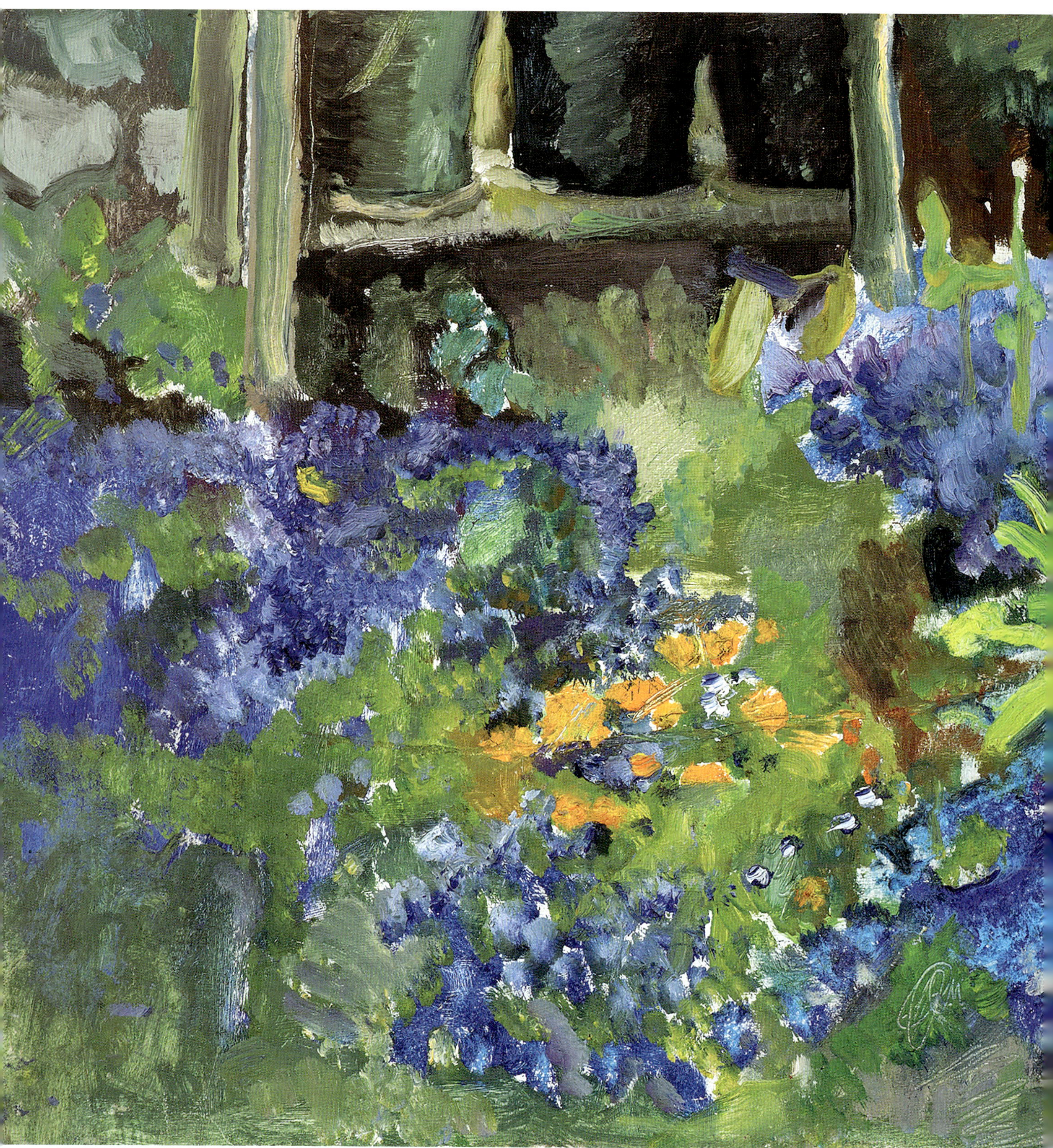

Blue Garden · c.1998 · oil on board · 31 x 46 cm

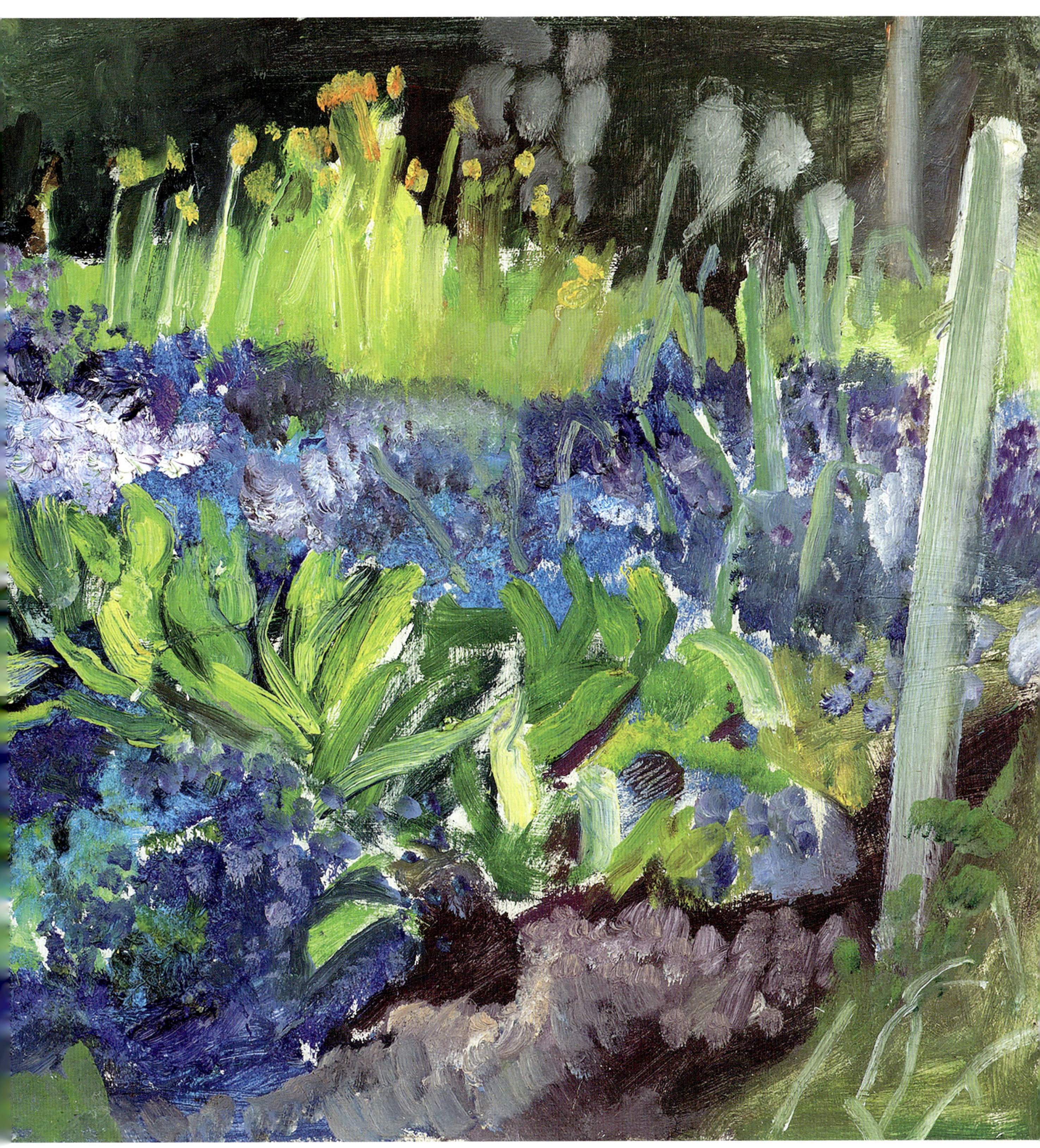

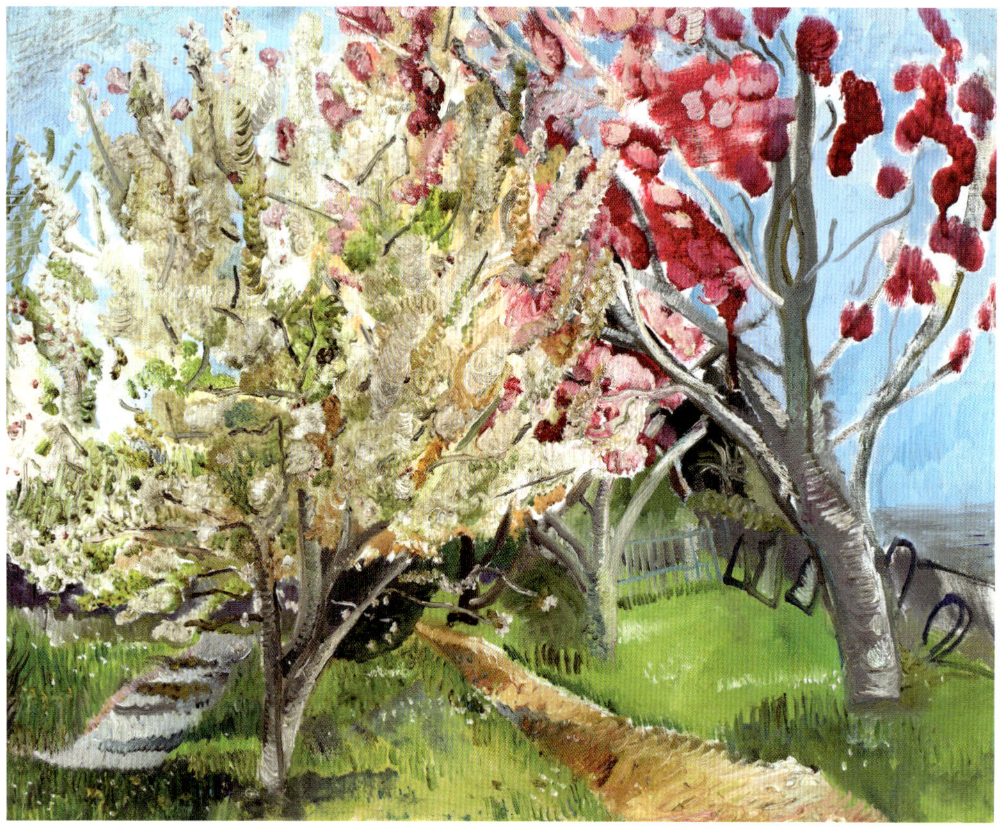

Quaker Cemetery · early 1990s · oil on canvas · 61 x 76 cm

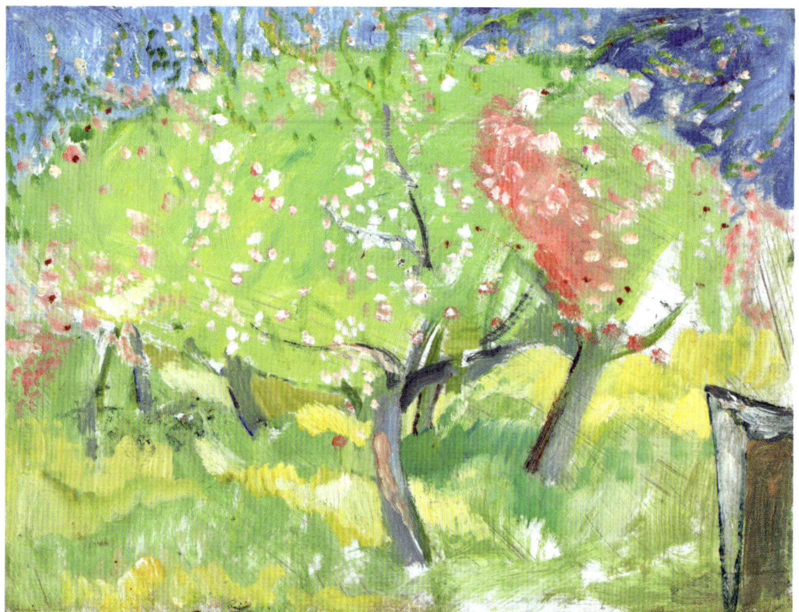

Quarryfield Orchard · c.1976 · oil on board · 46 x 61 cm

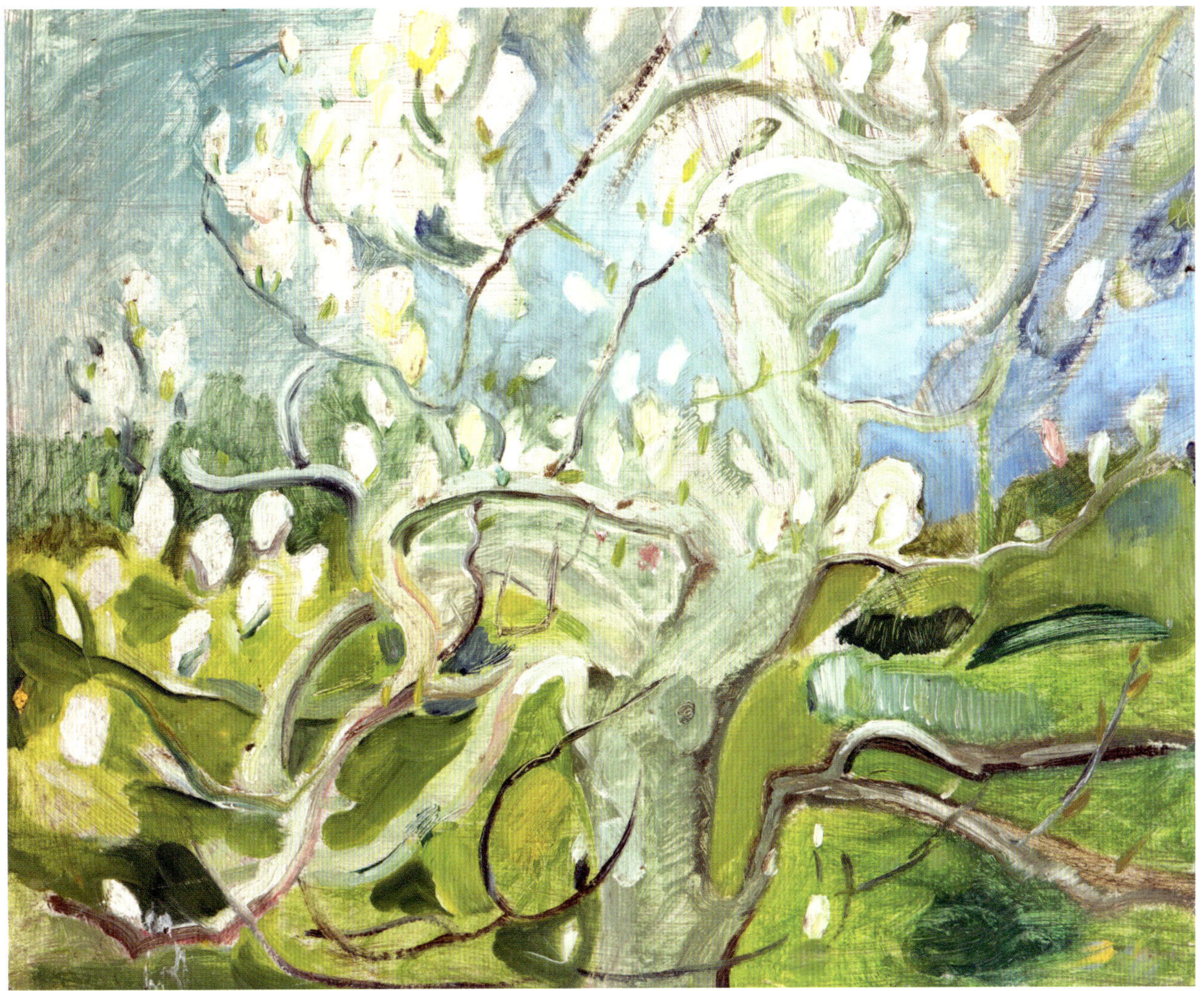

Magnolia Tree · late 1980s · oil on board · 76 x 92 cm

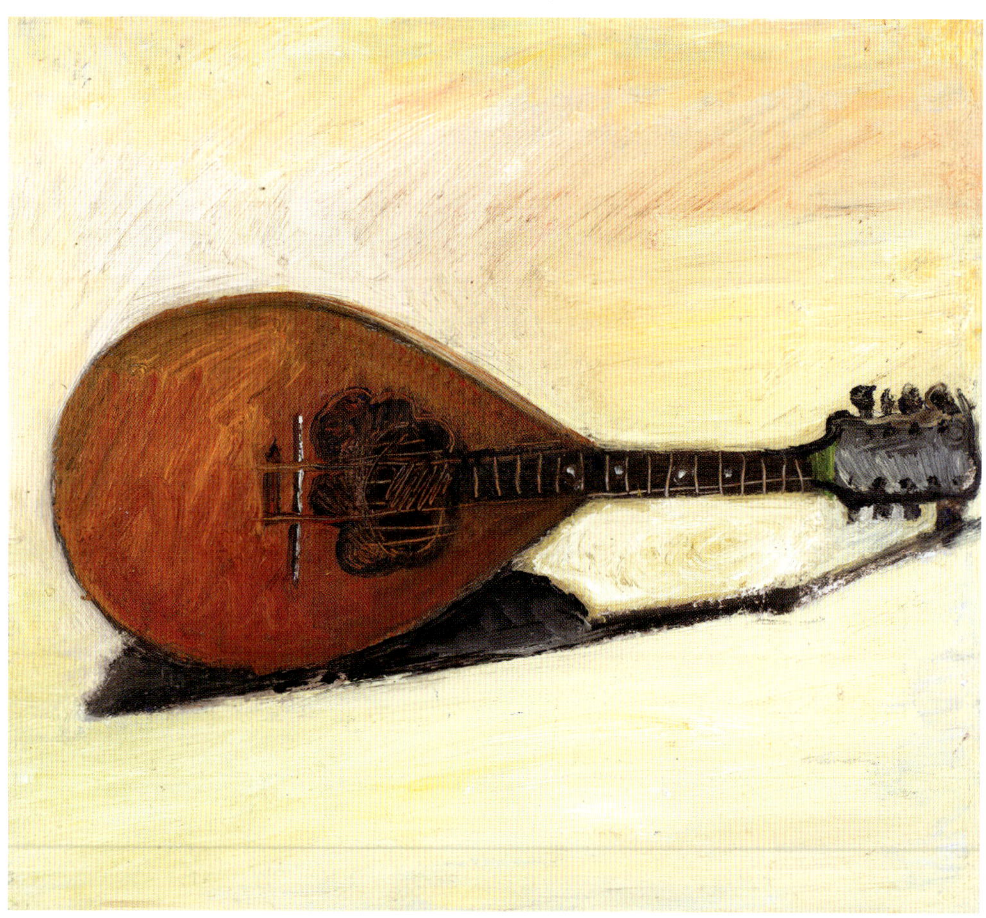

Mahogany Mandolin · c.1978 · oil on board · 46 x 49 cm

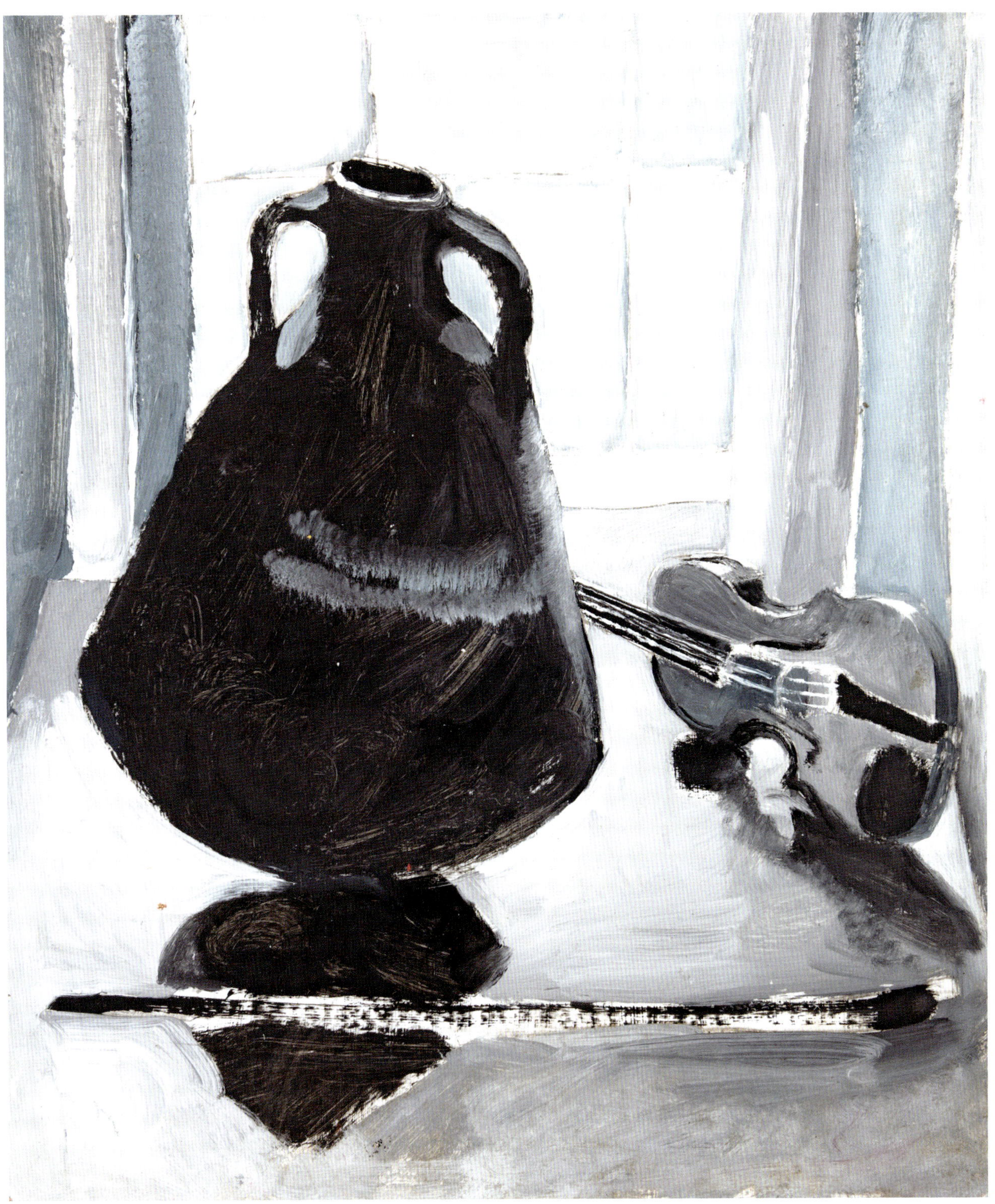

Pot and Fiddle (Greys) · c.1991 · oil on board · 71 x 61 cm

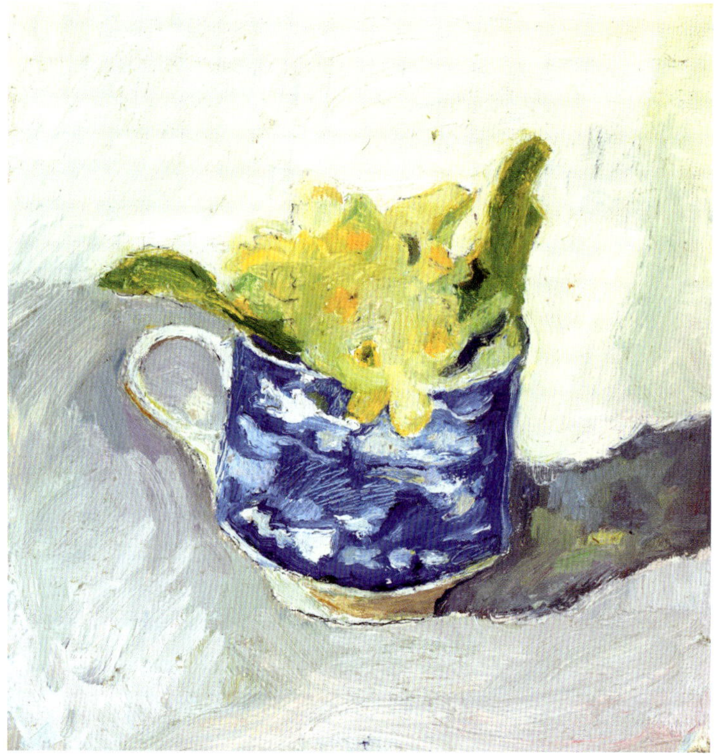

Primroses I · mid-1970s · oil on board · 31 x 30 cm

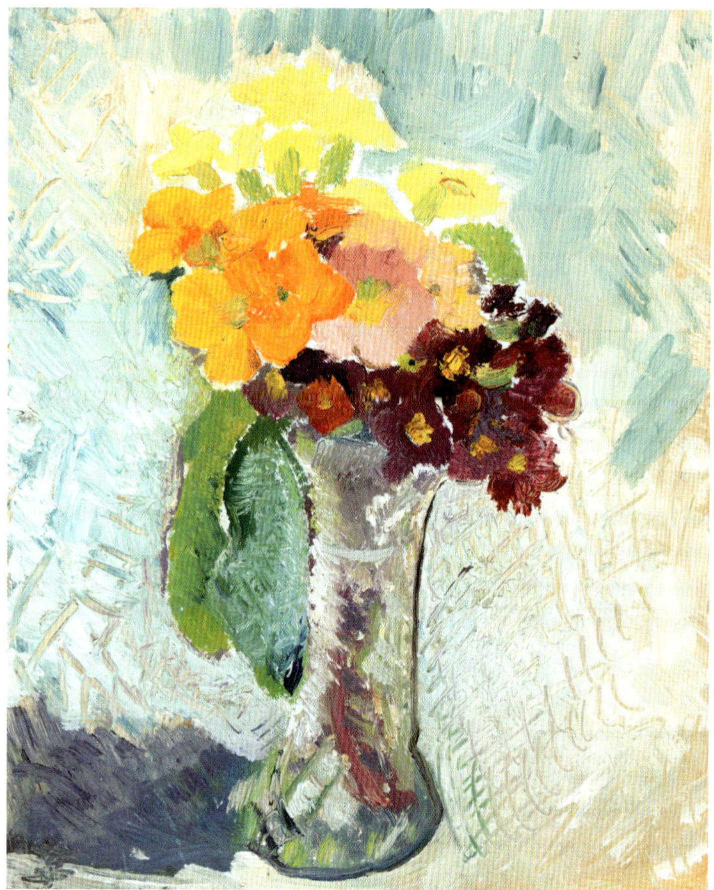

Polyanthus II · c.1985 · oil on board · 35 x 30 cm

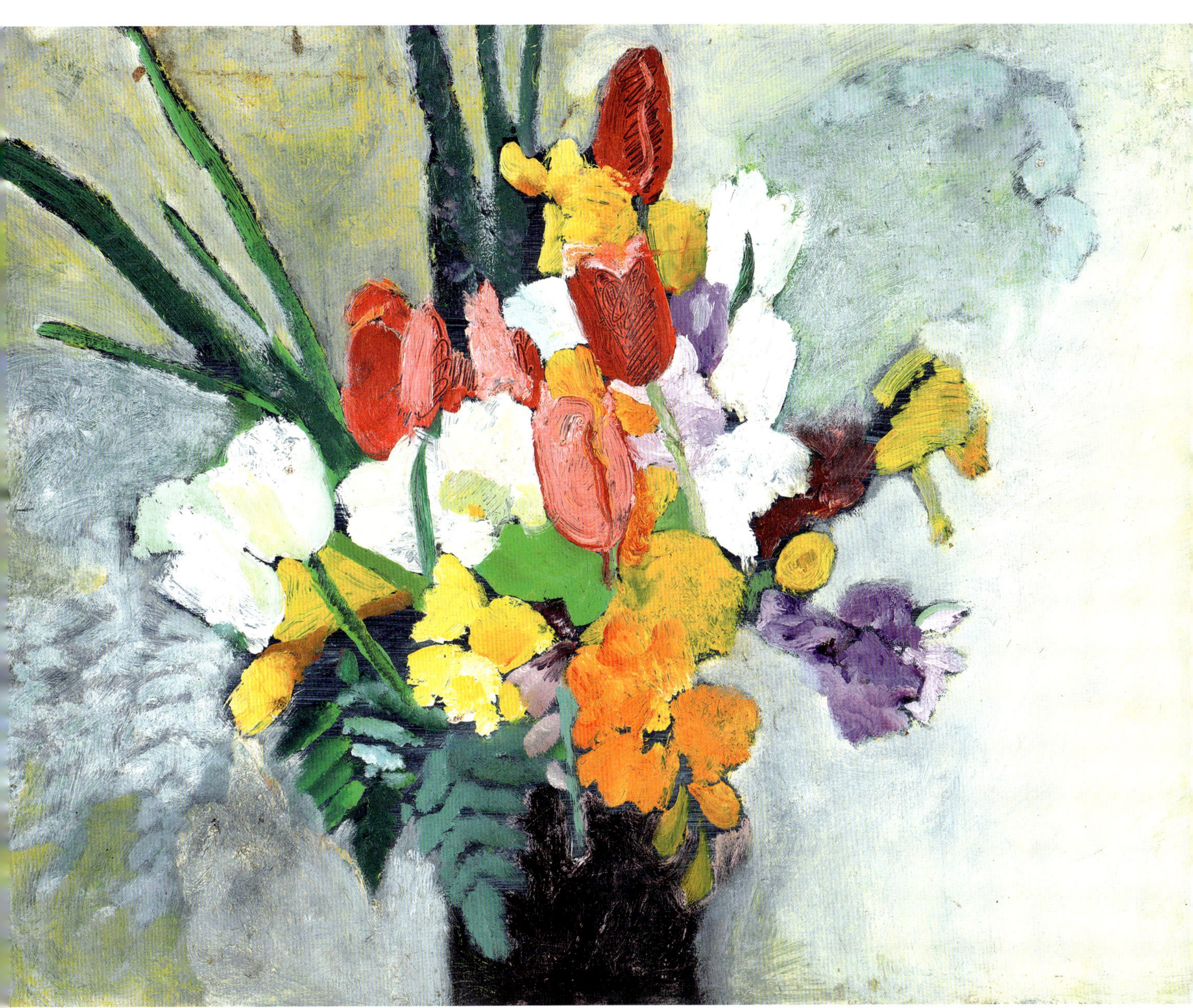

Tulips and Freesias · c.1975 · oil on board · 46 x 61 cm

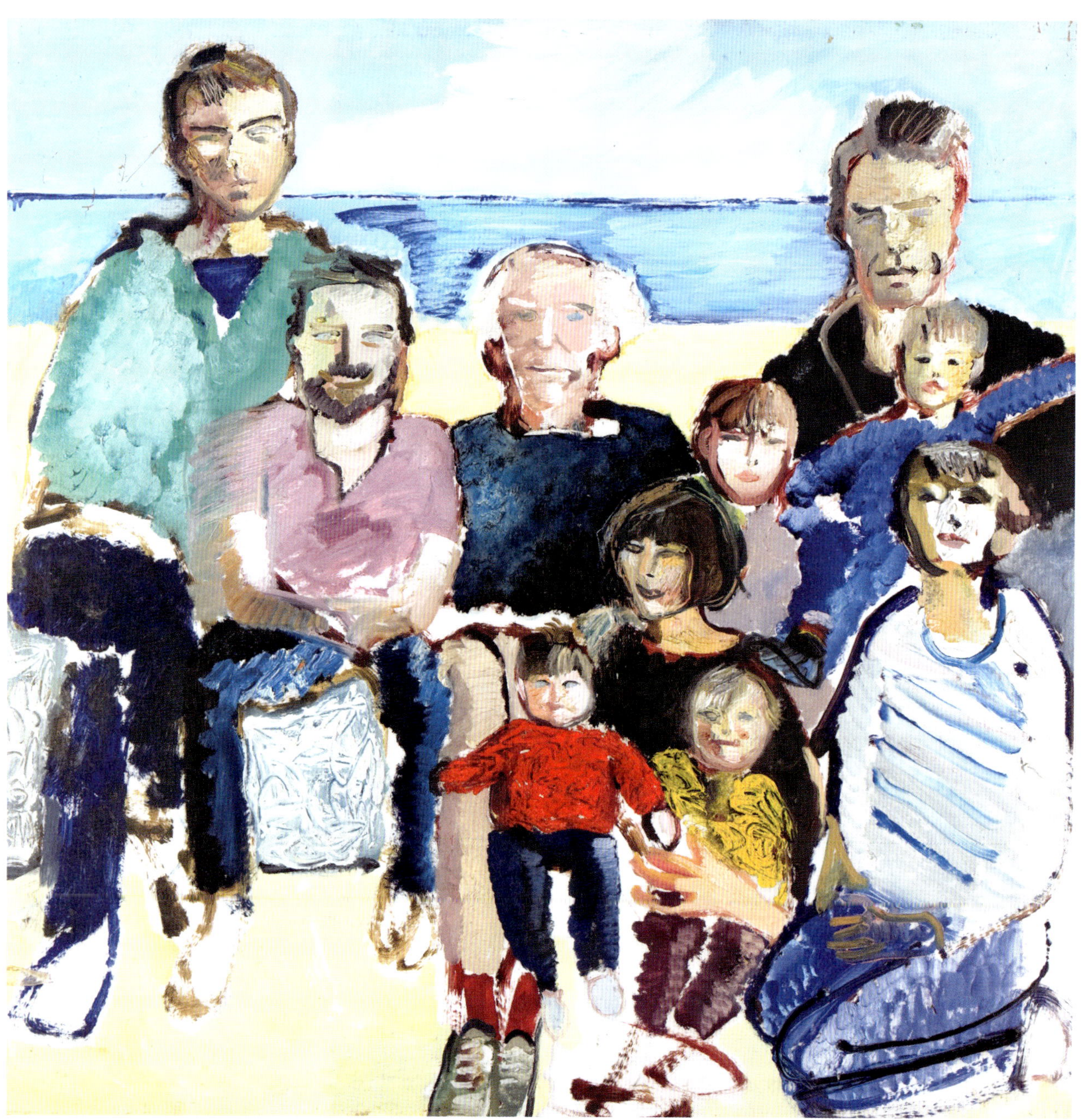

The Wollaston Clan · c.1987 · oil on board · 122 x 122 cm

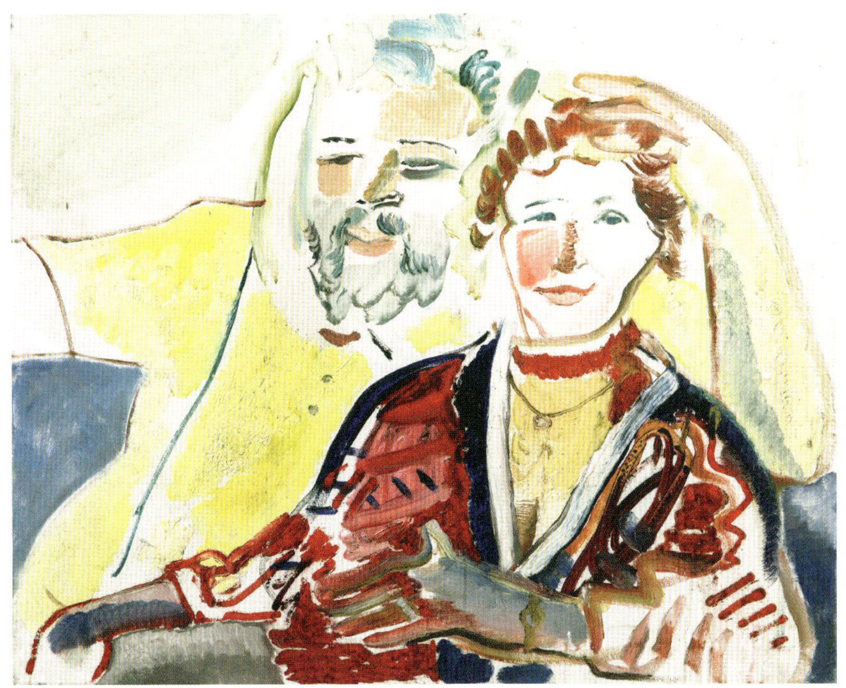

In Love (Rodney and Isabelle) · c.1998 · oil on canvas · 70 x 85 cm

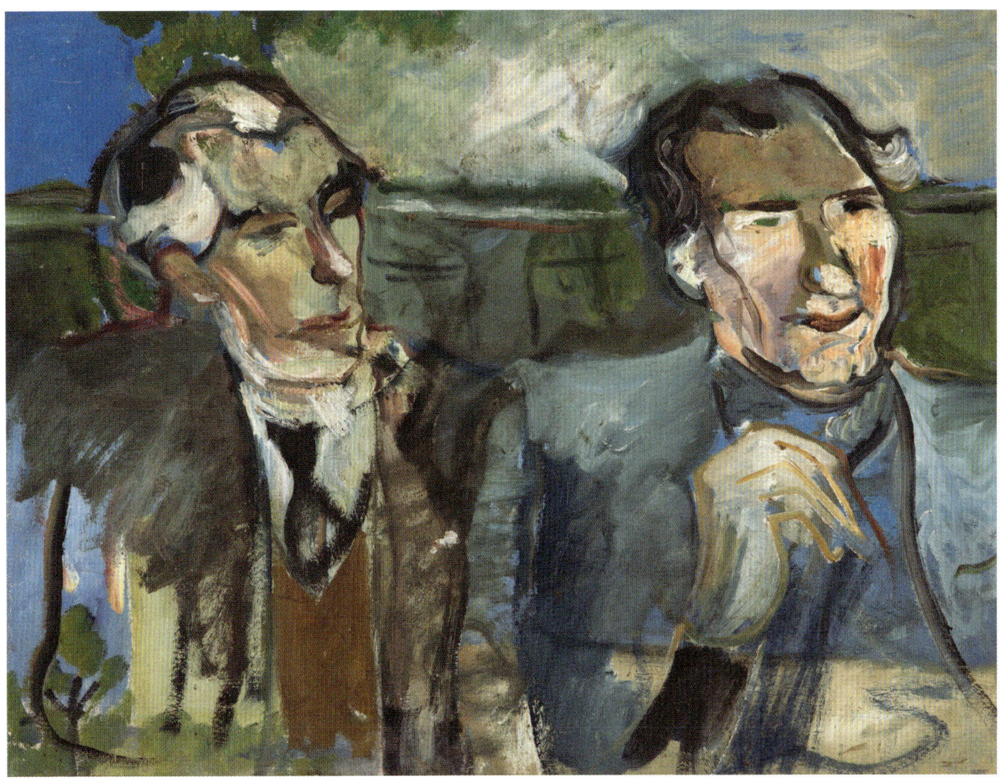

Piers and John St Aubyn · late 1980s · oil on board · 79 x 106 cm

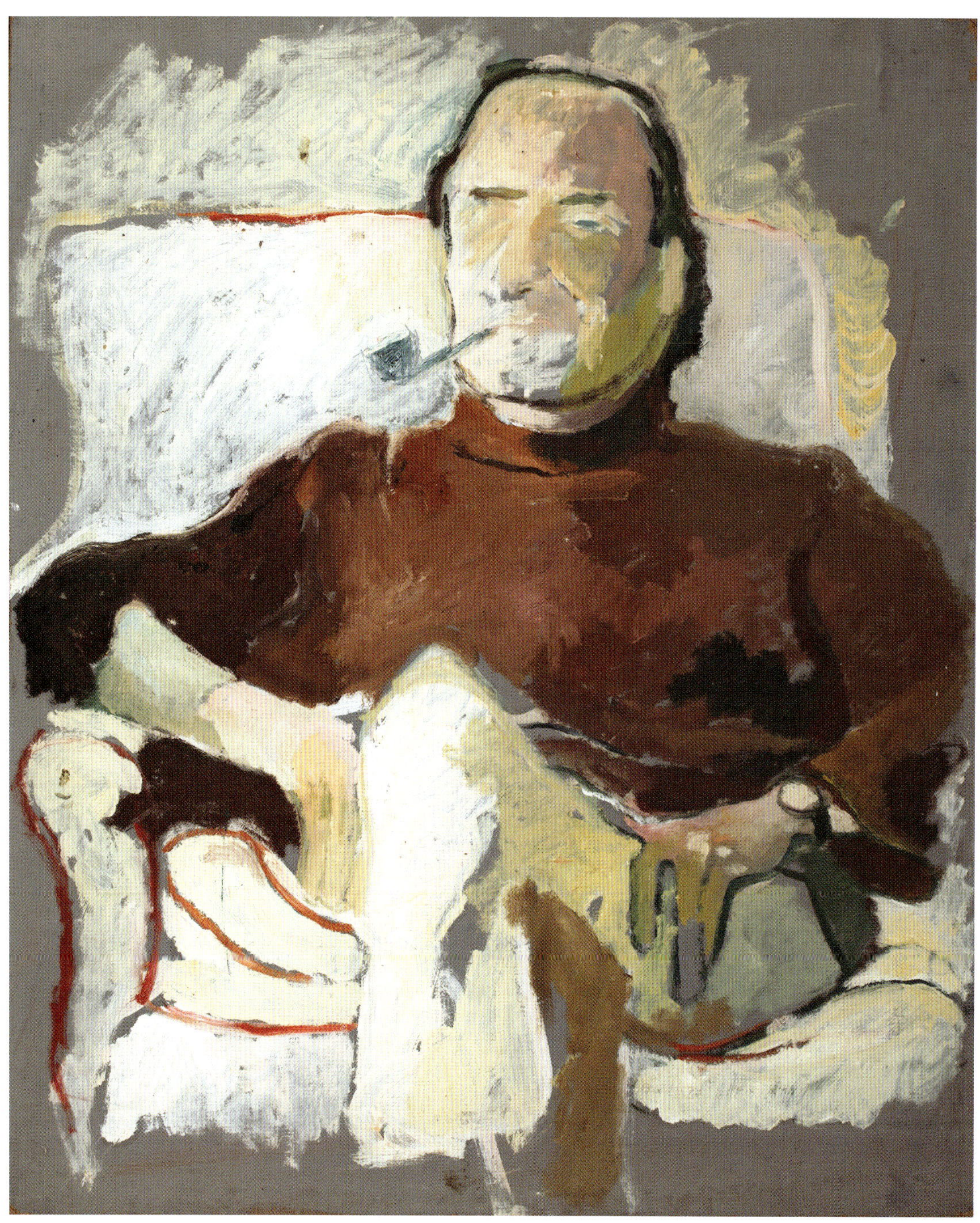

Austin Chamberlain · c.1975 · oil on board · 81 x 61 cm

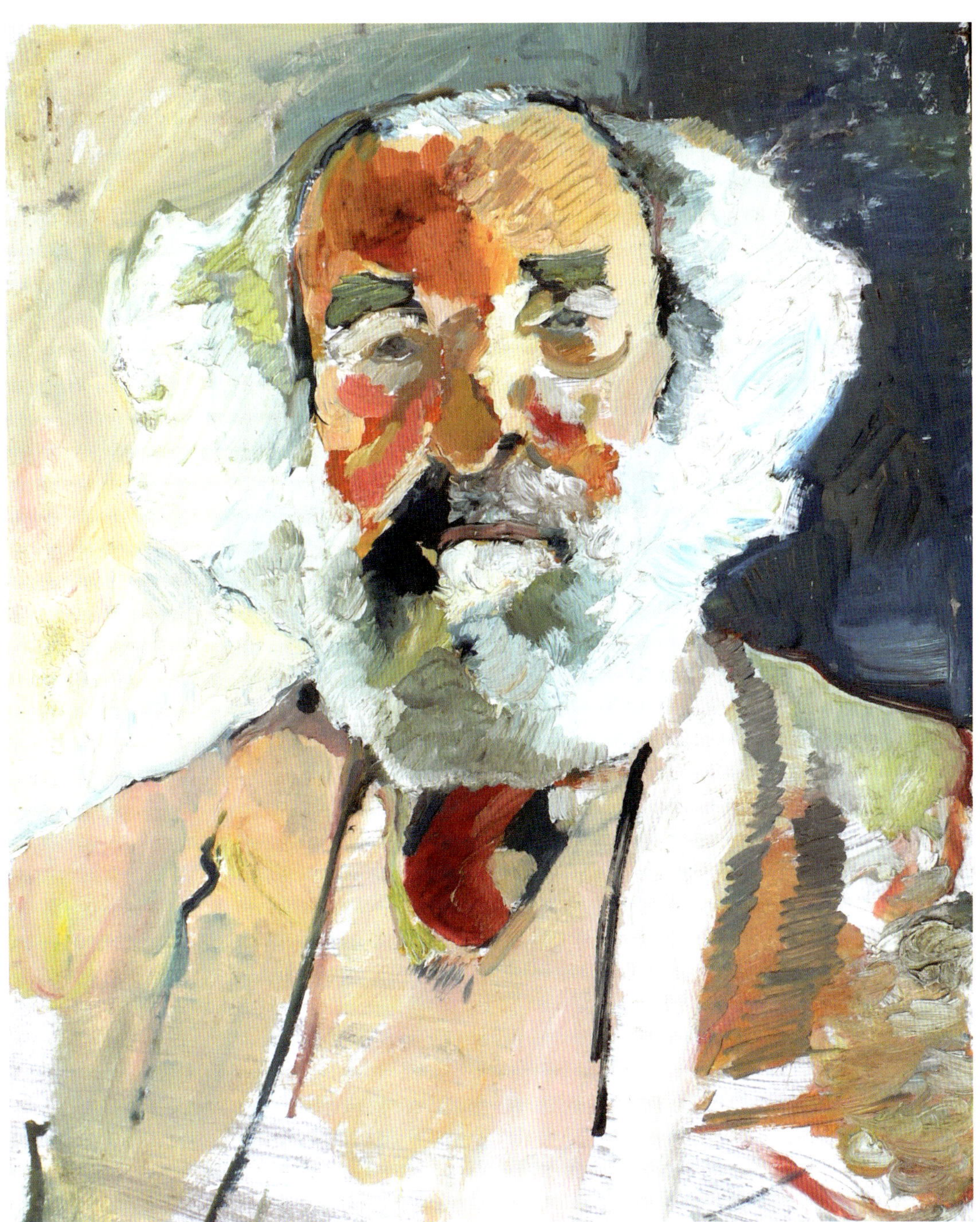

Michael Williams · c.1990 · oil on board · 81 x 61 cm

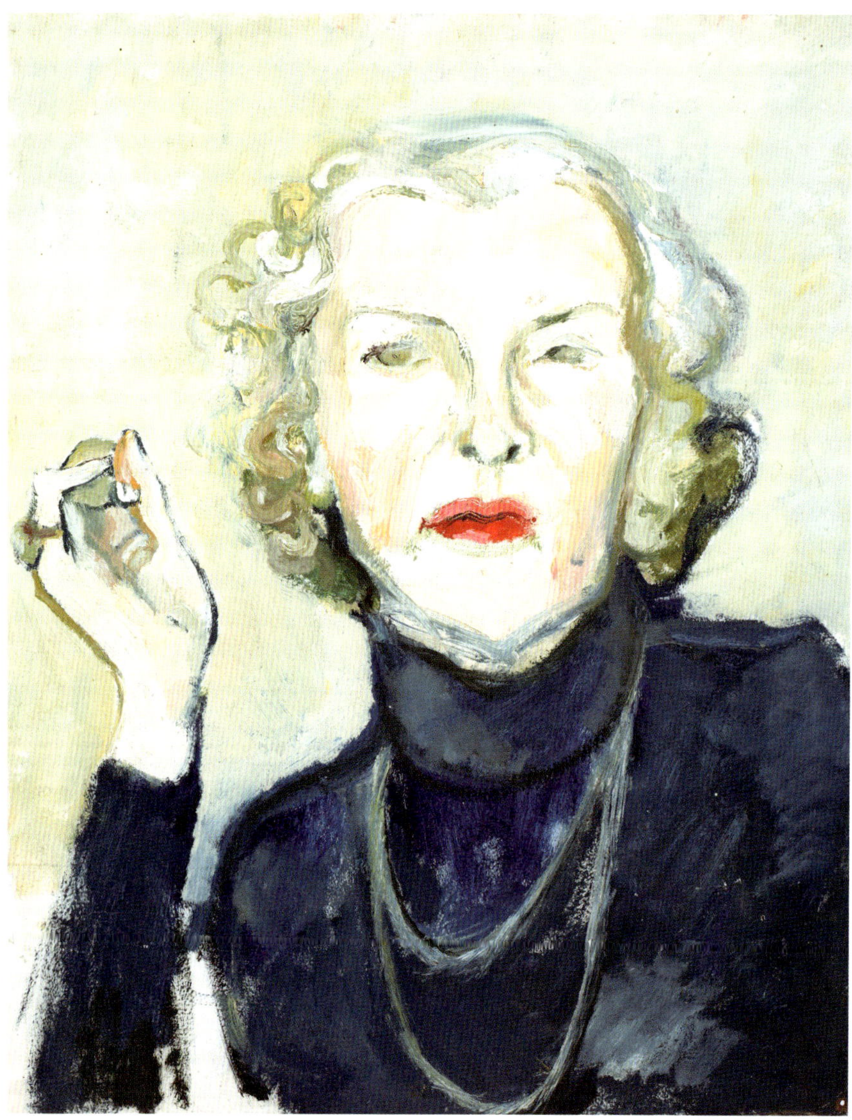

Griselda Kentner · c.1978 · oil on board · 61 x 50 cm

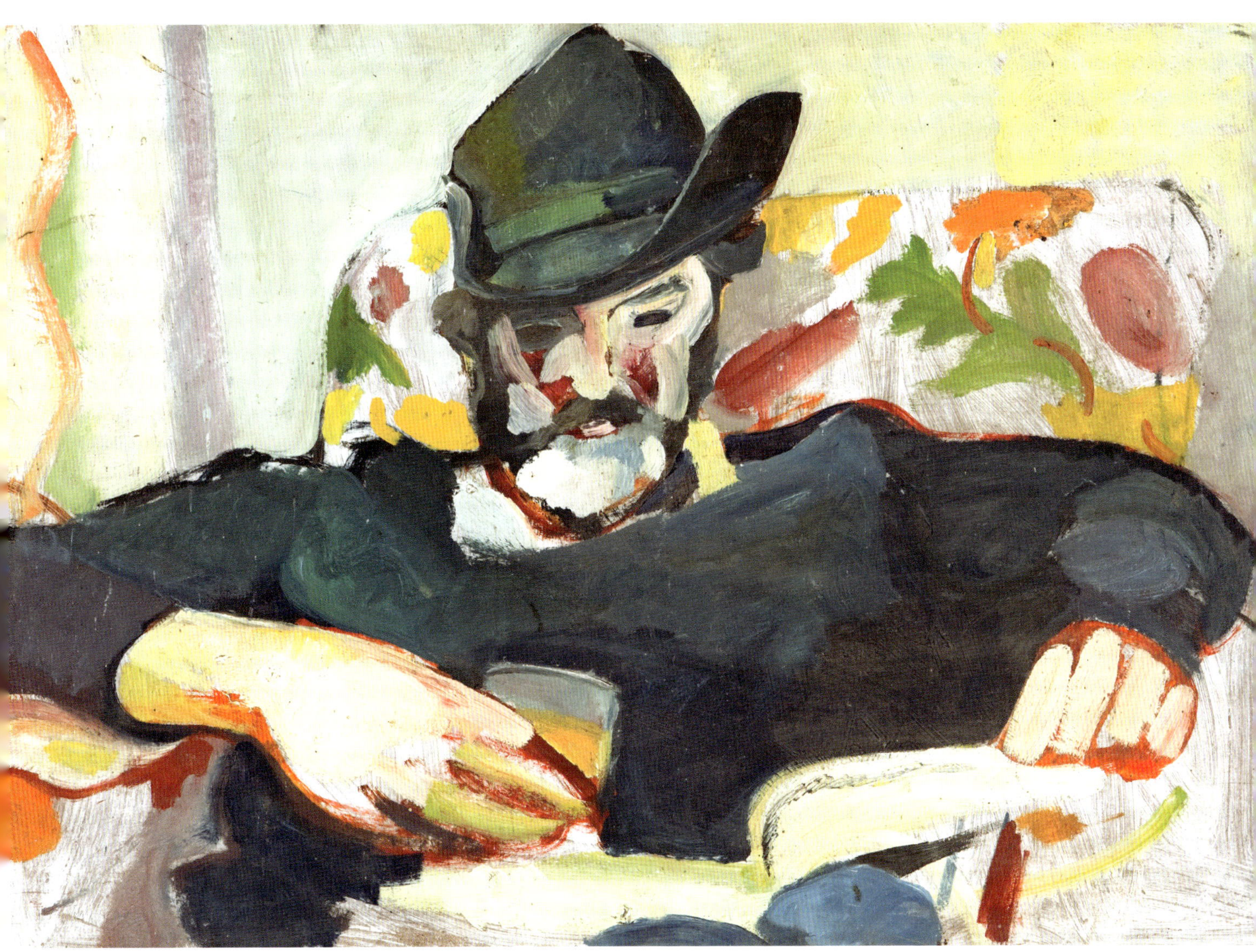

Whisky · c.1981 · oil on board · 62 x 90 cm

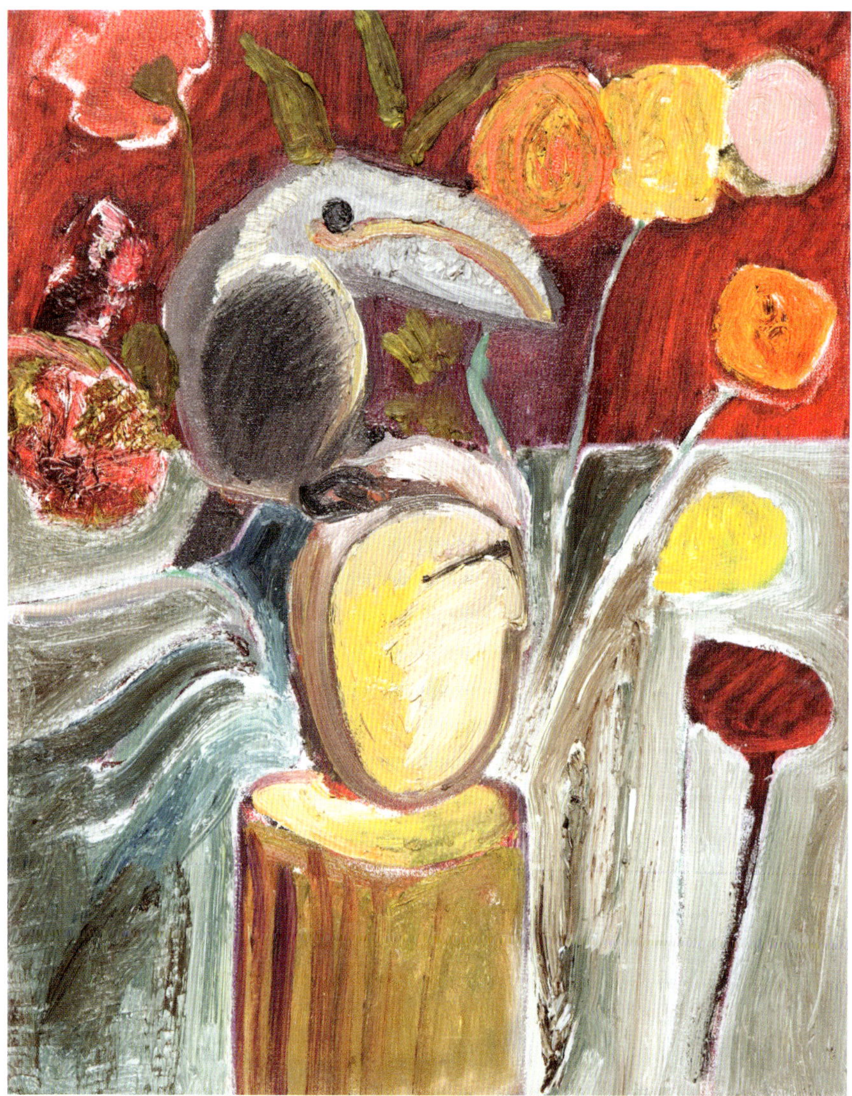

Toucan in the Flowers (Pausing) · c.2004 · oil on canvas · 51 x 41 cm

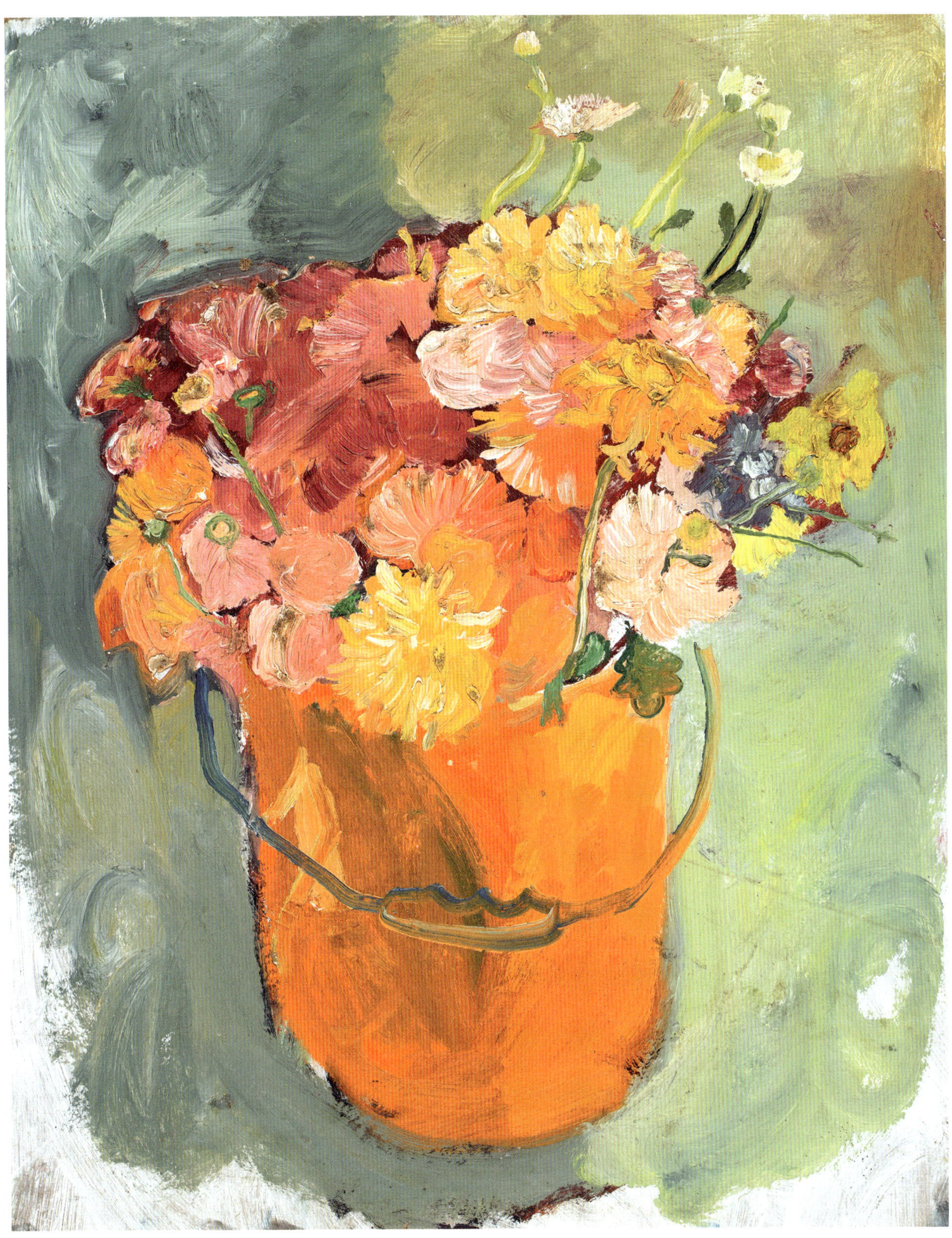

Chrysanths in Orange Bucket II · c.1989 · oil on board · 74 x 61 cm

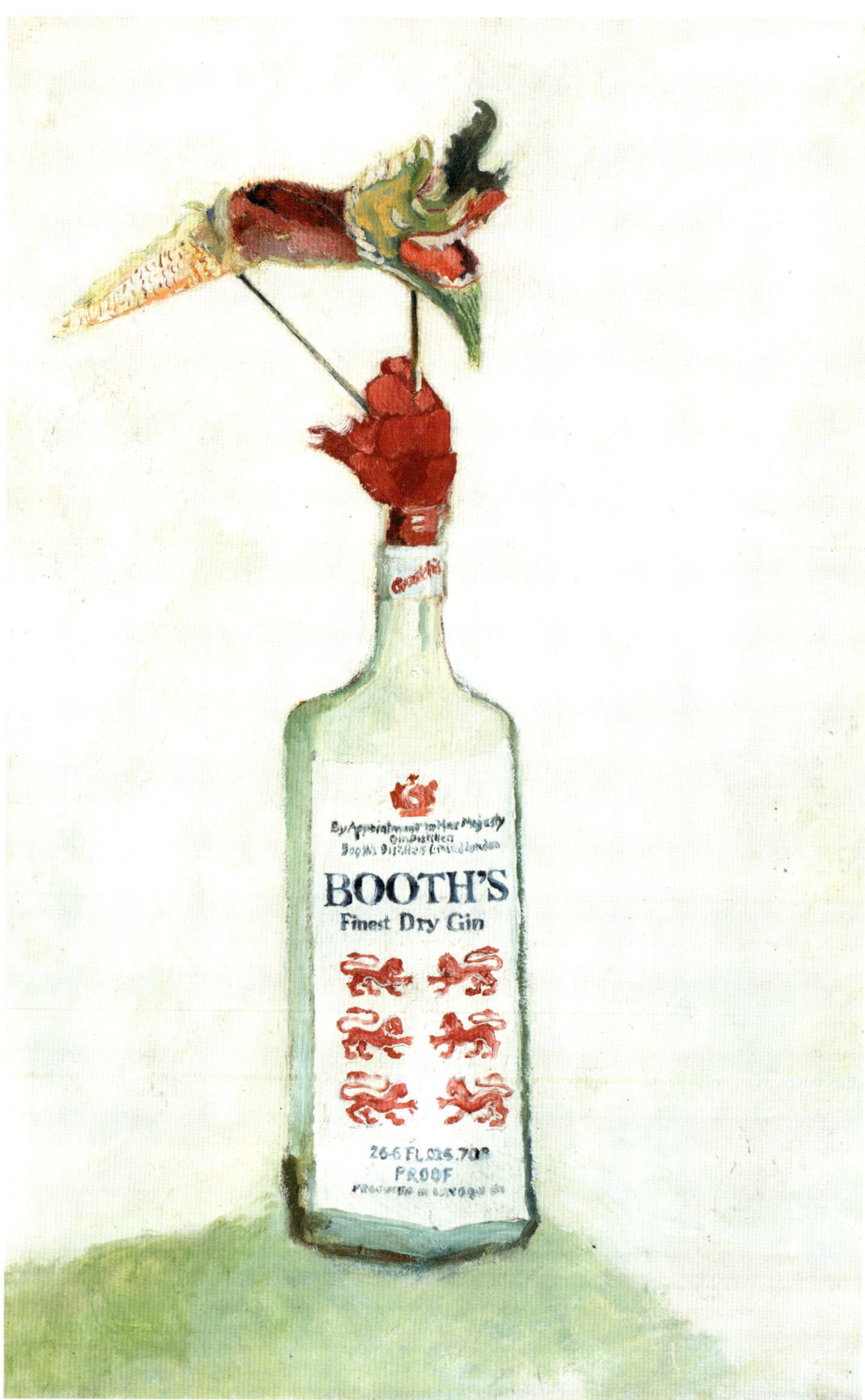

Booth's Gin · c.1974 · oil on board · 80 x 53 cm

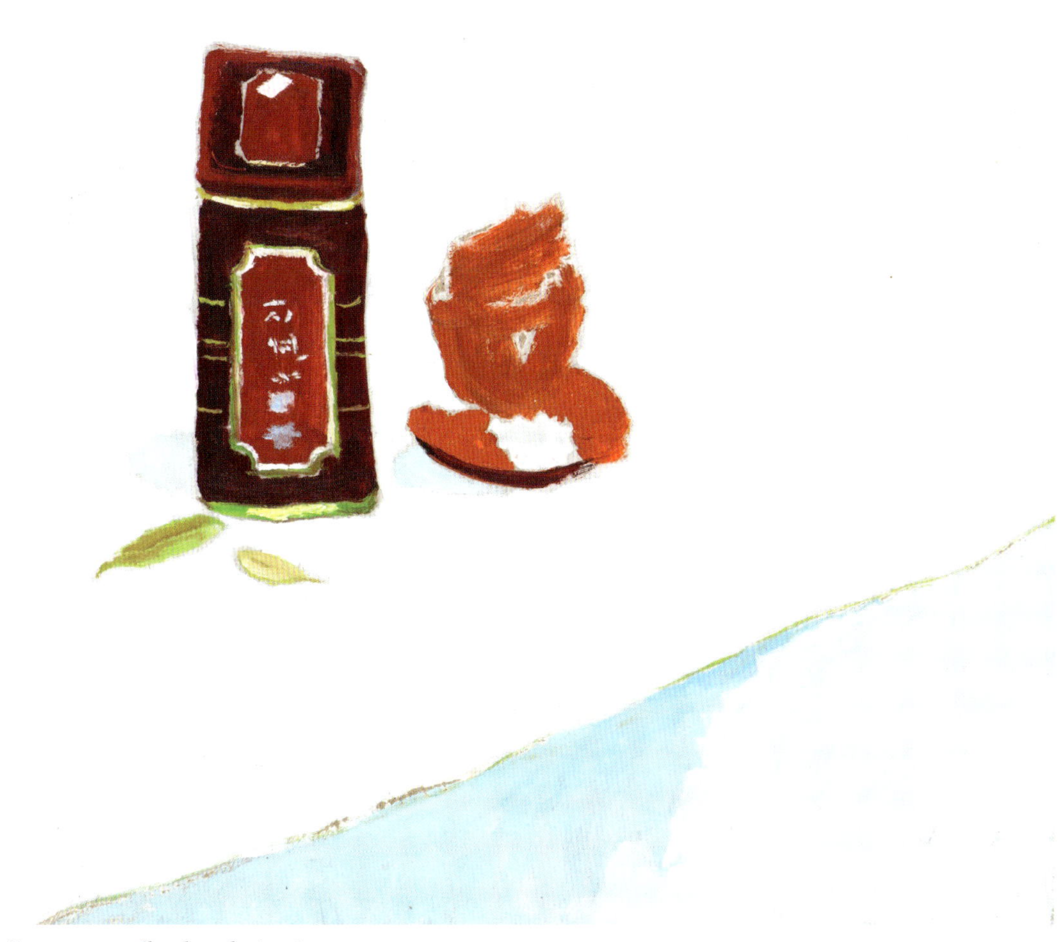

Tea · c.1992 · oil on board · 61 x 61 cm

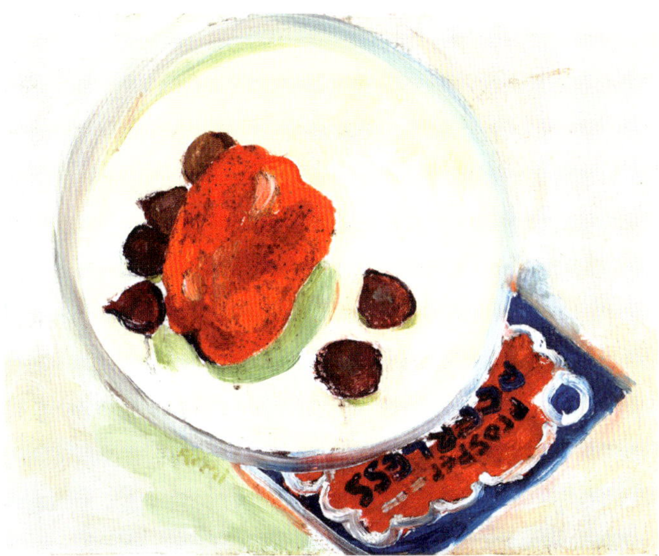

Pepper with Chestnuts · mid-1980s · oil on board · 30 x 39 cm

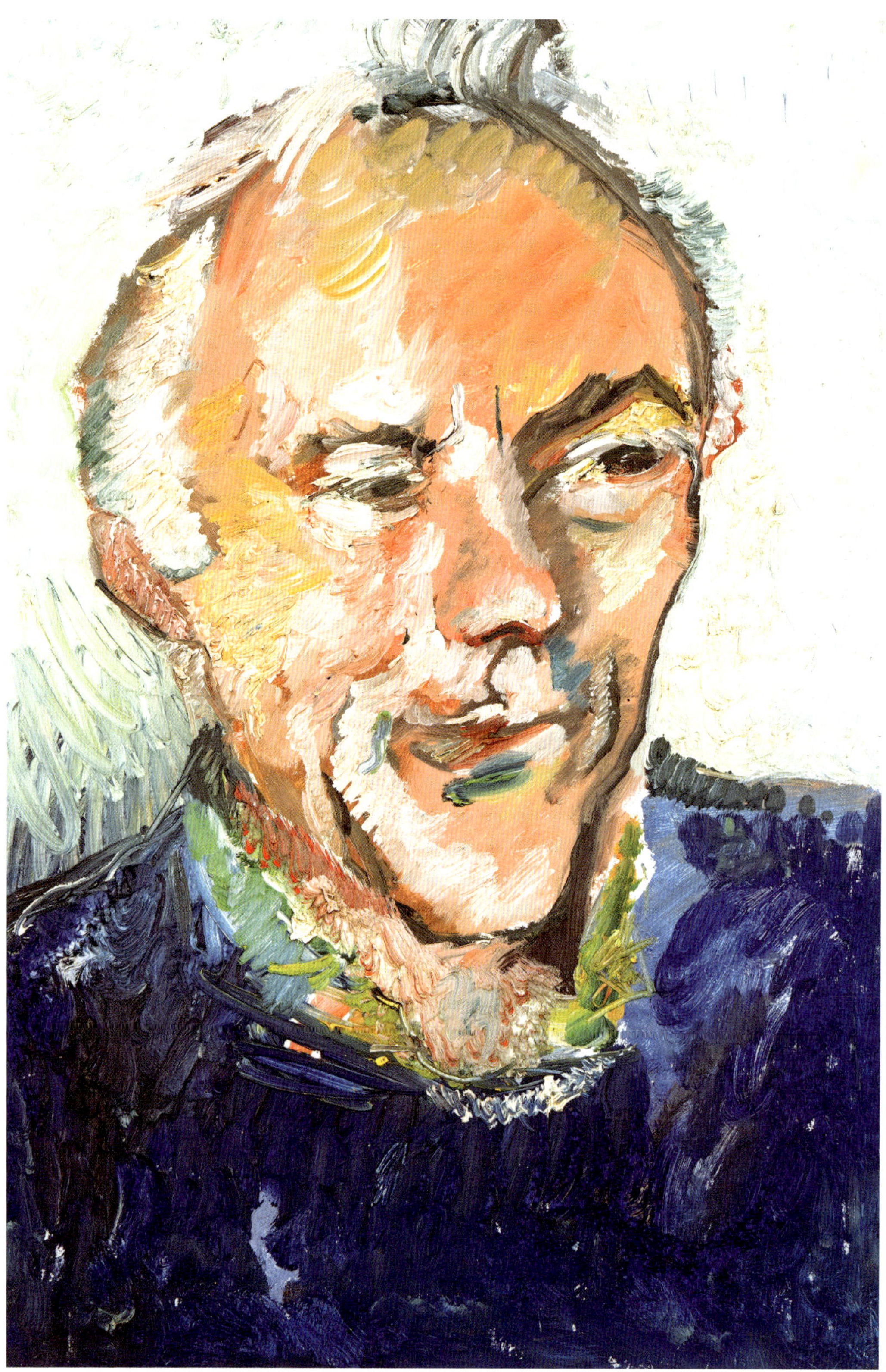

Patrick Heron II · c.1993 · oil on board · 61 x 41 cm

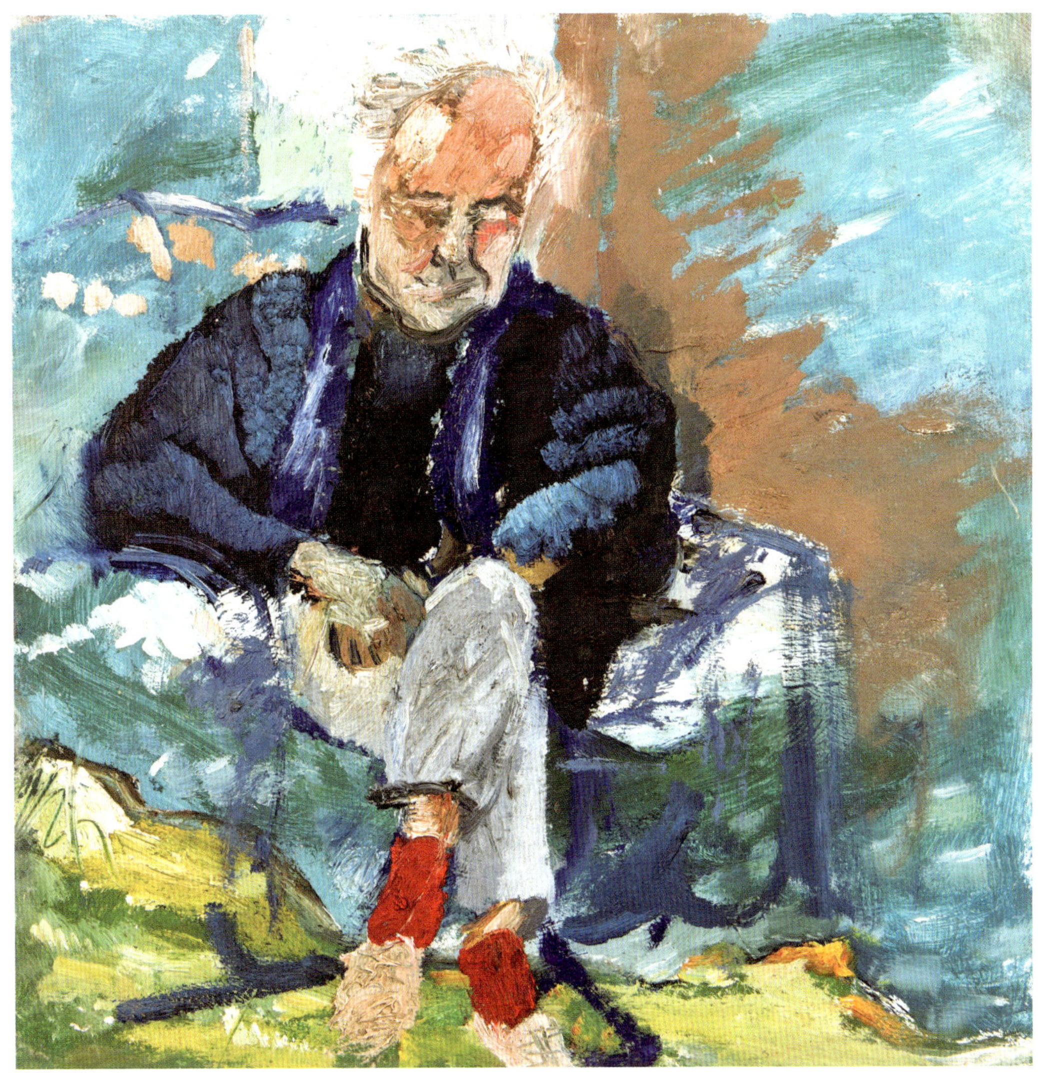

Patrick Heron III · c.1995 · oil on board · 41 x 41 cm

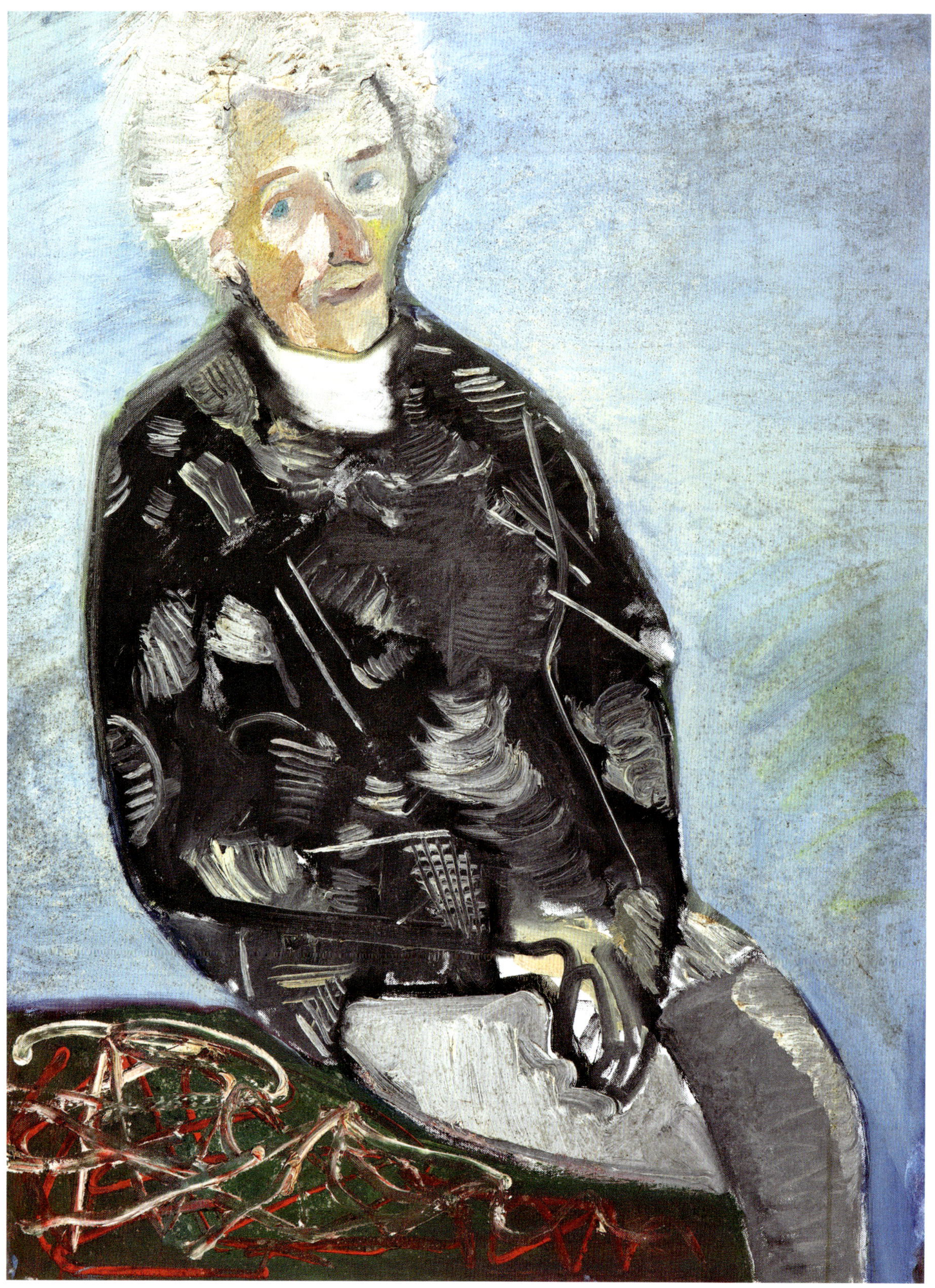

Wilmay Le Grice · c.2006 · oil on canvas · 102 x 76 cm

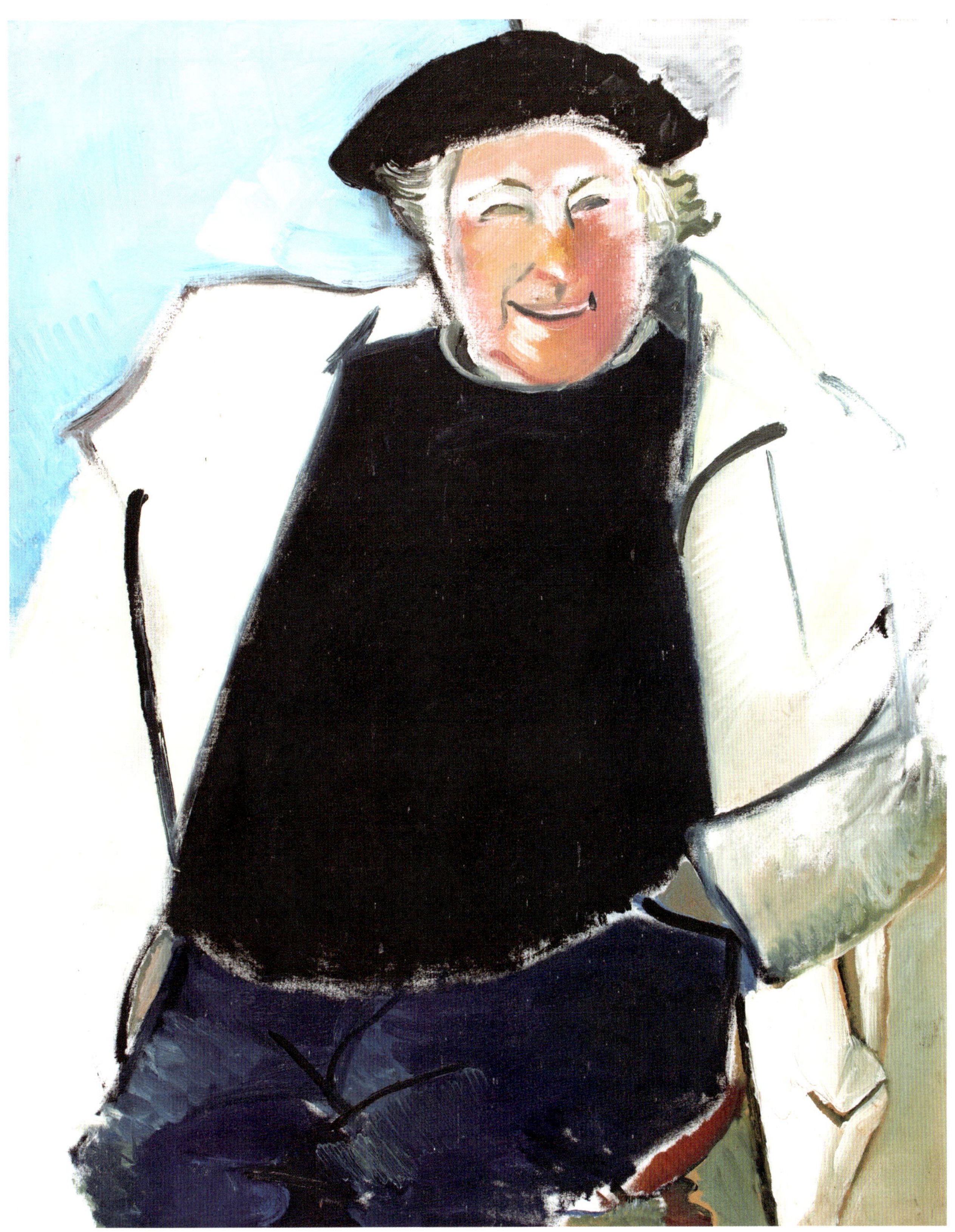

Jeremy Le Grice · c.1998 · oil on canvas · 102 x 81 cm

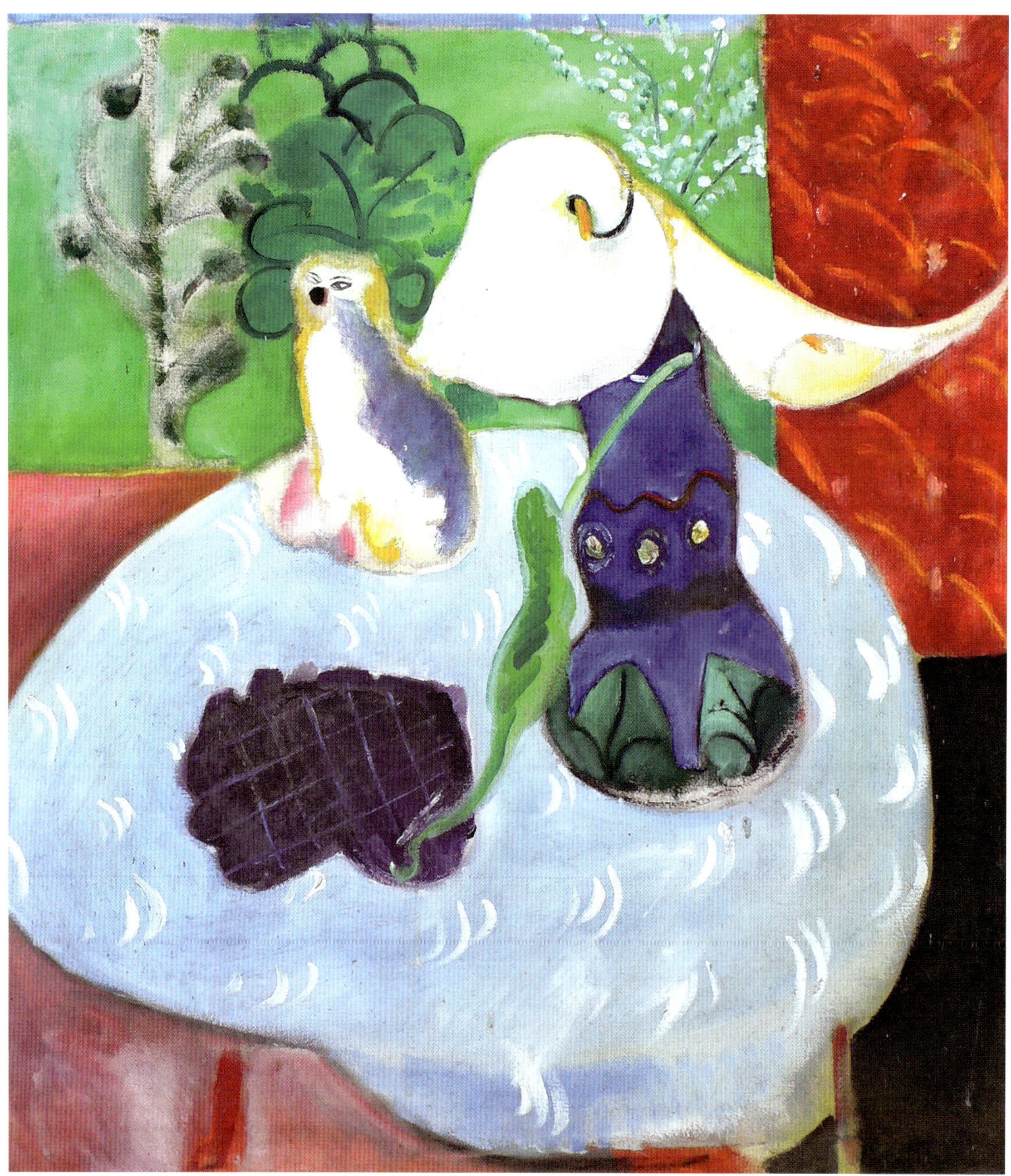

Hello Matisse! · c.1992 · oil on canvas · 102 x 92 cm

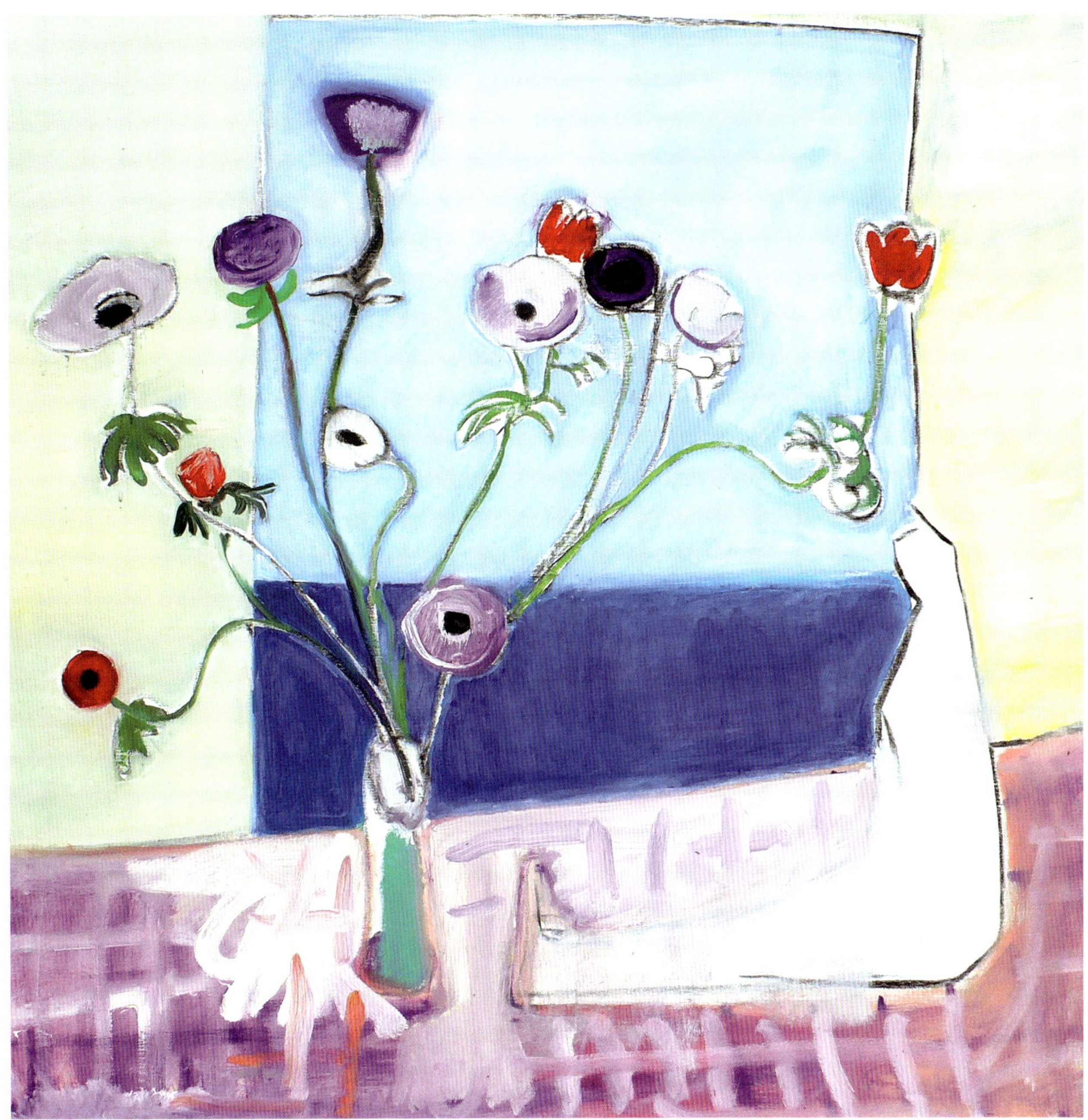

Anemones with Sculpture · c.2006 · oil on canvas · 102 x 102 cm

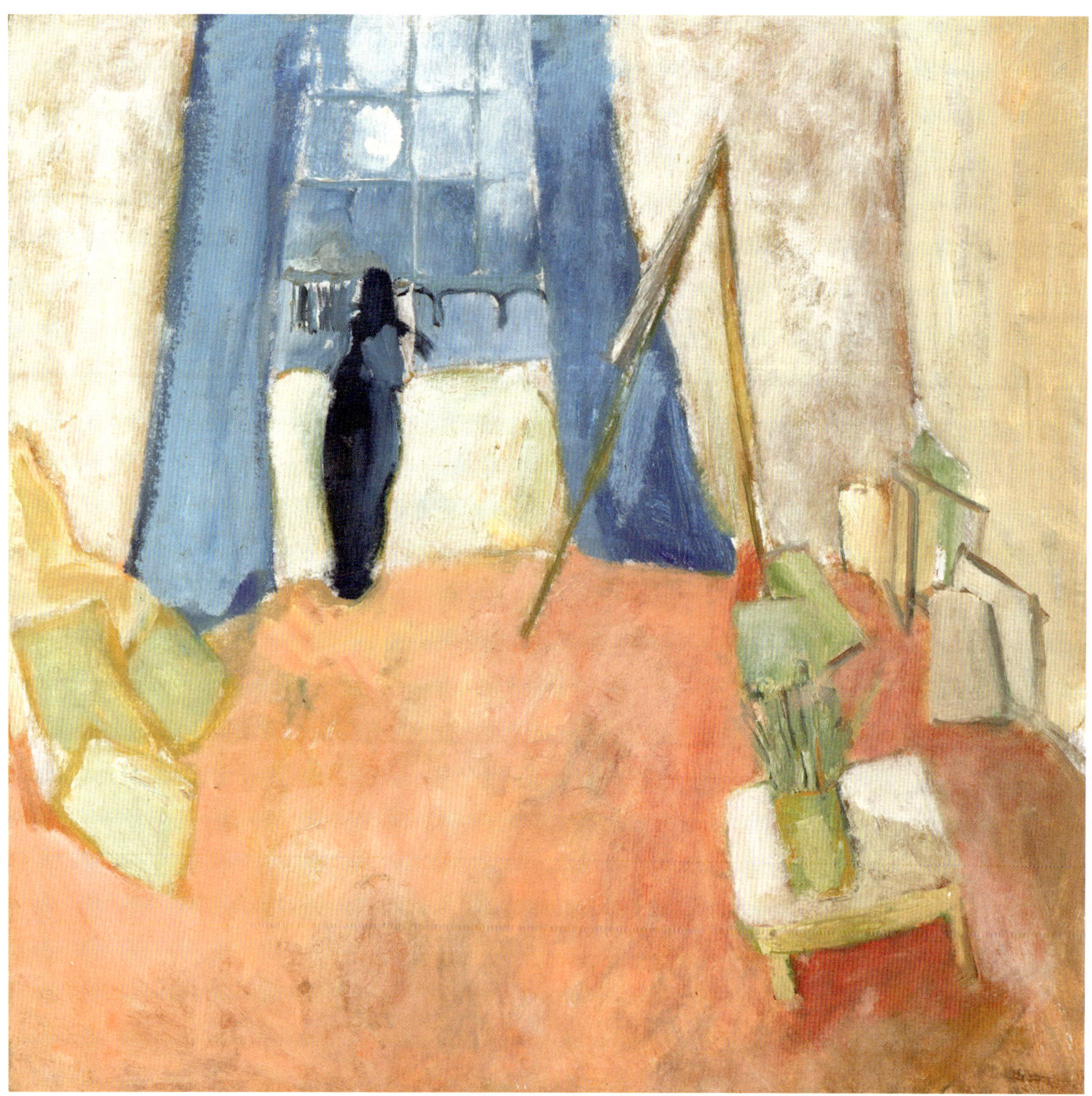

Last Evening, Self at Clevedon · 1982 · oil on board · 89 x 91 cm

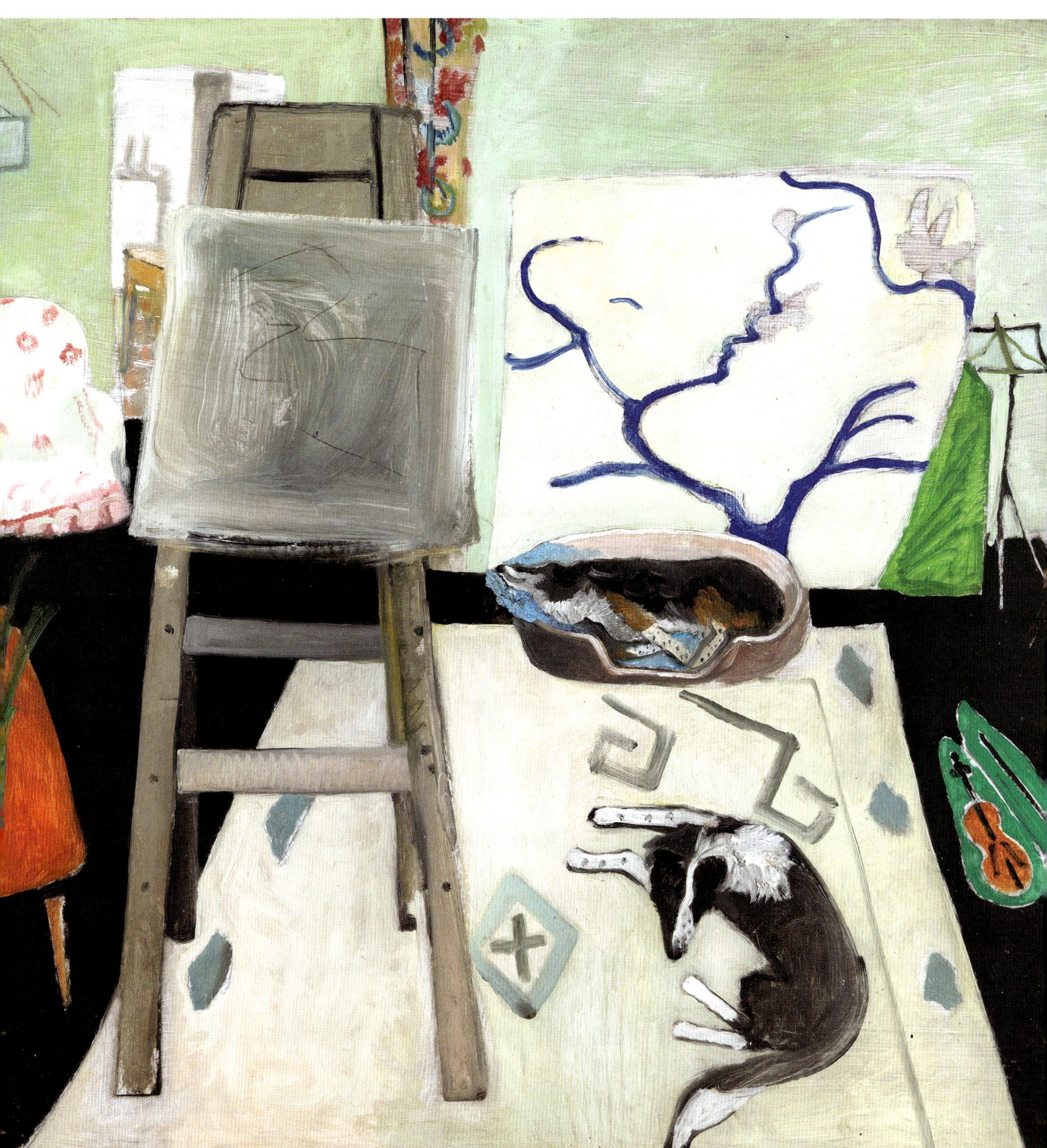

The Easel · *c.*1996 · oil on board · 122 x 122 cm

William Golding's Cloud · c.1993 · oil on canvas · 51 x 92 cm

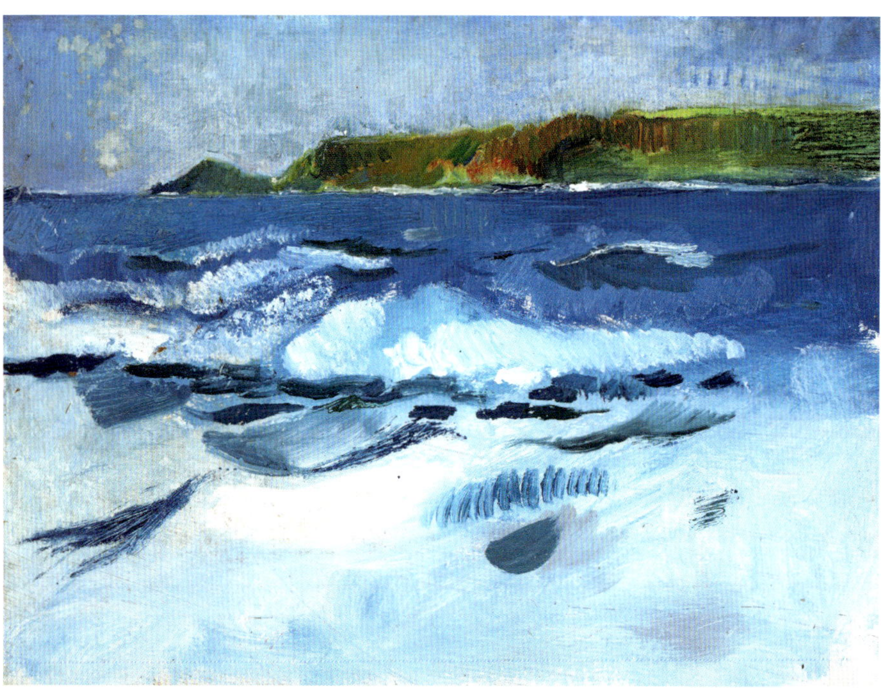

Sea at Sennen · c.1997 · oil on board · 41 x 61 cm

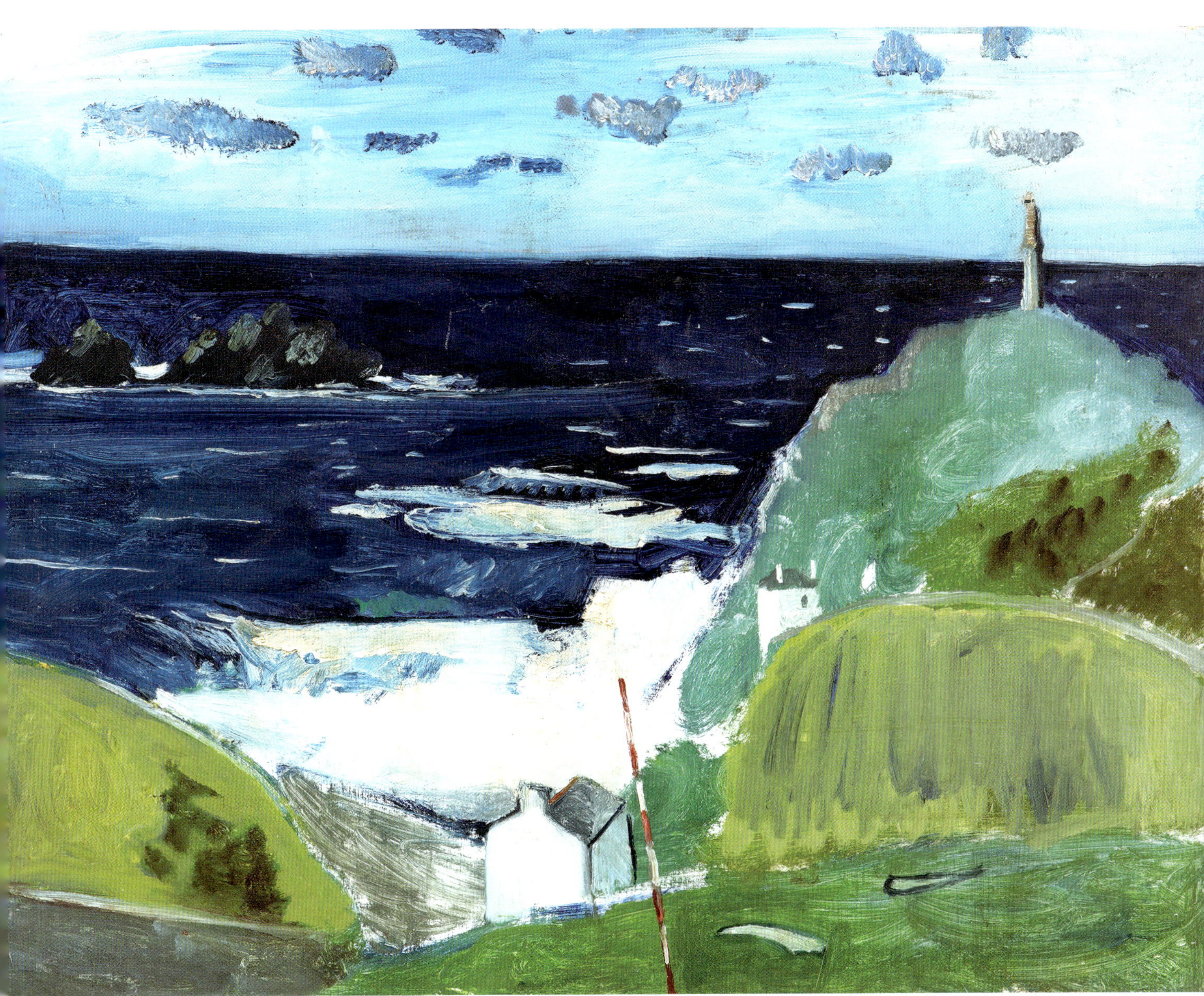

The Cape 1 · c.1998 · oil on board · 92 x 122 cm

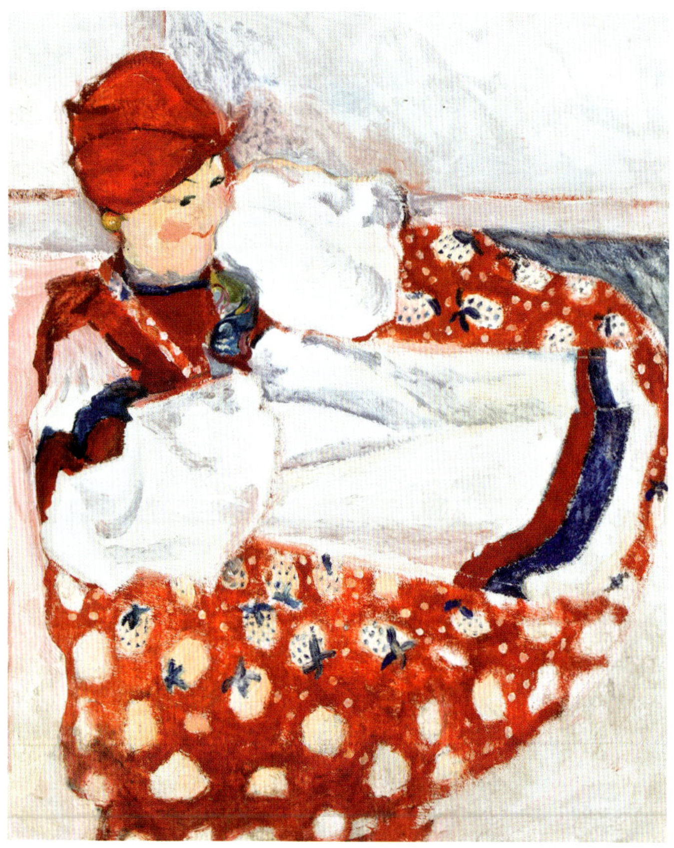

Doll · c.1976 · oil on board · 59 x 46 cm

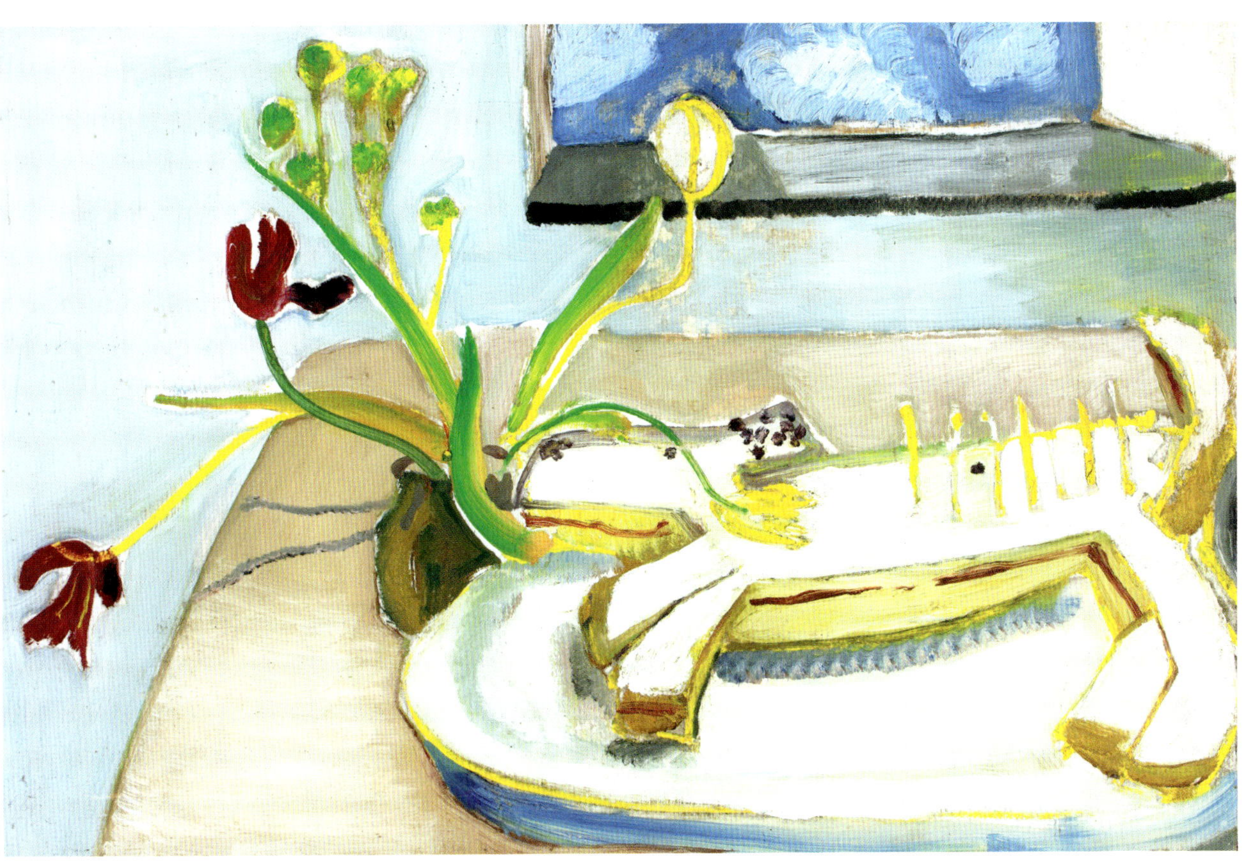

Tom's First Birthday Cake II · c.2001 · oil on board · 61 x 92 cm

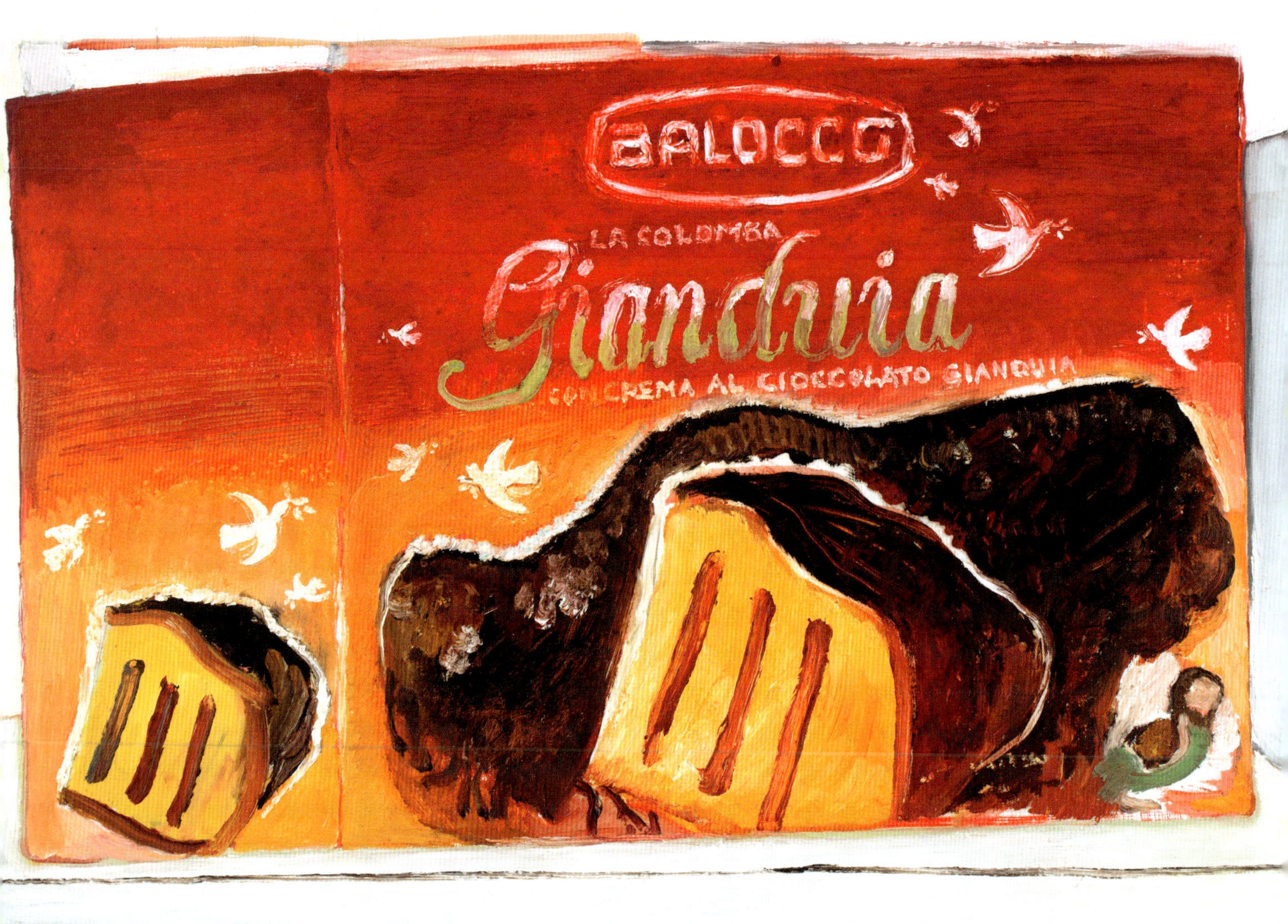

Panettone with Doves · c.2001 · oil on board · 61 x 76 cm

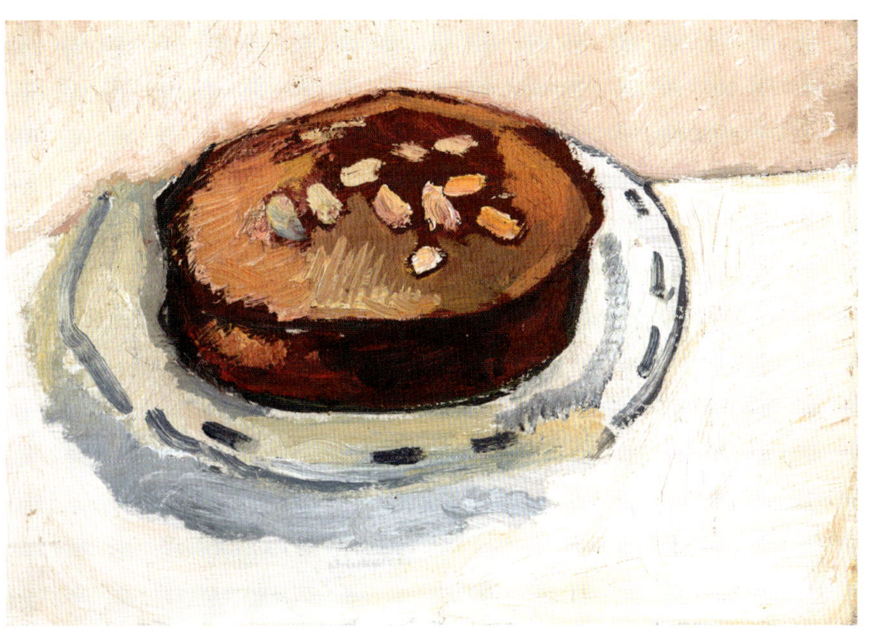

Cake with Almonds · c.2002 · oil on board · 23 x 33 cm

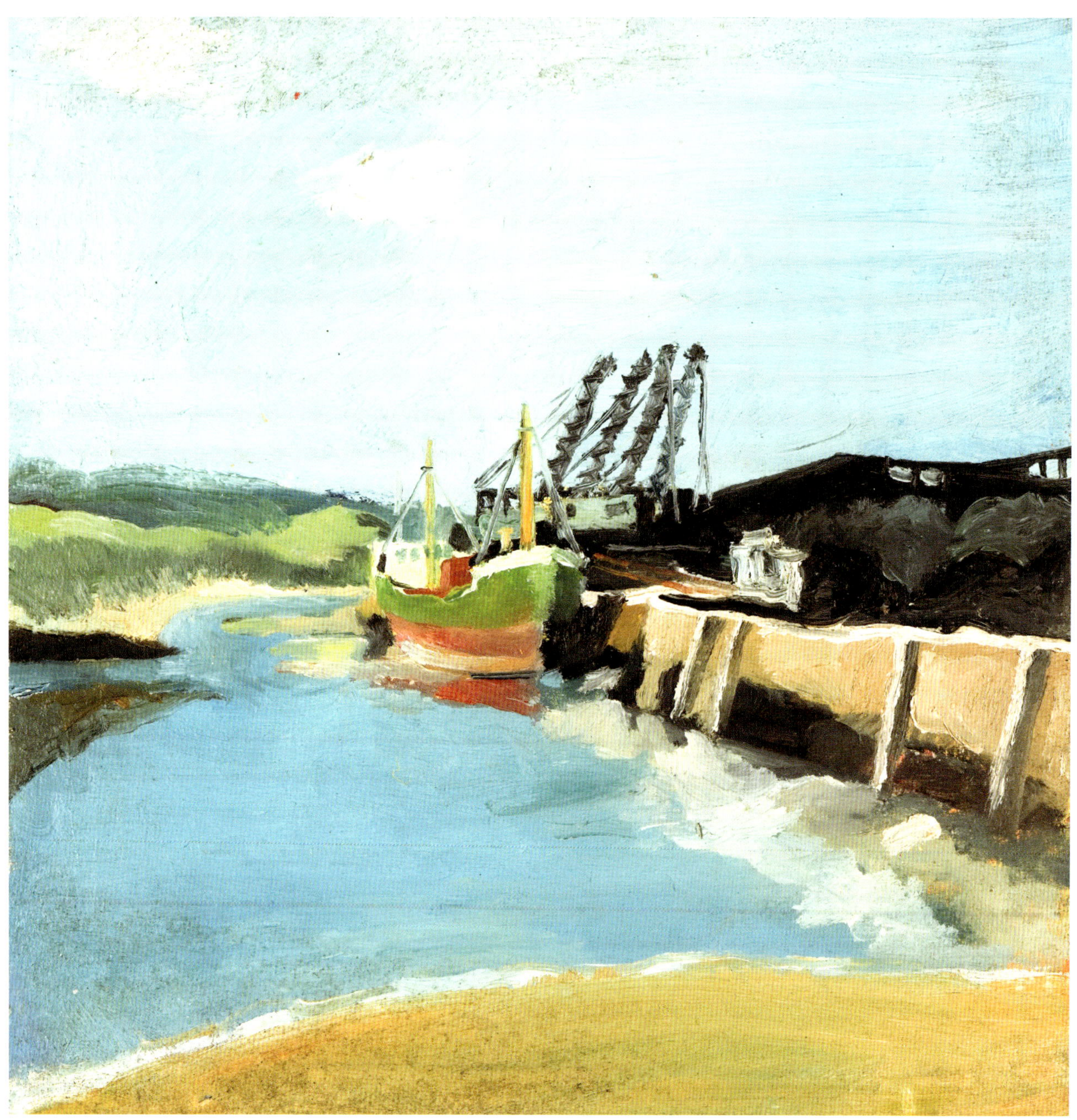

Boat at Hayle VIII · early 1980s · oil on board · 45 x 45 cm

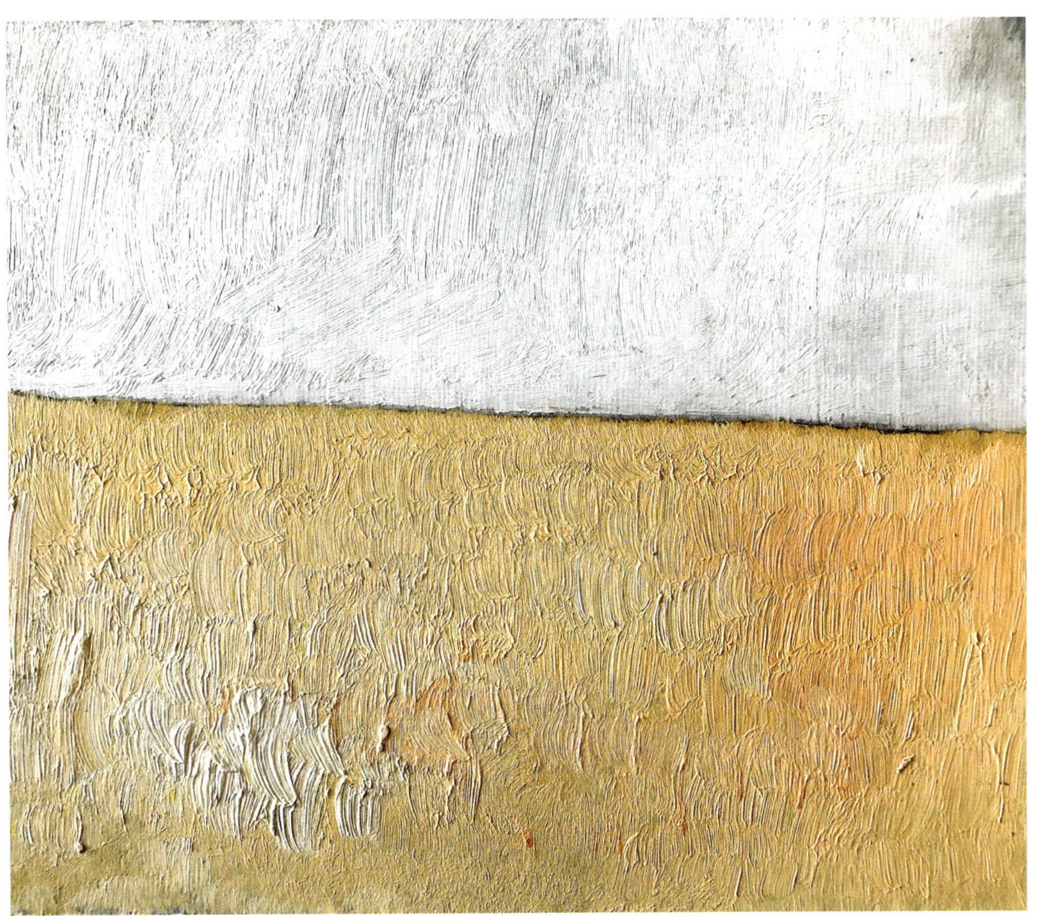

Signal Field · *c.*1987 · oil on board · 31 x 37 cm

overleaf · ***Red and Orange Boats*** · mid-1990s · oil on canvas · 41 x 61 cm

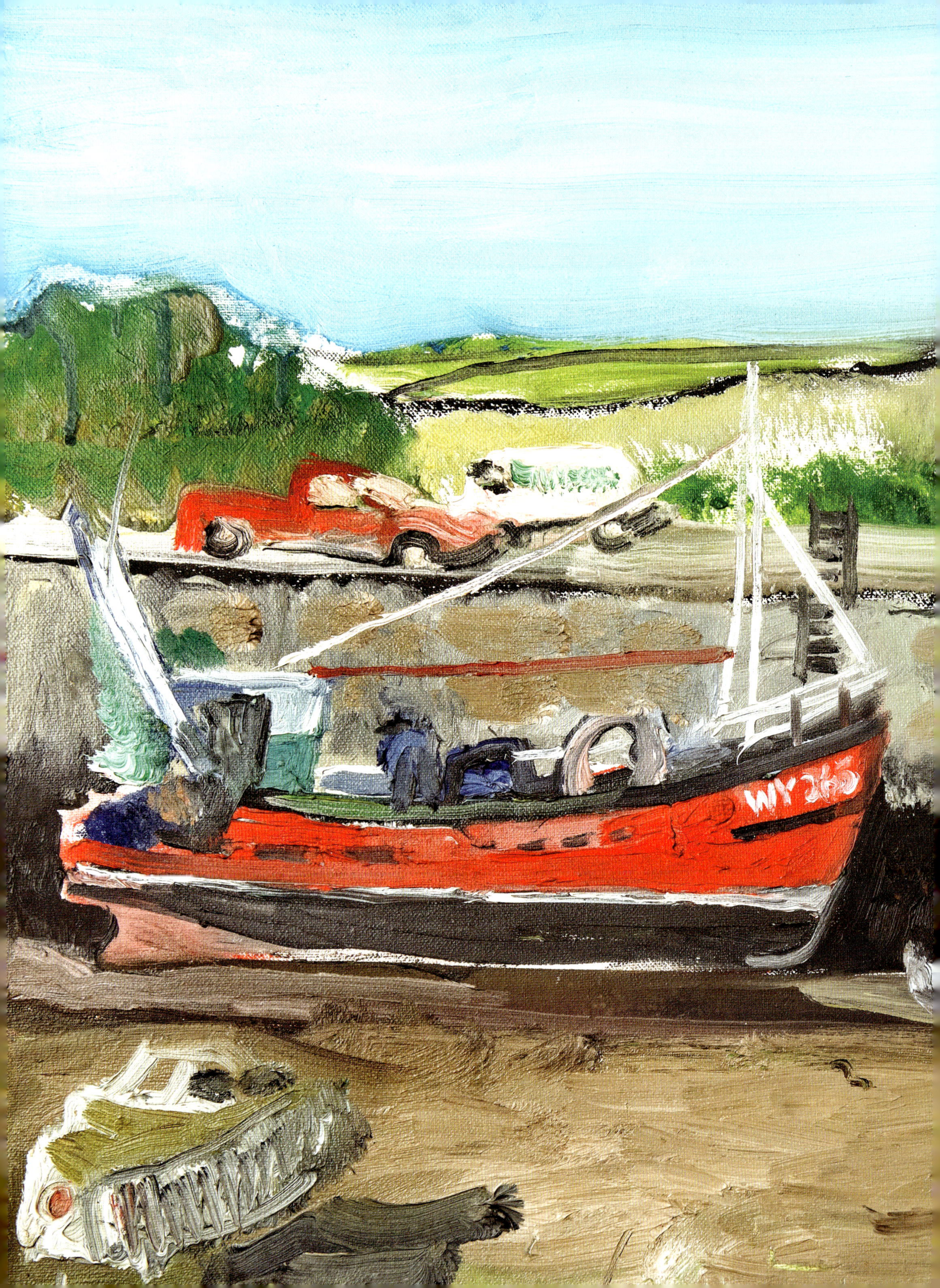

WY 240

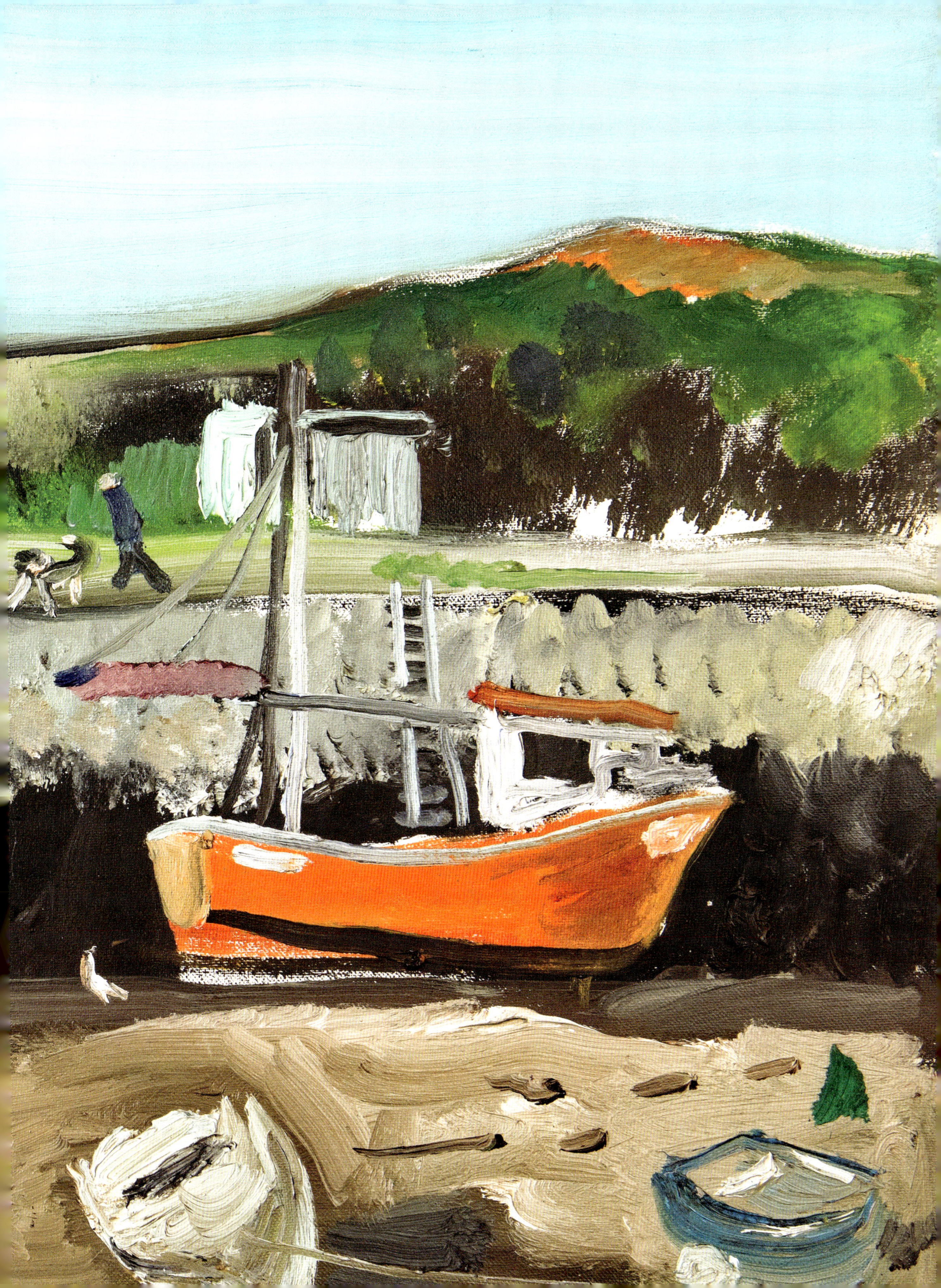

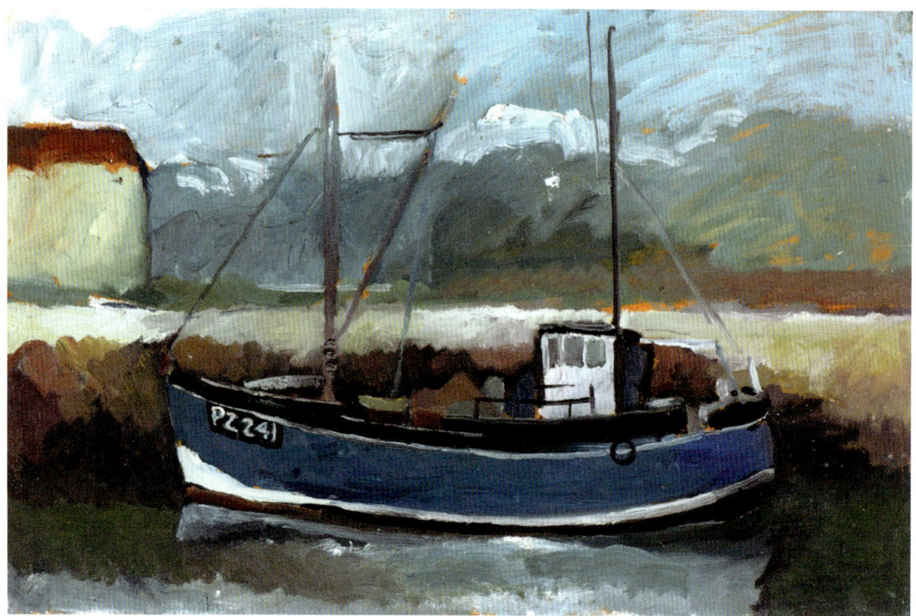

Boat at Hayle VI · late 1970s · oil on board · 42 x 66 cm

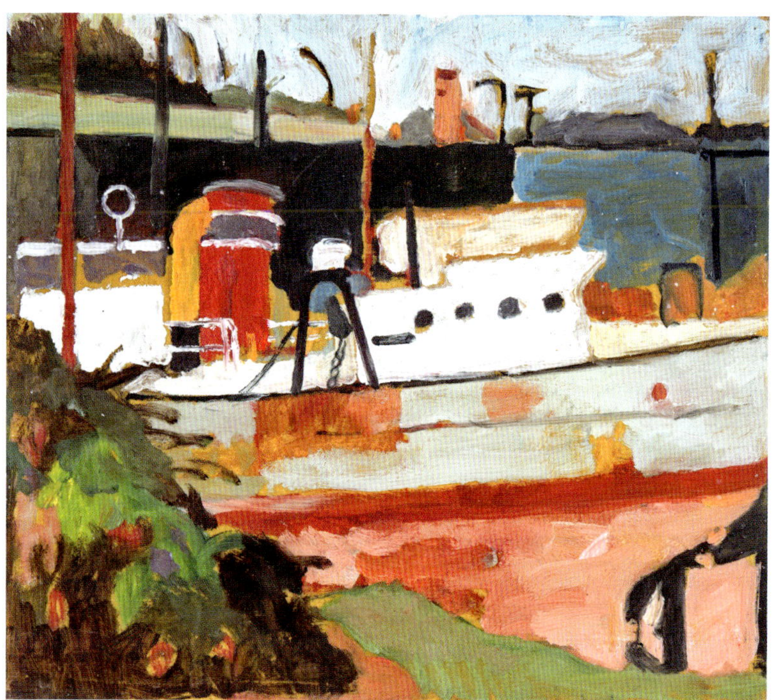

Boat at Hayle I (Red Funnel) · mid-1970s · oil on board · 48 x 56 cm

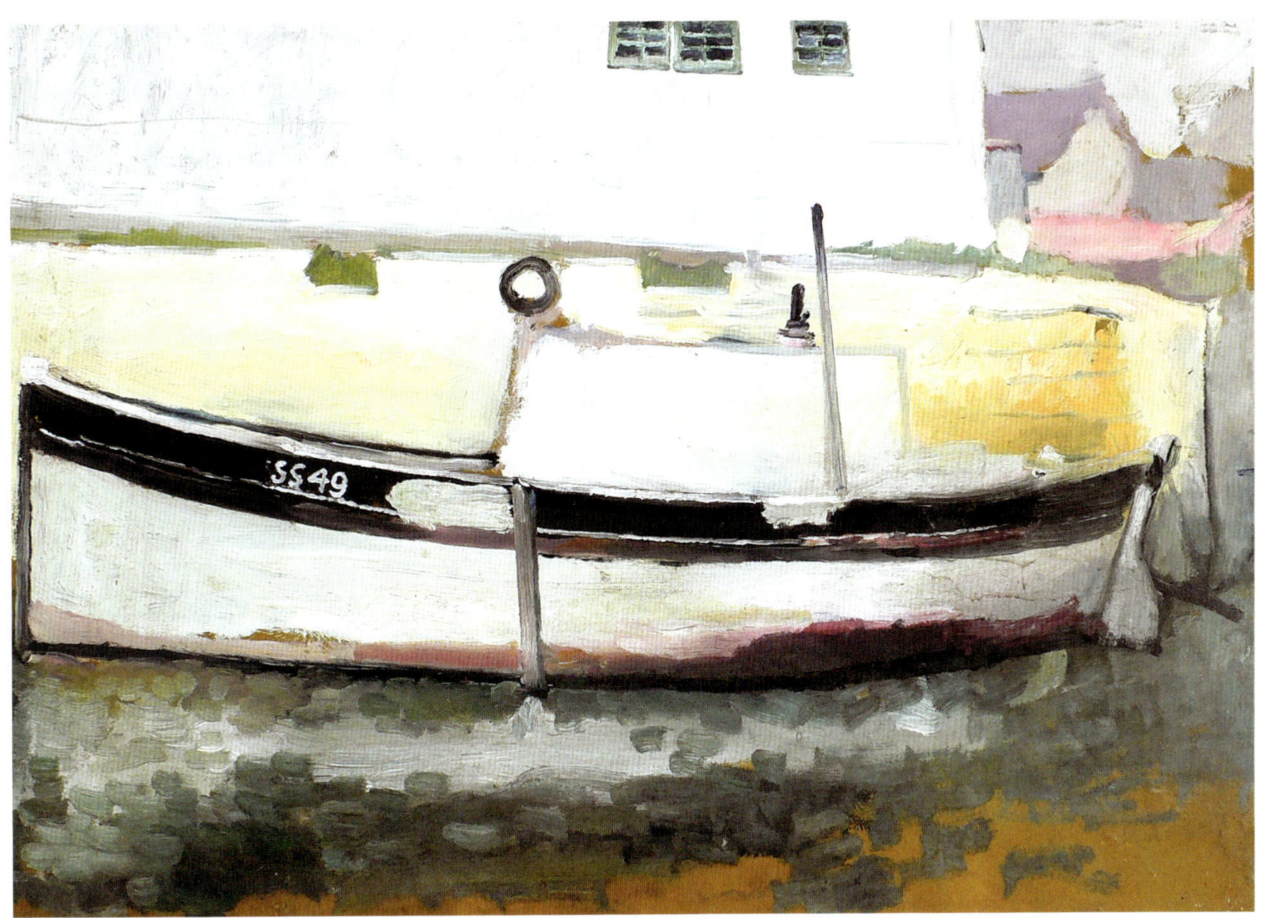

Penzance Fishing Boat · mid-1970s · oil on board · 64 x 89 cm

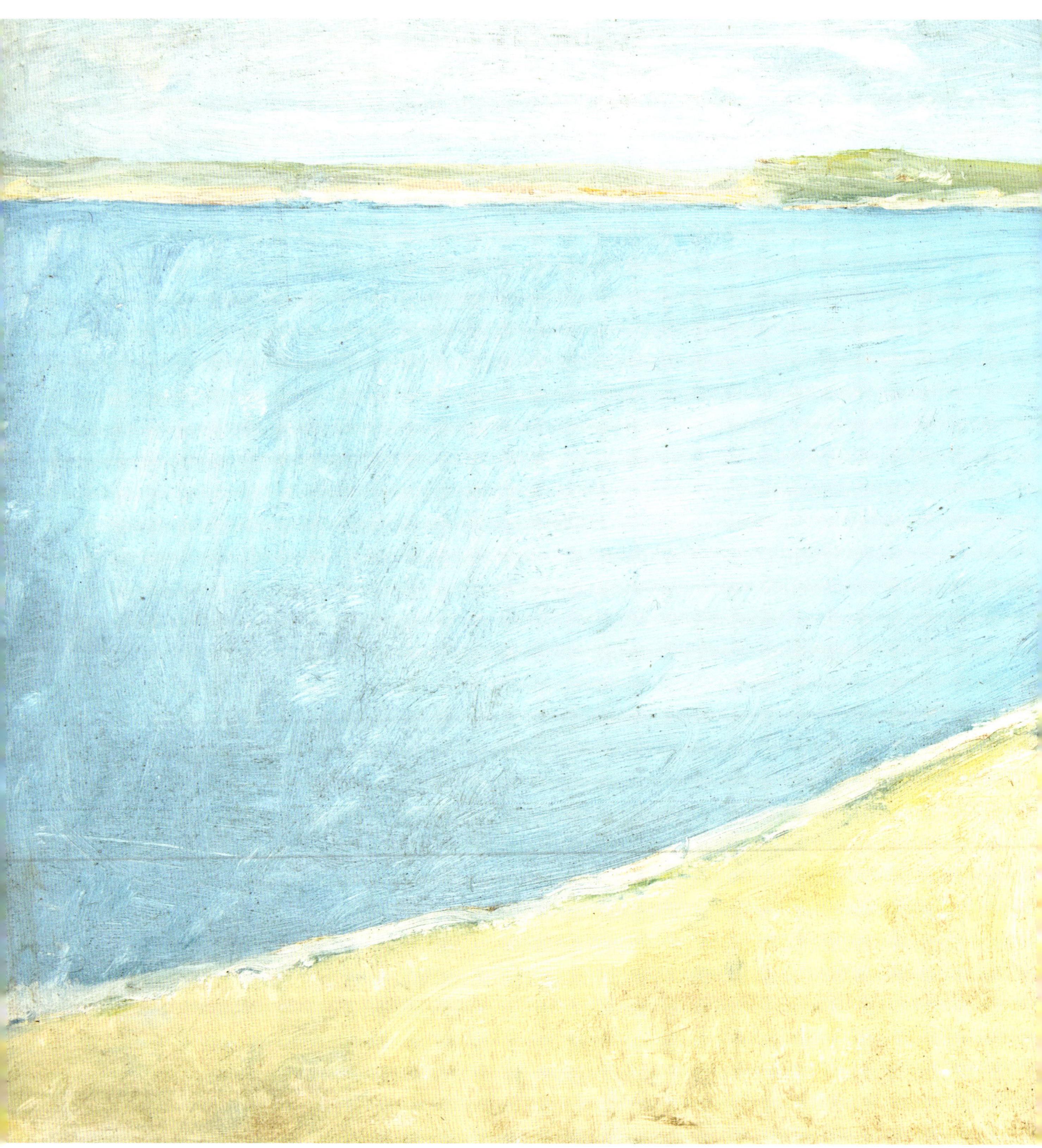

Empty Beach, St Ives · *c.*2004 · oil on board · 61 x 122 cm

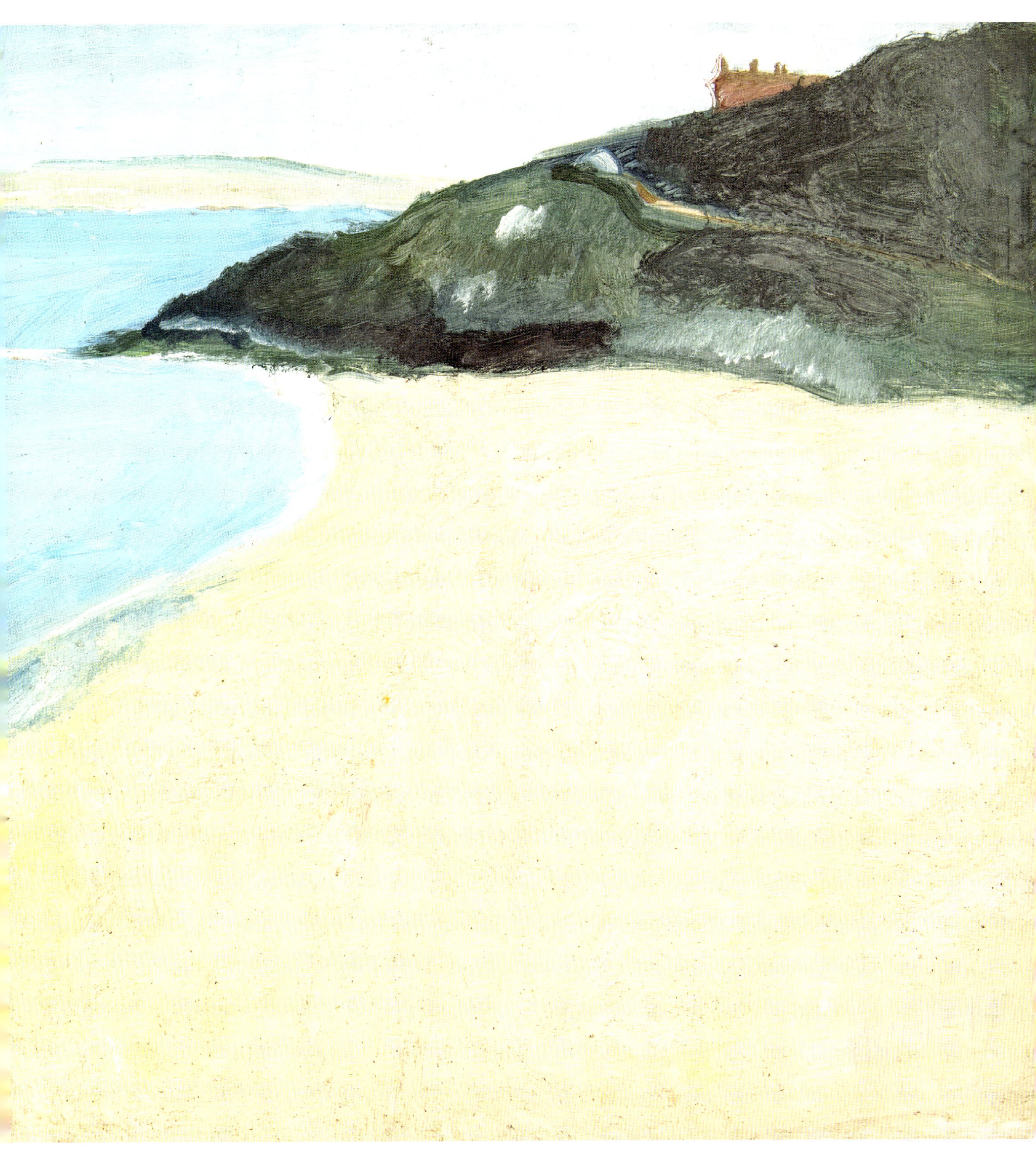

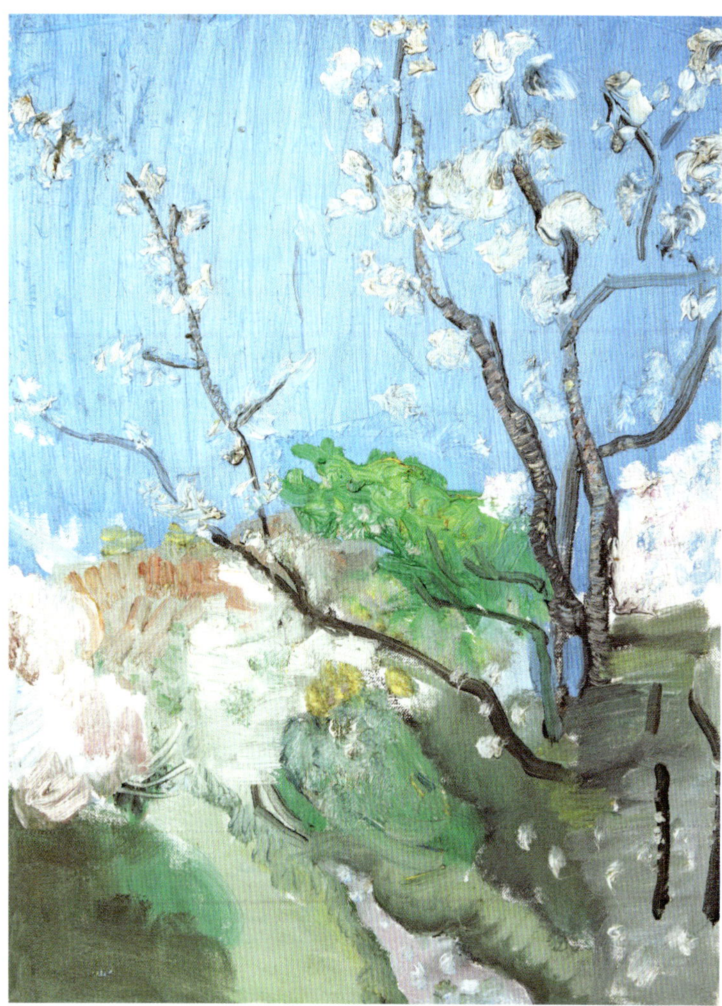

Blossom with Blue Sky · c.2005 · oil on canvas · 61 x 46 cm

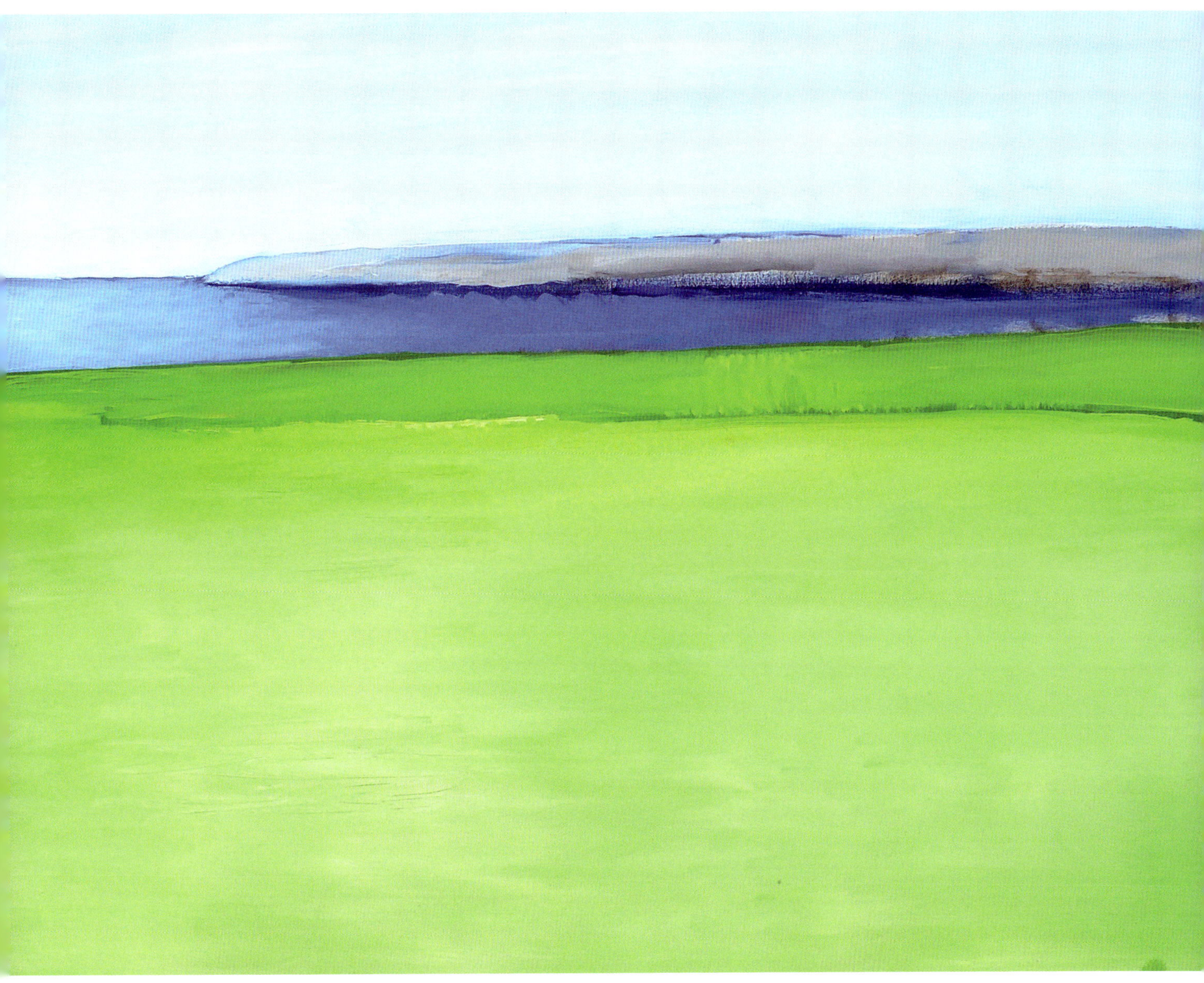

View from the Studio · c.2004 · oil on canvas · 76 x 102 cm

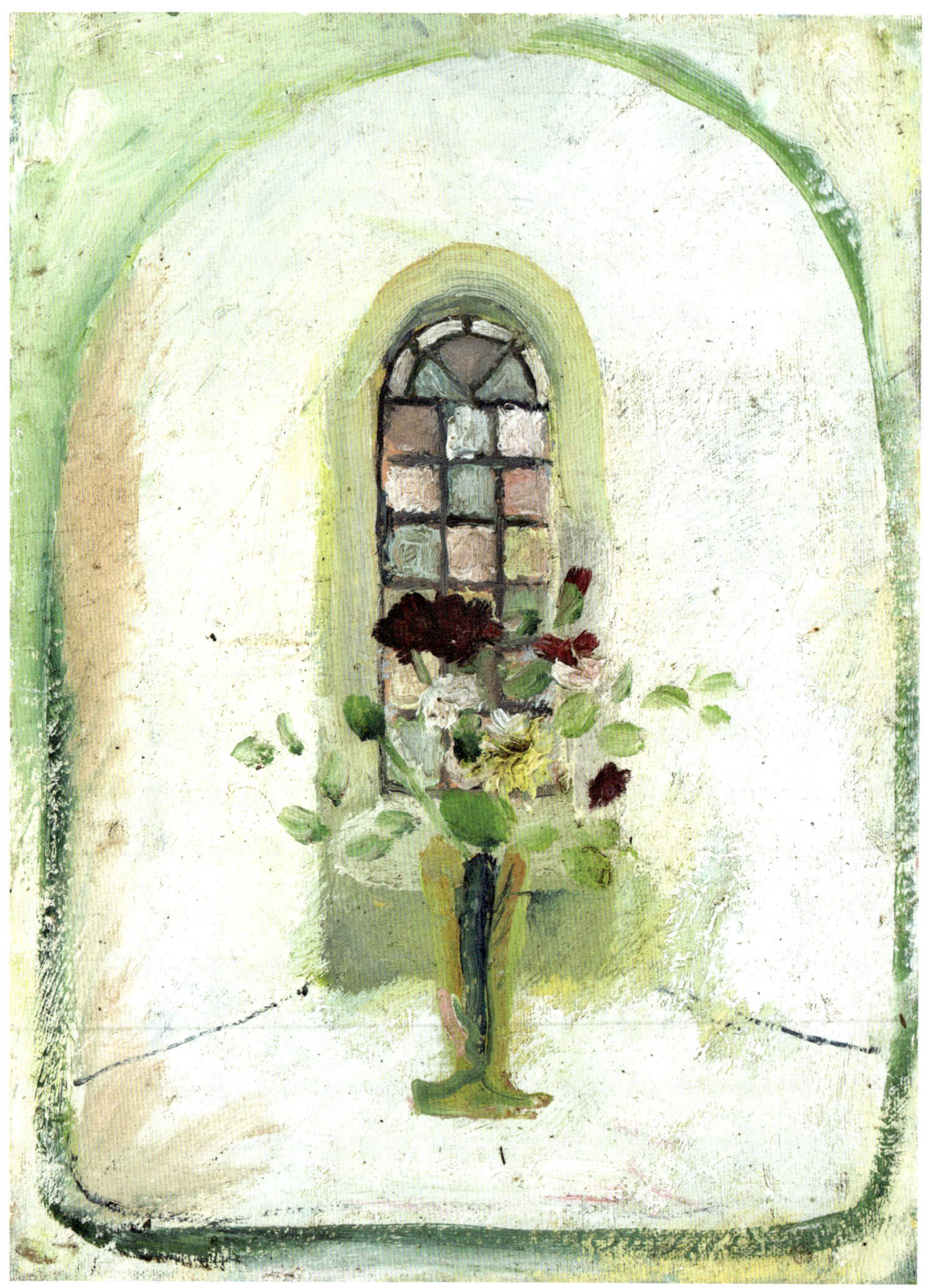

Germoe Window · c.1981 · oil on canvas · 41 x 31 cm

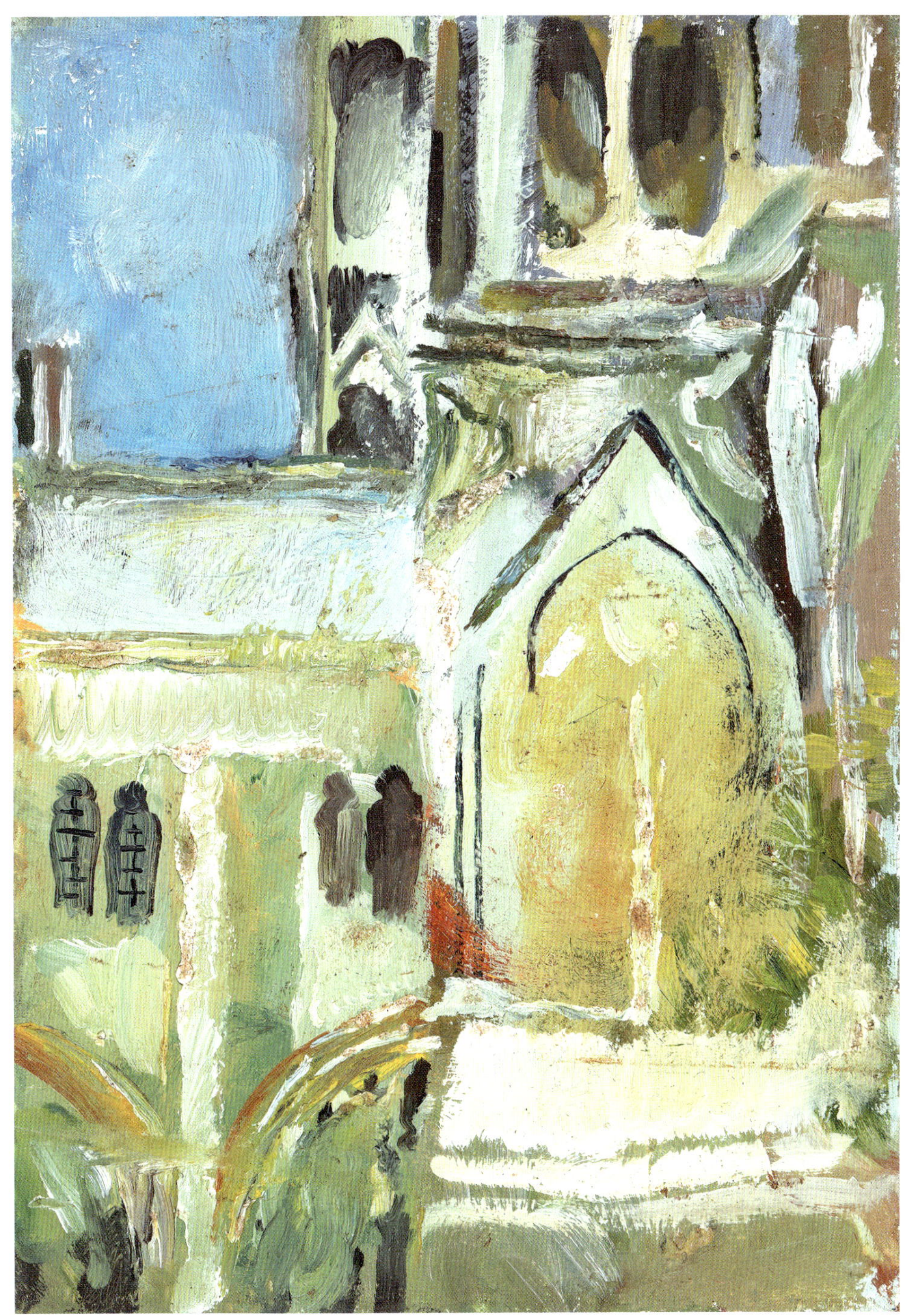

Wells II · mid-1980s · oil on board · 43 x 31 cm

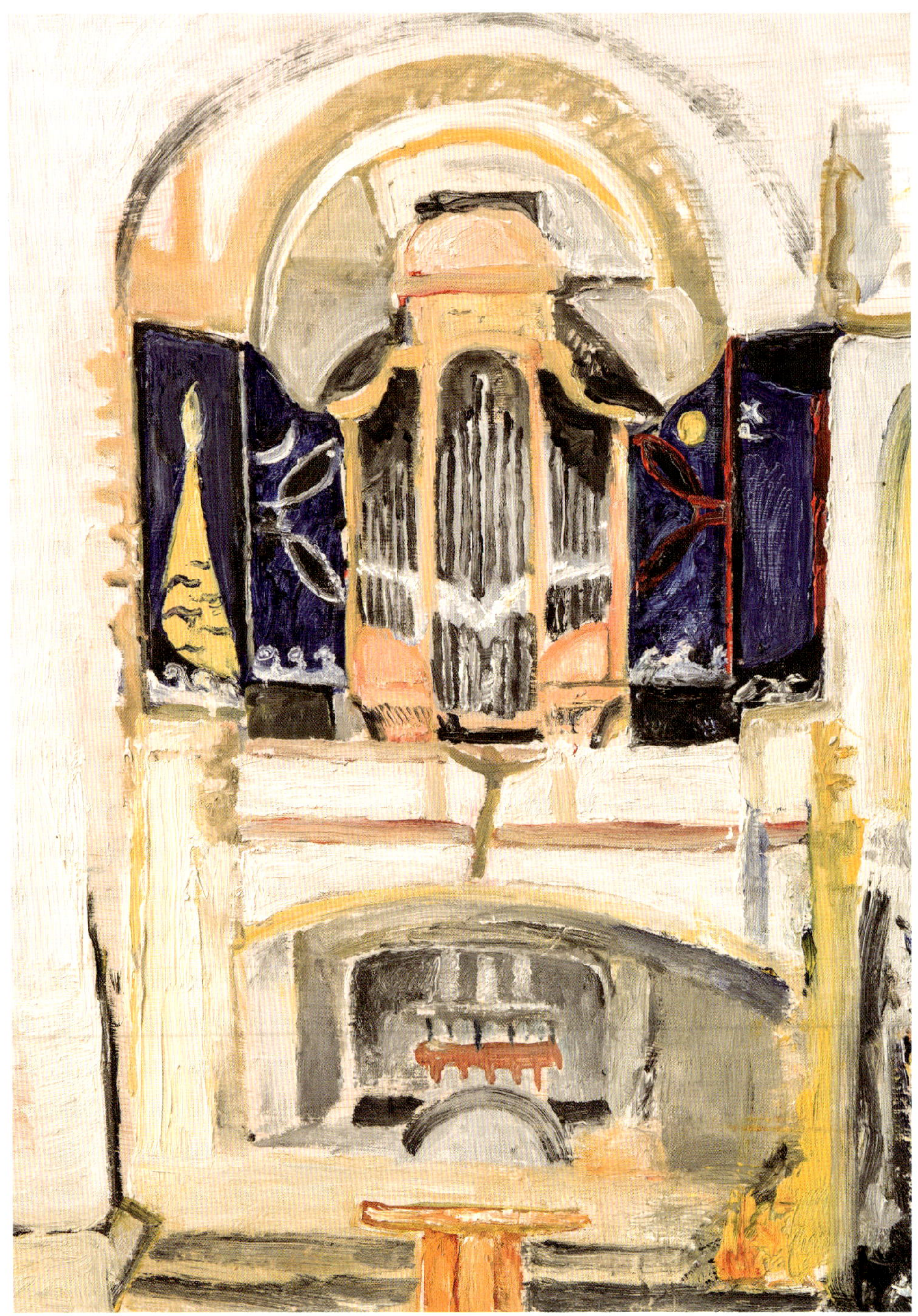

Organ, Portsmouth Cathedral · c.2014 · oil on board · 50 x 35 cm

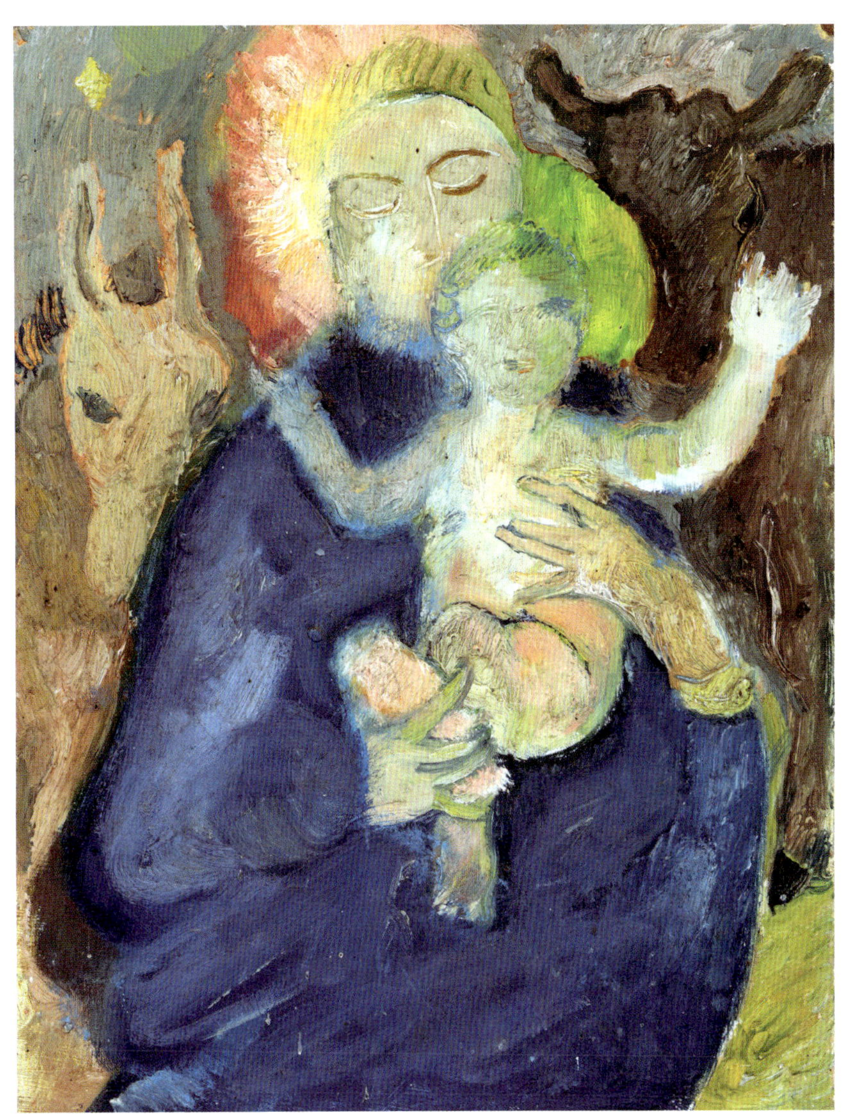

__Madonna and Child__ · c.1998 · oil on board · 40 x 31 cm

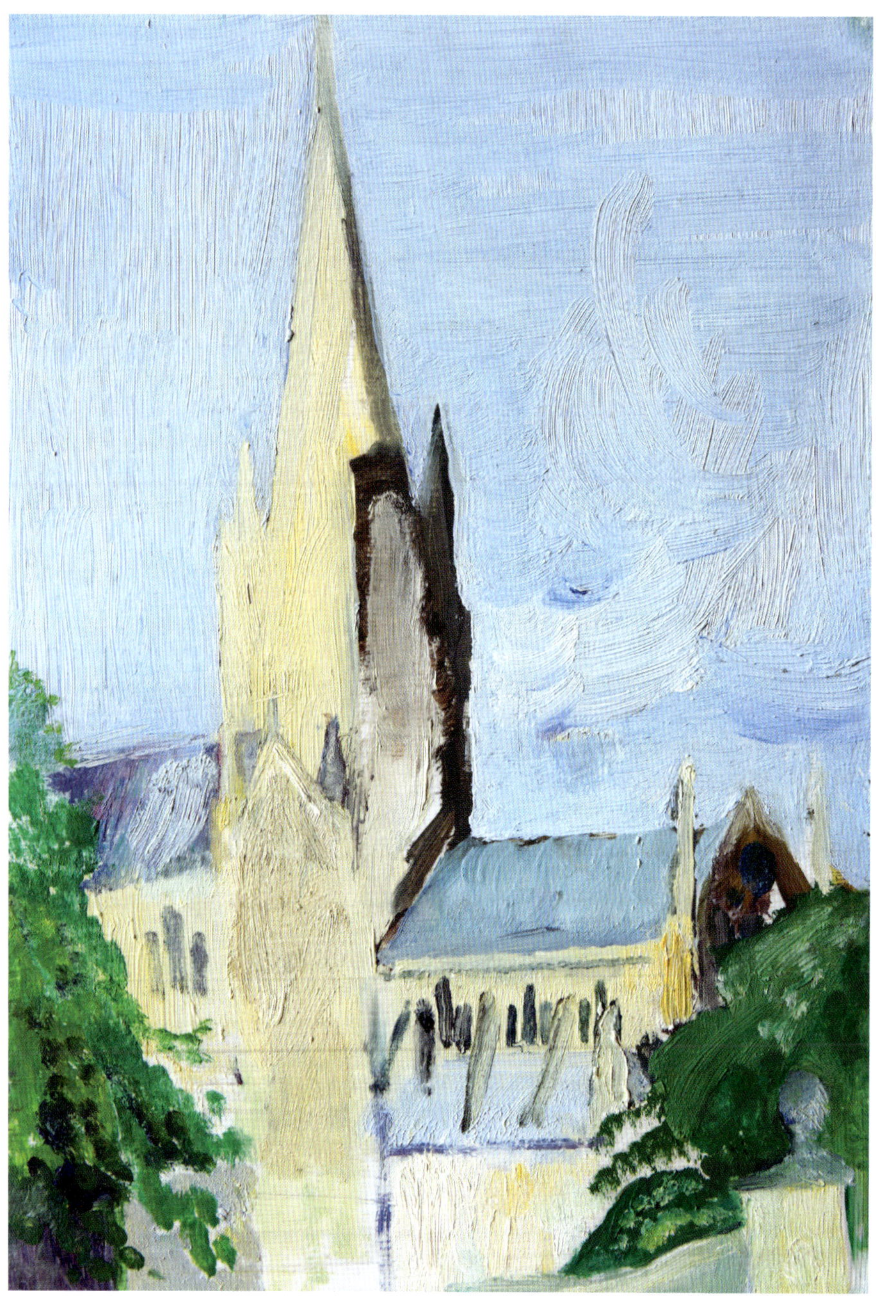

Salisbury from Sarum College · c.2014 · oil on board · 40 x 28 cm

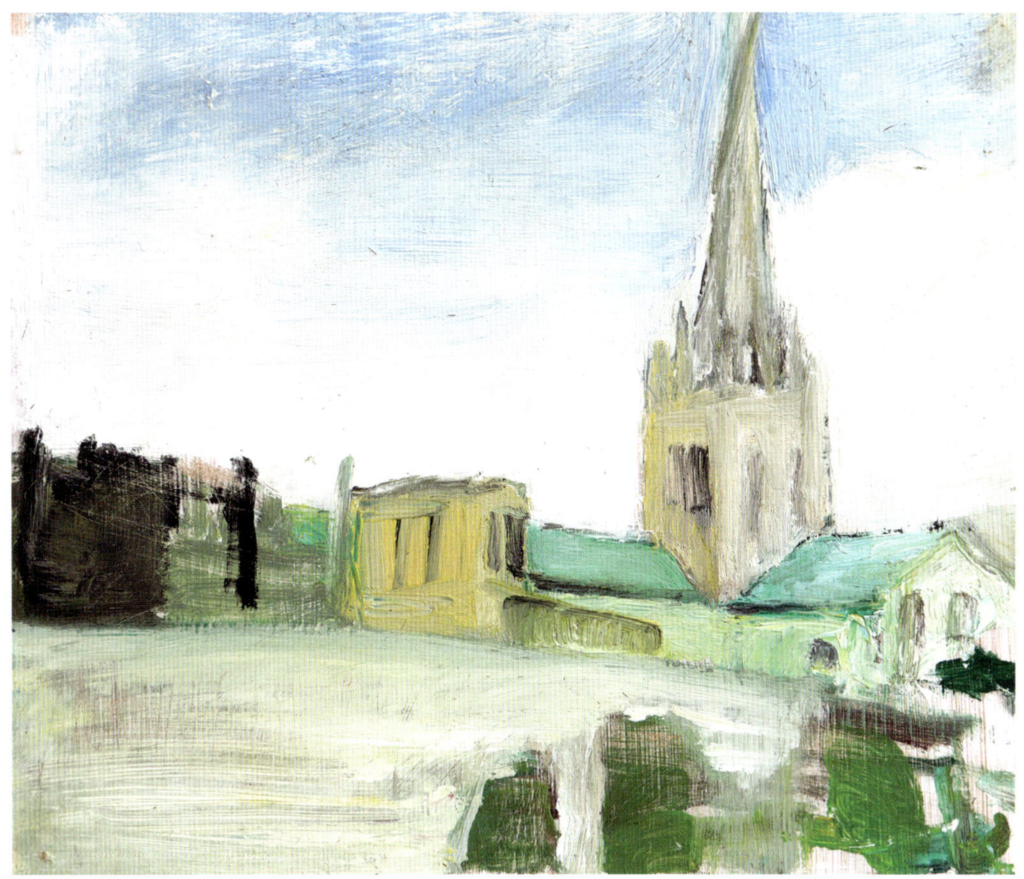

Chichester Cathedral 1 · 2014–15 · oil on board · 26 x 31 cm

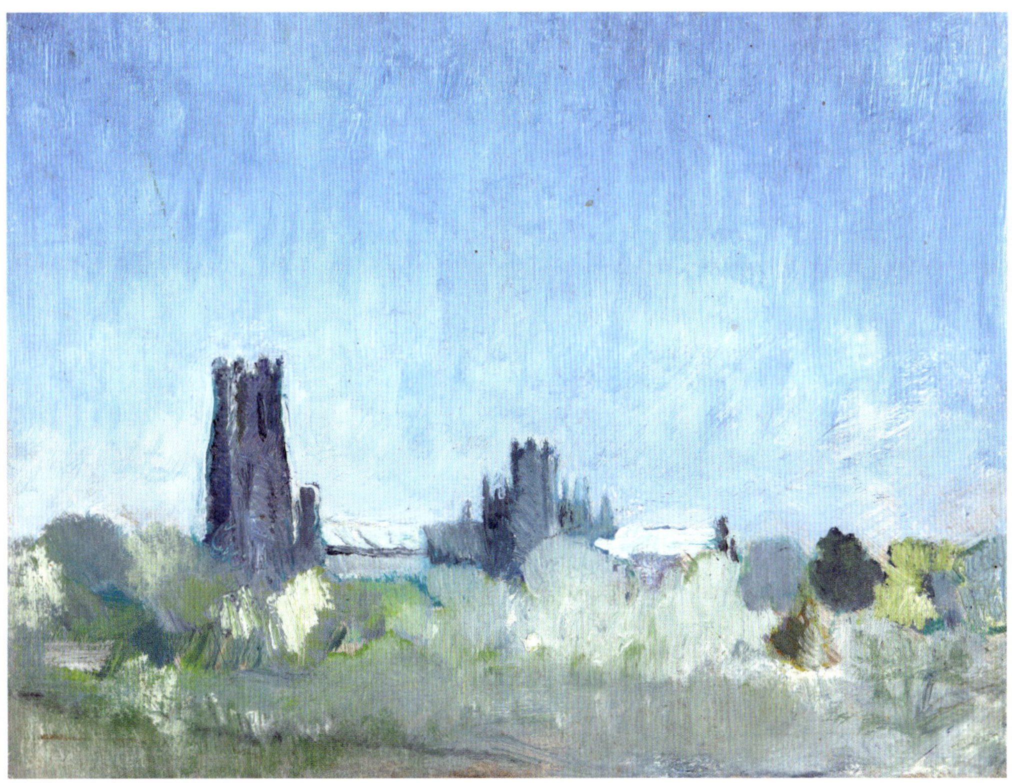

Ely, Ship of the Fens · c.1987 · oil on board · 23 x 31 cm

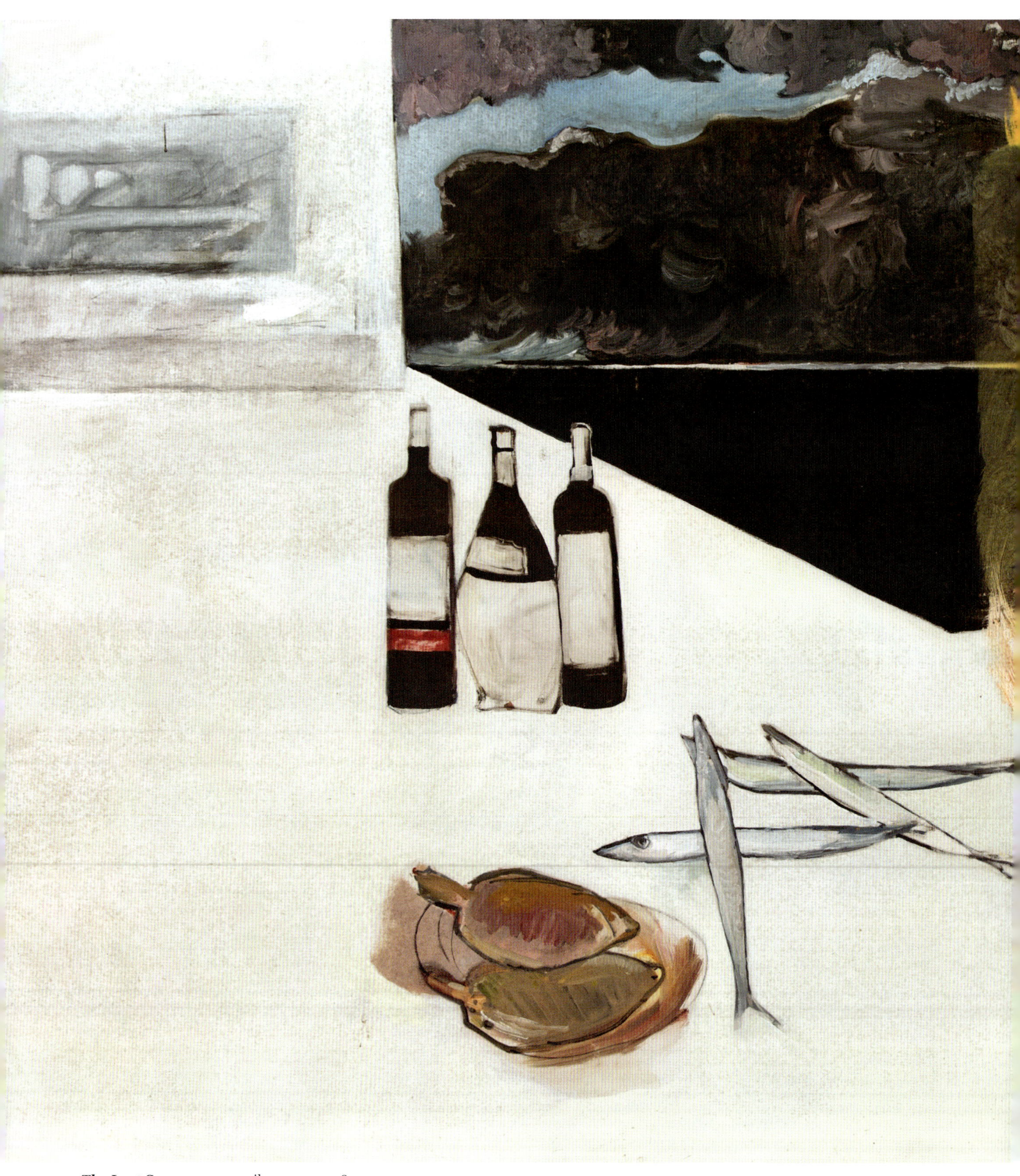

The Last Supper · 2013 · oil on canvas · 184 x 244 cm

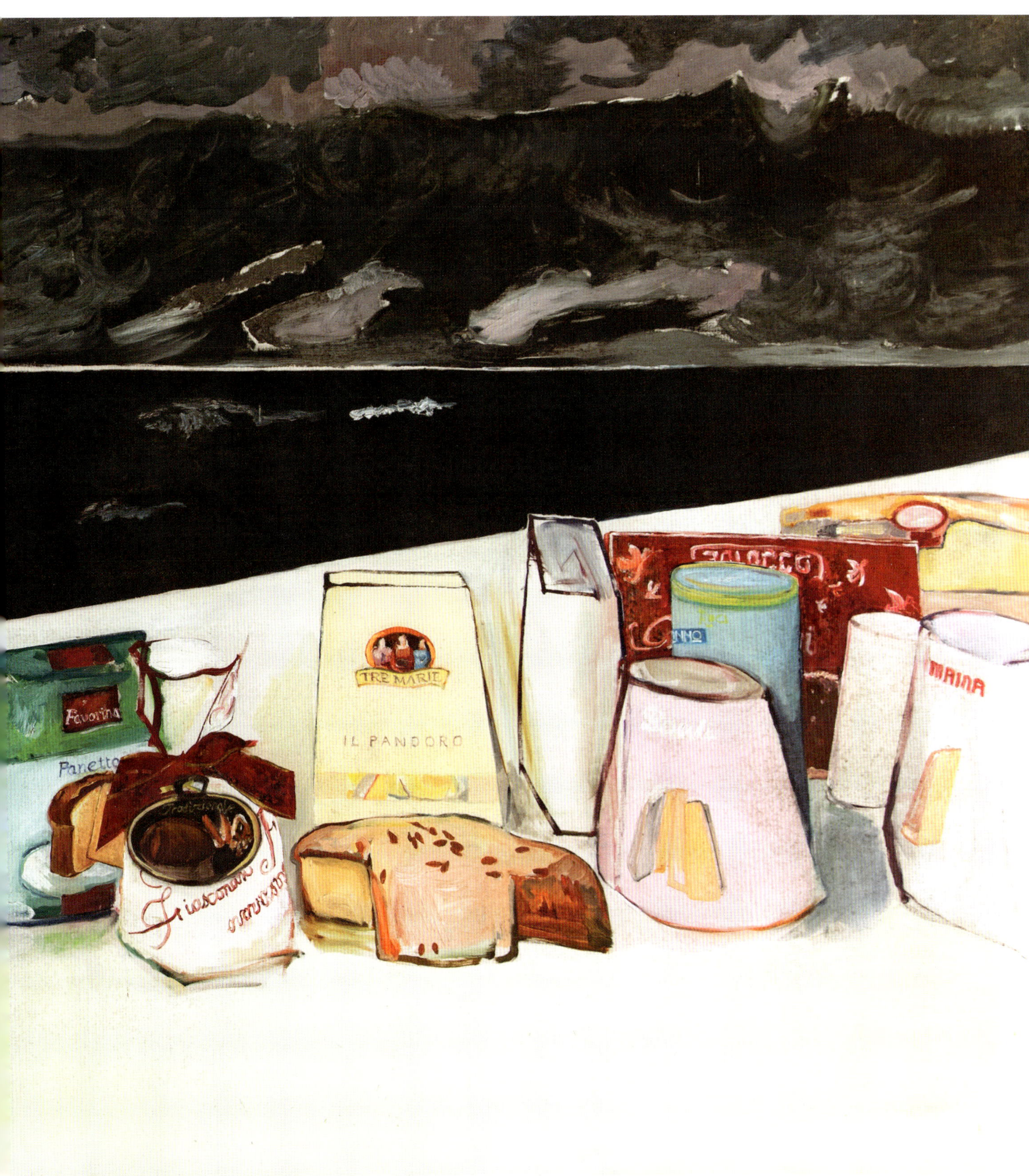

overleaf · *The Celtic Blessing* · 2014 · oil on canvas · 152 x 214 cm

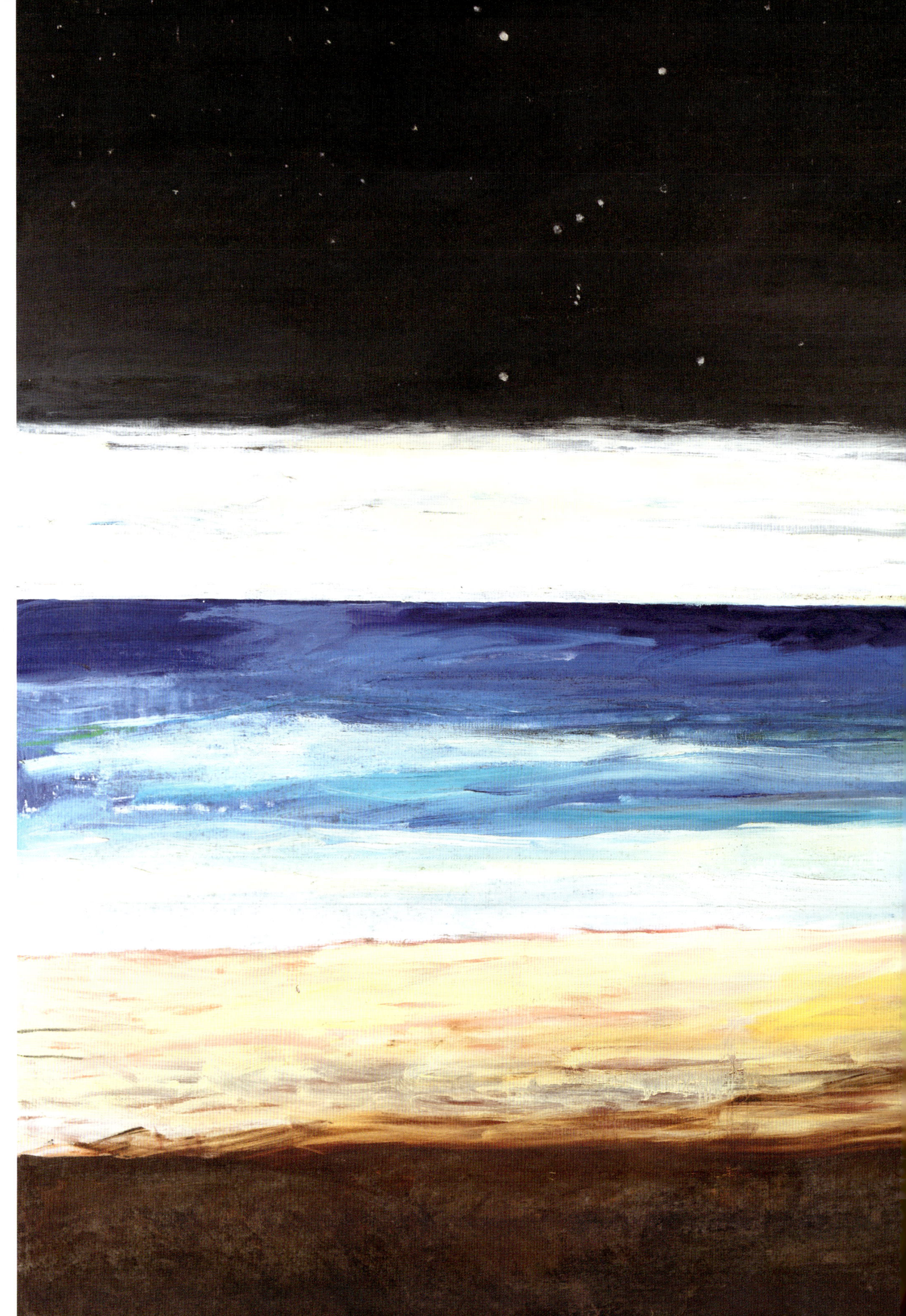

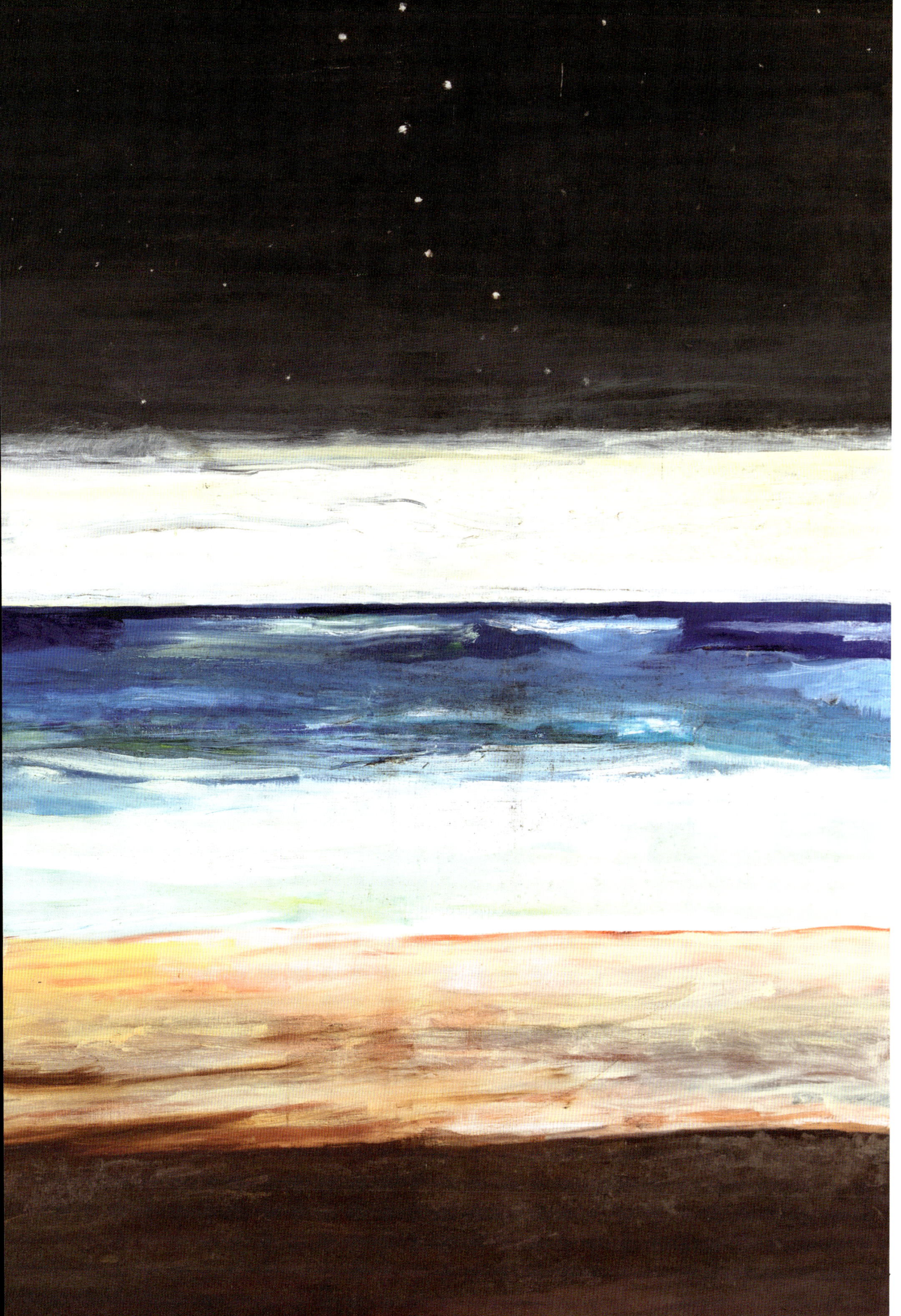

Romi remembered

Alice Mumford, Sue Norrington and Roz Quillan Chandler

Three of Romi's many friends share their thoughts and memories about her life and art.

¶

In our lifetime, we receive many friends and strangers into our homes. For Romi Behrens, it was a role that could have become an all-consuming definition. Not only did she welcome musicians from all over the world, but generations of families coming back to Porth-en-Alls for their treasured holidays.

I first became aware of Romi when I was a child of about nine. She and her family lived along the cliff path from where my mother had grown up in west Cornwall, a place where we would stay with my grandmother.

Romi and my mother had been at school together and were both painters. There was a mystery and intrigue about the Tunstall-Behrens household. Walking along the cliff path to reach the house, a sense of the unusual seemed to start miles before we got there. In fact, so strong was this sense that even the path itself had this association. Now when walking it, this sense has given way to the familiar.

After a forty-minute walk along a golden beach, then wild cliffs with an emerald sea below, we arrived outside an imposing three-storey house with a sort of courtyard. A grand front door with sweeping steps leading up to it. However, this was not the way into the house! I noticed an open window on the ground floor with a stone step in front of it. We followed Romi onto the stone and into the kitchen. While drinking tea and eating scones, people seemed to come and go through the window all the time we were there.

Romi and my mother shared an irreverence for convention, whether it was the way you entered a house

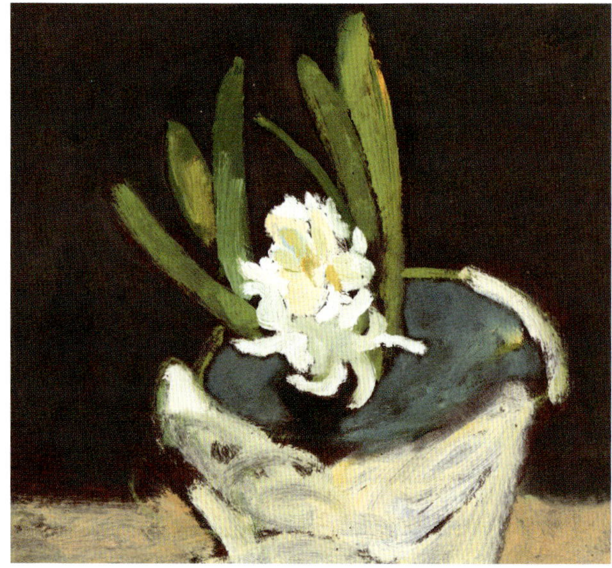

Hyacinth I · c.1978 · oil on board · 31 x 33 cm

or the way you talked to a nine-year-old. In part, I think, they were shaped by the elemental and wild landscape that surrounded them. Maybe that is what gave them an intrepid single-mindedness.

Romi chose, through her own sheer bloody-mindedness, not to be entirely defined by the estate where she lived and worked. She grabbed the smallest moment and she painted. This was an act of defiance, staking out her independence and identity through the oil paint. It is seen through her vigorous, energetic, confident, intuitive brushwork. If she was going to be a painter she had better get on with it; there was no time to dither. She painted the people that came and went. Through this practice of reading people quickly, she developed an uncanny ability to uncover sometimes uncomfortable things about the sitters – almost a second sight.

I suspect most people know Romi for her portraits, but she painted lots of other things: china dogs, jugs, boxes, her dogs and, memorably, panettone boxes set out as the 12 disciples. My mother owned a stunning painting of a pot of hyacinths just emerging. It has an element of a portrait but possibly a self-portrait. The sureness of the strokes in thick paint, juxtaposed with the sense of newness of growth, is very touching.

Romi was a generous painter and invited me to paint in her studio, and on one occasion go to Paradise Park in Hayle, which has a huge variety of birds. We settled down with oil paints in boxes and fold-out stools. With Romi next to me, it was like having a guide to lead one through a difficult pass. The unflinching ease with which she approached the moving subjects of little owls, cockatoos and ravens gave me great confidence. We packed up; I put my paintings in the boot of her car and she put hers on the roof. Soon after reversing, we realised we had just driven over two paintings that had slipped off! Quick as you like, she reconstructed the missing parts of the birds with her brushes and oils.

Remembering walking to Romi's as a child, and that undefined sense of intrigue and mystery, I think I can now better identify what it was. It was that Romi and her husband, Mike, lived by a different ethos to most people. There was a reverence for the fabric of the place – not just the buildings but the natural beauty – they were custodians rather than 'improving' it. This was the top priority; things were mended and looked after, not replaced with shiny and new. The needs of the buildings' inherent 'personality' were listened to, the sharing of an unspoiled cliff to be kept and passed on intact. Make do and mend, not for sentimental reasons or frugality, but because new things jar with the patina that time gives a place.

At that time in the seventies, this seemed obvious, but now it is a rarity. I am even more grateful for what Mike and Romi stood for. This ethos extended into her paintings and revealed a reverence for the wear and tear of life in things, listening to the nature of that person or object and revealing it to the viewer in paint.

Romi kept most of her paintings, and I think that might have been a way of asserting her identity. Maybe it was also a way of marking the extraordinary world of Porth-en-Alls, with all its comings and goings.

Alice Mumford *is an artist and teacher living and working in Cornwall.*

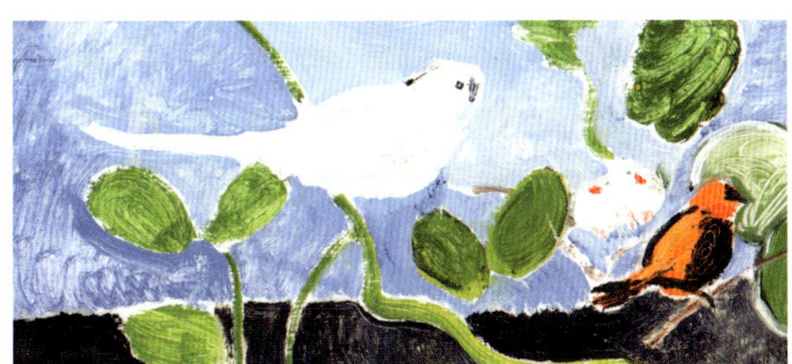

Budgies · c.1993 · oil on board · 15 x 46 cm

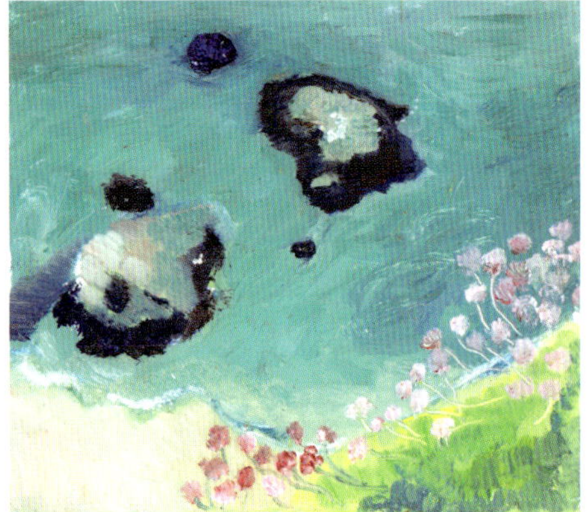

Looking down on Piskies (with Thrift) I
c.2001 · oil on board · 31 x 36 cm

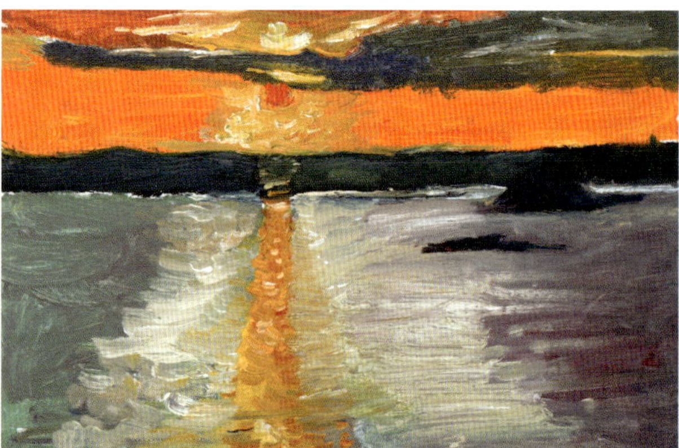

Presence over the Bay · c.1984 · oil on board · 39 x 61 cm

Stepping onto the stone, climbing through the window [used as a front door] into Romi's kitchen – nappies boiling, smell of beer brewing, bread rolls rising, paintbrush at the ready to capture any unsuspecting visitor …

These are my first memories of Romi in 1964. Enthusiasm and doubt intermingled, but boundless energy – loving and looking after Mike, Beccy, Emily and then Pete.

Over the years, more and more resolve and confidence with the painting. Fewer portraits were left unfinished and although many were minimally portrayed, more and more were ready to exhibit, stacked up in the studio. I remember the early Cornish houses, the glasses and the flowers, and am so happy to have some of those early works.

Romi knew that I really loved the thrift on the cliffs and, when I no longer visited in the spring, would send a bunch to me in a soggy envelope. She would write wonderful letters, from her heart, about the healing benefits of drinking your own pee,* and the joy of playing the violin in her orchestra, and whether or not she should vote for

Brexit, all in her characteristically generous writing, covering sheets and sheets of the thin paper she used.

We shared a magical picnic on Stackhouse rocks, overlooking St Michael's Mount, as the sun went down. That morning's lobster, cooked while she made mayonnaise, and served with homemade buns and beer. The tastes were the best ever, never to be forgotten. We clambered along the cliff after Mike, on his quest to show us the smugglers' cave where barrels of cognac would be sunk in a pool, which served as a trap for the police, while the pirates escaped from above! It was a very special evening, created by a very special couple.

Romi was herself – no one like her – and I appreciate having known her. I'm lucky to have so many of her paintings, but I miss our chats on the phone and the thrift in the spring.

Sue Norrington *was married to the acclaimed conductor Roger Norrington when she first came to Cornwall in 1964. She and Romi remained dear friends.*

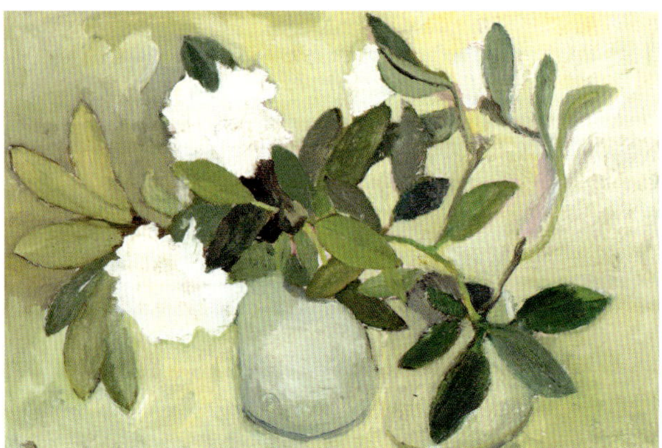

Mum's Rhodies · c.1966 · oil on board · 40 x 61 cm

*Romi became fanatical about urine therapy in the 1980s.

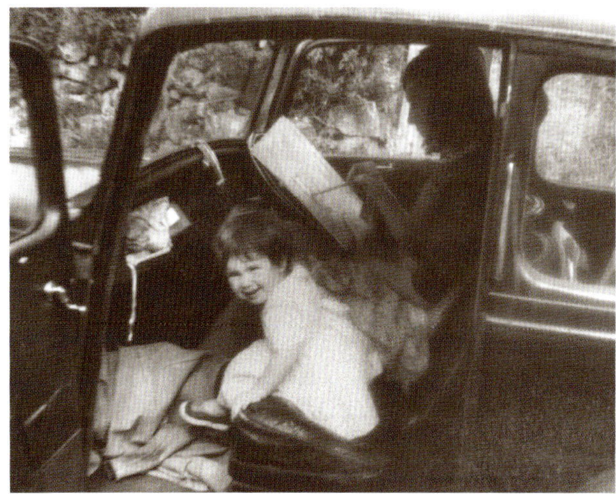

Romi, painting, and Rebecca, 1961

It's a grey and drizzling day, early 1960s, thin mist in the trees and on the hills, 'a perfect Cornish day' Romi would've called it, just the right sort of day to go and look at the land-/seascape!

Off we'd go in her rackety little car, leaving a platter of bread and cheese on the kitchen table, a large saucepan of home-made soup on the Aga and a note, written in big letters, propped against a vase of flowers for Mike, who would be out on the farm somewhere, probably fixing fences or dealing with a sheep's feet. It felt like bunking-off school, although I don't think Romi would ever have done that. Quite without warning them, we'd race over to see Alethea Garstin, Bryan and Monica Wynter, Johnny Wells or any of the many people she knew in West Penwith.

I think Romi found being a farmer's wife, housekeeper, cook, cleaner – and later on a mother with three small children – a sort of despairing situation, a tug of war for love of them and guilt over her need to paint (daily). She felt cut-off, far from the metropolitan world of art galleries. She'd constantly say how much she would love to live in London. People would look at her, at all she had – the beautiful family, the big houses, cottages, farm, wild cliffs, rocky coves, caves, clean sandy beaches … what they saw as a beautiful place, a wonderfully romantic situation – and think she was completely mad. In many ways she knew she was, which made it all the more difficult and frustrating.

Often, we'd sit in her studio, which changed places over the years from a converted pigsty to stable, shed, barn (they got progressively bigger as the paintings piled up), and would talk and argue for hours about life, love, books, religion, artists – and disagree fiercely about most things. We'd swear black was green and red was blue, until one or other of us had had enough and walked out.

Although she gave the appearance of total confidence, I always felt she lived with a terrible inner frailty. She had an endless need for approval of her paintings; she would drag anyone, almost off the streets, to look at them, to be as excited and as in love with them as she was. She would eagerly sort through a dozen or twenty paintings, some recent, some from way back, quickly changing them: 'What do you think of this, this, this?' Willing to listen to criticism, sometimes agreeing, sometimes not. Almost always, among the many, one would find a painting that absolutely took your breath away. She went through terrible angst as an exhibition grew closer – choice, price to put on them – and everyone would be asked, which, how much, how many?

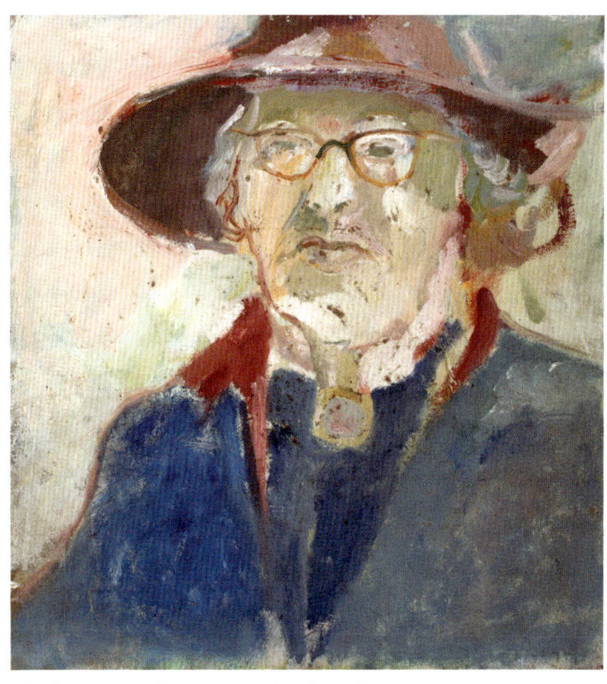

Alethea Garstin · c.1974 · oil on board · 61 x 57 cm

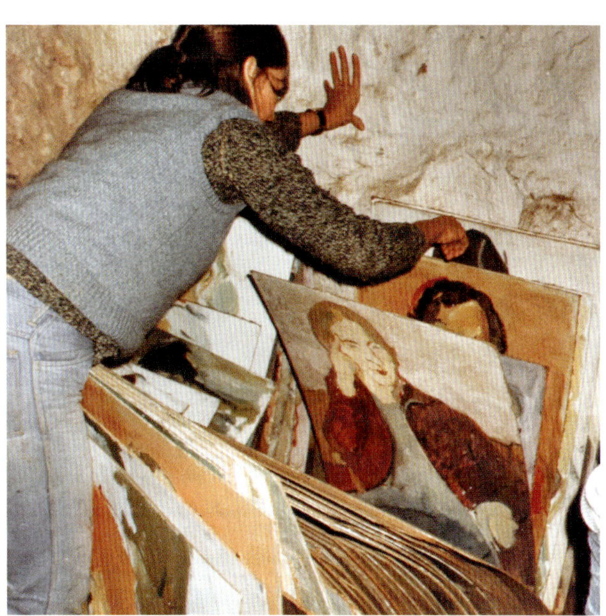

Paintings pile up in the studio, Trenalls, c.1974

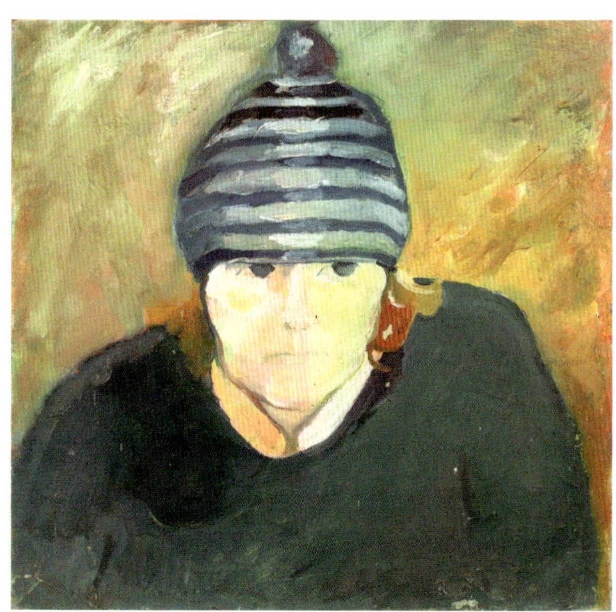

Roz Quillan Chandler · c.1975 · oil on board · 56 x 57 cm

She lived in a hangover from another era, circumstance of time (the difficulty for women to work without support), and having to divide her life between the responsibilities and demands of wife and mother and the need to be accepted as a serious painter, meant she endlessly fought with demons. Painting was her downfall and her salvation: she could be a monster or an angel – she knew she was both. Throughout her life, in some ways, she couldn't come to terms with the situation, but kept the faith and never gave up on any of it.

Roz Quillan Chandler *was a friend of Romi's from Salisbury School of Art and Crafts.*

'Microcosms of sheer delight'

Writings by Jeremy Le Grice

Selected writings about Romi by friend and artist Jeremy Le Grice (1936–2012), famed for his infectious enthusiasm for life, art and Cornwall.

¶

The individuality of Romi Behrens as a painter was assurcd the moment she started. In the mid-1950s [in fact, late 1950s–early 1960s] she was using as her motif modest buildings she loved. These paintings now stand as testaments in praise of old familiar out-of-the way places, many of which have since been spoilt. With the gradual expansion of her confidence and (self-taught) knowledge, those paintings led to a series of still lifes, more grandiose in character but involving things she had known well through the years. Dogs often sprawl on the floor beyond objects, their legs spread wide.

Step-by-step, portraiture became Romi's particular strength and celebration. For five or six weeks each year the International Musicians Seminar at Porth-en-Alls presented her with a chain of vivacious and fleeting subjects to whom she has responded with her live-wire vision. It is not only musicians who have been magnetised by Romi's brush; any haphazard visitor, a chance summer-let tenant, for example, or the passing doctor, odd-job man, child, friend, or sun-bather is liable to be whisked into her studio for a thorough going-over, or nailed down exactly where they stand or sit. But never easily so.

However, her responses to people remain amazingly direct and uninhibited. They are unhampered by pre-conceptions about 'art', untarnished by any inappropriate application of intellect; dependant only upon her intuition and deep-seated human sympathies. Her humour plays havoc with any pomposity – a bane with so much portrait-ure. Her brush sweeps precisely around the edge of a mouth, a particular hairline, snub of a nose or tilt of

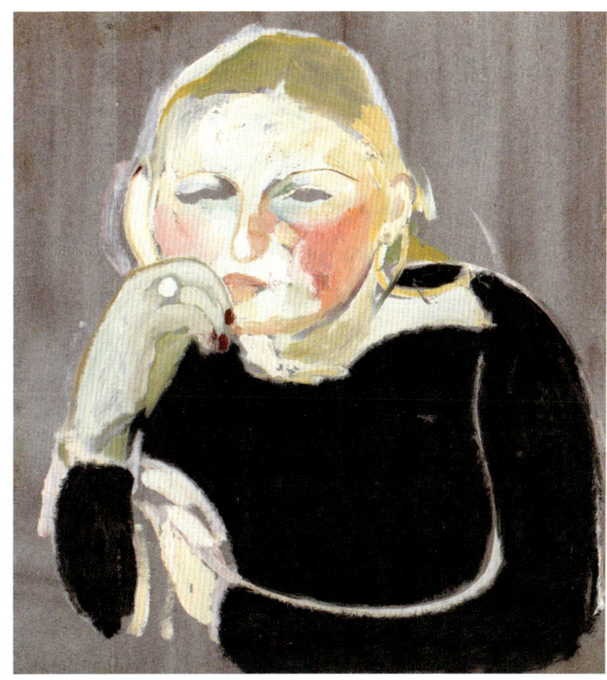

Woman with a Ring and Red Nails
c.1989 · oil on board · 49 x 46 cm

finger, but never descends to facility, so honest and accurate is her observation. Romi's reactions to accessories, belts, shoes, socks and brooches, astound by their pertinence. The manner in which she sees limbs – ladies' or men's, and children's especially – is never pedantic, always individual and infused with beauty. Eyes and mouths open and shut in her paintings; they appear to move or disappear, as in life. Her naked women are genuinely and blatantly sexy. Men breathe the credibility of their true natures; even a gentleman in uniform radiates a real, complex, personality. Images of her own offspring, grand-children and loved-ones are tender as dust and entirely without sentimentality.

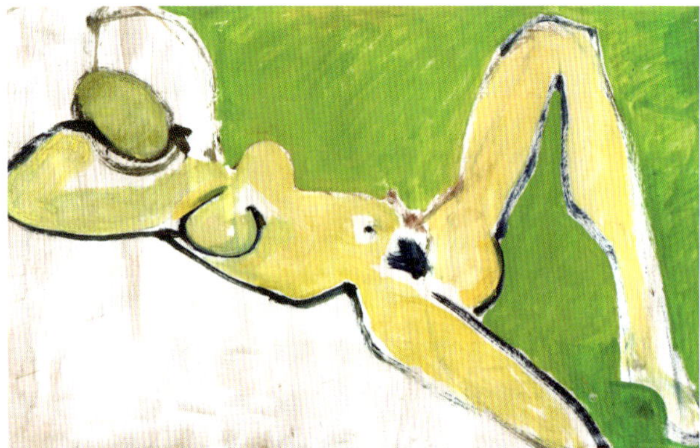

Just Imagine! · c.1988 · oil on board · 76 x 102 cm

Along with a number of prominent artists, I believe Romi Behrens' portraiture to be exceptional and her paintings to be important. Because they are genuinely gifted, their spontaneity, insight, courage, depth and verve are truly relevant to a hitherto eminent branch of art, now unfortunately so generally withered and unconvincing.

Portraiture can barely be presented as ordinary commercial-ware in West End galleries outside dull commissions. Therefore, although her 'cognoscenti' are widespread, she has enjoyed only relatively narrow public exposure. This has been limited to a few single-artist shows (Arnolfini [Bristol] being the most eminent), as well as haphazard showings at the RA and other mixed exhibitions. Leighton House would make a most suitable venue for this exceptional portraiture, which has never been seen in depth in London. It is now high time that it was.

Writing for the Romi Behrens exhibition, Leighton House, London, 1999 (note: very minor amendments have been made to the piece)

¶

Romi stands as one of the few painters around here now who works quite brilliantly on impulse. The paintings are uninhibited by the workings of the artist's consciousness; they consequently remain entirely fresh in their brush strokes and choice of pigments, displaying a confidence that amounts to 'blind' conviction, a quality too frequently trained out of artists during the creative journey from childhood's immediacy of response.

Her ability in pinpointing individuality in portraiture – where her reactions are as searing in their range as they are unpredictable and biting – is a gift she has worked at and nurtured relentlessly.

Personally, Romi is very generous and her work displays parallel qualities – grandeur of conception, breadth of treatment and a technique sure-fire in its execution. Her vision tends to land spot on target, too naturally truthful to become meretricious. A good Behrens amounts to a splendid treat, to be enjoyed time and time again and lastingly – for the best of these paintings becomes unexpectedly and surprisingly profound.

Writing about the Romi Behrens exhibition, Badcocks Gallery, Newlyn, 2005

¶

Romi 's portraits are microcosms of sheer delight. The intensity of her pleasure communicates instantly and the rapidity of her application is hard-pressed to keep up with the fleeting nature of her intuition and insight.

With the confidence and knowledge Romi now displays in her maturity, white areas of canvas speak for themselves in her paintings. This paradoxically increases the completeness, with the sitter spot-lit in a spontaneous blaze of brushwork and colour placed on an immaculate ground.

However, beyond exuberance, Romi carries into her work an essential humility. It is this quality that is taking her to ever greater heights as a portraitist.

From the catalogue '50 Years of Painting', Romi Behrens exhibition, Royal Cornwall Museum, Truro, 2009

Chronology

1939 · On 3 July, Rosemary was born in London, the youngest of three girls, to Humphrey and Marjorie Hall. The family left ten days later for Ramsbury Vicarage, Wiltshire, where Humphrey [Philip Humphrey Hall] was appointed vicar.

1954 · Expelled from St Brandon's Clergy Daughters' School, Clevedon (near Bristol).

1955 · Sent to the School of St Clare in Penzance.

1956 · Passed eight O-Levels.

1958 · Gained a further O-Level, in Art, from Salisbury School of Art and Crafts (see watercolour overleaf). She later described this as 'a general craft course'.

1959 · On 11 July, married Michael Tunstall-Behrens, at Bishopstone Church, Wiltshire. Moved to Trenalls, Porth-en-Alls Estate, Cornwall, with her husband.

1960 · Began attending classes at Penzance School of Art. On 3 August, birth of first child, Rebecca Rose.

1961 · Continued with art classes at Penzance School of Art.

1962 · In February, became a life member of the Newlyn Society of Artists, with 10 paintings accepted by Michael Canney, curator at Newlyn Art Gallery. In April, at Porth-en-Alls, the Easter Musical Festival began with Roger Norrington (later Sir) as the conductor. Romi recollected:

> *My brother-in-law, Hilary, had a brain wave (he had lots!). Dreamed up the Porth-en-Alls Music Festival, which took place at Easter every year down here in what was then far-off Cornwall. My husband, Mike, had the cottages, Hilary had the London contacts – professionals, brilliant amateurs and very good local singers – for a week of fabulous music with Roger Norrington conducting. We did 'Poppea' with Heather Harper in 1962, for example. We think that was the first time it was done in England. Absolutely amazing! Ben Luxon, Duggie [Dougie] Cummings, Terence Weil, Yfrah Neaman.*[1]

On 15 May, birth of second child, Emily Frances.

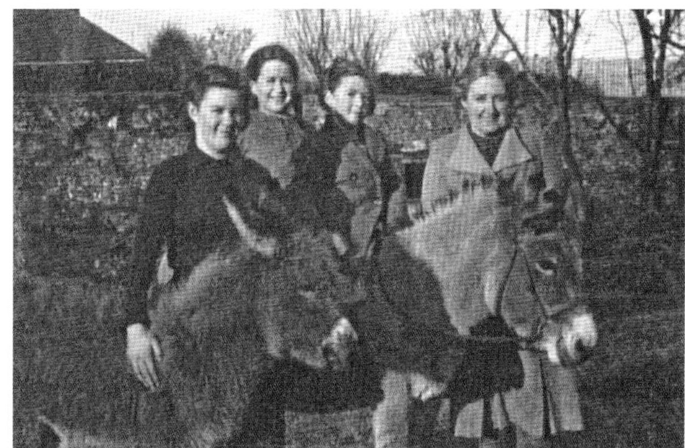

Mother, Marjoric (right), with daughters Susan, Gillian and Rosemary (Romi), *c.*1949

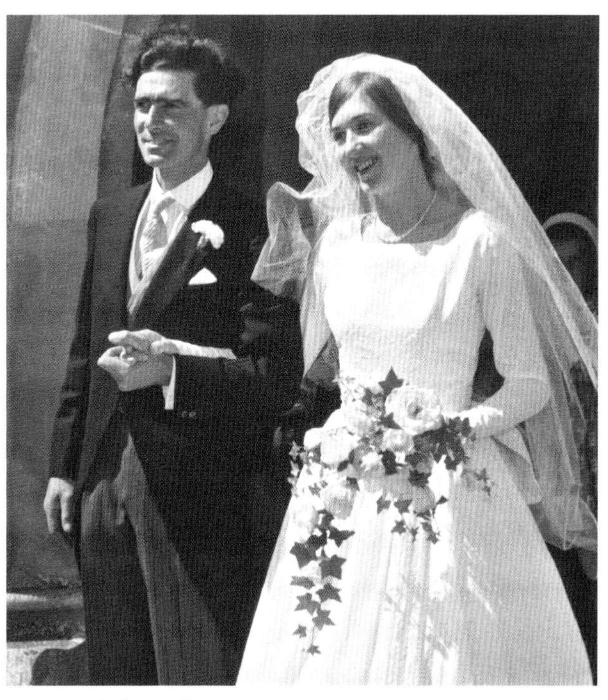

Just married! 11 July 1959

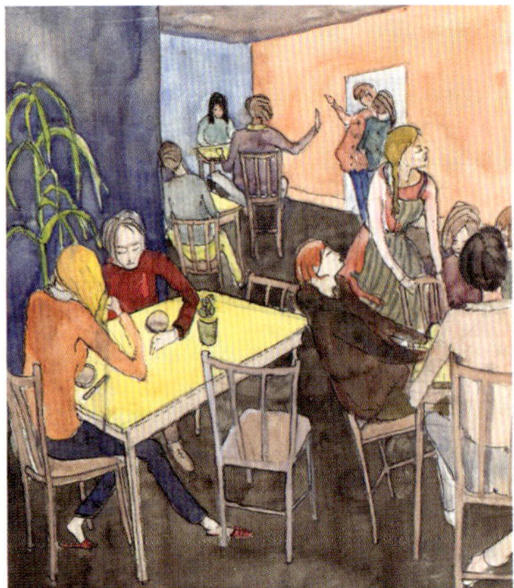

Classroom Scene
1958 · watercolour on paper · 41 x 36 cm
signed R. Hall [Romi]

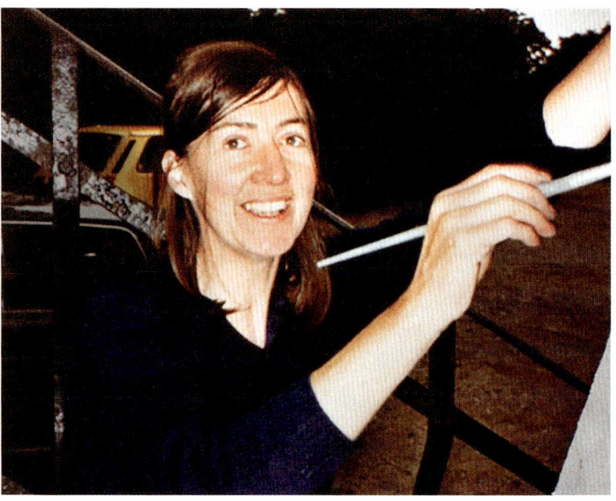

On the steps outside Trenalls, *c.*1967

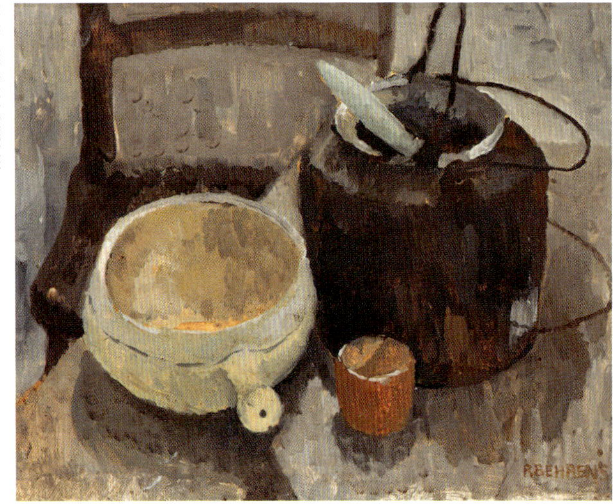

The Glue Pot · *c.*1962 · oil on board · 30 x 46 cm

1963 · In April, four more paintings were accepted at Newlyn Art Gallery, Cornwall, because they were selling.

1964 · Michael and the farm provided a haven for the sons of friends, usually aged 18–20 (such as Chris Aarvold, below). They would work as farm hands for a few months at a time.

1965 · On 6 March, birth of third child, John Peter Poingdestre.

1966–7 · These early years in Cornwall were both challenging and rewarding. Romi used every opportunity, visitor and event as a subject to paint.

1968 · During the summer, Romi was taken by a friend to see the Matisse retrospective at the Hayward, London: 'I was bowled over and never quite recovered, stayed all day.'[2]

1970 · Focus on portraits, notably of local Cornish characters (see pp. 45–8).

1971 · Romi began to experiment with painting nudes,

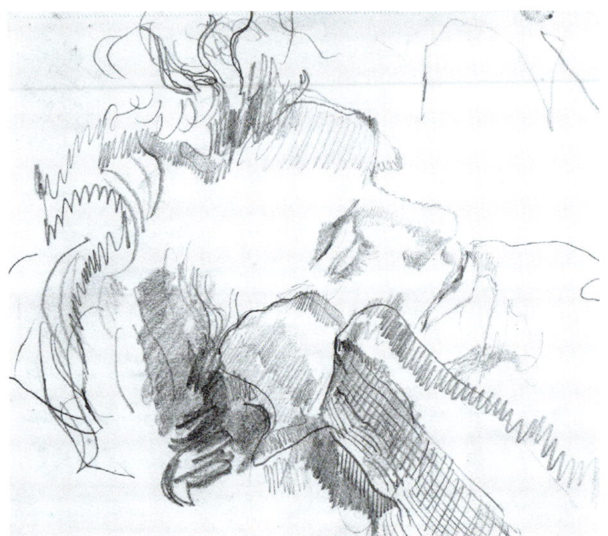

Chris Aarvold · *c.*1964 · pencil on paper · 21 x 30 cm

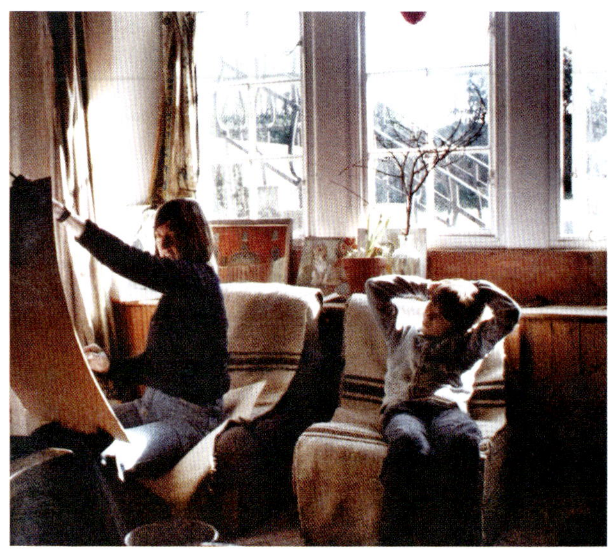

In the kitchen, Trenalls, late 1970s; the window (right) was used as a front door (see pp.158 and 160)

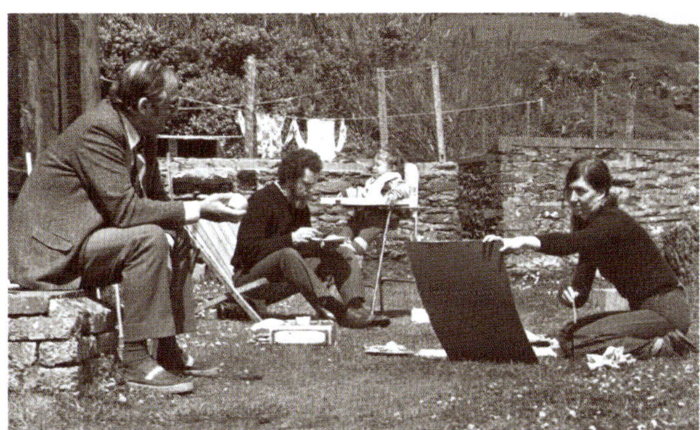

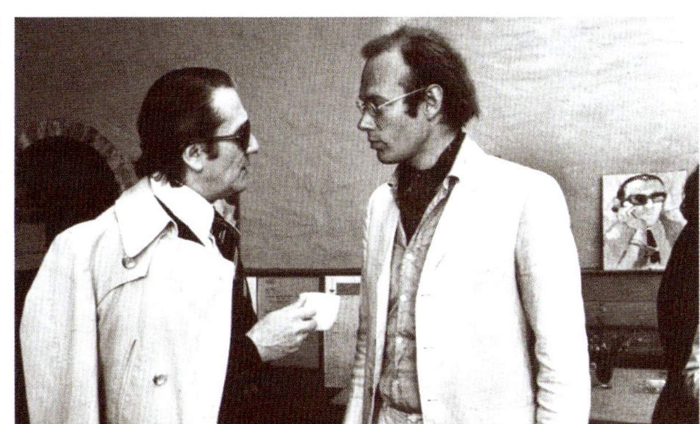

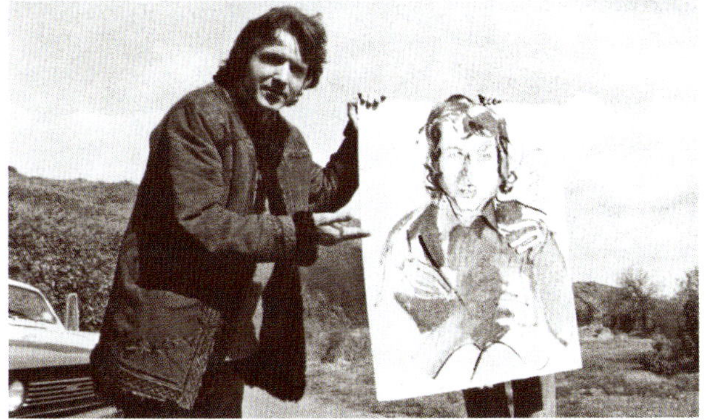

Painting musicians, International Musicians Seminar, mid-1970s; Radu Aldulescu and Robert Etherington, *c.*1976; Johannes Goritzki, portrait held by Romi, *c.*1980

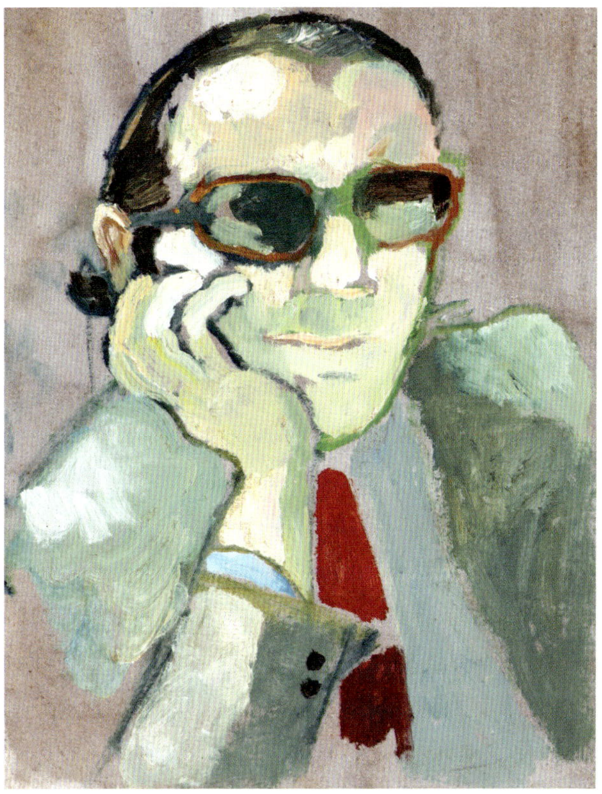

Radu Aldulescu · *c.*1976 · oil on board · 48 x 38 cm

starting with herself (see p. 43).

1972 · In April, the International Musicians Seminar (IMS) began, founded by Sándor Végh (and Hilary Tunstall-Behrens) who invited different *maestri* each year. Early students included Stephen Isserlis, Krysia Osostowicz and Susan Tomes. Romi painted 'everybody'.[3]

1973 · Stayed alone for a week in Coastguards No. 6, a cottage on the estate, to paint (see p. 35).

1974–6 · These years of the IMS provided irresistible material for Romi.[4]

1977 · Painting, *Heather and Teapot*, accepted for (and sold at) the Royal Academy Summer Exhibition, London.
1978 · In April, first solo exhibition, Brunswick Gallery, London; curator Ron Field, He discouraged Romi from hanging portraits but thought 'instant portraiture could be an interesting publicity gimmick'.[5]
1979 · Artist and friend, Jeremy Le Grice, introduced his second wife, Lyn, to Romi, who painted her portrait there and then:

> *It wasn't Romi's physical presence, it was her mind. I could hardly tell you what clothes she wore, it was her way of expressing things, the words she used, that were so interesting and powerful. It was the impression she gave or the way she would tell you about people in her excitable and explosive voice. Everything was a little bit more remarkable than the last thing.*
>
> *She was at every exhibition opening, for example the Penwith in St Ives, and she had a huge personality. She was a big scale artist, not domestic. Her paintings were so powerful and pure. She painted exactly what she was looking at and she was so quick. Jeremy thought she was a fabulous painter.*[6]

1980 · In January, solo exhibition, Arnolfini, Bristol; curator Lewis Biggs. On 18 October, mother, Marjorie, died: 'She never told me what to do; she always let me be myself.'[7]
1981 · In October, Rebecca married Robert Derry-Evans.
1982 · In January, rented a cottage in Clevedon, near Bristol, for a month, to paint (see pp. 80, 86–9 and 128). In August, joint exhibition at Halesworth Gallery, Suffolk, with ceramicist Tessa Fuchs.
1983 · In February, Ted Graham, Labour MP, helped Mike and Romi oppose a local caravan site development. Romi later painted a still life, given to Lord Graham, to say thank you.

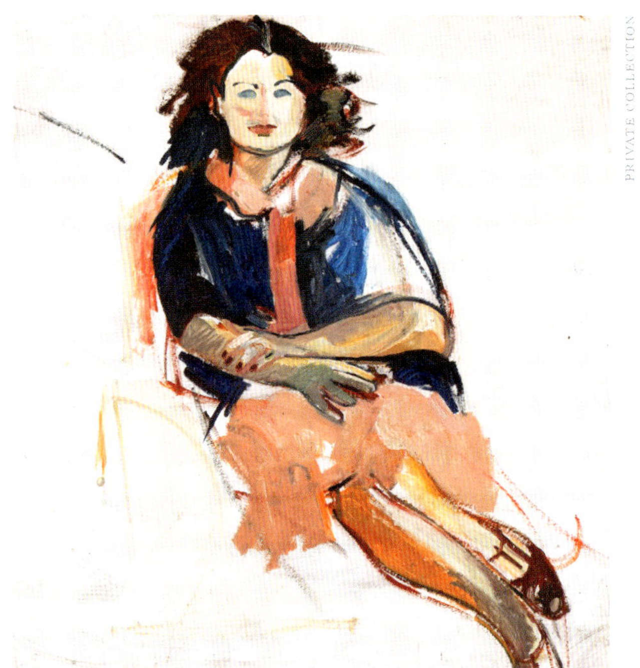

Lyn Le Grice · 1979 · oil on board · 124 x 93 cm

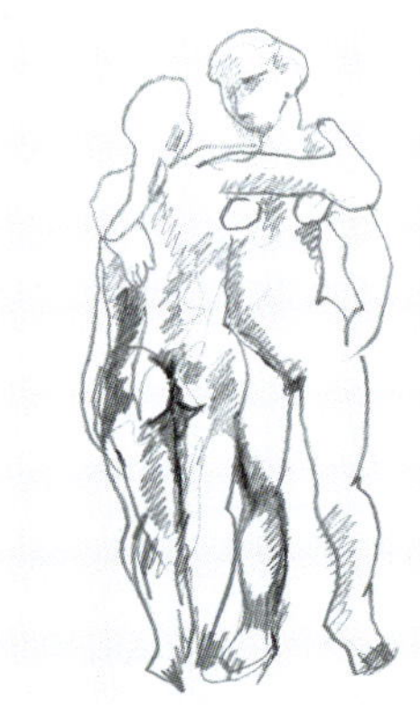

Matisse Sculpture
*c.*1988 · pencil on paper
30 x 21 cm

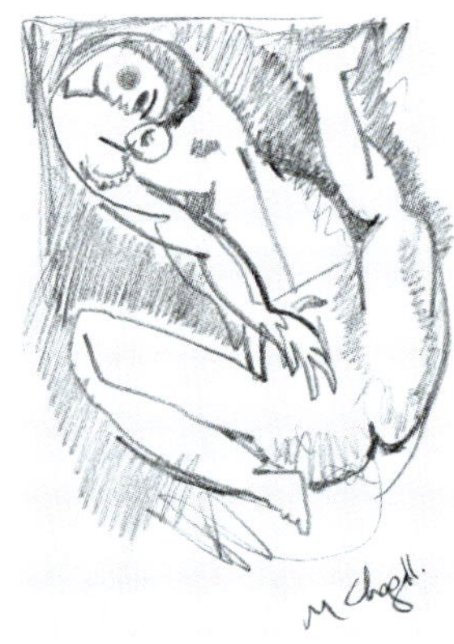

M. Chagall
*c.*1988 · pencil on paper
30 x 21 cm

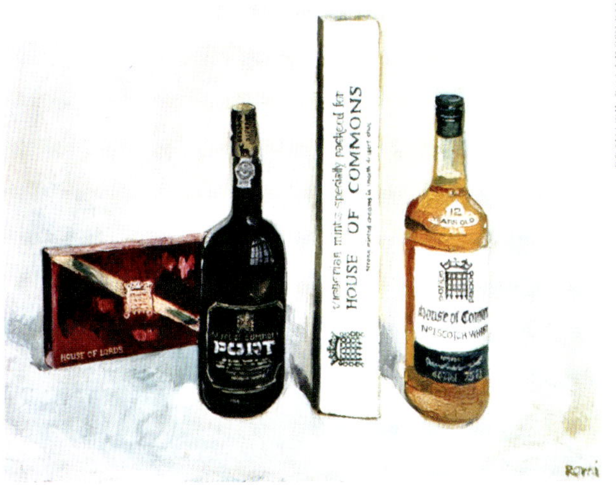

Gifts from Lord Graham · 1983 · oil on board · 61 x 93 cm

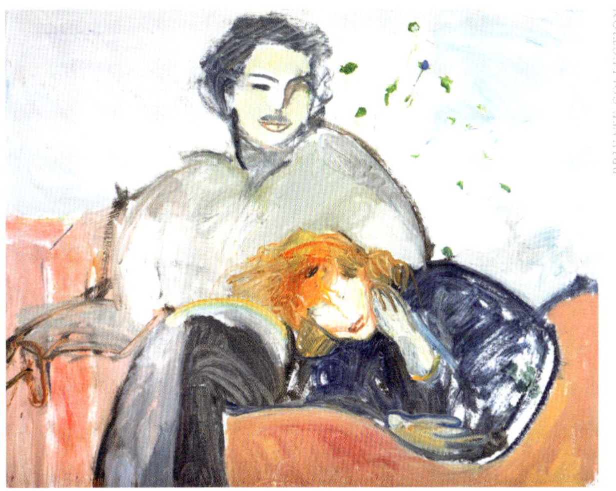

The French Lieutenant · c.1984 · oil on board · 95 x 122 cm

1984 · In March, solo exhibition at Margaret Fisher Gallery, London. Lord Alan Bullock and Douglas Cummings (leader of cello section of the London Symphony Orchestra) spoke and played. In May, *The French Lieutenant* (Mike came up with the title) accepted for (and sold at) the Royal Academy Summer Exhibition, London.

1985 · In April, illustrations for a book, *Peter & Zeb, the Magic Zebra*, by Mark Eliot (see overleaf). Sadly, not published.

1986 · Visited daughter, Rebecca, in Hong Kong and was inspired by Chinese objects (see pp. 90, 103 and 121).

1987 · On 11 March, father, Humphrey, died.

1988 · Romi's fascination with the nude continued and developed (see p. 27, note 31; pp. 164 and 168).

1989 · In July, mixed exhibition, Michael Parkin Fine Art, London.

1990 · The friendship between Patrick Heron, Mike and Romi deepened. Patrick respected Romi as both an artist and a friend. In October, solo exhibition, Michael Parkin Gallery, London.

1991 · In February, Romi became fascinated by intaglio

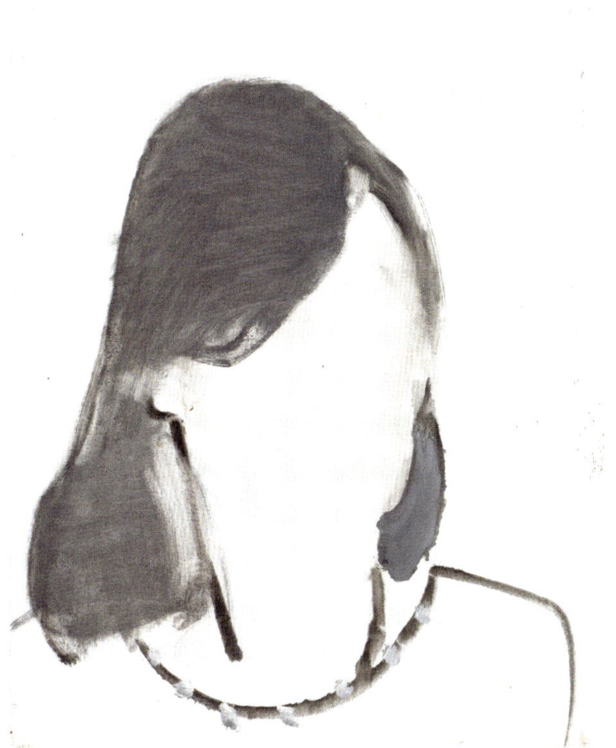

ROMI : c.1990 · Patrick Heron · oil on canvas · 52 x 41 cm

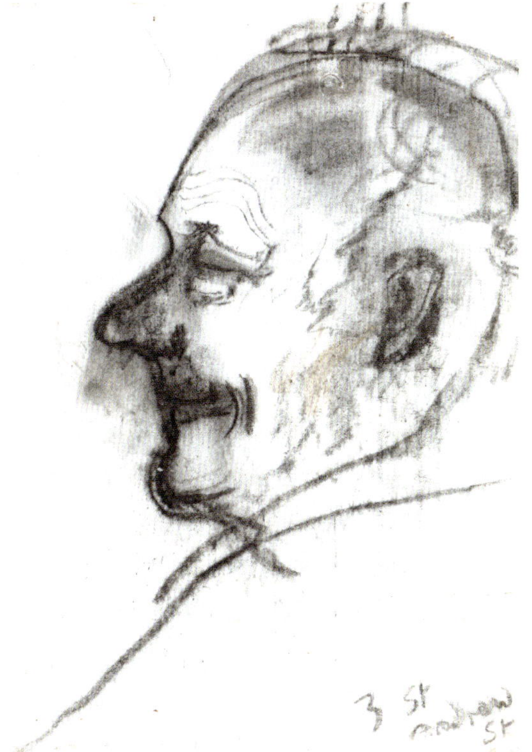

Patrick Heron · c.1990 · charcoal on canvas · 50 x 36 cm

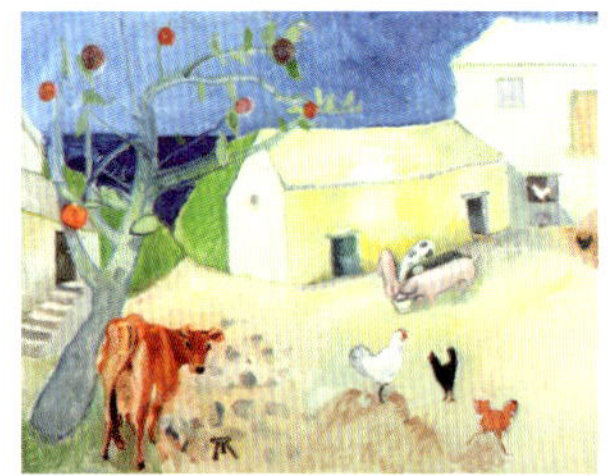
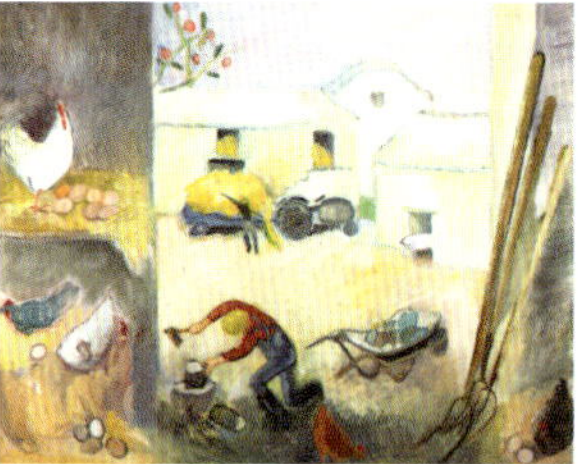
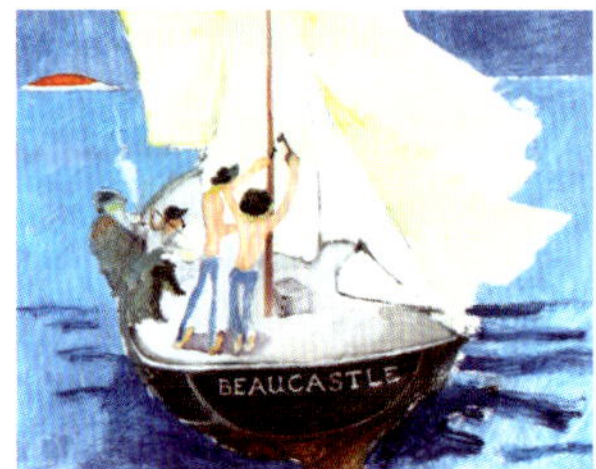
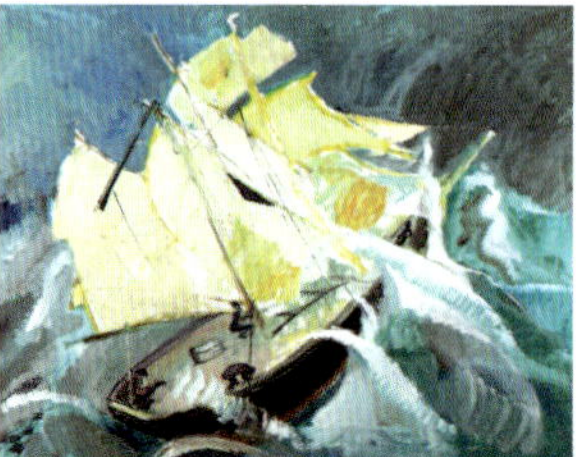

Illustrations for *Peter & Zeb, the Magic Zebra*, 1985

printmaking, producing many images and using a variety of techniques. In December, solo exhibition, 'The Seaview Paintings', Rebecca Hossack Gallery, London.

1992 · In June, mixed exhibition, 'Music of the Spheres', Rebecca Hossack Gallery, London.

1993 · In January, mixed exhibition, 'Cornwall: A Painter's Choice', Cadogan Contemporary, London. Other exhibitors: Jeremy Le Grice, Tamsin Woodford, Clive Blackmore, Bob Bourne, Daphne McClure.

1994 · In July, mixed exhibition, Cadogan Contemporary, London. Romi's painting was on the flyer.

1995 · Mike and Romi moved out of the family home, Trenalls, across the farmyard to the old tractor shed they had converted together: Tares.

1996 · Silver anniversary concert of the International Musicians Seminar was 'a smash hit' for Romi.[8]

1997 · In June, mixed exhibition, 'St Ives: The New Generation', presented by Terrain at Curcurrian Valley Studio, San Francisco. In December, art auction in aid of St Teresa's Cheshire Home, Longrock, Cornwall, including Terry Frost.

1998 · In March, Romi visited the Bonnard exhibition at the Tate Gallery; she was clearly influenced by his painting throughout her life (see pp. 25 and 72).[9]

1999 · In February, joint exhibition, Rainyday Gallery, Penzance, Cornwall, with Jeremy Le Grice. In October, solo exhibition, Leighton House, London; curator Jessica Wood – *The Guardian* review read:

> *For Patrick Heron, Cornwall was a palace of light which served up an endless palette of painterly possibilities. This is true for Romi Behrens, a friend of Heron's and nearby resident down at Prussia Cove. Behrens also has a love affair with colour inherited from Matisse. Whether in portraits or still lifes, she manages to balance bright tones with a seeming ease, with gestural marks that might look like chance but reveal a reductive, considered approach.*[10]

2000 · In the autumn, Mike and Romi moved again, from Tares to Trewartha, a farmhouse on the edge of the estate.

2001 · In September, Emily married Cengiz Saner. In December, Peter married Hannah Freeman.

2002 · Numerous paintings submitted to mixed shows in London and Cornwall.

2003 · In February, joint exhibition with printmaker Bridget Holden, North Cornwall Museum, Camelford.

2004 · In April, all-female group exhibition, 'The Artful Sex', in Fowey, Cornwall, including Mary Stork. On 25 December, Romi's limerick, *Babe in a Manger*, won the BBC4 Christmas competition and was broadcast:

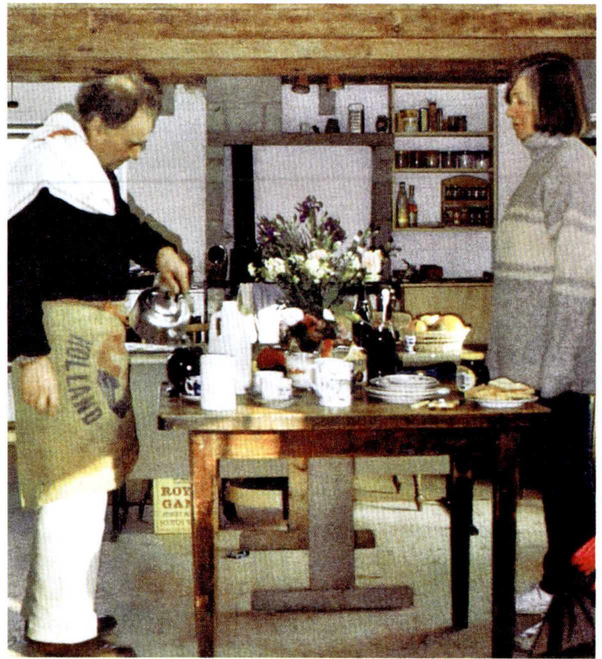

Mike and Romi, Tares kitchen, 1995

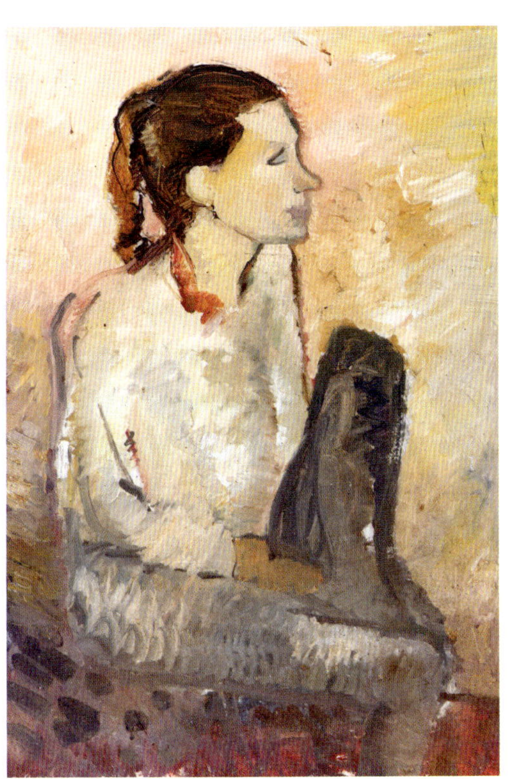

Kate Feiler · 1986 · oil on board · 122 x 80 cm

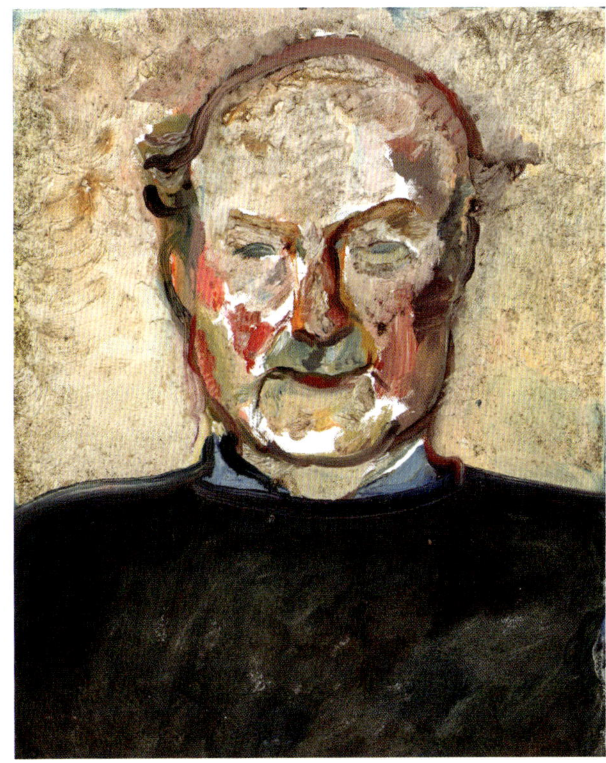

Paul Feiler · 2008 · oil on canvas · 51 x 40 cm

There once was a babe in a stable
Whose life was all set to enable
Us lot to be FREE
Of the bad things that we
Have all done –
This is true, NOT A FABLE!

2005 · In April, solo exhibition, Badcocks Gallery, Newlyn, Cornwall; curator Nickie Carlyon.
2006 · In June, solo exhibition, 'The Le Grice Family Portraits', Trereife House, Penzance, Cornwall. Romi painted portraits of anyone who came to the exhibition and accepted commissions throughout the summer.
2007 · In June, solo exhibition, Badcocks Gallery, Newlyn, Cornwall; curator Nickie Carlyon.
2008 · Mike's health was declining and Romi became his carer, so was constrained. She painted this portrait of Paul Feiler at his home on 17 May. A portrait of his wife, the artist, Catharine Armitage (known to Romi as Kate), was painted earlier.
2009 · On 14 January, Mike died. In October, major retrospective exhibition, Royal Cornwall Museum, Truro.

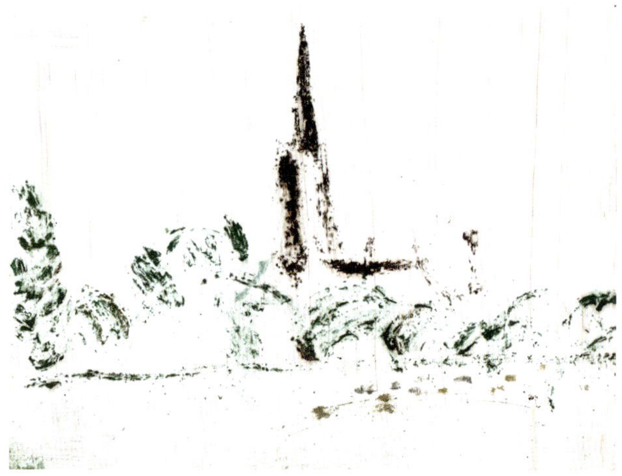

My Cézanne, Salisbury Water Meadows I
2014 · oil on board · 46 x 61 cm

A catalogue, *50 Years of Painting*, was produced.
2010 · In December, solo exhibition, Old Methodist Chapel, Gulval, Cornwall. Romi gave 10 per cent of her earnings from the exhibition to the switching on of the Gulval Christmas lights.
2011 · In February, solo exhibition, 'Toucan and Friends', Illustration Cupboard, London; curator John Huddy. The exhibition was inspired by a model Romi found in a charity shop: 'When subject matter or inspiration seem to be lacking, this little bird, the toucan, always rescues me, as fifteen years ago, I had rescued him from a junk shop in Penzance!'[11] In April, Romi was the inspiration for an exhibition, 'The Female Perspective', at the Chapel Gallery, Gulval, Cornwall.
2012 · In December, Romi donated a painting for an auction of contemporary Cornish art at Christie's, South Kensington, London, in support of the IMS.
2013 · Religion had always been important. Romi painted *The Last Supper*, the subject for a huge canvas (see pp. 154–5). She developed a breast lump. It was removed and she recovered.

2014 · In March, a project to paint all the cathedrals in England began. Although not completed, Romi achieved nine; several paintings of each exist (see pp. 150 and 152–3). In July, Romi painted *The Celtic Blessing* on another huge canvas (see pp. 156–7). In October, solo exhibition, Penwith Gallery, St Ives, Cornwall; curator Peter Eadie: 'Romi was one of the few unsung artists of British Modernism. Her art so very honest. A very rare talent.'[12]
2015 · In July, solo exhibition, Silk Mill, Frome, Somerset. A space generous enough to show *Sophie and Scarlett (The Sirens)*, painted in 2011 (see frontispiece).
2016 · In January, solo exhibition, The Gallery, Shepherd Market, London.
2017 · In April, mixed exhibition, Newlyn Art Gallery, Cornwall; curator Ben Sanderson.
2018 · Final solo exhibition, Tremenheere Sculpture Gardens, Penzance, Cornwall. Romi was in a wheelchair.
2019 · On 6 March, Romi died peacefully at home. In December, posthumous entry in *Bible of British Taste* blog.[13]

Notes

1. RB archive.
2. RB archive.
3. See Peter Tunstall-Behrens, 'Introduction', *Romi Behrens: Portraits of IMS Prussia Cove. Musicians, Patrons & Helpers, 1972–2010*, catalogue, 2021.
4. See www.i-m-s.org.uk.
5. Correspondence. RB Archive.
6. Interview, October 2022. RB archive.
7. Conversation with daughter, Emily Saner, in 2018.
8. *The Cornishman*, 11 April 1996.
9. 'Bonnard', Tate Gallery, 12 February–17 May 1998.
10. Simon Grant, *The Guardian*, 23 October 1999.
11. Conversation with curator. RB archive.
12. Conversation with curator, 2024. RB archive.
13. Ruth Guilding, *Bible of British Taste*, 17 December 2019, https://bibleofbritishtaste.com/i-am-a-painter-and-i-paint-every-day-romi-behrens-at-prussia-cove.

The Twinkling Toaster –

It was a twinkling toaster
My father gave to me –
On our silver wedding anniversary

The Golden Golden toast it makes
Has given us new life
Breakfast is now as happy
As new husband + new wife –

A toaster is two circles
Joined by a piece of wire
To stop the bread from burning
Or falling in the fire

A marriage is two people
Joined by a band of gold
To keep each other happy
While they are growing old –

We love our twinkling toaster
So bright to start the day
And endeavour to be like it
From sun till Saturday

P.T.O

Our father gave it to us
To toast our daily bread
And this we will remember
long after he is dead
~
This made sound rather callous
– but not to you or me
As we don't think our darling
Dad will toast eternally –

More likely he'll be twinkling
'mongst stars so clear & bright
And there we hope to join him
If we keep our toaster right –

———

written clean out of the blue
on a train to plymouth about
1984 (married '59) Mike & I added
another verse later "its 30 40 – now its
deuce – togetherness the
game, with our twinkling tennis racket we
will make love just the same

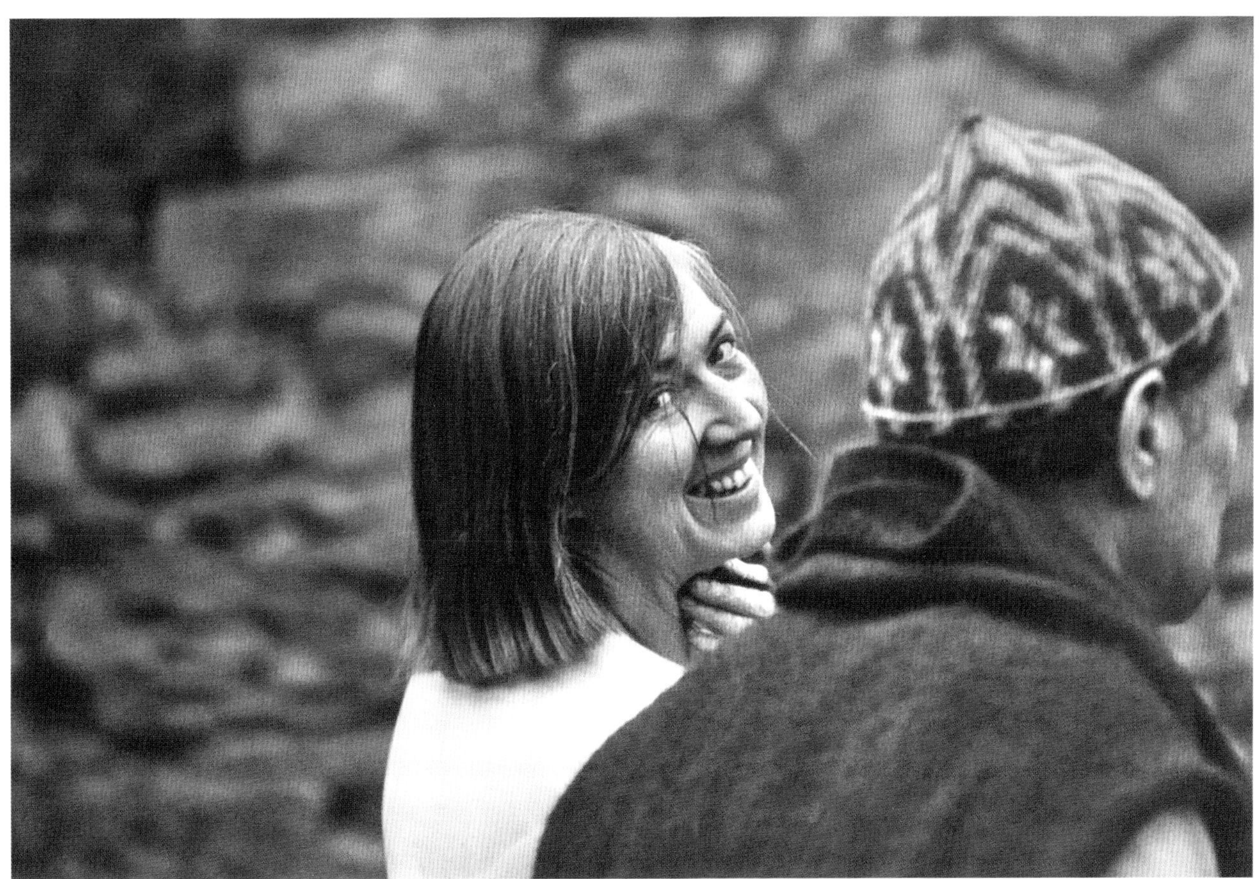

Romi and Mike, Cornwall, *c.*1993

Acknowledgements

Thank you to Chris Stephens, Rachel Rose Smith and David Ward for their time and effort in producing the foreword, 'Becoming Romi Behrens' and 'I paint every day!' respectively. (Lines from Mary Oliver's poem 'Don't Hesitate' in David's essay are reprinted by the permission of The Charlotte Sheedy Literary Agency as agent for the author. Copyright © 2010, 2017 by Mary Oliver with permission of Bill Reichblum.)

Thank you to the contributors and writers for 'Romi remembered': Alice Mumford, Sue Norrington and Roz Quillan Chandler.

Thank you to Lyn Le Grice for meeting and talking to us and (posthumously) to Jeremy Le Grice for his constant support for Romi. For Jeremy's piece for the Leighton House exhibition (1999), thanks to: Leighton House, Royal Borough of Kensington and Chelsea.

Photography of artworks by Simon Cook, Beata Cosgrove and Otto Saner. Restoration of paintings by Alison Smith. Framing by Richard Guy. Research, chronology and preparation of paintings by Rebecca Derry-Evans and Emily Saner.

Thank you for permission to reproduce paintings or portraits: Prach Boondiskulchok, Hugo and Adam Feiler, Scarlett Fishburn, Delia Goddard, Allie Heath, Katharine Heron, Susanna Heron, Adele Herson, Lyn Le Grice, Tim Le Grice, George Misiewicz, Nick Murray, Sir Roger Norrington, Robert and Debbie Porter, Peter Quicke, James St Levan, Ceola (Sophie) Tunstall-Behrens, Hilary and Tatiana Tunstall-Behrens, Peter Tunstall-Behrens, Wollaston Family.

Thank you to Elena Hill and Harriet Löffler for their enthusiasm and support.

¶

If you would like further information about the artist, please go to the website **romibehrens.art**